EXTRÊME
OCCIDENT

EXTRÊME

OCCIDENT

*French Intellectuals
and America*

JEAN-PHILIPPE
MATHY

The University of Chicago Press

Chicago and London

Jean-Philippe Mathy is assistant professor of French at the University of Illinois, Urbana-Champaign.

The University of Chicago Press, Chicago 60637
The University of Chicago Press, Ltd., London
© 1993 by The University of Chicago
All rights reserved. Published 1993
Printed in the United States of America
02 01 00 99 98 97 96 95 94 93   1 2 3 4 5
ISBN:0-226-51063-8 (cloth)
ISBN: 0-226-51064-6 (paper)

Library of Congress Cataloging-in-Publication Data

Mathy, Jean-Philippe.
     Extrême-Occident : French intellectuals and America / Jean-
Philippe Mathy.
          p.   cm.
     Includes bibliographical references and index.
     1. French literature—20th century—History and criticism.
     2. United States—Foreign public opinion, French.   3. France—
Intellectual life—20th century.   4. French literature—American
influences.   5. America in literature.   I. Title.
PQ143.U6M37   1993
840.9'3273—dc20   93-16456

⊗ The paper used in this publication meets the
minimum requirements of the American National Standard
for Information Sciences—Permanence of Paper for
Printed Library Materials, ANSI Z39.48-1984.

For Rosemary

CONTENTS

ACKNOWLEDGMENTS

A book is, in more than one way, a collective enterprise. Many colleagues, students, and friends contributed stimulating advice and criticism. Special thanks are due to Evelyne Accad, Nancy Blake, Paul Bové, Douglas Collins, Carl Estabrook, Peter Garrett, Stan Gray, Gordon Hutner, Myra Jehlen, Harry Liebersohn, Marc Lilla, Patricia Merivale, Robert Nelson, Allan Stoekl, and Paul Vieille. I am particularly grateful to Thomas Pavel, for his acute comments and unfailing help and encouragement, and to Doug Kibbee, for his careful reading of the manuscript and detailed suggestions.

I also wish to thank the Center for Advanced Study, the Program for the Study of Cultural Values and Ethics, and International Programs and Studies at the University of Illinois for providing the grants and fellowships that enabled me to complete this book. I wish to express my gratitude to Emile Talbot for his guidance and support in these matters.

Portions of chapters 3, 4, and 6 appeared in *Contemporary French Civilization* (1988), *The French Review* (1989), *American Literary History* (1990), and *Stanford French Review* (1991). I am grateful to the editors and publishers concerned for permission to reprint the material.

Finally, I should like to thank all those who helped make the manuscript into a printed volume: Alan G. Thomas, Randolph Petilos, and Jean Eckenfels of the University of Chicago Press.

There is more ado to interpret interpretations than to interpret things; and more books upon books than upon any other subject; we do nothing but comment upon one another.   *Montaigne*

Les États Unis d Amerique, ce pays d' outre-Occident . . . The United States of America, this land beyond the west   *G. Duhamel*

INTRODUCTION

THE RHETORIC OF "AMERICA"

For some reason or other, the European has rarely been able to see America except in caricature. *James Russell Lowell, "On a Certain Condescension in Foreigners"*

Our critics are not aware that . . . no European society has ever had to face the problem of say, 100,000,000 people who possess the purchasing power to satisfy their impulse to entertainment and instruction. In a closed society, those millions could be ordered to read, hear and see what their masters thought "culture"; in a democratic society, cultural despotism cannot be imposed; every movie producer, comic-book publisher, TV manager is free to solicit the patronage of those millions—and he does. *Lewis Galantiere*

French intellectuals, with a few rare exceptions, have failed to grasp the new rhythm of the planet as it developed in the USA. They were philosophers, rationalists, Mediterraneans, humanists with a big thesis, Aristotelian-Platonists, post-Proustians, aphorists, shameful Zhdanovists, refurbished Stendhalians, children of the Third Republic—institutionalized, universalized, normalized. *Philippe Sollers*

In a short essay called "Une Amérique inattendue," André Maurois quotes an old friend of his, a Frenchman who has never crossed the Atlantic, but professes "violent and precise ideas" on the United States. When Maurois informs him that he has been invited to spend a semester at Princeton University as a visiting professor, his friend embarks upon a spirited critique of American society and culture:

My dear child, he said to me, don't do such a thing! You won't come back alive. You don't know what America is all about. In that country, restlessness is such that you won't be allowed a minute of leisure; noise is so pervasive that you won't be able to sleep, or even rest; in that country, men, at forty, die of overwork, while women leave their home early in the morning to participate in the universal restlessness.

1

Spirit and intelligence are of no value over there. Freedom of thought does not exist. Human beings do not have a soul. All they ever talk about is money. You have known, ever since your childhood, the sweetness of a spiritual civilization; a civilization of bathrooms, central heating and refrigerators is awaiting you. . . . Did you read, my friend, the description of Chicago's slaughterhouses? It is a monstrous vision, I assure you, an apocalyptic one. . . . And what about those stories in the newspapers, the gangs of outlaws who commit murder in broad daylight, with the complicity of the police themselves? . . . Truly, I am terrified for you. You have a wife and children. . . . Please, give up on this trip. (*L'Amérique inattendue*, 6–7)[1]

I have quoted this humorous passage at length because it lists most of the criticisms directed at American culture by French intellectuals, whether conservatives, liberals, humanists, nationalists, libertarians, or traditionalists. We will encounter this complex set of representations time and again in the following chapters, in the works of writers as different in their ideological, aesthetic, and political views as Simone de Beauvoir, Georges Duhamel, and Louis-Ferdinand Céline.

The anti-American sentiment prevalent in most French intellectual circles from the twenties to the seventies aimed at two related phenomena: technological *production* and its social and political consequences, on the one hand, and the rise of mass *consumption*, on the other. In the aforementioned passage, allusions to restlessness, noise, the emancipation of women, and the "civilization of bathrooms, central heating, and refrigerators" belong to criticisms of the first category.[2] The considerations on materialism ("all they ever talk about is money") and the related absence of spiritual values ("soul," "freedom of thought") exemplify the cultural and moral indictment of American consumerism. Both discourses, however, are suffused with the same apocalyptic tone, the same horrified fascination for the brave new world across the Atlantic. In contrast, France becomes both a threatened paradise and a bulwark against the contamination of Europe by crass materialism and decadent hedonism. Most critical accounts of American modernity share in this *paradigm of discontinuity* between the two civilizations. The genuine concern and horrified warnings of André Maurois's friend uncover the paranoid obsession with contamination, corruption and infection that underlies many a description of the inevitability of the American threat. "Don't do such a thing! You won't come back alive!"

This set of commonplaces belongs to a long tradition of French narrative constructions of America, which are based on a corpus of texts widely circulated among educated readers. Such a collection of textual references common to most accounts of life in America constitutes what is called to-day an *intertext*.[3] The descriptions cite one another, exhibiting similar features and repeating familiar readings, thus producing a complex signifier, a contested textual construct that bears the name "America." The slaughterhouses in the quotation from Maurois probably refer not only to Sinclair's *The Jungle*, but also to a chapter of Georges Duhamel's *America: The Menace, Scenes from the Life of the Future* (1931). In a passage entitled "The Kingdom of Death," the author offers a vivid and particularly repugnant description of the systematic slaughter of pigs, cattle, and sheep, which can be taken as a metaphor of the massive destruction of human lives and souls in modern industrial cities.

Duhamel's book triggered a heated debate in the French press and was obviously part and parcel of every conversation on the monstrosities of *outre-Occident*, as the author had called the United States.[4] Paul Morand's *New York*, published in France in 1930, which Maurois praised at the end of his essay as "quite accurate and brilliant" (12), was also widely read and quoted at the time. Twenty years later, Simone de Beauvoir contrasted in *America Day by Day* (published in France in 1948) her perception of the American landscape with the disparaging comments found in Duhamel's book, thereby attesting to the latter's impact on French readers: "Now we would thread our way through lonely mountains; there was not one car on this narrow twisting road; it became even wilder, and we thought that M. Duhamel could have travelled but little in America to have dared pretend that the countryside was hidden by advertisement hoardings" (104).

In Maurois's quote, the references to the "universal restlessness" of the Americans, or to the absence of freedom of thought in the land of liberty, go all the way back to Alexis de Tocqueville, whose analysis inaugurated a long line of French interpretations of America. In a chapter of *Democracy in America* entitled "Why the Americans appear so restless in the midst of their well-being," the French observer constrasted the carefree happiness of the oppressed people of feudal Europe with the "serious" and "even sad" demeanor of the "freest and most enlightened men" in the world. "It is a strange thing," he wrote, "to see with what feverish ardor the Americans pursue their own welfare; and to watch the vague dread that constantly torments them lest they should not have chosen the shortest path that may lead to it" (144). Such stigmatization of the American angst, in the French *moralistes'* vein, will crop up time and again in most of the works I will be examining.

On the prevalent anti-intellectualism of American culture, Maurois's friend quoted Tocqueville almost word for word. Consider the following passage in which the French historian attributes the absence of genuine artistic and literary life in the United States to a lack of "true independence of mind and freedom of discussion": "In America, the majority raises very formidable barriers to the liberty of opinion. . . . If great writers have not at present existed in America, the reason is very simply given in these facts; there can be no literary genius without freedom of opinion, and freedom of opinion does not exist in America" (Tocqueville, 1: 269). The peculiar combination of restlessness and monotony that struck Tocqueville as one of the main characteristics of American society also impressed Simone de Beauvoir, Louis-Ferninand Céline, and Georges Duhamel when they encountered the lonely crowds of the New World. In his analysis (in vol. 3 of *Situations*) of the "system of Americanism" and the pervasive "tyranny of public opinion," Sartre echoed, also almost verbatim, Tocqueville's reflections on "the tyranny of the majority" in America.

The advocates of a balanced, "objective" view on the subject, such as Maurois or, more recently, Raymond Aron, have repeatedly questioned the validity of most narrative constructions of American life, contrasting these mythological Americas with the complex and diverse empirical reality of the United States—which is, after all, a plural substantive. It was often easy to point at the inconsistencies and contradictions of many critical accounts of life in the United States, but the appeal to fairness and coolheadedness was largely unheard, given the passions aroused by the American experience. Mary McCarthy, for one, took obvious pleasure in listing the catalog of Simone de Beauvoir's errors and misinterpretations in *America Day by Day* (see McCarthy quoted in Lasky, 584). For McCarthy, as for many others, the Left's ideological representations of America were not necessarily totally inaccurate, but they were one-sided, caricatural, and reductive, since they only concerned themselves with some aspects of American life (urban life, industrial and racial relations) and specific places such as New York City, Chicago, and, after 1945, the West Coast.

André Maurois noted that his friend had never crossed the Atlantic: "And so, the unbearable confusion of real facts never came to upset the marvelous simplicity of his judgment, and he can therefore remorselessly curse with all his heart a country that he has never seen and where he does not know anyone" (5). Maurois went on to disprove, in a tone of candid puzzlement, most of his compatriot's clichés. Strangely enough, Princeton, New Jersey, did not seem to correspond to the apocalyptic description he had been given of the United States. In this "pretty, provincial town," there was less traffic than in Tours or Avranches, and the silence at night was so deep it could wake up the foreign city dweller, who always expected to hear in the distance the rumble of Parisian tramways. "I think that you would find a rather faithful image of what life . . . is like [here] by reading those novels of Balzac that take place around 1835, in Touraine or in Poitou. So much for noise and agitation" (9).

The French humorist went on to say, in the same tongue-in-cheek manner, that he unfortunately never encountered anything even close to "a civilization of bathrooms and central heating." On the contrary, the only drawback of his little house was the lack of comfort. The antiquated heating system, too hot in the summer and too cold in the winter, could no longer be found in Europe. As for the bathroom, "it is quite pleasant to look at, but it would be totally unrealistic to expect to find hot water in it, which, incidentally, enabled me to revive a habit of my youth, replacing the hot bath with the cold shower" (11). On the topic of widespread criminality, Maurois found his neighborhood so secure that "when I happen to leave [my house] for two or three days, I don't lock the door, to allow the mailman to leave letters and packages in the lobby" (11). His friend's picture of American reality was as inaccurate on the life of the spirit as it was on the subject of technology:

> I talk a lot with my students, with my colleagues, with their wives. Shall I dare say that they have souls, and some of them quite delicate ones? . . . What are our conversations like? . . . My God, how strange, they are strikingly identical to the ones I can have in Paris, with intelligent friends. One talks about the same things and the same books. Marcel Proust, Balzac, Flaubert, Sinclair Lewis and André Siegfried play a great role in our conversations. (9)

Although highly critical narratives of life in the United States have been dominant among the twentieth-century French intelligentsia (at least up to the mid-1970s), there has always existed a countermythology fascinated with the innovative (rather than alienating) dynamics of American modernity. A kind of reverse snobbery, it often implied a solid dose of self-doubt and some anxiety about a Europe behind the times and marginalized. The nationalist pamphleteer Jean Cau satirized, and excoriated, the attitude in the following passage:

> All that comes from the United States is "new" and "big." How could we not, then, genuflect before the Great Novelty? . . . Here intellectual cosmopolitanism teams up with "reason," whose arguments rest on numbers, statistics and arid demonstrations. One goes from a noble form of cosmopolitanism ("We need to open up to foreign in-

5

fluences") to the cold reasoning . . . that concludes: America is *great* and Europe is *little*. . . . There is a form of bourgeois dandyism, unbearable and despicable, which plays at being cosmopolitan. "When you go to New York, you realize that France is the pits. . . ." Very well, you jerk, why didn't you stay in New York, instead of coming back? I, for one, would not have cried over the loss. (*Pourquoi la France*, 25, 27, 104)

For Melvin J. Lasky, the wheel of transatlantic images has been making the same circle, round and round, for centuries: "In Europe, a utopian pro-Americanism in times of adventurous hope, and then the turn to a grumbling anti-Americanism in times of stress. In America, a naive and nostalgic pro-Europeanism when life was raw and difficult, and then the turn to a strident anti-Europeanism when prosperity made for power and national confidence" (466). In France, pro-Americanism was predominant during the eighteenth-century revolutions, in 1848, immediately after the two world wars, or during the past fifteen years; anti-Americanism was more widespread during the July Monarchy and the Second Empire, in the 1930s, and during the Cold War.

The two competing narratives of America have also coexisted within the same individual or literary circle, as well as within most of the intellectual Left during the fifties and sixties. A few years ago, Jean Daniel, editor-in-chief of *Le Nouvel Observateur*, discussed the "two successive—and sometimes also simultaneous—mythologies" that had divided the French Left for decades: "A negative one, which expects America to uphold a few Marxist theses, by the way generally oversimplified, on the contradictions of capitalism, the wrongs of imperialism, the civilization of material profit, etc. [and] the other, a positive one, which fascinated the *blasés* of old Europe, mainly through America's culture, its daring architecture, the richness of its cinema, the freedom of its universities, its lead in technology, and, above all, the unbelievable ability of Americans to imagine the unforeseeable or put their own society on trial" (110).

In a recent study of the relationship between American intellectuals and popular culture, Andrew Ross denounced what he called "an unlikely consensus among certain voices of the right and the left about the intrinsic evils of new technologies and the monstrous mass cultures to which they give birth" (209). The anti-Americanism of the French intellectuals exhibits similar patterns and often cuts across political and ideological lines. Time and again, we will encounter the same conservative-radical consensus over the nature of American culture and society (which makes for strange bedfellows, as Ross puts it). In fact, this consensus explains the strong cohesion of the French intertext of America and the continuity of this interpretive tradition over time. Judgments passed on the United States *from* France must be read as discourses *about* France; they tell us more about an author's position in French intellectual and ideological fields than about social and cultural processes within American society.

The main assumption of this study is that many French intellectuals' perceptions of America, from Tocqueville to Beauvoir, are rooted in a humanistic and aristocratic ethos derived from models of intellectual excellence and critical practice born in the Renaissance and refined in the age of French classicism. The traditional emphasis on intellectualist, universal categories of judgment, the cult of abstraction, and the rejection, on moral and political grounds, of economic and financial activities unbecoming *les gens de lettres*, helps explain the widespread condemnation of the "materialism" and "pragmatism" of American culture. It is in large part because they share homologous positions in the social structure—equidistant from the popular classes and the business and professional establishment—and subscribe to the model of cultural excellence that has prevailed for centuries among the cultivated elites, that most French literati agree across widely diverging political and ideological commitments in their criticism of American culture.

The advent of a market society was the undoing of the traditional intelligentsia. It is ironic because the progressive fractions of the Western European secularized clerisy had played a major role in the legitimation of modern political and economic structures, and had often hastened their development by direct political action. What happened is that the triumphant bourgeoisie did not only emancipate itself from the fetters of dogmatic church and absolute monarchy; it also freed itself, to a certain extent, from the authority of the traditional guardians of knowledge and good taste. In Zygmunt Bauman's words, "The middle-class juxtaposed to the power of intellect the power of money; left to its own discretion, it would conceivably make the power of intellect hollow and ineffective, without even bothering to challenge it on its own territory—the theoretical judgment of taste" (136).

More and more often, the middle classes deferred to the decisions of the market, not the authority of the scholarly elites, in forming their cultural judgments. Whatever sells is good, and whatever sells is what pleases the consumer. Throughout the nineteenth century, the citizens of the republic of letters discovered, with growing dismay, that freedom from feudal patrons also meant their own increasing irrelevance to the central value-creating mechanisms of a capitalist economy. Gradually dispossessed of their monopoly on aesthetic tastemaking and intellectual trendsetting, the intellectuals reacted strongly against the pretentions of the *nouveaux riches* to define the true, the good, and the beautiful independently. High modernist writers and artists proclaimed their scorn for petty bourgeois aesthetic categories, which they ridiculed, like popular tastes in previous eras, as "vulgar" and "philistine." One needs only to think of the anathema Baudelaire and Zola hurled at the Parisian public, whom they accused of completely misunderstanding the achievements of Delacroix or Manet. "It is," Bauman remarked, "the autonomy of artistic judgment—autonomy in regard to the judgment of the elite—that invites rage and condemnation" (136).

Not only were the literati expropriated by economic processes (the verdict of the market), but their authority was also threatened by certain cultural aspects of the new social order, namely its reliance on science and technology. The control over the discourses of truth, judgment, and taste, which define and orient social practices, was being assumed by autonomous institutions of specialized research and learning that were funded by the state and peopled with professionalized experts. In the eyes of those who stood to lose the most in this process, namely Bauman's universalist "metaspecialists," who still pretended to legislate for the whole of society in matters of aesthetics, ethics, or politics, the whole process of modernity had somehow gone awry and was definitely getting out of hand. As Bauman rightly suggests, "the sorcerer's apprentice's feeling of having lost control over his own product and heritage" (a dominant theme in 1920s and 1930s narrative constructions of America) probably expresses, in a phantasmic way, the deep anxieties of increasingly marginalized poets and philosophers, all those prophets and legislators whose expertise had grown obsolete (158).

In France, the power over the minds of a century-old literary culture, the prestige of *ancien régime* models of taste and behavior among the bourgeoisie, and the capacity of a centralized school system to instill in the middle classes and the people a quasi-religious respect for the sanctity of elite classical culture, enabled the literati to retain some ascendency over the whole cultural process. The United States, by contrast, appeared to French intellectuals as the perfect expression of what they had such a hard time containing at home: the triumph of expert knowledge, petty bourgeois taste, and the disenchantment of the world. If it is true that modern society, to quote Ernest Gellner, "is inherently protestant, in that it cannot seriously bring itself to hold important cognition to be accessible only to a ritually segregated minority" (262), then American civilization was the quintessence of modernity and the archenemy of the intellectuals.

Despite their common origin in macrohistorical conditions of possibility, French interpretations of America do not make up a homogeneous bloc: traditional intellectuals have always struggled over the definition of cultural excellence, whether it was grounded on reason and the culture of Enlightenment, on a romantic rejection of technological mastery over nature, or on the nostalgic appeal of tradition and precapitalist life-styles and moral beliefs. The one thing on which they would agree, however, is the validity of debating such questions, which defines, precisely, the legitimate activity of their corporation. In any case, to reduce the complex set of French narrative constructions of America to a neat opposition between romantics and rationalists, or liberals and radicals, or, more recently, between elitist foes of mass society and postmodern supporters of popular culture, is to simplify matters unduly.

I have identified at least six major types of discourse on the United States in the twentieth century (see diagram).

These, of course, are ideal types, theoretical constructs, and analytical tools; they do not exist in pure form as actual descriptions of the United States. One should not overemphasize their coherence, either. Although most of the texts that I will discuss would generally fit in any of the broad categories outlined above, themes belonging to various types can be found in any specific text or within the same individual's trajectory. These interpretive clusters do not fit neatly, either, in a political grid constructed in terms of right and left, revolutionary or reactionary. *Postmodern* and *humanist* discourses, for example, although they often mirror each other as opposite positions on the question of modernity, cannot readily be classified as "progressive" or "conservative" viewpoints. A traditional humanis-

Pro-American

countercultural (libertarian)	*postmodern*	*liberal-democratic* (Atlanticist)
(para)Marxist	*humanist*	*nationalist*

Anti-American

9

tic approach, while it usually precludes any kind of extremist or collectivist ideology (both fascism and communism contain strong antihumanistic elements), is compatible with progressive or conservative views on a particular topic. As for postmodernism, its ideological and political significance is still highly debated, as witnessed by the recent polemical exchanges between Jean-François Lyotard and Jürgen Habermas, and it would be better to talk about various postmodernisms, each with diverse aims and consequences in terms of collective mobilization, historical agency, or transformative impact on social structures.

Some of these discourses may overlap. Specific brands of postmodernism incorporate liberal-democratic elements, others are clearly of a radical, libertarian type (e.g., the 1960s counterculture minus its romantic idealism). A particular author may, at various moments of his or her career, or, even simultaneously, espouse conflicting views on the United States. Céline's anti-Americanism, mainly cultural and antitechnological in the *Journey to the End of the Night*, became more political in the wartime pamphlets. In *Bagatelles pour un massacre*, for example, Céline espoused classic fascistic views of the United States as an aggressive capitalist nation dominated by international Jewish interests. Sartre's own brand of criticism evolved from a youthful passion for jazz and American movies to philosophical and humanistic considerations on "the objective spirit of the United States," and finally to the militant anti-imperialism of the sixties.

This study of French representations of America exhibits a tension similar to the one Edward Said pointed to in his introduction to *Orientalism*. Here, he delineates the tension between collective discursive formations, which are the creation of no one in particular, as the product of the dynamics of a social field, and the individual expressions of these collective ways of making sense of the world in particular texts written by specific authors. Said remarked that "one must repeatedly ask oneself whether what matters in Orientalism is the general group of ideas overriding the mass of material . . . or the much more varied work produced by almost uncountable individuals and writers, whom one would take up as individual instances of authors dealing with the Orient" (8). The maintenance of this uncomfortable tension in fact prevents the social history of intellectual production from falling into the twin pitfalls of sociologism and idealism. Ideas are neither directly "determined" by social and economic processes, nor are they free-floating entities submitted to the sole constraint of inner consistency or place within a tradition. The notion of the "relative autonomy" of the intellectual field is central to any critical enterprise that examines the complex relationship between authors, texts, and (historical) cultures.

The principle of a complex set of shared categories, political investments, and imaginative projections at work within individual texts also enables Said to free himself from the erudite, scholarly obsession with exhausting the corpus of orientalist material. In the same way that a given language can produce an infinite number of meaningful sentences, a discursive formation can generate countless individual, and specific, expressions of what Raymond Williams called its "structure of meanings." However, one does not need to examine all of the possible utterances of a given language (an impossible task by definition) to understand it, or all the texts produced within a given universe of discourse to account for it. "It should be said that even with the generous number of books that I examine," Said writes, "there is a much larger number that I simply have had to leave out. My argument, however, depends neither upon an exhaustive catalogue of texts dealing with the Orient nor upon a clearly delimited set of texts, authors, and ideas that together make up the Orientalist canon" (4). Similarly, I have obviously not examined the entire corpus of French views of the United States; I nevertheless hope to show the consistencies and articulations, as well as the structure of differences and inconsistencies, that make up the complex of descriptions that forms our intertext.

The seven major narrative constructions of America I propose to examine in the book can be briefly characterized as follows.

1. In the 1920s and 1930s, most critical accounts of American culture were humanistic in content. In the manner of André Maurois's friend, traditional humanists saw American civilization as the collapse of Western intellectual values, which were quickly replaced by a mass culture made up of technological hubris, positivism, and the uncontrolled pursuit of pleasure and profit. These accounts tend to demonize American culture as the absolute Other of Europe and stress its difference with classical and Renaissance civilization. Conservative in its outlook, the humanist tradition opposed the American technological nightmare with a highly idealized version of European culture that was based on moderation, refinement, disinterestedness, and the cultivation of aesthetic and spiritual values. The views of Duhamel and the early Céline clearly belong to this category, and will be discussed in chapter 2.

2. While the humanistic approach was mainly cultural and philosophical, the intellectual Left of the 1950s and 1960s centered its criticism on economic, political, and racial issues in the context of American capitalism

and imperialism. The works of Jean-Paul Sartre represent what I call, in a broad sense, Marxist or para-Marxist interpretations of the United States. Chapters 3 and 4 examine the existentialist Left's denounciations of the hegemonic claims of the United States, from the Cold War to Vietnam.

3. Right-wing nationalist and antidemocratic descriptions of the United States are inspired either by Gaullist principles or by a conservative tradition that goes back to Jacques-Bénigne Bossuet, Joseph de Maistre, and Charles Maurras. This brand of cultural nationalism is based on a up-dated critique of the influence of Lockean and Rousseauean principles in the New World (what Louis Hartz has called the "natural liberalism" of American culture). The wartime writings of Céline, Jean Cau's anti-American pamphlets, and recent developments within the French *nouvelle droite* will be examined in this context (chaps. 1 and 6).

4. Up to the 1960s, positive accounts of American society came mainly from the liberal Right and from Christian-Democratic quarters (the Atlanticist camp). The works of Raymond Aron, although at times critical, best represent such a position, which I call *liberal* (in the "European" sense of the term, i.e., opposed to authoritarian, state-centered political regimes, whether monarchist, fascist, or Stalinist. This is quite different from its "American" meaning, i.e., progressive, in favor of state intervention in economic and social matters, and left of center.) I discuss the views of the Atlanticist intellectuals of the postwar period in chapter 4.

5. The worldwide diffusion of American counterculture in the 1960s and 1970s and the decline of Marxism as *the* legitimate theoretical horizon of the critical clerisy gave rise to a new brand of pro-Americanism, and further divided the French Left. This *libertarian* or *countercultural* discourse emphasized the social and cultural diversity and the political experimentalism of contemporary America, which was seen as the only alternative to bureaucratic socialism or European moral and political decadence. Works by Jean-François Revel and Edgar Morin best exemplify this position (see chap. 5).

6. In the past fifteen years, a *postmodern* version of American culture has gained prominence among French intellectuals. In the wake of a strong anti-Hegelian reaction in philosophical circles after 1968, postmodern critics entertain ambiguous and sometimes contradictory notions on the newest technologies of the postindustrial world. Although they often lament the dehumanizing and standardizing aspects of life in modern bureaucratic societies, they also celebrate the liberating effects of the information revolution (Lyotard) or the pragmatic and egalitarian American utopia as the reign of the simulacrum (Baudrillard). The main tenets of the

postmodern vision will be examined with the notion of the United States as the "end of history" in the last chapter of this book.

7. While philosophers and social scientists have tended to judge America in the light of their own assessment of the rise of a democratic worldview, poets have created more lyrical, and often more sympathetic, descriptions of the New World, celebrating American history as a metaphor of *poesis*, and its geography as an imaginary (often female) body on which all the desires, fantasies, and phobias of the Old World converge. I have devoted a good part of chapter 5 to these poetic constructions of the American space.

This book is not concerned with representations of the United States in the mass media or popular literature, which could provide the subject matter for a very interesting study: in France, as in most Western European countries, nonintellectuals, rich and poor, have usually been much more attracted to the American way of life than the cultivated elites.[5] Besides, the corpus I have examined in no way pretends to exhaustivity. I have chosen to study texts belonging to various domains of intellectual creation, such as poetry, novels, essays, travel narratives, historical or social scientific analysis, deliberately cutting across traditional genres, treating all these texts as so many "fictions" of America (in both senses of the term, imaginary accounts and "facts," i.e., things made, cultural constructs). I have focused my attention on the content of these texts rather than on their form, although I have taken into account the role the formal properties of texts play in the construction of their referent (especially in chap. 5).

For the most part, the order of exposition is chronological, from the interwar (chap. 2) and the Cold War (chaps. 3–4) to the 1960s (part of chap. 5) and the contemporary period (chap. 6). I found such a linear structure best suited to what intends to be essentially a historical narrative of the literary and philosophical descriptions of America by prominent French intellectuals. One of the major points of this study, however, is that the different views of the intelligentsia on the United States do not proceed through a neat series of distinct phases easily identified by a discrete set of specific features. Themes, stereotypes, and clichés often born in the prerevolutionary period recur and overlap throughout the nineteenth and twentieth centuries, and the first chapter briefly examines their genealogy.

These ideological building blocks are often modified and rearranged in new configurations called forth by new historical contexts, the transformations of French and American cultures, and the changing structure of the relations of power between the two countries. Moreover, some considerations are dominant at times, but lose their importance at others: American consumer culture comes to the fore during the critical interwar or more favorable contemporary period, while foreign policy and race relations constitute the core of Cold War Americanophobia. Although I have adopted an overarching linear framework, I have also tried to describe as well as possible the relational and recursive nature of this American mythology, mainly by juxtaposing texts from different periods.

Let me end on a more confessional note, since our self-conscious, skeptical, and suspicious fin de siècle is growing increasingly aware that "all research is autobiographical" or, to paraphrase, and slighty subvert, a well-known feminist slogan, that "the personal is the theoretical." As a Frenchman living in the United States, I could not deny that my study reflects a personal experience of uprooting and acculturation. Still, the question of the specificity, of the "exceptionalism" of American society and culture started to puzzle and interest me long before I decided to live in this country. Once I did emigrate, however, I experienced what many travelers, immigrants, and exiles have gone through. As I was revising the long held views and familiar clichés I had inherited from my French upbringing, American culture, paradoxically, became more foreign to me, although I was growing accustomed to it and was even getting better at living in the midst of it. Simultaneously, I realized I shared many of the views of the United States I was reading about. As one (European) student once remarked to me, American reality is so diverse that French critics of any persuasion could always find in the United States the opposite of their own beliefs and commitments. I soon found myself confronted with a double complexity: that of the "object" of the study, namely, a set of representations of life in the United States, and that of the referent of these representations, namely American culture and society (or subcultures and societies). I hope I have conveyed a sense of that complexity in the following pages.

As I became more familiar with the American academic world, I found myself challenged in two distinct but convergent ways. Confronted with the amazing success of those theoretical models referred to as "French theory" (I discovered the existence of an American Foucault and an American Derrida), I started to reread books of philosophy and literary theory I had not opened since my student days in Paris in the mid-seventies (this setting aside occurred in part because I had gone on to graduate work in history and the social sciences, disciplines then generally inimical to the poststructuralist paradigm, which would eventually come under attack in philosophical circles after 1975).[6] I was even more puzzled, and intrigued, at seeing that most indigenous of all American schools of thought, pragmatism, strategically allied with the most arcane and elaborate products of Parisian intellectualism in the works of American theorists such as Richard Rorty, Barbara Herrnstein Smith, Cornel West, and Stanley Fish. This series of surprises rekindled my interest in the comparative study of French and American intellectual traditions and histories.

Since I share, to a certain extent, the current epistemological modesty of many philosophers and literary critics, I certainly do not subscribe to a realist, "God's eye view" conception of knowledge, according to which it is possible to step outside of one's field of inquiry to give a complete, accurate account of one's object of study. In that sense, there is no last word on America, French culture, or anything else in this book. On the other hand, I take the works of historians or sociologists of culture too seriously to adopt an all-out subjectivist position and to deny that anything meaningful, communicable, and somewhat comprehensive can be said on the French intellectuals' perceptions of America. I find retaining a concept of totality still useful, if not in the closed, metaphysical sense to be found in some quarters of the Hegelian tradition, at least as a horizon of possibility, an unreachable, always receding, limit toward which one is constantly striving.

Spatial metaphors may help here. Although I think it illusory and counterproductive to try to present a total picture seen from above, there is another way in which one can try to account for as much of the field as possible: horizontally, and serially, by visiting in turn all, or most, of the positions one takes to constitute the field. This is what I have tried to do: not to apprehend the object all at once, as in the structuralists' synoptic, objectivist diagrams of a myth or a kinship structure, but to cover descriptively as much of the terrain as possible, exploring it on foot rather than looking down at it from an airplane. To describe the (shifting) positions of the players, the structure of the field, and the relations between them is not to play the game, to be sure, but it is the best one can do to convey a feel for it through the objectifying tool of language.

The human mind helps us in this critical task, I think, since its capacities for symbolization and rationalization are limited and somewhat repetitive through time: there are just so many ways of celebrating or denouncing such cultural realities as Incan sacrificial rituals, Chinese mandarinism, or American modernity. Despite the innumerable individual variations in the expression of beliefs and values, representations nevertheless form interpretive clusters around which people rally and sometimes mobilize. Otherwise, collective action and shared practices would never be possible.

15

The observer, while trying to see the whole space of positions is himself positioned. Traveling on foot and spending some time with the locals allows him to see more of the country, and in more detail, but he is still looking at it from a distinct perspective, albeit an (ideally) comprehensive one. The question of perspectivism, of the preconceptions critics bring to their object by virtue of their own position, is at the core of the current debates over relativism and the status of cognitive truth in the human disciplines. The problem is heightened when, as in the case of intellectual history and the sociology of intellectuals, the student belongs in some way or other to the population under scrutiny. I am not sure that the debate can be put to rest by philosophical arguments and sophisticated epistemological and methodological considerations alone, however. Ultimately, it is the *practice* of historians, literary critics, and social scientists, that is, the empirical study of particular fragments of the social (and the textual), that will enlighten us on the possibility of making sense of symbolic worlds without unknowingly taking up one of the positions which constitute them.

I do believe, obviously, that it is possible to a certain extent for the critic to objectify the space of possible positions, including his own, in order to reach some kind of nonideological understanding. Otherwise, I would never have attempted this discussion. To understand, of course, does not mean to approve, excuse, or justify. Understanding should not lead, either, to indifference or neutrality. Hence, the *critique* of the French intellectuals' views of the United States implies, at times, a *criticism* of their mandarinal, socially authorized, stance. The attempt to describe the entire field of discourses on a given question inevitably leads one to see the limits of each discourse and, beyond, to question the power, and arrogance, of those who try to impose their perspective as the only valid one. I believe that intellectual history, when aware of the social determinants of culture and knowledge, cannot but reinforce a healthy skepticism as to the wisdom and legitimacy of intellectuals who pose as arbiters of taste and truth, whether in an elitist or a populist register.

My own social and intellectual trajectory can certainly account for a good part of the skepticism with which I have often viewed the French mandarins' pronouncements on American culture and society. As a first-generation intellectual, I owe my ability to speak in culturally legitimate ways of the cultivated world to an elitist and highly selective school system; thus, I cannot look at such a world without a mixture of fascination and detachment. When a desire to belong does not make them fanatics, converts often stand both inside and outside the sacred precincts of the social:

they are more likely to see the limits of what goes on within, and more likely to blow the gaff. In many respects, this study was also a way of answering for myself the question of how one could be an intellectual.

In the following pages, I have gone from one text to the next, often retracing my steps, trying to suggest the interrelatedness of all these interpretive clusters, the way they echo each other through time and space. The debate over the future of learned culture, and the role "America" plays in it, is often cacophonous, made up as it is of entangled, overlapping lines of conversations between (and within) individuals, some alive, some dead. The topic is incredibly vital to French intellectuals; it is a question of life and death indeed, for it involves their most sacred beliefs and, ultimately, the justification of their being as intellectuals. To build a mirror gallery, or an echoing chamber, of all these conflicting versions is to me what "culture criticism" is all about. It is a genre of writing that aims not to anathematize or celebrate, but to understand, albeit with a dose of irony, in the hope that, in the words of Richard Rorty, "if one understands enough poems, enough religions, enough societies, enough philosophies, one will have made oneself into something worthy of one's own understanding" (*Consequences of Pragmatism*, 66). In my wanderings through text after text, from one cultural form to another and back again, I have entertained some of that hope.

ONE

THE CONTEST OF AMERICA
A Historical Perspective

In the course of history, Mother Europe has sent to New York the children she wanted to punish—for being Huguenots or Quakers, poor or Jewish, or simply for being younger sons. She thought she was shutting them up in a dark closet, and it turned out to be the jam cupboard. Today those children are grown up; they are the center of the universe. *Paul Morand*

One nation that manages to lower intelligence, morality, human quality on nearly all the surface of the earth, such a thing has never been seen before in the existence of the planet. I accuse the United States of being in a permanent state of crime against humankind. *Henri de Montherlant*

There are foreign travelers who are struck right away with what we call in French *le coup de foudre*, love at first sight. . . . A friend of mine . . . likes to think of the French people who got in this way, at one stroke, some inner understanding of this country, as constituting a group of privileged people, a sort of club, in which each one is on brotherly terms with the others by reason of the common understanding in question. *Jacques Maritain*

The old quarrel between the ancients and the moderns over the meaning and value of democratic modernity, has recently turned into a fierce battle between the moderns and the postmoderns. The moderns have now become the new ancients, paradoxically borrowing from traditional classical humanism criticisms against our decadent and cynical fin de siècle. It is an ironical twist of historical fate that the old foes of church and state, the progressive, secular heroes of yore, from Locke and Descartes to Rousseau (that rabble-rouser), not to mention Sartre himself, are now seen by many critics as fossilized representatives of oppressive, "unreconstructed" ethnocentric or misogynous views. The postmodern debate, however it may contribute to a change in the rules of the game, has in no way modified the fundamental issues at stake.

In a sense, contemporary critics of the American scene face the same alternative Karl Popper defined, some sixty years ago in *The Open Society and Its Enemies*. Popper's "moral decision" amounted to a choice between "the revolt against reason" and a "minimum concession toward irrationalism." The point was to adopt a kind of (self-) critical rationalism based on "the awareness of one's limitations, the intellectual modesty of those who know how often they err, and how much they depend on others even for this knowledge" (227). The anti-Americanism of the 1920s and 1930s was a symptom of the anxiety Popper called one of the nightmares of our times, namely the fear that "the development of mass production and collectivization may react upon men by destroying their inequality or individuality" (234). He was thinking of Huxley's *Brave New World*, but the same could be said of Duhamel's *America: The Menace, Scenes from the Life of the Future* or Céline's *Journey to the End of Night*.

In many ways, the current battles over the closing of the American mind, the culture of narcissism, and the imminent collapse of Western civilization (at least in academic curricula) proceed from the same sets of assumptions and beliefs that framed the debates of the interwar period, or the seventeenth- and eighteenth-century indictments of the new social and intellectual developments, as in Pascal's criticism of Montaigne's self-indulgent epicurism, or Rousseau's attack on the corruptions of civilization. The anxiety over its own imminent collapse and erasure seems to have been part and parcel of Western culture's self-description ever since its beginnings. The debate over decadence, more than any other issue in the Western tradition, bears out the impression that modern and contemporary European intellectual history is often no more than a series of slight displacements within recurrent problematics, a process of repetition within change.

Questioning Modernity

Although most French accounts of the American way of life between the two world wars were motivated by the advent of technological culture (Henry Miller's "air-conditioned nightmare"), the responses to American modernity differed from one author to the next and depended heavily on his or her interpretation of what was wrong with the United States. The most radical critics of America were not all "irrationalists." Some, like Georges Duhamel, contrasted the technical rationality of industrial civilization with a humanistic definition of reason patterned after ancient and Renaissance ideals of moderation and genteel culture. Others, like the wartime Céline or fascist writers like Drieu la Rochelle, favored a more radical response to the decadence of the West: an appeal to nationalistic pride, a call for action, a celebration of effort and self-mastery, a rejection of materialism in the name of pagan, anti–"Judaeo-Christian" spiritual values. The alternative was to resist what Popper called "the myth of the lost tribal paradise, the hysterical refusal to carry the cross of civilization" (245). Those who refused to throw the baby of modernity out with the bathwater of corporate or state bureaucracy or to equate the liberal rationalist tradition of the Enlightenment with the development of mass production and collectivization, usually refused a polarized vision of the relationship between Europe and America.

While the radical critics, whether on the right or the left, adhered to what I have called a paradigm of absolute cultural discontinuity, the liberal interpreters of America underscored the philosophical and political continuities between both cultures and usually downplayed the demonic side of the modern. Alexandre Kojève saw the United States as nothing but "the North American extension of Europe" (161). André Maurois would certainly have agreed. For him, Americans shared common concerns and a common cultural tradition with Europeans. He tirelessly reminded those who deplored the absence or marginalization of learned culture in the New World of the similarities between intellectual and academic life on both sides of the Atlantic. In an essay published in *L'Amérique inattendue*, he gave some advice to a young Frenchman about to leave for America: "Of all the false ideas that you can bring her, the silliest one is the legend of an American indifference to things of the mind" (171). A few years later in a short text entitled "Return from America," Maurois acknowledged that the six years he had spent in America had taught him "the growing importance of culture in the United States," a country where education amounted to a religion. American materialism, the love for industrial organization, was not to be taken as greed, but as "pleasure of achievement" (*From My Journal*, 176).

Maurois saw the threat of modernity not in the destruction of *belles-lettres*, but in their accelerated consumption, in the built-in obsolescence of ideas: "The universal curiosity [of the Americans] is naturally not without its dangers. The life of the mind suffers, in the United States, from the evils of our times, but they have taken over there a more virulent form. The most serious one is the short shelf-life of ideas" (*From My Journal*, 174). Maurois also shared one of the fundamental beliefs of the liberal tradition, that is, the faith in the sound common sense and natural good taste of "the people." The poor quality of mass culture, he argued, need not be attributed to the innate vulgarity of the masses, but rather to the preconceived notion of popular tastes and demands entertained by the producers of collective entertainment. In a journal entry dated 11 May 1946, the French writer noted that "it is not the public that requires Hollywood to distort the lives of great men. . . . I have never seen spectators hostile to a really fine work of art," he added. "Tastes and demands are attributed to them that are not actually theirs" (*From My Journal*, 80).

Maurois urged his young listener to free himself from what I have called the French intertext of America, for it is mostly made up of necessarily incomplete, and flawed, journalistic essays and travel narratives. "You have read, since you started preparing for your trip, hundreds of books on America: forget them. The traveler is tempted, when describing a foreign country, to exaggerate its strangeness" (*L'Amérique inattendue*, 163). Maurois viewed travel narratives as the product of a particular kind of gaze, which, like a magnifier, distorted the facts of ordinary experience. As a literary genre, travel narratives often aimed at entertainment rather than education:

> As for me, whose goal is not to please, but to inform, I will say that the beings with human faces whom you will meet on the other side, after six days on the ocean, are not as different as you think from your friends in Europe, or from yourself. They are people who, like us, work, suffer, eat, drink and make love, read poetry, build temples and then destroy them, are born and die. After noticing that some of them, just like yourself, love Proust and Valéry, after seeing in their homes paintings by Degas and Renoir and hearing in their concert halls Debussy, Dukas and Ravel, you will undoubtedly cast away with some shame the spiritual explorer's extravagant equipment you are now sporting. You are going to America, not to the moon. (164)

Maurois's avowed distrust of most European accounts of American life stemmed from his humanist belief in the universality of human experience and his insistence on the common cultural heritage shared by the educated classes on both sides of the Atlantic. The critics of American life in the 1920s and 1930s were likely to respond that the genteel, patrician atmosphere described by Maurois was precisely the most Europeanized aspect of American culture, a protected and somewhat artificial material and symbolic environment that thrived on the past and was in no way representative of what lay in store for an Americanized Europe. Indeed, Maurois

21

acknowledged that "if few people spend their leisure time in the slaughter-houses of Chicago," it was also true that "America is not Princeton." He earnestly advised the young traveler to avoid the simplifications of ideology:

> The truth, you see, my dear sir, is that the world is not made of the simple and brutal oppositions our passions would often wish for. Burke, in 1793, speaking of France to the English, used to say: "One cannot condemn a whole nation." When this nation is young, lively and only wishes to get better acquainted with us, doesn't it seem more human and more wise to try to understand it rather than condemn it? (12–13)

Transatlantic Conversations

Andrew Ross's recent account of the conflict between American intellectuals and U.S. popular culture in the twentieth century sounds familiar to the student of French interpretations of life in the United States. Ross's thesis is that the views of many American high intellectuals are in fact patterned after those of their European counterparts: until the fifties, they swore "unswerving allegiance to the printed word and the dictates of European taste" (11). Drawing on Gramsci's and C. Wright Mills's analyses of the specific situation of American intellectuals, Ross argues, rightly I think, that the "cultural establishment" in the United States has lived on borrowed, "foreign" capital, on the profits of a precapitalist prestige imported from Europe. Even after its ascendance, the European bourgeoisie, excluded for so long from political and cultural recognition by the nobility, kept looking to aristocratic life-styles and humanistic education to consolidate, justify, and idealize its new position of power. Its American counterpart, in contrast, shared with the popular classes a national identity informed by the resistance to feudal society and a strong "protestant" dislike of the monopolization of knowledge by a priestly caste of high-culture worshippers.

The American middle classes never really needed the legitimating services of a semiautonomous class of literati, whose social function, patterned after the European model, was to reproduce and inculcate the traditional values of classical excellence. Estranged in a business and political "populist" culture that did not value the legitimation of genteel, aristocratic taste (usually reserved to the marginalized world of bourgeois women), many American intellectuals have been reduced, in Ross's words, to simulate the position of a rentier class in "a national culture without a historical rentier class given over to the cultural pursuits that were once thought requisite to the life of a gentleman" (62).

The commonality of taste and values between the high-culture intellectuals of Europe and America accounts for the relative similarity of their reactions to "masscult and midcult." During the Cold War, traditional humanists and anti-Stalinist leftists alike strongly resisted the mass media and the culture of kitsch; today, many in the younger generation of intellectuals celebrate pop culture and the collapse of the old hierarchies of taste. A similar evolution affected French perceptions of America, from the anathema of the 1930s and 1950s to the enthusiasm for the counterculture of the 1960s and the recent postmodern praises of U.S. fashion and pluralistic consumerism.

Ironically, the tables seem to be turned today: European intellectuals subscribe in greater numbers to the "cool," anti-elitist, populist mood of their American counterparts, and have replaced the traditional Jacobin and Leninist cultural vanguardism of old with a pragmatic rejection of metaphysics, metanarratives, and universalist propheticism. It is not by chance that deconstructionist attacks on the Western tradition have found such an echo in American academic circles; the ground had been prepared by two centuries of empiricist, pragmatic, populist, and "ethnocentric" criticisms of Old World classicism and scholasticism. To put it more crudely, the attack on the Western European canon looks much like the completion of the American Revolution (and its attendant Emersonian declaration of intellectual independence) in the last strongholds of European high humanism on the American soil—that is, in academic departments in the humanities, which John Dewey himself, among others, strongly criticized long before today's cultural radicals.

The convergence between postanalytic American philosophy, especially in its neopragmatist form, and European poststructuralism, which Richard Rorty so enthusiastically documents and advocates today (pragmatists and deconstructionists, he says, are natural allies) may signal a growing pragmatization of North Atlantic academic culture (I discuss these trends in more detail in chap. 6). Now that the winds are blowing the other way, this may constitute the final stage of the Americanization of Europe: the New World is not only exporting its songs, situation comedies, buttons, and faded leather jackets, but its philosophical categories and radical, antifoundationalist discourses as well.

The European and American traditional clerisies also share similar anxieties concerning the future of the relations between their respective cultures. In the past, both groups have been strongly divided over paradigms of continuity or rupture between the mother culture and her wayward and independent-minded child. Many Europeans have favored views of a growing rift between the two continents, while some entertained strong beliefs in a commonality of destiny among North Atlantic nations. American humanists, on the other hand, tenaciously clung to a narrative of continuity, fearing that a total rejection by their European counterparts would deliver them to the anti-intellectualism of some of their compatriots. For a Mark Twain who wondered what there was in Rome to see that others had not seen before him, for a Malcolm Cowley who once burst out that "America is just as god-damned good as Europe . . . and French taste in most details . . . [is] unbearable" (quoted in Lasky, 488), scores of academics, artists, and journalists have overlooked the patronizing contempt of some of their European counterparts and embraced a belief in their participation in a common Western intellectual and moral enterprise. Things appear to be changing today, as voices in the cultural Left urge the American academic community to wrench itself from the fetters of Eurocentrism.

Often, those who insisted on the radical difference between both civilizations had the choice between a nostalgic yearning for European cultural distinction and the decision to become altogether European. Even Walt Whitman, for all his buoyant enthusiasm for his country's democratic vistas, was not immune to what Melvin Lasky has called "the temptation of Europe." Thus, our democratic society," Whitman wrote, "possesses nothing . . . to make up for that glowing, blood-throbbing, religious, social, emotional, artistic, undefinable, indescribably beautiful charm and hold which fused the separate parts of the old feudal societies together, in their wonderful interpenetration" (quoted in Lasky, 473).

T. S. Eliot wrote of another famous exile, Henry James, that "it is the final perfection, the consummation of an American to become, not an Englishman, but a European—something which no born European, no person of any European nationality can become" (quoted in Lasky, 483). Paradoxically, even those who had most radically reversed America's drift away from the old continent by choosing to become European, or rather Europeanized Americans, often had done so in the hope of maintaining American literature within the ancestral fold. Eliot endorsed the paradigm of continuity, urging his readers not to give up what he called "the historical sense," which involves "a perception, not only of the pastness of the past, but of its presence; the historical sense compels a man to write . . . with a feeling that the whole of the literature of Europe from Homer and within it the whole of the literature of his own country has a simultaneous existence" (quoted in Lasky, 488).

Populist Minds, Aristocratic Souls

Heeding Eliot's call to sharpen our sense of history, I will briefly place the study of French interpretations of the United States within the broader context of social and political history, since anti-Americanism among European elites is hardly limited to the twentieth century. When the United States became an independent nation, there was a short burst of elation at seeing the mighty British ridiculed by their colonies; still, the main tenets of anti-Americanism were already present across Europe. The major sin of the citizens of the new republic was their unabashed materialism, their unquenchable thirst for money, and the plebeian vulgarity of their mores and cultural tastes.

The British, of course, especially those of Tory persuasion, were among the fiercest critics of the barbaric egalitarianism of the Jacksonian era. How could such a boorish, unrefined sample of humanity ever have come out of English civilization? The problem was not so much that America was full of common folks, for there were lots of these in Britain, too, but that they were so unashamedly conspicuous, bent on running things and conquering positions of power and leadership. John Keats scoffed at the petty middle-class thriftiness of the two American heroes of European democratic and revolutionary circles, Franklin and Washington. The former, he wrote, was "a philosophical Quaker full of mean and thrifty maximes," while the other stooped so low as to sell "the very charger who had taken him through all his battles." Anyone familiar with the English reverence for humankind's most noble conquest will understand Keats's disgust and amazement. "Those Americans are great," the poet said, "but they are not the sublime Man—the humanity of the United States can never reach the sublime" (quoted in Cunliffe, 508).

In the first half of the nineteenth century, critical reports on American society by conservative British soldiers and explorers, such as Basil Hall or Thomas Hamilton, outnumbered sympathetic accounts, such as those of Frances Wright or Harriett Martineau (*Society in America*, 1837). Fanny Trollope, author of *Domestic Manners of the Americans*, who had departed for the New World a Whig, came back a Tory, inflamed against the leveling populism of Jackson's supporters. Dickens, for his part, wrote in his *American Notes* (1842) of his profound disappointment at seeing the culture of the common man in action: "This is not the republic I came to see; this is not the republic of my imagination. . . . The more I think of its youth and strength, the poorer and more trifling in a thousand aspects it appears in my eyes" (quoted in Lasch 1961, xi).

Most of these accounts of America were immediately translated into French and exerted a strong influence on the cultivated readership's perception of the young republic. In those days, French critics usually deferred to the judgment of their British counterparts; the latter were believed to possess, by virtue of the commonality of language and cultural origins, a privileged insight into things American. Parisian publishing houses waited for the reaction of the English public before launching a translation of James Fenimore Cooper or Washington Irving on the French market.

In the early years of the American republic, the main lines of opposition regarding the New World were already drawn within French educated opinion. During the Empire and the Restoration, liberals, republicans, and democrats had held fast to eighteenth-century idealized images of the American Arcadia as the land of happiness, an agrarian paradise where good savages, altruistic Quakers, modern-day Catos and Cincinnatis, and freedom-loving farmers shared the stoic virtues of the ancient world and the tolerant, enlighted rationalism of Thomas Jefferson. As René Rémond has argued in *Les États-Unis devant l'opinion française, 1815–1852*, most intellectuals in the political opposition during the Empire and the Restoration, from the Idéologues (around Destutt de Tracy) to the small, but active, liberal circles of Benjamin Constant and Germaine de Staël, were staunch admirers of the new republic.

The main purveyors of anti-American images before 1830 were the *ultras*, the hard-line royalists who anathematized the American Revolution as a prelude to the French one. Their vision of the United States, strongly influenced by recently translated Tory pamphlets, was undissolubly political *and* cultural in character. Criticisms of the boredom, utilitarianism, and lack of refinement of American life were welded with political considerations on the powerlessness and lackluster demeanor of the executive government, the weakness of the military, and the abstract rationalism that had given birth to the U.S. Constitution and the institutions of the new regime. "The babe in swaddling clothes," as Joseph de Maistre, a leading exponent of *ultra* ideology, had contemptuously called the young nation, had all the vices of modernity and none of the redeeming moral and humanistic features of ancient republics.

The European nobility, with its taste for panache and chivalrous deeds, elegant salon conversations, and the refined codes of sociability displayed in its *fêtes galantes*, felt only scorn for the humdrum life-style and acquisitive ethos of the American middle classes. Romanticism, steeped in history and a fascination for medieval times, gave the old patrician class additional reasons to reject the ridiculous pretentions of the Founding Fathers, who wished to start from scratch, with the help of universal reason, and build a wholly new society on the basis of a decisive break with tradition. "The United States, this republic born yesterday," the marquis de Custine wrote to the marquis de Dreux-Brézé, "full of stiffness and Puritan sadness, with its mores so monotonous and so cold, has none of the national memories that lend so much charm and color to our old Europe. . . . That country lacks a past, no monuments and no traditions. There, all is serious, cold, and dry. Between the existence of this republic so poor in memories and the annals of our old monarchies, there lies the same difference as between the black frock of the President of the Union and the royal cloak of Charlemagne or Louis XIV" (quoted in Rémond, 648). American society lacked soul and poetry because it lacked that essential romantic ability: imagination. "In this country," the French aristocrat Hyde de Neuville wrote in his *Mémoires*, "imagination finds little nourishment, for it is everywhere at grips with reality. . . . [America] had neither past nor infancy, which deprives her of poetry" (quoted in Rémond, 648).

Ironically enough, the patrician vision of the French Tories, embattled and often ridiculed while they ruled the country, gradually became prevalent among the French elites when the Liberals took power. There was an outburst of enthusiasm for the United States as the "model republic" after the upheaval of the Trois Glorieuses (27–29 July 1830) and the return to prominence of Lafayette and his "American school," but the image of the United States as agrarian myth and the most perfect form of republican government gradually lost support among the liberal and democratic Left. The rapid urbanization of the country, the growing political role of the lawless, uncivilized plebeian West (exemplified by Jackson's rise to prominence) and the expansionist implications of the Monroe Doctrine soon led the French public to wonder if the United States were not closer to Carthage or Babylon than to democratic Athens and republican Rome.

Long before the 1840s, many commentators, even in the progressive camp, thought that the land of Spartan simplicity and Jeffersonian farsightedness had fallen victim to its own success: excessive freedom and the love of money were sure to turn republican virtues into democratic vices. The Chevalier de Beaujour wrote as early as 1814 that, if virtue had traditionally been considered as the principle of republics, that of the American republic seemed "a frenetic love of money" (quoted in Cunliffe, 506). Too plebeian for the reactionary aristocrats, American culture was too acquisitive for those who believed in republican virtues. Pessimistic and anxious descriptions of the United States as a power-hungry mercantile nation, blindly headed toward an uncertain future, replaced the traditional vision of an eternal, motionless agrarian order, blessed with civil peace and forever removed from the vicissitudes of history. The disillusionment with which travelers, confronted with a reality quite different from the myths that had circulated among their peers, viewed the American experience is reflected in Chateaubriand's account of his first visit to the New World in 1791 (from *Travels in America*, originally published in 1827):

> A man landing as I did in the United States, full of enthusiasm for the ancients, a Cato seeking everywhere the rigidity of the early Roman manners, is necessarily shocked to find everywhere the elegance of dress, the luxury of carriages, the frivolity of conversations, the disproportion of fortunes, the immorality of banks and gaming houses, the noise of dance-halls and theaters. At Philadephia, I could have thought myself in an English town: nothing proclaimed that I had passed from a monarchy to a republic. (15)

This first impression, which led to what Chateaubriand called his "political disappointment," proved to be misleading, the result of a youthful attachment to ancient, outdated forms of republicanism. Reflecting on the experience four decades later, and letting his admiration for American political freedom and economic growth override his monarchist convictions, Chateaubriand claimed to have realized that the classical opposition between wealth and virtue, democracy and morality, agriculture and commerce, had been superseded in the new nation. "I did not know," he wrote self-critically, "that there was another liberty, daughter of the enlightenment of an old civilization, a liberty whose reality the representative republic has proved. It is no longer necessary to plow one's own little field, reject art and science, have ragged nails and a dirty beard, in order to be free" (*Travels in America*, 15).

Such considerations formed the core of the liberal celebration of American politics in the early years of the nineteenth century. One of Lafayette's companions during his glorious return to the United States in 1825 wrote enthusiastically that the prosperity of New York showed that "republican principles are not incompatible with luxury and the pleasures of wealth, but such luxury is only the result of industry, the daughter . . . of freedom" (quoted in Rémond, 513). That it would become increasingly difficult for the supporters of the American experience to reconcile wealth and equality, republican virtues and the drive for profit, is witnessed in the following remarks by Victor Jaquemont, who had been raised in the progressivist circle of the Idéologues, staunch opponents to Bonapartism and fervent supporters of Jefferson. During his visit to the model nation his father had so much admired, Jacquemont quickly grew disenchanted with what he described as a contradiction between the tolerance guaranteed in the laws and the religious fanaticism of the American sects, a topos destined to enjoy lasting success in French descriptions of the United States. "The Bible," he wrote, "seems to me to be the curse of America" (quoted in Rémond, 678).

In the eyes of disillusioned liberals, the Voltairean deism of Jefferson and the genteel culture of aristocratic Virginia, which had given three presidents to the new nation, had degenerated into a petty bourgeois commonwealth dominated by greedy Yankees and uncouth frontiersmen. "M. de Chateaubriand," Jacquemont wrote in reference to the passage of *Travels in America* quoted above, "talks of the elegance of modern republics, alluding to the United States. That is because, when he came to this country, all the men of the American Revolution were still alive, who were republican in principle but aristocratic in their mores, or at least in their manners elegant and polite, because they had received the monarchist English education of the times. These men are dead" (quoted in Rémond, 679).

By 1830, the younger generation of liberals had tired of hearing the praises of a country in which they could not see the virtues extolled by their seniors, men who, like Saint-Simon, had fought alongside Lafayette for American freedom and had never recanted the republican idealism of their youth. The establishment of a constitutional regime in France after 1830 made it less necessary to praise the United States as an alternative to the absolute monarchy. Evils such as slavery and the growth of a miserable industrial working class were more apparent now that it was no longer politically expedient to downplay their existence. The younger disciples of Saint-Simon did not share the master's enthusiasm for the future of the new nation and refused to see it as a model of a free and democratic social system. In 1832, Emile Peirere wondered in the *Revue encyclopédique*, the organ of the left-wing Saint-Simonians: "What is the use of comparing the finances of France and the United States? What connection can there be between a nation at the head of the civilization of Europe and a new people with endless explorations ahead?" (See Tillett, 15.)

The French enlightened, modernist elites of the 1830s, like many of their now deceased American heroes, were often liberal in principle but aristocratic in taste and behavior. They would go as far as liberalism, but not beyond. Sympathy for the republican ideal and repulsion for the reality of American popular culture were at the root of the equivocal position many French literati held regarding the United States. The same ambiguity could be found in their assessment of the French lower classes, in their tastes and politics; they shuttled back and forth between populist, progressivist political principles, and elitist social and aesthetic judgments. French popular wisdom captures this in the commonplace, "les Français ont le cœur à gauche, et le portefeuille à droite" (The French have their hearts on the left and their wallets on the right).

The fundamental ambiguity of the French intellectuals' political stance comes in large part from their position within the social structure, where, as Pierre Bourdieu would say, they occupy the "dominated pole of the field of power." Economically and socially dominated by the propertied bourgeoisie, many intellectuals are prone to rebel against the status quo. Their contempt for the narrow-minded philistinism of the establishment often drives them to side with the popular classes and to mistake, like Hugo, Zola, or George Sand, revolutions in the realm of aesthetics for those in the social order. When a crisis arises, though, and a choice must be made between maintaining the freedom conducive to creative experiments and unorthodox life-styles, and submitting to the distinct social desires and political demands of the lower classes, most writers and artists will side with law and order, as the condemnation of the Paris Commune of 1871 by the vast majority of the intelligentsia, regardless of political persuasion, amply demonstrates.

Théodore Jouffroy, a political commentator during the July Monarchy, grasped the dilemma of the European intelligentsia confronted with the impossible choice between the abstract symbols of American freedom and equality and their concrete, historical *mise en œuvre*. This latter was represented through the practices and cultural categories of the most democratic society that had ever existed, a world suffused with (but not entirely dominated by) the representations, tastes, feelings, and habits of the lower middle classes. Fanny Trollope's experience, Jouffroy contended in an article published in *La Revue des deux mondes* in 1832, was typical of French travelers as well. "What happened to her, is the simplest thing in the world. She left England with ideas and habits that were not of the same color; her ideas were democratic and her habits aristocratic. . . . Forced to choose between habits compatible with her ideas, or ideas compatible with her habits, [she] did not hesitate: revolted by democratic habits, she renounced the principles which engender them." Mrs. Trollope's book highlighted a contradiction that she, and "all of us European democrats," had overlooked, that is, "the deep antipathy between our mores and the habits of democracy." "We only know half of this truth," Jouffroy concluded, "because we know only its ideas and are ignorant of its ways. To learn it whole, all of us, great and small, would have to make a trip to America. There, we would witness democratic mores such as true democracy made them" (quoted in Rémond, 720).

Stendhal, who never made the trip, but felt early in life a deep admiration for the young republic, finally saw the truth and noted in his journals: "Until recently, I thought I hated aristocrats; my heart sincerely believed to be in step with my head" (quoted in Rémond, 682). "The most unhappy place in the world," he remarked in his *Life of Rossini*, published in 1825, "is assuredly Boston, precisely where the government is just about perfect. Isn't Religion the key to the enigma?" (quoted in Rémond, 683). Freedom and happiness may well be incompatible, for how could someone raised in the refinements of high culture be happy in a land without opera or literature, where the stern divinity of the Calvinists was gradually being replaced by the "Dollar god," as one character remarked in *The Charterhouse of Parma*.

What the intellectual elites, whether royalist or liberal, could not accept was the New World's insistence on consensus and uniformity, which Tocqueville had called the "tyranny of the majority" and Michel Chevalier termed "popular autocracy." This standardization meant adopting, as legitimate culture, the values and behaviors of the same petty bourgeois classes the European elites despised so much at home. Auguste Comte summed it up in a letter to his friend Valat, in April 1818, in which he contrasted collective freedom and the sacred independence of the (creative) self:

> If in Paris one enjoys far less political freedom than in Washington, one has much more civil liberty, i.e., freedom to act and to live as one pleases. . . . It is no doubt nice to speak one's mind openly on the affairs of the State and even to be able to print it . . . but it is, I think, much more pleasant to be able to do at home whatever one wants without having to fear the despotism of gossip, to dress, eat and make a home as one sees fit, and, in brief, to live according to fancy. (Quoted in Rémond, 682)

The incompatibility between the two conceptions of freedom became another illustration of the chasm between Europe's north and south, between Latin Catholicism and Anglo-Saxon Protestantism, an opposition destined to generate volumes of comments and exhortations. How could anyone, asked the viscount of Arlincourt in 1848, dream of transplanting the American republic on French soil? "One would have to transform the entire French character beforehand, dim its spirit, freeze its imagination, and destroy its memories. It would amount to forbidding its glory. Could anyone grow an Egyptian palm on the coast of Norway? Would you turn an English Methodist lady into a Spanish gypsy? . . . No, these ideas are absurd, these chimera pure madness" (quoted in Rémond, 866).

And so it happened that the version of American life that had been the hallmark of legitimist circles came to dominate the liberal intelligentsia as well. Its basic themes (materialism, egalitarianism, utilitarianism, positivism, pragmatism, bigotry, and anti-intellectualism) soon became enduring motifs that would be woven time and again into the French tapestry of America by successive generations of critics, well into our century, as I hope to show in the following chapters. The story of how French liberals such as Tocqueville, Stendhal, or Jacquemont, became disenchanted with the American dream and traded, like Mrs. Trollope, their admiration of the *political* achievements of the new republic for a deep distrust of the *cultural* constraints of a democratic society, would repeat itself over and over in the decades to come. From then on, the liberals, fearing "the people," would almost always side with the Right in times of crisis, thereby splitting the Anglo-American model, using Disraeli's England against Jackson's America.

But if the United States was too illiberal for the European liberals, the country was definitely not democratic enough for the European democrats. American civilization never made up on the left for the support it lost at the center. To be sure, references to the model republic surfaced again in 1848 as they had in 1830 and 1789, perhaps because, in those short and violent moments of revolutionary epiphany, the voices of the masses rose to profess a deep attachment to the mythical aspects of American democracy and briefly overcame the usually dominant voices of the skeptical elites. Those were fleeting moments in the saga of the French democratic and socialist camp: its most enduring trait, after this period and up to the 1960s, would be a profound hostility toward the American experience. "Let us beware of believing," a republican pamphleteer wrote in 1833, the year of Lafayette's death, "that the emancipation of America was a triumph for the cause of humanity. The name of republic was given to the new federal power; but it was an order of things in which the rich were the only masters. . . . The thought which directed the founding of the American federation was an aristocratic and egotistic one" (quoted in Rémond, 669).

Its Jacobin roots prompted the French Left to reject federalism and bicameralism as ploys against the popular will, and its collectivist principles inclined it to dismiss "English individualism" as a divisive, demobilizing ideology. In the nineteenth century, slavery and the subjugation of Native Americans convinced left-wing militants that there was definitely something wrong with the Land of the Free. The criticism soon displayed the vehemence and righteousness one would find almost a century and a half later in Sartre's diatribes against the United States during the Rosenberg trial and the Vietnam War. In 1835, a certain Docteur Cerise drew the following conclusions from reading Tocqueville's *Democracy in America*, which he discussed in *L'Européen:*

> Our debate is not over with this hideous gathering of aristocratic bourgeois and bourgeois aristocrats who proclaimed so loudly Christian freedom, and rebelled against the Motherland not to pay a few extra pennies on a pound of tea; this bunch of slave-drivers who speak of fraternity and equality, and engage in the shameful traffic of human flesh; a people of ignorant shopkeepers and narrow-minded industrialists, who do not have on the whole surface of their huge continent a single work of art . . . who do not have in their libraries a single science book not written by the hand of a foreigner; who do not have a single social institution not patterned after an ancient one, and not constituting a flagrant rebuttal of the Christian principle from which it pretends to emanate. (Quoted in Rémond, 671)

Americanization and Its Discontents

As the United States gradually attained, after 1917, a dominant position in international relations, the evaluation of American society and culture became an issue in *domestic* ideological debates throughout Europe. It is not surprising, therefore, that conflicting representations of America mirrored the ideological and political divisions within the intelligentsia and the cultivated public at large. In this respect, the study of the various interpretations of America becomes a tool for understanding French cultural and political history in the twentieth century. Conversely, the content analysis becomes more meaningful when it can be related to changes in the French intellectual community and to the broader context of American economic, political, and cultural influence on French society.

French anti-Americanism, alive and well throughout the second half of the nineteenth century,[1] gained momentum between the two world wars, one of the darkest and most tragic periods in European history. But in the United States, the 1920s correspond, on the one hand, to the consolidation of consumerism and, on the other, to the gradual rise of the country's prominence as an international diplomatic and military power. The two divergent processes were of course closely related in the European consciousness, and the leitmotiv of the 1920s and 1930s will be that the two empires rising on either side of Western Europe were partly responsible for the crisis and imminent collapse of civilization. For the most pessimistic of European minds, the reign of the machine and its gradual "planetarization," as Heidegger used to say, would soon be equated with, and made responsible for, the moral decadence of the Western world. In France, the theme of the twin evil empires—America and the Soviet Union—resurfaced during the Cold War and became the core creed of neutralist circles as well as the basis for Gaullist foreign policy. It was still alive and well a few years before the collapse of Soviet communism, as demonstrated by the views of three prominent authors who are situated on opposite ends of the political spectrum. Régis Debray, then one of President Mitterrand's advisors on foreign policy, wrote an essay in 1985 called *Les Empires contre l'Europe*, in which the empires are, once again, the United States and the Soviet Union. Jean-Marie Benoist, an avowed admirer of General de Gaulle had claimed in 1976 in *Pavane pour une Europe défunte* that "the two empires that share out the planet between themselves" are "twin monolithic tyrannies of uniformity . . . almost obscenely symmetrical in their hegemonic ambitions." The two cultural imperialisms, he went on, take the form of "a paranoid desire for uniformity and integration into monolithic blocs, alongside which Jacobin uniformity looks very amateurish stuff" (quoted in Lacorne et al., 19, 21). As for Alain de Benoist, one of the leading figures of the extremist *nouvelle droite*, he was quoted in the newspaper *Le Monde* (1981), saying that "there exist two distinct forms of totalitarianism, very different in their effects, but equally fearsome. The Eastern variety imprisons, persecutes and mortifies the body, but at least does not destroy hope. Its Western counterpart ends up creating happy robots. It is an air-conditioned hell. It kills the soul" (quoted in Lacorne et al., 21).

Europe's feeling of being squeezed between two equally threatening entities reached its climax in Weimar Germany. It had taken the Germans a good part of the nineteenth century to achieve their political unity. The destiny of the fatherland was suddenly threatened by the arrival on the international scene of two nations perceived as both hostile and alien to German identity and the culture of *Mitteleuropa*. "This Europe," Heidegger wrote in the 1939 edition of his *Introduction to Metaphysics*, "in its ruinous blindness forever on the point of cutting its own throat, lies today in a great pincers, squeezed between Russia on one side and America on the other. From a metaphysical point of view, Russia and America are the same; the same dreary technological frenzy, the same unrestricted organization of the average man" (37).

The French intellectuals, unlike their German counterparts, did not feel threatened solely in their long-established *national* identity, but also in their role as self-proclaimed leaders of a *universal* republic of letters, an exemplary role their forebears had claimed for themselves ever since Joachim Du Bellay wrote his famous ode to France as "mother of arts, arms and laws," in 1558.[2] The realization of this decline in French intellectual and political leadership took on new meaning after 1945, when it became clear that (1) European democracies could never have won against Hitler without the help of both the United States and the Soviet Union and that (2) America's rise to superpower status meant, as so often in history, that the patron would meddle in the economic and cultural life of its dependents. The first fact indebted the French intellectual elites and the rest of the nation to the United States, the second turned them into potential victims of America's cultural and ideological leadership.

As "Patrie des droits de l'homme" (birthplace of human rights) and land of liberty, respectively, France and America had competed as universalizing symbols, mythical expressions of the political hopes and dreams of oppressed classes and nations all over the world, ever since their revolutions had dealt a blow to the joint domination of church and monarchy. In the early nineteenth century, however, the balance was far from being equal: America was nothing more than a symbol in European democratic and republican circles, a fast growing, recently decolonized republic separated from Europe by a vast stretch of ocean and dismissed with a good deal of patronizing ignorance. In 1945, the symbol had become a threatening superpower which was exporting its dollars, G.I.'s, platinum blondes, and soda cans around the globe, from Berlin to Tokyo.

Fighting the Americanization of French culture became the rallying point of the vast majority of the intellectuals. Raymond Aron, who, with a handful of liberal thinkers, was trying to keep things in perspective and to escape the dichotomized, Manichean views so characteristic of the Cold War period, ascribed the resentment of postwar high-brow anti-Americanism to the particular historical heritage of the critical clerisy. What the French literati could not forgive American civilization, Aron wrote in *The Opium of the Intellectuals*, was its scorn for the thinker or the social prophet, its (mis)use of the intellectual as expert and specialist, its narrow, utilitarian professionalization of the mind. If France, and especially the Parisian Left Bank, were the paradise of the intellectuals, then the United States was undeniably their hell on earth. The intellectual bred in the European tradition, Aron wrote in the mid-1950s, "jumping to unfair conclusions, attributes to the realities or rather to the words he does not like the cost (which is perhaps inevitable and probably only temporary) of the advent of the masses. The vulgar magazines and digests or the productions of Hollywood are compared to the highest literary works which are enjoyed by the privileged few and not to the intellectual pabulum which used to be provided for the common man. The suppression of the private ownership of the means of production would not alter the vulgarity of films or radio" (228).

Aron's point suggests that the left-leaning proclivities of the youngest members of the French cultural elites and educated public in the immediate postwar years cannot account entirely for the widespread anti-Americanism of the intellectuals. In the 1920s and 1930s, at least up to the Popular Front, the most prominent writers and journalists hailed from the Right, whether in its moderate or radical form, and many of them, such as Maurras, Montherlant, Duhamel, Céline, or Valéry, were harsh critics of American civilization. The physical elimination or banishment of the collaborationist and pro-fascist intellectuals after the fall of the Vichy regime prompted a radical redistribution of positions within the French intellectual field, and somewhat changed the direction, if not the fundamentals, of highbrow anti-Americanism. Gone or discredited were the literary stars of yesterday, guilty of having answered a little too enthusiastically the famous rallying cry of the conservatives after the Popular Front: "Better Hitler than Blum!" The new generation of postwar prophets came from the Underground, where they had forged strong affective and intellectual ties in the common struggle against fascism. Malraux, Sartre, Beauvoir, Camus, and René Char were the new heroes of the intellectual youth.

The active, and often exemplary, role of the French Communists in *la Résistance* after Hitler's break with Stalin, and the collapse of liberal democracies made Marxism and socialism, in their various forms, the only credible, mobilizing answers to the immense reconstructive challenge that lay ahead. To the traditional moral and cultural denunciations of the technological nightmare, postwar anti-Americanism added a distinctive political component. Not only was American civilization threatening both the time-honored values of European humanism and the very role of the intellectual as universal, critical, and prophetic conscience of the people, but the United States were taking the lead in an international crusade against communism, using the threat of the atomic destruction of the planet to further its own imperialistic claims.

The new leader was attracting criticisms on all sides—moral, political, and economic. It was hard to find any redeeming quality in such a negative composite. For pro-Americans such as Aron or Jean-François Revel, the United States had become the scapegoat of European decadence, the demonized Other on which were projected all the anxieties and phobias of a threatened intellectual caste. In Revel's eyes, hostility toward American civilization stemmed from a feeling of "resentment at the thought that a civilization other than their own has come to serve as a clearinghouse for the problems of the world" (144).

Far from being the distinctive mark of the reactionaries, this intellectual case of bad faith was, paradoxically, shared by the Left as well. Both parties were acutely aware, Revel argued, that something had gone wrong in European history in the nineteenth century, although they disagreed on what it was that sent the old continent reeling in its downward course. For the Right, the spread of the Enlightenment's democratic and capitalistic ideals had had a "corrupting effect" on traditional societies. As for the Left, it longed "for the nineteenth century—a century at the end of which the 'classic' transition from the first industrial revolution to socialism was supposed to take place" (Revel, 144). Since this did not happen, "the absence, or failure, of socialist revolutions is what must be explained, and the invention of a foreign scapegoat provides a much needed balm for the ego of the Left which has been so bruised by so many defeats and betrayals." America bashing had become an "excuse for disappointed socialism as well as for frustrated nationalism" (Revel, 145).

French discourses on America *do* cut across traditional political and ideological boundaries. Jean-Paul Sartre and his former secretary, the right-wing pamphleteer Jean Cau, often agreed in their condemnation of American conformity and materialism, while the French Left in the late 1960s and early 1970s was bitterly divided on such issues as the interpretation of American counterculture or the necessity to "Americanize" French society by decentralizing it. The French Communists even coined the phrase "American Left" to discredit those within the social-democratic fold who felt attracted to some political and cultural features of the American democratic and reformist traditions.

Revel agreed with Aron's reading of anti-Americanism as a symptom of the European elites' deep chauvinistic resentment at not having answered the challenge of modern times by failing to maintain Europe's intellectual and economic leadership. Jean-François Revel ascribed the furor aroused in the French Left by Jean-Jacques Servan-Schreiber's *American Challenge* (1967) to the central thesis of the book: American successes and advances in electrical engineering, computer science, and the third industrial revolution were due "more to intelligence than to force or the abundance of natural resources" (Revel, 138). "The most humiliating kind of defeat," Revel argued, "is a cultural defeat. It is the only defeat that one can never forget, because it cannot be blamed on bad luck, or on the barbarism of the enemy. It entails not only acknowledgment of one's own weakness, but also the humiliation of having to save oneself by taking lessons from the conqueror—whom one must simultaneously hate and imitate" (139).

A Model of Intellectual Excellence

It should be apparent by now how, in my view, French intellectual anti-Americanism is rooted in the specific social and political history of the French learned classes. The critique of the "holy trinity" of the bourgeois ethos—materialism, positivism, and philistinism—needs to be examined in the context of the extremely elitist model that has dominated French culture, high and low, ever since the end of the Middle Ages. I think the most convincing (if oversimplified) narrative of the genealogy of the French fascination for *le commerce des belles-lettres* as an individual's highest activity, is one that connects the rise and hegemony of the intellectual function to the gradual emergence of the national state.

In the days of Saint Louis and Philippe-Auguste, the French monarchy sought ideological legitimation from the one institution that held the monopoly on the representation of the world, that is, the Roman Catholic church. Later, the kings, finding themselves increasingly opposed both to the pope and the nobility, fell into the habit of enlisting lay bourgeois elites, rather than religious clerics, as legal counsel and political administrators in their struggle to subject to their authority the local and regional power of feudal barons, free cities, and recently annexed provinces. The new elite of royal legists created by Philippe le Bel was closely tied to the monarchy both by conviction and self-interest, since the purchase of royal offices soon became one of the quickest paths to nobility for wealthy and learned, but untitled, Frenchmen.

Contrary to the old feudal aristocracy, which derived its power from land and military skills, the *noblesse d'Etat*'s rise to prominence was linked to its cultural capital, its monopolistic knowledge of law and tradition. To legitimate their function, the grateful servants of the state and faithful instruments of royal power elaborated a new model of distinction, separate from the old military and chivalrous ideal of the nobility of the sword, as well as from the monastic ideal of the church clerics and the acquisitive, secular, and utilitarian ethos of the commercial and financial middle classes, not to mention the indignant practices of those who owed their survival to the work of their hands. The new aristocracy of the mind mixed the traditional elitism of the nobility with the otherworldly asceticism of the monastic tradition and felt nothing but scorn for professional special-ization and the pursuit of monetary or otherwise "interested" benefits. Their worldview privileged juridical and linguistic competence, the ability to deal in logical abstractions and universal generalizations, over and against the technical or financial skills of the rising, but intellectually and culturally unqualified, money-making bourgeoisie.

As the concentration of power and prestige within the court society forced more and more aristocrats to trade their swords and their soldierly, boorish manners for the refined etiquette of the literary salons, the cultural model of *l'honnête homme* was forced upon the entire population as a set of educational principles that governed the entire school system from the ur-ban colleges of the Renaissance and the Jesuit colleges of the seventeenth century to the church-controlled village schools for the peasantry.[3] Nor-bert Elias, in *The Court Society*, has shown how classicism as an aesthetic doctrine is the highly stylized and formalized transcription of the "virtues" necessary to succeed in the competitive world of the royal court and its salons: the sense of honor and the care for appearances, the cult of deco-rum, form, and formula, a gift for keen psychological observation (trans-posed as the art of the portrait, and, later, as a taste for the psychological novel), the mastery of emotions and the manipulation of interpersonal re-lations through the power of the word, elegant conversation as a strategy of survival and promotion (French classical theater, contrary to its English counterpart, privileges speech, verbal sparring matches, and battles of wits, rather than "action"). The humanistic ideology of *culture générale*, the scorn of practical life and fondness for ideological debate (patterned after the scholastic *disputatio* of medieval times), continued to dominate French life long after the Revolution of 1789 and the historical demise of the *no-blesse de robe*. It played no small role in the resistance of many of the eco-nomic and political elite to capitalism, industrialization, and technical ra-tionalization in the nineteenth and early twentieth centuries.

Social historians have underscored the ambiguity of the courtly model of cultural distinction. On the one hand, its emphasis on the aristocratic overcoming of the self and the heroic cultivation of individual wisdom (as exemplified in Montaigne) leads to a form of haughty ascetic elitism, to the proud awareness of belonging to a chosen few, and to the ideal of a life well spent in uplifting conversation with the atemporal community of great souls. On the other hand, intellectual distinction, because it is the

result of the cultivation of the universal qualities of "man," is not determined by birth or wealth and is therefore theoretically available to any
individual, regardless of social or regional origin and, later, regardless of
gender, provided he or she is determined to pay the price for this radical
transformation of the self.

The meritocratic, even sometimes democratic, character of the humanistic model of excellence explains its easy transference to the republican school system in the last part of the nineteenth century. "Republican
elitism," a doctrine recently revived in some sectors of the French Left,
combined a belief in the superiority of literary endeavors with the claim
that education as self-fulfillment had to be available to everyone. The success story of the son of illiterate peasants, who, as a *boursier de l'Etat*, had
been educated with the financial aid of the Republic and had become a
cabinet member, a renowned writer, or both, was hailed as living proof that
the welding together of democratic processes of selection and republican
excellence in leadership was both feasible and desirable.

A cultural matrix of this type could only reinforce the anti-Americanism of many French intellectuals.[4] Historically inclined to abstract univer-
salism and scorn for purely monetary pursuits, *and* increasingly threatened
in their national prominence, they felt only contempt for the pragmatic,
capitalistic, and scientistic outlook so central to American culture. Conversely, the ethos of the traditional European savants often put off their
American counterparts. When pushed to an extreme, the love of abstract
reasoning could (and did) lead to a refusal to "pay attention to the practical
peculiarities of everyday life, and to the reality of social differences," according to the French historian André Burguière (152). The dominant
French cultural model, then, often appears to Americans as the epitome of
the rationalistic, metaphysical, and reductive kind of patrician and priestly
weltanschauung, which, for pragmatists like John Dewey, had to be superseded if one wanted to solve the "real" problems of humanity.

France may have been America's oldest ally, the home of Lafayette
and Bartholdi (who gave the country its most potent symbol, the Statue of
Liberty). However, as Robert Nelson has pointed out in his book, *Willa
Cather and France*, the country is also "the emblem of that high culture, an
aristocratic and foppish fanciness and elegant *savoir-faire*, against which the
American democracy in its pragmatism pits its rough-and-ready, democratic know-how" (20). Nelson goes on to show that Willa Cather herself
was one of the most passionate partners in the cultural and political love-
hate affair between France and the United States. As early as 1898, she had
developed a view of Gallic culture as deeply antagonistic to her own ro-

mantic aesthetic and metaphysical views, which favored doing over talking, song over speech, the seen over the said, and the image over the idea. She wrote in an article comparing French and English literature (published March 1898 in *The Atlantic Monthly*), that the former was not capable of high religious expression, or exalted spiritual fervor, because it was "born of a language in which faith was dead" (quoted in Nelson, 12).

In Cather's view, Gallo-Roman culture, born of the decadence of a universalist and learned empire, had it too good. Unlike the Anglo-Saxon tribes, who "came without an inherited classical sense of fitness and proportion, into a language as dark and unexplored as their own forests," the French nation never had to fashion itself, and its people were born "old, wise, critical, cynical," armed from the start with a medium which had "the fatal attribute of perfection." Hence the French concern with the visible rather than the unseen, and their gift for the "enjoyment of the tangible," which, for many Americans, translates all too often into an overindulgent propensity for the erotic and the decadent.[5] But the perfection of the French idiom as a critical tool, so wonderfully equipped to "describe, nay, almost reproduce, an artistic effect, a physical sensation, a natural phenomenon," was also, in Cather's eyes, its most crippling shortcoming. For if it excelled in the sympathetic criticism of life, manners and arts, it could do no more than that. Only in as imperfect a tongue as that of the Anglo-Saxon tribes could humanity strive to express the unseen and the imaginary and give voice to the oversoul. Deprived of a literary idiom, unable to fit his thoughts exactly into words, the Saxon seer had to learn "how to mean more than he said," and make his reader feel it, inventing as he went along his own "tongue of prophecy," writing in "a language apart from words":

> You feel it in Emerson, when his sentences seem sometimes to stand dumb before the awful majesty of the force he contemplates; it is in the pages of Carlyle, when those great, chaotic sentences reach out and out and never attain, and through them and above them rings something that they never say, like an inarticulate cry. That is the cry of the oversoul, present to a greater or lesser degree in all the English masters. (Quoted in Nelson, 13–14)

Cather, of course, situated herself within that transcendentalist tradition, pursuing what Nelson calls, after John T. Irwin, her "pictographic" quest for verbal images that alone could suggest "the inexplicable presence of the thing not named" (2). These images would restore writer and reader alike to that "prelapsarian moment of language in which signifier and signified were one," that Edenic state in which seeing is also saying. The

French, on the other hand, are doomed by their ritualistic fascination for the signifier, their cult of style, precision, and the Flaubertian *mot juste*. They are incapable of writing apart from words, of doing away with mediating structures of meaning, and of freeing themselves from the prison of language.[6] In psychoanalytic terms, one could say, following Nelson, that their "lexical" culture is dominated by the symbolic instances of the superego, while the Anglo-American romanticism Cather advocates aims at the imaginary realm of the Freudian id or the Jungian archetypes. Time and time again, in the course of this study, we will encounter the inverted French versions of Cather's fundamental rift, from Sartre's characterization of the American literature of his days as spontaneous and free of self-consciousness to Julia Kristeva's descriptions of the aphasic, and hysterical, character of American art, where colors and sounds scream, but can never be articulated in speech. In a striking passage, Régis Debray brings together all the components, linguistic as well as cultural and economic, of the deadly threat Americanization poses for the French tradition: the rise of "the Empire" and its media at the expense of the French specificity implies the ascendency "of *information* over *instruction*, of the *image* over the *idea*, of *oral* expression over *writing*, of the *instant* over *memory*, and of *economics* over *politics*" (*Les Empires contre l'Europe*, 119; emphasis in original). Which is to say that a society's views on language involve at the same time a relationship to time, nature, power and knowledge, all constitutive of a particular cultural figuration.

The abstract universalist bend of their ethos also predisposed many French intellectuals to take a prophetic stance in social and political matters. Many of the leading literary figures of the sixteenth, seventeenth, and eighteenth centuries, like Montaigne, Descartes, Bossuet, Boileau, Pascal, La Fontaine, La Bruyère, Montesquieu, and Voltaire came from or belonged to the class of royal officers, jurists, and parliamentarians that had elaborated the dominant model of intellectual excellence. Because the most faithful servants of the state and the most successful thinkers and artists in the nation shared similar social origins, structures of thinking and feeling, and moral-political values and ideological commitments, there existed strong organic ties between literature and politics, intellectuals, and state power. French politicians write novels and dream of being admitted to the sacred precinct of the Académie Française, while novelists and artists are regularly appointed to ministerial and high civil service positions.

In *The Old Régime and the Revolution*, Tocqueville argued that the French Revolution, far from having broken with the past, had in fact strengthened the two distinctive, and closely related, features of French society in the Age of Classicism: the centralization of the state and the intellectualist, meritocratic model of cultural excellence. In the absence of any viable alternative to the crisis of monarchical institutions in the mid-eighteenth century, the citizens of the Republic of Letters became the self-appointed representatives of the alienated, discontented, and disenfranchised segments of French society and the only effective counterforce to a now-contested absolutism. "In the nation-wide debacle of freedom," Tocqueville remarked of pre-revolutionary France, "we had preserved one form of it; we could indulge, almost without restrictions, in learned discussions on the origin of society, the nature of government, and the essential rights of man. All who were chafing under the yoke of the administration enjoyed these literary excursions into politics. . . . Thus the philosopher's cloak provided safe cover for the passions of the day and the political ferment was channelled into literature, the result being that our writers now became the leaders of public opinion and played for a while the part which normally, in free countries, falls to the professional politician. And as things were, no one was in a position to dispute their right to leadership" (142).

After the French Revolution, the two Napoleonic empires and the republican state did nothing but reinforce this peculiar organic relationship between the intellectual and political fields. In the words of André Burguière, French "men of letters, in view of their social and intellectual proximity to men of power . . . but also because of their propensity for abstract reasoning and generalization . . . feel entrusted with a privileged mission regarding the powers that be, a mission of enlightenment, support and criticism if needs be" (152). Voltaire, Lamartine, Hugo, Flora Tristan, Sand, Zola, Sartre, and Beauvoir were exemplary figures of these literary prophets. All felt they were "invested with an intellectual responsibility to society and history; that of thinking the world for the rest of society, of lending voice to its aspirations and of showing it the way" (Burguière, 152). The idealistic and strongly romantic nature of literary propheticism after the French Revolution accounts for a great part of the anti-Americanism of the intellectual Left, which has traditionally been turned off by the prosaic, anticlimactic character of America's contribution to world history. In contrast to the Soviet Union, France, or China, the United States cannot serve as a mythical reference for the revolutionary tradition. American political principles, frozen as they were in the bourgeois optimism of the late eighteenth century, are totally lacking in the sublime and romantic elements that used to appeal to large parts of the progressive clerisy: the American past is as boring as its technological, mass-marketed present. As Raymond Aron remarked in the ideologically charged atmosphere of the 1950s:

> An empirical success, American society does not embody a historical idea. The simple, modest ideas which it continues to cultivate have gone out of fashion in the old world. The United States remains optimistic after the fashion of the European eighteenth century. . . . There is no room there for the Revolution or for the proletariat— only for economic expansion, trade unions and the Constitution. The Soviet Union purges and subjugates the intellectuals, but at least it takes them seriously. . . . The United States does not persecute its intellectuals enough to enjoy in its turn the turbid attractions of terror; it gives a few of them, temporarily, a prestige and a glory which can compete with that of the film stars or baseball players; but it leaves the majority in the shadows. Persecution is more bearable to the intelligentsia than indifference. (*The Opium of the Intellectuals*, 228)

In *The Genius of American Politics*, Daniel Boorstin emphasized how the attitude toward life and its aesthetic expression separated the old world from the new. The optimistic utopianism of the immigrant popular classes excluded both the Platonic quest for the sublime and the anguished cult of the tragic character of the human condition that remain the hallmark of European high culture:

> The very commonness of American values has seemed their proof: they have come directly from the hand of God and from the soil of the continent. This attitude helps explain why the martyr (at least the *secular* martyr) has not been attractive to us. In the accurate words of our popular song, "The Best Things in Life Are Free." . . . The character of our national heroes witness to our belief in "givenness," our preference for the man who seizes his God-given opportunities over him who pursues a great private vision. Perhaps never before has there been such a thorough identification of normality and virtue. . . . Our ideal is at the opposite pole from that of a German Superman or an irredentist agitator in his garret. We admire not the monstrous, but the normal. . . . Our national heroes have not been erratic geniuses like Michelangelo or Cromwell or Napoleon but rather men like Washington and Jackson and Lincoln, who possessed the commonplace virtues to an extraordinary degree. (28–29)

When divorced from immediate political considerations, the European distaste for American populism may turn into what the Roman Catholic philosopher Jacques Maritain described as a spiritual distaste for the prosaic, democratic "materialism" of the land of the common man. Maritain quotes a long passage from Lawrence's *The Plumed Serpent* as a perfect illustration of the nostalgic and elitist paganism of those contemptuous of the American nightmare. The heroine of Lawrence's novel, Kate Leslie, goes to New Mexico in quest of a more authentic form of spirituality and ponders over "the enigma of America":

> And sometimes she wondered whether America really was the great death-continent, the great No! to the European and Asiatic and African Yes! . . . Was it the continent of the great undoing, and all its peoples the agents of mystic destruction . . . Was it so? And did this account for the great drift to the New World, the drift of spent souls passing over to the side of Godless democracy, energetic negation? The negation which is the life-breath of materialism. And would the great negative pull of the Americans at last break the heart of the world? (quoted in Maritain, 122)

Maritain labeled such a position a "pseudomystical" hatred for everything represented by American egalitarianism. The pseudomystics, Maritain said, are "bored to death by [what they believe to be] such lukewarm . . . and vulgar ideals as human freedom and human brotherhood. They hate the common people" (124). The vengeful resentment of those who mistake "the effort to turn matter in the service of man" for materialism leads to a deep scorn for the American experience, "that swarming of all colors and races, that great drift of souls coming over to leave oppression and humiliation behind and to work together in hope and liberty" (124). Maritain could not find harsh enough words to condemn the pseudospirituals, whom he saw as the natural enemies of America, a country which genuine spirituals, on the other hand, can only love, in spite of "all human defects, such as those mentioned in this book" (126). Echoing other defenders of the American way of life, such as Aron or Jean-François Revel, Maritain found the mechanism of the sacrificial victim at the root of the pseudomystics' "grand slander" of democracy: "To compensate for their frustration and resentment they need a world-wide scapegoat, a symbolic continent great and powerful enough to arouse mankind's hopes, and perverse enough to betray them—the nightmare of *their* America" (127).

The intellectuals' evaluation of the American populist ethos is one instance of the complex relation between the secular, modernist clerisy and "the people." In the eyes of the intellectual vanguard, there have always been two kinds of popular classes: the good, that is, the irreligious, anticlerical, and rebellious members of the European working classes, and the bad, that is, the highly unsecular and consequently deeply alienated masses who, especially in America, are still in the grip of Christian moralism. In the same way, there are two kinds of "popular culture" in the United States: the intelligentsia embraces the grass-roots radicalism of working-class European immigrants in the 1920s, the militancy of black Americans in the 1960s, and the protests of gay and feminist activist organizations in the 1980s (although the "popular" character of gay liberation is, in a sociological sense, highly debatable); but the Southern Baptist worldview, which is shared by large segments of the rural popular classes, and the urban "white ethnic" populism à la Archie Bunker are rejected.[7] American cultural modernists, to the extent that they borrow intellectual categories and ideological models from Europe, have been forced to do battle on two fronts, against the materialistic philistinism of the bourgeoisie on the one hand, and against the moralistic fundamentalism of the "common folks" on the other. American conservative ideologues, for their part, have always been quick to drive the wedge of moral issues between the "silent majority" and those they portray as decadent, libertine "eggheads" or "cultural elites," in the hope of preventing any alliance between the intelligentsia and the popular classes, as in Europe or Latin America. In the old world, even the revolutionary Left is elitist; in America, even the patrician Right is populist.

American Paradoxes and the Interpretive Double Bind

Americans and their supporters have often pointed to the contradictory nature of the demands anti-Americanism makes on the civilization it criticizes. As Christopher Lasch states in his introduction to the 1961 edition of Dickens's *American Notes,* "Any country regarded by so much of the world as a land of special promise and opportunity should expect to find itself judged by standards more exacting that those applied to countries which do not have to live up to such an exalted reputation" (1). Lasch concludes with the typically American tolerance to criticism that infuriates critics and indeed sometimes inspires the criticism in the first place: "If people criticize us with particular violence, we should be reassured even though we may suffer pangs of shame; the violence of the criticism implies that the old promise still raises hopes throughout the world. We should be grateful to our critics. We need them to hold us to the mark." To the foreign critic, America is as much a missed opportunity, a god that failed, or a dream that did not come true, as it is a demonic monstrosity or a spiritual nightmare.

The contradictory nature of foreign (and domestic) expectations of the United States imposes a kind of interpretive double bind on the competing versions of the New World. In the words of Jean-François Revel, "When the American work week is shortened through automation, we [the French] say that Americans are technological slaves. When they reduce poverty, we sniff and talk about the 'consumer society.' And yet, the latter accomplishments are two of the secular goals of utopic or 'scientific' socialism" (139). Not only is the corpus of interpretations of life in the United States extremely diverse and conflictual, but the object itself is often seen and described as a dichotomized, contradictory reality. On the one hand, we have the United States, a nation among others, which should be submitted to the same standards of praise and condemnation, as say, Italy, Nigeria, Brazil, or Burma. On the other hand, there is America, an incarnated idea, endowed with mythical status as the repository of the hopes, desires, fantasies, and phobias of millions of freedom-loving, money-grubbing, or pleasure-seeking individuals around the globe. The judgment passed on the former (a nation among others) can never be dispassionate, for it rests too heavily on how the latter (the incarnated idea) has been fulfilled or betrayed in the unfolding of its history. The tension has never been resolved, and never will be, as long as the United States remains a symbolic, dual entity, for the tension lies at the core, not only of the judgments foreigners have passed on America but also of the very dynamics of the country's political and cultural history.

The paradoxical nature of American civilization in turn justifies the extreme polarization of the judgments passed on it. Consider the traditional oppositions, seen as constituting the whole fabric of American life and characteristic of the American "exceptionality," between the system and the people, or the structure and the ideal, which in turn duplicates the disparity between what ought to be and what is, between the (American) dream and the (air-conditioned) nightmare. Jacques Maritain, who lived in New York during World War II and later taught at Princeton University, described his very first impression of the United States in the following terms: "It was quite definite, though difficult to express in words. I felt I was obscurely confronted with a deep-seated contrast of immense bearing, a sharp, far-reaching contrast between the people on the one hand, and, on the other hand, what I would like to call the externally superimposed structure or ritual of civilization" (21). This ritual of civilization "dedicated to some foreign goddess," was, Maritain reminds us, born in Europe and transplanted on American soil. "Originally grounded as it was on the principle of the fecundity of money and the absolute primacy of individual profit," the ritual of industrial life was "inhuman and materialist" (21). However, Maritain argued,

By a strange paradox, the people who lived and toiled under this structure or ritual of civilization were keeping their souls apart from it. At least as regards the essential, their souls and vital energy, their dreams, their everyday effort, their idealism and generosity, were running against the grain of the inner logic of the superimposed structure. . . . Thus the basic thing in my first impression was the sharp distinction to be made between the spirit of the American people and the logic of the superimposed structure, . . . and not only the distinction, but the state of tension, of hidden conflict, between this spirit of the people and the logic of the structure; the steady, latent rebellion of the spirit of the people against the logic of the structure. (22)

Maritain's dynamic distinction, however, is not restricted to positive, heroic descriptions of the American enterprise. One finds a similar contrast between the spirit of the people and the logic of the structure at war within American culture in the highly critical portrait Georges Duhamel had published thirty years earlier. In *America: The Menace, Scenes from the Life of the Future* (1931), Duhamel also distinguished the people from the structure, although he drew opposite conclusions from his observations: the ritual of civilization had an overwhelming power of corruption and dehumanization. "I can't see the Americans for America," Duhamel remarked. "Between the American and me there rises I know not what monstrous phantom, a collection of laws, institutions, prejudices, and even myths, a social machine without an equal in the world, and with no analogue in history. I see a system rather than a people" (42). The same opposition colored Sartre's early impressions of America. In *Force of Circumstance*, Simone de Beauvoir noted that although there were "many things in the civilization of the Western hemisphere that shocked him," the philosopher "had been greatly moved by the crowds of New York and felt that the people were worth more than the system" (33). Sartre elaborated further on the matter, describing the struggles of individuals against the inhuman "system of Americanism."

Reflecting on the celebration of America's Bicentennial in 1976, Jean-Marie Benoist, a professor at the Collège de France and an assistant to Claude Lévi-Strauss, pondered the "enigma" standing at the core of the American experience. How can one account, he wonders, for the fact that "the nation born of the freest revolt is sometimes reduced to support regimes and governments whose kinship with the worst regimes of Antiquity is obvious?" (96). Benoist embarks upon the quest for the "ideological, psychological and political forces" that allowed a nation to proclaim freedom as its fundamental principle while "reaching a type of rationality and technical organization commanding it to encourage, if not create, fascism and tyranny all over the world" (98). The answer to the hybrid character of the American destiny, "this strange alliance between a frantic desire for freedom and an obstinate will to dominate," lies for Benoist in the persistence of the categories of English colonial ideology in American culture. It is as though the American colonies, however skillful they had been in shaking the political and economic yoke of the motherland, had "agreed to keep the ideological and cultural hegemony of their former masters." It is as though "the declaration of independence and rebellion had stopped halfway, so deeply had the categories of English ideology, puritan and missionary, instilled itself in the underlying code of the men who were then boldly challenging the old Europe" (99).

Having ascribed the contradictory character of the American experience to its having insufficiently freed itself from British imperialism, Jean-Marie Benoist advocates a "reversed Marshall Plan," through which (continental) Europe would help the United States finish its revolution by shedding the last remnants of its English past, all those "ferments left behind by the old imperial power . . . whose names are repetition, uniformity, homogeneity, profitability, pragmatism and empiricism" (102). This salutary program would imply the "uprooting" of these "Anglo-Saxon elements" masking the cultural diversity of the United States. The country ("Worth more," concedes Benoist, "than the picture painted by some of its methods of cultural export" [109]) would then recover "the perception of the subtleties and nuances that make up the riches of Europe, as well as its own," and open itself up to "the wisdom of the lessons of the Third World" (103).

The gap between an idealized and mythical utopian America and the complex and flawed reality of the United States is as wide, if not wider, today as in the past. The French "media intelligentsia" and its public, who dream of sharing the life-styles and intimate secrets of the American "gliterati" often choose to overlook the social and economic problems that have plagued the United States since the 1960s. Crime, drugs, the AIDS epidemic, urban decay, budget deficits, financial scandals, skyrocketing education and medical costs, increasing inequalities, and so on, are emphasized and exaggerated by those who remain staunch Americanophobes. They paint the picture of a nation nearly threatened to extinction by its social and economic processes.

Indeed, the basic tension between the ideal and the real allows critics to compile a long string of American paradoxes: a Puritan country steeped in sexual licentiousness; a federal republic fraught with the problems inherent in a centralized, powerful executive; a receptive, pragmatic, tolerant, pluralistic civilization that appropriates and transforms human culture—whether food, music, or ideas—into soulless, lifeless, mass-produced simulacrum; a Christian, idealistic nation awash in greed and materialism; an imperial republic that long advocated decolonization and national self-determination only to replace declining European powers in dominating undeveloped countries; a technological, engineering culture obsessed with naturalness and simplicity; a democracy based on universal rights and free contractual relations but tainted by racial discrimination and ethnocentric ideologies; an optimistic, boisterous, forward-looking capitalist nation with an educational system based on Rousseauean beliefs in the goodness and creativity of children, full of television preachers gloomily lamenting the corrupt, sinful, unredeemable nature of human beings; a society that rewards conformism as the highest achievement of individuality; a land of independence that thrives on the pressure to belong; a multicultural, multiracial, geographically diverse continentwide nation that offers from coast to coast the same standardized motel room, complete with bedside lamp and a free copy of the Bible; a non-traditionalist, anti-intellectual culture that holds sacred a two-hundred-year-old Constitution based on the abstract principles of Old World Enlightenment philosophy.

This multifaceted kaleidoscopic image, America seen through French eyes and described in French words, is the subject matter of the following chapters. Its complexity lies as much in the object of the representations as in the representations themselves. In a sense, America, that historical construct, that most ideological of nations, does not stand apart from the descriptions found in so many different accounts, whether domestic or foreign. America *is* constituted from those very dreams, fears, and desires themselves. In the words of Marcus Cunliffe, "America has never existed as a real place for Europeans. . . . The New World was invented before it was discovered. Mythology preceded exploration; and discovery happily fitted previous invention" (494). The (positive) picture of a mythical civilization that had dominated the European mind for centuries after the Renaissance became for many twentieth-century French intellectuals the (negative) universe of mythical, and mystifying, images. "What is real, in fact, is not (or is not only) the reality aimed at by the text," Roger Chartier has remarked, "but the very manner in which the text aims at it in the historicity of its production and the strategy of its writing" (40). Because it has been a cultural experiment and an ideological laboratory from the start, the United States *as* America, more than any other nation in the world, partakes of this ambiguous ontological status.

TWO

AMERICAN DYSTOPIA

I assert that any people subjected for half a century to the actual influence of the American 'movie' is on the way to the worst decadence. The cinema is the skillfully poisoned nourishment of a multitude that the powers of Moloch have judged and condemned, and whose degradation they are accomplishing. *Georges Duhamel*

Through the Hudson estuary the American car spreads out over the world, the instrument of escape, the tool of speed, which, after freeing the United States, is shattering Puritanism, volatilizing savings, demolishing the family, reversing the law, leading the world toward catastrophe and the glory of adventure. *Paul Morand*

The idea that we were brought up on, that Europe is the home of civilization in general—nonsense! It's a periodical slaughterpen, with all the vices that this implies. I'd as lief live in the Chicago stockyards. *Walter Hines Page*

Georges Duhamel attained literary fame with a book ironically entitled *Civilization*, in which he described the self-destruction of European culture and society, drawing on his own experience as a physician during World War I. Throughout the old continent, the nightmare of the trenches triggered a revolt against the scientist and positivistic ideals of the previous generation, whose belief in progress had been ridiculed and shattered by the bloody encounter between the wealthiest and most "enlightened" nations on earth. In the introduction to *America: The Menace, Scenes of the Life of the Future*, Georges Duhamel summed up the new zeitgeist in the following sentence: "An enthusiastic respect for the word 'future,' and for all that it conceals is to be ranked among the most ingenuous ideologies of the nineteenth century" (xii). In the 1920s and 1930s modernity meant the "planetarization" of technique, and technique meant America. France, Germany, Spain, and Italy, the whole of Europe rang with shouts of "Americanism," "Fordism," and "Taylorism." In intellectual reviews and academic journals, people traded insults and clichés on the advantages and drawbacks of the motion picture and social security.

The American threat had come to be seen as part of the same process of technical rationalization of the physical and natural world that had contributed to the destruction of millions of human beings during World War I. In France, the influence of Bergson's philosophy of creative intuition, the belated success of André Gide's *Fruits of the Earth*, an exalted paean to the life of the senses, and the rise of a new generation of writers who, like Malraux, Montherlant, Saint-Exupéry, or the surrealists, searched for spiritual meaning and human solidarity through exotic adventure or political activism, attest to the widespread "revolt against reason" shared by many of Europe's intellectual youth in the aftermath of the war. In Germany, the philosophers of the *Unterdang des Westens* anathematized the mass civilization of industrial democracies.

In a lecture delivered at the University of Freiburg in Breisgau in 1935 and reprinted in *Introduction to Metaphysics*, Martin Heidegger called the whole process "the darkening of the world" and "the enfeeblement of the European spirit." The darkening of the world, he told his audience, "means emasculation of the spirit, the disintegration, wasting away, repression, and misinterpretation of the spirit" (45). Although this spiritual decadence with its attendant calamities—the prevalence of "extension and number" and the rise of conformity and routine—had originated in Western Europe, it was in America and Russia that this development had grown "into a boundless et cetera of indifference and always-the-sameness—so much so that the quantity took on a quality of its own." The crux of the matter, the root of all contemporary evils, was for Heidegger the "reinterpration of spirit as intelligence" or, worse, "cleverness." This meant the degradation of true spirit into a tool for the "domination of the conditions of production" (as in Soviet Marxism) or for the ordering and manipulation of the material world (as in American positivism). In those two civilizations, "the domination . . . of a cross section of the indifferent mass has become . . . the onslaught of what we call the demonic (in the sense of destructive evil)" (46).

Not everybody, to be sure, agreed with the German mandarins' narratives of decadence and demonology: the liberals, worried by the rise of totalitarianism, still upheld the values of democracy, even in its industrial version. The Marxists viewed the transformations of the process of production induced by automatization as a decisive step in the evolution of capitalist society toward communism. The new forms of the rationalization of labor, they argued, by speeding up industrial concentration and

turning more and more skilled workers into proletarians, could only en-
hance the revolutionary consciousness of the masses and exacerbate the
contradictions of the Old World. In Italy, the debate opposed the communists to the conservative intellectuals who loathed the "Americanization of
Europe." In his *Prison Notebooks*, Antonio Gramsci poked fun at the great
fear of the traditional elites, threatened in their cultural hegemony by the
rise of new social relations. In response to Luigi Pirandello, who, in an
interview given to the review *L'Italia Letteraria* (14 April 1929), had warned
that "America is swamping us" and that "a new beacon of civilization has
been lit" in the United States, Gramsci countered that "all that they do in
America is to remasticate the old European culture." He went on: "We
are dealing with an organic extension and an intensification of European
civilization, which has simply acquired a new coating in the American climate" (318). Gramsci saw the critique of the "new culture" of Americanism
as an expression of the moral and intellectual reaction of declining social
strata to the (inevitable) rise of the modern: "In Europe it is the passive
residues that resist Americanism (they 'represent quality,' etc.) because
they have the instinctive feeling that the new forms of production and
work would sweep them away implacably" (305). In "Americanism and
Fordism," he argued that "what is today called 'Americanism' is to a large
extent an advance criticism of old strata which will in fact be crushed by
any eventual new order and which are already in the grips of a wave of
social panic, dissolution and despair" (317).

Ideological politics in the 1930s opposed democrats, fascists, and communists, all of whom often insisted on viewing the game as a clear-cut
binary struggle: each camp piled the other two into one single abhorred
entity. To the democrats, Stalinism and Nazism were two faces of the same
coin, while the Left rendered bourgeois liberal parliamentarism responsible for the advent of fascism. Meanwhile, the Right claimed that Soviet
society was nothing but the product of the French Revolution, liberalism
gone mad. As years went by and the tension rose, each camp accused its
opponents of being the epitome of technological hubris. Heidegger, an
avowed supporter of the Third Reich in the mid-1930s, argued that Russia
and America were, "from the metaphysical point of view, the same thing:
same ominous frenzy of technique let loose, of the rootless organization of
standardized man" (37). On the Left, Walter Benjamin described fascism
as the exaltation of technique and the aesthetization of politics as technological war. "Imperialist war," he wrote, "is a revolt of technique, which
claims in the form of 'human material' what society wrenched from it in
the form of natural matter" (244).

This view of modernity as violence against nature, which humanity must eventually expiate and repay with the sacrifice of its humaneness and its existence, is central to many of the texts I shall discuss. Duhamel's description of the United States is replete with animal metaphors, and the Chicago stockyards clearly symbolize for him those other infamous human slaughterhouses, the trenches of Verdun. Duhamel drew a contrast between "the concept of an essentially moral civilization, fit, according to Humboldt, to 'make people more human,' . . . [and] the concept of another civilization that is predominantly mechanical and that may be described as Baconian, since it is wholly based on the applications of the inductive method" (viii). The latter was simply taking new, pacified forms after the mass slaughter that had almost bled the old continent to death. The growing threat of the "Baconian civilization" from the New World was in fact, to paraphrase Clausewitz, the old war of the barbarians against culture waged by other means:

> No nation has thrown itself into the excesses of industrial civilization more deliberately than America. . . . No one can any longer doubt that their civilization is nevertheless able to conquer the Old World and has begun to do so. America, then, represents for us the Future. . . . Our future! Before twenty years have passed, we shall be able to find all the stigmata of this devouring civilization on all the members of Europe. For a handful of men who view the phenomenon with distrust and sadness, there are thousands who hail it with loud shouts. (Duhamel, xiii–xiv)

Duhamel felt that popular classes and trendy writers, artists, and journalists were ready to welcome and celebrate the diffusion throughout French society of American standards of taste and behavior. He staunchly refused to surrender the values of the humanistic tradition either to the lure of material progress or to its opposite, the profound despair that had seized another physician, Céline's alter ego Ferdinand Bardamu, in the streets of New York and Detroit. Duhamel claimed that his criticism was directed at American civilization, not at the "American people, among whom I have found many excellent friends. . . . The judgments that I form . . . bear no mark of passion if it be not the passion that I consecrate to the triumph of mind" (xv). His account, however, is a perfect illustration of the dual character of the critique of American culture and society in the interwar period. On the level of social and economic organizations, on the side of production, we have the threats of mechanization (the theme of the sorcerer's apprentice), the disappearance of individuality within the mass conformism of a bureaucratic order, the puritanical obsession for control and for physical and moral hygiene. On the level of culture and ideology, on the side of consumption, there are moral and spiritual decadence, the new religions of sport and cinema, and, half a century before postmodern semiotics, the apocalyptic description of the empire of the sign and the simulacrum, the proliferation of images, the triumph of kitsch, plastic, icons, and holograms.

The Anthill and the Slaughterhouse

Two metaphorical lines borrowed from the animal kingdom structure Georges Duhamel's narrative of the technological nightmare: the anthill and the slaughterhouse. While the stockyards attest to the destructive effects of industrial *production*, the ant's nest, the termite heap, and the beehive refer to the functional side of modernity that represents collective *consumption* of material and symbolic goods. The image of insect societies also underscored the deep conformity produced by what Duhamel had called a "Baconian civilization." The abattoirs foretell the death of man, while the entomological model illustrates the decline of the individual. Given the intellectual tradition to which he belonged, Duhamel was more inclined to emphasize the contamination of humanist culture by the virus of Americanism while Céline, say, was more likely to celebrate the "existentialist," anarchic individualism embodied by his anti-hero, Ferdinand Bardamu.

The two threads of the modern, dehumanization and the loss of individuality, are symbolized by the concurrent destinies of sheep and ants and are tightly interwoven in Celine's *Journey to the End of the Night* and Duhamel's *America: The Menace, Scenes from the Life of the Future*. The apocalyptic description of the Chicago meat-packing industry in the central chapter of Duhamel's book has contributed greatly to the success of his narrative of America. Entitled "The Kingdom of Death," the stockyard passage is set between a criticism of urban landscape and a satire of Prohibition. To the narrator, "the abattoirs are a city within the city, a world in the bosom of the world, the sanctuary of carnivorous humanity, the realm of scientific death," and he tried to imagine it while "the Elevated express was carrying [him] at full speed into the middle of a taciturn and, as you might say, a sacrificial crowd" (93). A certain Pickleton, the executive in charge of taking visitors for a tour of the facilities, asks whether Monsieur Duhamel is easily upset. Unimpressed by the fact that Duhamel was a doctor and had "served in the War," Pickleton implies by his skepticism that the peacetime butchery may be more unbearable than the bloodiest episodes of the war of trenches.[1] The scene the narrator is about to witness will in fact exceed all expectation: "Suddenly, behind a red door, we heard the cries of animals. We entered. The cry made, as it were, a bold leap in intensity. It now filled the universe to its very edge. Could it be that they did not hear it, over there, on the other side of the Atlantic?" (101). Industrial death is not simply death on the assembly line, it is staged as an unbearable ritual, a parody of ancient sacrifice, a technological version of Antonin Artaud's theater of cruelty:

> The butcher was a brawny Negro. He wore a suit of overalls that was sticky with blood to the arm-holes. . . . The chain passed in front of him and the hogs . . . were presented to him at the proper height. Then, with a calm, sure gesture, he pierced their necks with his cutlass. . . . The steel buried itself without haste. A stream of blood gushed forth. . . . I have seen hundreds of men die, but deep in my heart the capacity for horror is not extinct. Death, even when mechanized in this way, even when reduced strictly to the proportions of an industrial process, remains a great mystery. I could not take my eyes from the cold, expressionless face of the Negro who distributed those hammer-strokes on the foreheads that Homer called "majestic." (Duhamel, 101–2, 105)

The visit takes the narrator through Dante's circles of Hell: after the pigs, the cattle, then the sheep, and then the various stages on the disassembly line, the division of sacrificial labor, the devils who cut, those who chop and mince, burn and scrape, and shave the skin, from the "suffocating steam-room, where quarters of meat danced in vapor," down to the "workrooms on a lower floor where wholesale cooking is done" (107).

The "empire of the sausage" is a microcosm of society, each race, each gender in its place, the female typists in the upstairs offices, the black executioners down below, and, in between, the white male executives like Pickleton, who, unlike the tens of thousands of men and women who "consume all their existence" in the stockyards, goes home every evening to his family in the suburbs, away from the urban hell. Following his visit, as he rides home on the elevated train, the narrator cannot cleanse his mind of the nightmarish visions; he falls prey to various hallucinations. The passengers packed in the train are nothing but "a jumbled herd." "Would a Negro pass along the length of the car," he wonders, "and free us from this bestial existence by hitting us a dexterous blow on the forehead with a sledge?" (110). As he looks through the window, the slow motion of the people lining up in front of movie theaters reminds him of "the animals who mounted the incline to their slaughter" (111). A hunted beast himself, his hotel room has become his burrow, his shelter, his "refuge from this crazy town" (111).

The tired, huddled masses of Chicago's working-class neighborhoods are not the only ones to be sacrificed on the altar of the gods of modernity: the whole American experience, regardless of class distinctions, partakes of the horrors of the stockyards. At a party celebrating the 1928 presidential election, the sight of a rich, elderly matron covered with jewels triggers another bout of hallucination. Duhamel writes, "Her dress was gold and her slippers were gold. Of gold, too—red and green gold—was her old, a hundred times retinted hair. And behind all that jeweler's shop, I seemed to see a hundred thousand squealing pigs whose throats were being cut by a Negro all covered with blood. It was not the pigs that were screaming; it was the enthusiastic dancers" (125). Black workers are forced by society to carry out the collective slaughter of animals, but black men are also often portrayed as beasts, whether by Duhamel himself or by one of his white interlocutors. Discussing the "Negro question" with a white American and noting that in view of their "highly prolific" nature, the black population will soon reach twenty million, the author ironically asks his interlocutor what he proposes do with a "burden like that huge herd" (150), while a white creole from New Orleans proudly declares that his family has "always treated the colored people with kindness and pity, like domestic animals" (142).[2]

The description of the collective aspect of American life, such as lines at the movies or the mass hysteria of sporting events, provides ample occasion for comparisons with the animal kingdom. Here, the sacrificial theme gives way to the traditional topos of the beastly, irrational side of human nature, especially as displayed in collective behavior. For example, Duhamel contrasts the brutality of football games with the "harmonious dance" of Greek statues; the players are compared to a "pack" of wild, carnivorous beasts watching one another "like dogs pointing." The stadium is the new temple where the masses of modern Rome enjoy the decadent barbarity of ancient circus games. Football has "no elegance, no imagination, above all, no beauty, unless it were that repellent beauty you may find at times in a display of savagery" (154). "The powdered rouged girl students" who cheer the players are likened to "parakeets on the perch" endowed with a budding, childish sexuality: "from their bosoms, still as immature as apples in July, they sent forth shrill penetrating cries that seemed to have a tonic influence on the nerves of the competitors" (155). One of the cheerleaders, however, displays a more mature, animal sensuality: "With a megaphone in hand, and with her skirts flying in the wind, she screamed, flounced about, gave play to leg and haunch, and performed a suggestive and furious *danse du ventre*, like the dances of the prostitutes in the Mediterranean port. From time to time, she reassembled her aviary and encouraged it to a fresh outburst of shrill screaming" (156).

Duhamel's now amused, now horrified description of the hysterical crowd of spectators displays the characteristic fantasies about the over-sexed, promiscuous, vulgar, undifferentiated, and fanatical "masses" that were to become one of the privileged themes of the zeitgeist of the 1930s, a decade haunted by the specter and the spectacle of totalitarianism: "The common herd filled the gigantic shell. The plebeian crowd, without distinction and without authority, was there, and knew that it was there, only as ballast, as padding, as the odd change that made up the bill. In it you could recognize and count five hundred times the same masculine hat—gray with a black ribbon—and a thousand times the same feminine hat. . . . In short, here was the mob in all its colorless horror" (155). Like Durkheim or Wilhelm Reich, Duhamel interpreted the exaltation of the sport fans in terms of "mass psychology"; he viewed it as a deep-seated desire for the surrender of individuality, as emotional fusion with a powerful entity, as collective self-hypnosis and group narcissism: "Did you not come, O crowd . . . to get drunk on yourselves, on your own voice, on your own noise; to feel yourselves numerous and full of strength, to be charged with one another's emanations, and to taste the mysterious pleasures of the herd, the hive, and the ant-hill?" (157).

While the theme of the slaughterhouse illustrates the dehumanizing effects of the rationalization of labor and leisure, the anthill and the termite heap point to the mass conformism that most French observers, starting with Tocqueville, have found prevalent in American life. The hierarchical, holistic order of insect "societies" has traditionally served as an allegory of totalitarian utopias, and Duhamel, after Maurice Maeterlinck, makes full use of the ideological connotations of entomological metaphors: "In the United States . . . what strikes the European traveler is the progressive approximation of human life to what we know of the way of life of insects—the same effacement of the individual, the same progressive reduction and unification of social types, the same organization of the group into special castes, the same submission of everyone to those obscure exigencies that Maeterlinck names the genius of the hive or of the ant-hill" (194).

The functional integration of insect societies, which "extend over the continents," offers an obvious political advantage, for there are no revolutions among the insects. Thus, Duhamel remarks, "no revolution in the American ant-heap can be imagined—unless indeed some day . . . the incredible machine goes off the track, collapses, and falls in cinders" (214). The theme of the impossible revolution, which will haunt leftist representations of American capitalism all the way into the 1960s (e.g., Marcuse's "repressive desublimation") is linked to the critique of the overwhelming bureaucratic control exercised by social apparatuses upon a growing number of human activities, including entertainment, health, and sexuality. America, says Duhamel, hides the Americans: "The ant-heap prevents me from seeing the ants. . . . Men, about whom I always feel an eager curiosity, in this country seen to me like pure ideograms, like the signs of an abstract, already fabulous civilization" (42).

The Epidemiology of Bourgeois Communism

For Duhamel, the "dictatorship of counterfeit civilization" (44), which echoes Tocqueville's tyranny of the majority, is all the more powerful since this insidious domination, unlike that of regimes based on forceful repression, rests on the manipulation of desire by legions of cultural or ideological, rather than political, experts. Americans are the slaves of their professional class, "your moralists, your lawyers, your hygienists, your doctors, your city planners, even your teachers of aesthetics, to say nothing of your police [and] your publicists" (45). The cultural cohesion engineered by what we would call today modern technologies of the image, the self, and the body, amounts, in Duhamel's eyes, to "a sort of bourgeois communism." And he tells a bewildered friend that American clubs remind him, "on a much more luxurious scale, of course," of the Soviet houses for peasants or writers: they signify a similar suppression of the individual. In the same vein, the comfortable atmosphere of the Pullman cars struck the foreigner as a plush version of the Stalinist state, a sort of "communism of the rich. The men's washroom provides for five persons at a time, like the common washroom of the House of Scholars at Moscow" (163).

Nowhere was the disappearance of individual autonomy more obvious, in Dr. Duhamel's eyes, than in matters of health. America was in the grip of a hygienic hysteria, an obsession for sanitary control, a paranoid phobia of contamination from the outside. Years before jogging and aerobics became the hallmark of yuppie culture, Duhamel remarked that Americans were superstitiously attached to health and dieting (15). Reminding his interlocutor that, "as a Frenchman from France," he did not take hygiene more seriously than necessary, he went on to say that he believed in "things enough to be their master, and not enough to be their slave" (15). Scientific faith, he added, does not bring peace to the Americans, their torments only change places and forms. When a vaccine for every single disease has been found, people will suffer from health. Instances of the American "hygienist and puritanical dictatorship" abound in the book. As his ship neared Havana, the French traveler was informed by the captain that the passengers were soon to leave board so that the ship could be fumigated with prussic acid. Later, everybody was required to fill out and sign a long questionnaire demanding a "swarm of important serious declarations" with respect to religion, politics, private life, marriage, financial resources, and "the constitutional or contagious diseases with which we might be afflicted" (4).

The political side of the American fear of European contamination appears in Céline's *Journey to the End of the Night*. As the "slave ship" on which he crossed the ocean is kept offshore weeks and weeks for observation, Bardamu informs the reader, perhaps in reference to the trial and execution of Sacco and Vanzetti, that "these people in America hate galley slaves coming in from Europe. 'They are all anarchists,' they say" (184). Duhamel, for his part, being anything but a slave and an anarchist, naively assumed that, having already produced a host of documents justifying his trip, he was done with "operations of police and hygiene." ("In order to be able to set foot in this Paradise, I have made more calls and gone to more trouble than would be required to get into revolutionary and bureaucratic Russia" [6].) He was sadly mistaken however, for a young physician in military uniform, "booted and equiped as for a colonial expedition," and accompanied by a nurse, comes aboard. Having ordered the passengers to stand single file, cattle-like, on the deck, the physician puts a thermometer in each mouth. When he tries to stick his finger under the author's eyeglasses, the latter vehemently refuses to allow any further manipulation of his body. "I do not much care to have a gentleman, even though he has the appropriate diploma, finger any part of me after he has manipulated some dozens of my fellow beings" (9). A similar scene occurs in Céline's narrative: the newly hired workers at a Ford factory are submitted to a medical examination before being assigned various tasks on and around the assembly line. Standing naked in single file, the workers are stripped of their social identity. Instead of isolating possible diseases to prevent contamination, however, the systematic screening of possible ailments or deformities helps the Ford management to optimize the use of a disabled labor force. Although he is found to be in "terrible shape," Bardamu is given a specific task to do: "They seemed very happy to find invalids and wrecks in our little lot" (223).

The American fear of infection by outside elements, however, had its counterpart in the European obsession with the inevitable corruption of civilized life by technological barbarity. American culture is described as a frightening epidemic in the opening pages of Duhamel's essay, and the book ends with the horrifying prophecy of the American disease silently spreading across Europe and the world, like a colony of termites eating away at the very core of civilization. "There are on our continent, in France as well as elsewhere, large regions that the spirit of old Europe has deserted. The American spirit colonizes little by little such a province, such a city, such a house, and such a soul" (Duhamel, 215). The good doctor wonders whether "the American fever" will ever be cleansed from his body and soul: "How long," he asks in fear and trembling, "would it take me to be cured of Chicago?" (112).

The Circles of Hell

When dealing with the city, anti-American discourse resorts to a more demonic register, still keeping animal and medical metaphors handy. Duhamel's Chicago is an underground jungle, the kingdom of night and insanity, "the tumor, the cancer, among cities" (78), a chaotic underworld in which all traces of the good, examined life have been eliminated, hell indeed, but "hell that lacks a Dante" (85):

> Night fell. A thousand lamps lighted and clashed like so many daggers. I did not see the lake, but I divined its presence on my right— an abyss of silence, an infinity of cotton-wool in which the noise of the demonic city was lost. . . . At the base of the bridges appeared clusters of lights, linked intimately with a coincident medley of noises. Groups of red lights, raised high, blazed from moment to moment with convulsive flames, and each flame was accompanied in perfect time by a harsh, strident ringing, a clattering storm of sound. The flame and the noise were so perfectly mingled that you heard the light with your ears, and that the sound dazzled and blinded you. (Duhamel, 80, 82)

The urban hell has its Lethe, too, a genuine stream of oblivion and death: the "ancient" Chicago River, on the marshy banks of which Cavelier sieur de La Salle camped, has been turned into a sewer, carrying foul garbage to Lake Michigan.

Céline's New York City is hardly more endearing. Dr. Ferdinand Bardamu's first impression of Manhattan, besides the banal reference to verticality, is that of the "sickening" standardized duplication of buildings *and* beings, the endless repetition. "Lifting up my nose toward these bulwarks,

I felt an upside-down sort of giddiness, because there were really too many windows up there and they were all so much alike eveywhere you looked that one felt sickened by them" (*Journey to the End of the Night*, 191). Bardamu is concerned with not being too *visible* amid the crowd, as he feels overwhelmed by a sense of shame at his worn-out clothes and unhealthy physical appearance. He quickly realizes that he need not worry, for with the first contact with the crowd he experiences a total loss of individuality, a sudden loss of physical presence and self-consciousness; his being is reduced to an anonymous ghost, a mere shadow: "But I needn't have felt ashamed. There was nothing to bother about. The street I had chosen was easily the narrowest of all. . . . So many other people, both large and small, were already walking along it, that they carried me with them like a shadow" (191).

Bardamu has truly become, in his instantaneous dilution in the urban masses, an invisible man. After a few days in the "isolation of the American ant-heap," which is "more shattering" than "the frightful kind of loneliness" he had known in Africa, the narrator meditates on the process of self-fragmentation he has been undergoing. The American experience, by dissolving the reassuring landmarks of a familiar environment, acts as a revelator of the meaninglessness of life, of the ultimate illusion of self-identity, of the disgusting presence of being that Sartre's Roquentin experienced in *Nausea*. Bardamu reflects, "I had always suspected myself of being almost purposeless, of not really having any single serious reason for existing. Now I was convinced, in the face of facts themselves, of my personal emptiness. In surroundings much too different from those in which I had previously had my meagre being, it was as if I had at once fallen to pieces. . . . It was a disgusting experience" (202).

The American city, far from offering an antidote to the inescapable ennui of industrial life, is the concrete manifestation of that boredom. The good doctor cannot find any solace in walking the neighborhood streets, for it is nothing but "an unsipid carnival of vertiginous buildings. My lassitude," he tells the reader, "deepened before a row of these elongated façades, this monotonous surfeit of streets, bricks, and endless windows, and business and more business, this chancre of promiscuous and pestilential advertising. A mass of grimy, senseless lies" (203). The Baudelairean boredom of modernity is painted on the expressionless faces of the anonymous crowd, whom Bardamu allows to carry him, aimlessly drifting in a sea of joyless, indifferent shadows.

The most salient feature of street life is the absence of communication, especially between men and women, which, given Bardamu's permanent state of sexual arousal, is of great wonder to him. "The sexes seemed to keep each to itself in the street. . . . You didn't find any old people in this crowd. Nor couples either. No one seemed to think it at all odd that I should be sitting there hour after hour, watching the people pass" (194). City dwellers do not seem to communicate any better in the privacy of their bedrooms, for that matter. Shamelessly voyeuristic, Bardamu witnesses from his hotel room the nightly rituals of hundreds of human insects going through the motions of life, with the indifference of zombies:

> The women had very pale, very full thighs, at least, those I could see properly had. Most of the men shaved, smoking a cigar, before going to bed. Once in bed, they take off their spectacles first, and then remove their dentures, which they put in a glass, and then place the whole lot on show. . . . You'd say they were fat, very docile animals, very used to being bored. I saw in all only two lots do, with the lights on, at any rate, what I was waiting for, and not violently at all. The other women just ate sweets in bed, while waiting for their husbands to finish their toilet. And then they all put out the light. (199)

From the window of his hotel room, the invisible voyeur tries in vain to break through the catatonic indifference of the city dwellers. When his cries for help are not answered, he finally comes to the realization that he is the inaudible man as well, his imperceptible, antlike existence always on the verge of dissolution:

> In my room the same thunderings continued, in snatches, to shatter down their echoes . . . and then as well that soft murmur of a moving crowd, always hesitating again and coming back. The bubbling, like jam, of people in a city. . . . I called to them "Help! Help!" Just to see if they'd take any notice. None whatever. . . . They don't give a damn. And the bigger the town and the higher the town, the less they bloody well care. I'm telling you. I've tried. And it's no use. (208)

Unable to make up with his former lover, Lola, Ferdinand sees the urban environment as the embodiment of the silent hostility that keeps them apart. Céline, like Duhamel, makes frequent use of animal metaphors. Here, he compares the city to a crouching wild beast, watching its prey: "After that, it was quite cold between us two in the car. The streets we went along seemed to threaten us with all their silent stones, armed and towering above us . . . A watching town, a monster bituminous and rain-sodden, ready to pounce" (219). Céline's New York is another hell without Alighieri. The narrator is surrounded with threatening, dark enclosed spaces he calls caves: his room, the subway, the underground toilets, the "cage full of flies" that is the Ford factory, the dark womb of the movie theater, the frightful labyrinth of office buildings, and his hotel, "a gigantic, odiously animated tomb" (204). The description of his first journey along the dimly lit corridors of the Gay Calvin Hotel, under the guidance of a childish bellhop, reads like a grotesque descent into hell:

> First along a corridor . . . we forged, determined and in darkness like an underground train. . . . Is this it? No, another corridor. Darker still, ebony panelling all the way . . . I was lost in a tornado of unfamiliar sensations here. There comes a moment between two civilizations when one finds oneself struggling in a vacuum. Suddenly, without warning, the bell-hop swung around. We had arrived. I hurled myself through a door into my room, a large, ebony-pannelled box. Only on the table did a lamp cast a glimmer of dim, greenish light. . . . As soon as I was alone, it was much worse. All this America was nagging at me, asking me huge questions and filling me with horrible presentiments, even here in this room. (197–98)

Ferdinand Bardamu's urban inferno has two major components: the promiscuity of the people (Céline's version of Sartre's "hell is the others") and the unbearable vibration of things, the constant aggression of industrial noises (in Céline's African chapters, odors were dominant). In Chicago, Georges Duhamel experienced with great distress the irresistible invasion of his being by the metallic clamor of the city, which robbed him of his intellectual abilities: "It was seven o'clock in the evening. The Elevated express was crowded. It clattered across the tumultuous city. It was useless to try to arrange my thoughts. I was in the grip of Chicago, as I might have been in that of some fell disease" (109–10). In the same way, the rumbling noise of the New York elevated trains prevents Bardamu's escape from anxiety into sleep, and his remarks echo the chilling prediction of André Maurois's friend: "You will not be able to sleep, let alone find some rest."

> With rumbling regularity the walls by my window trembled at the passing of an elevated railroad car. It hurtled along opposite between two streets, like a shell filled with quaking, jumbled flesh, careering from one district to another across this lunatic city. You could see it down there, rushing over a network of steel girders whose echo groaned on long after it had passed at a hundred miles an hour. . . . It was above all else this frantic railway that wore me down. (Céline, 198)

An even worse experience awaits the narrator as he later finds a job on the assembly line in a Detroit automobile plant. The "slow-moving files and hesitant groups" of the newly hired employees on their way to "where the vast crashing sound of the machines came from" recall the reluctant herds of sacrificed animals in Duhamel's slaughterhouses and underground trains. "The whole building shook," Céline goes on, "and oneself from one's soles to one's ears was possessed by this shaking, which vibrated from the ground, the glass panels and all this metal, a series of shocks from floor to ceiling" (224). Céline offers his version of Marx's analysis of an industrial capitalism that reifies the proletarian into a mere appendage of the machine: "One was turned by force into a machine oneself, the whole of one's carcass quivering in this vast frenzy of noise, which filled you within and all around the inside of your skull and lower down rattled your bones, and climbed to your eyes in infinite, little, quick, unending strokes. As you went along, you lost your companions" (224). It is the whole of America that has become a living hell for Europe's invisible man, who can only find solace in the dreamlike, phantasmic universe of the movie theater and the brothel. Asked about his first impressions of the New World by his former lover, Lola, Ferdinand confesses that "her country terrified me quite definitely more than the whole sum total of threats, actual, hidden and unforeseen which I found it contained, particularly on account of the vast indifference towards me which, as far as I was concerned, was what it stood for" (212).

That mass society is hell is most eloquently suggested in the famous passage on the underground toilets, where Bardamu discovers the underside, as it were, of Puritanism. Trying to escape the suspicious look of a policeman, Bardamu sees on his right a "great wide hole in the middle of the pavement, rather like our métro at home." This "subterranean resort" however, is deceitfully familiar: it turns out to be the place where city dwellers "go about Nature's needs." In the hole, "filled with a filtered, dying daylight fading on the backs of unbuttoned men," a horrible vision, a collective nightmare akin to Duhamel's slaughterhouse, awaits Bardamu: dozens of individuals, "red in the face, in the midst of their own stinks . . . attended to their dirty business in public, to an accompaniment of frightful noises. Among men, that way, without fuss, and to the tune of laughter and encouragements from all around, they settled down to it as to a game of football. . . . Many groaned like wounded men or women in labour. The constipated were threatened with ingenious tortures" (195).

Above and beyond his disgust, Bardamu is "nonplussed" and "disconcerted" by the contrast between the "absolute restraint" exhibited by men in the streets and "the easy shamelessness, the stupendous intestinal familiarity" they display in the underworld. "The stricter, the more mournful even, the behavior of these men out there in the street, the more the prospect of having to empty their bowels in tumultuous company appears to solace and inwardly delight them" (195). Bardamu finds his way out of the "fecal cave" and back to the light of day without having even approached the men, "because of their smell." He is left to ponder the frightfully schizophrenic behavior of the American people and the meaning of such a display of "vulgar, digestive debauchery, a joyous communism in filth" (196), the underside of Duhamel's bourgeois communism. Unable to "find a synthesis" of all the aspects of the question, the narrator yearns for the forgetfulness of sleep.

The once-familiar landscape of American urban life that so thoroughly repulsed Bardamu must have shocked quite a few foreign visitors in its days, since Georges Duhamel also devoted a few lines to New York's underground toilets, a passage which, interestingly enough, does not appear in the English version of *America: The Menace*. Like Céline, Duhamel tried in vain to understand their meaning and likewise, after failing to do so, his only recourse was to flee:

> It stands on the banks of the East River, at the foot of the Brooklyn Bridge, on the Manhattan side. One of these buildings, so rare in this country, that gentlemen appreciate at certain times. I walk in out of curiosity . . . if only to honor one of our old French traditions. . . . What do I see? Lord of my Fathers, what do I see? Ten guys, glaring fixedly, looking strangely preoccupied. They raise toward me faces full of the same sleepy indifference one notices among the crowds in cinemas, restaurants or other places of pleasure. Why these open toilets? Is it, once again, out of moral concern that the doors have been taken off? What care? What morals? (Duhamel, 210)

No more Celinian luxuriance and raciness here, but a mixture of panic and puzzlement. "It is not Rabelaisian. Not at all. It is lugubrious, it is pitiful, and, above all, humiliating. Let's run, let's run, O Europe!" The modern individual, whether attending to natural or cultural needs, does not seem to be able to escape the dehumanizing glare of others. One can probably read in this phobia for promiscuity an effect of the extension of the logic of production—to the private sphere, to leisure, psychic life, and sexuality—that characterizes our contemporary social universe. In Céline's narrative, the collective release of excrement is no liberation of repressed instincts or drives. The "joyous communism in filth" is no romantic utopia of natural desire freed from social constraintss. The collective production of organic refuse, just like that of fantasies or gadgets, is not an alternative to Puritan repression; it is, rather, its obscure, but complementary, underside. No consumption without scarcity, no transgression without forbidding: liberation only makes sense if there exists a constraint from which one needs to be freed at any cost. Since nothing shall be hidden, forbidden, or repressed any longer, then everything has to be said, meant, and brought to light, until all meaning is spent and all remnants transformed and recycled.

In Chicago, Georges Duhamel was given a tour of the museum for by-products of industrial animal slaughter: drums, tobacco pipes, buttons and knives, harnesses and rackets, toothbrushes and clothes-brushes, shoes and gloves, suits of clothing, drugs, chemical products, toys and soaps, "everything that can be made from horns, hides, bones, and fat, from blood and other fluid substances of the body, and from whatever else remains after the great butchery. 'At Chicago,' says a famous apothegm, 'they use every part of the pig except the squeal'" (98). In fact, Duhamel argues later, the scream is so strong and so alive that "the packers will make something of it some day," for "it is absurd that this enormous sum of energy should thus evaporate and lose itself in space" (104).

The logic of rationalized production implies that nothing is ever wasted, lost, or totally sacrificed, as it is, for example, in the potlatch of primitive societies, that gratuitous gift without reciprocity, absolute sacrificial *dépense*, and excess of desire over death, which so fascinated the anthropological imagination of Marcel Mauss and Georges Bataille. The break in the sacrificial cycle means that the spirits of the slaughtered animals, since they have not been properly propitiated, will come back to haunt the writer, in the guise of the myriad lifeless objects in which they have been reincarnated:

> Finally, I reached the hotel, my own shelter, my own burrow, my own refuge from this crazy town. At last I should have a bath, and perhaps attain forgetfulness. Well, no! The soap . . . smelled strongly of the abattoir. Moreover, it undoubtedly *came* from there. . . . The dropped eggs—Heavens! they were cooked in lard! . . . The binding of the Bible placed on the table by the bed . . . No, that at least was nothing worse than imitation sheepskin. But what of the comb, the brush, and the little horn-handled knife lying warm in my pocket? "Keep cool," I said to myself; "Be calm." (Duhamel, 111–12)

Similarly, human beings can be recycled, endlessly reinserted in the process of labor and production, even if they are apparently unfit for it. Céline, a physician, had been sent to the United States to study the organization of social medicine. In the report he wrote on medical practices at the Ford Motor Company (*Œuvres*, 1:712), he noted that the hiring of disabled individuals helped solve one of the major problems of American industry, that is, labor mobility. The physically and psychologically ailing employees knew they could not find wage labor anywhere else, so they were more than happy to work for $6 an hour. In the same way, the very obscenity of the subterranean toilets lies in the fact that the most discrete, the most personal, the most intimate is open, visible, available, preferred to the gaze of others, summoned, called upon to appear, to reveal and manifest itself. The ob-scene—the word says it—is what shows and shows off and displays itself complacently on the public stage of the theater of modernity. As Jean Baudrillard remarked, and as Céline and Duhamel suggested, the imperative of production, spreading as it is today to all domains of reality, whether economic, sexual, or intellectual, means the end of intimacy, secrecy, and dissimulation:

> Let everything be produced, be read, become real, visible, and marked with the sign of effectiveness; let everything be transcribed into force relations, into conceptual systems or into calculable energy; let everything be said, gathered, indexed and registered: this is how sex appears in pornography, but this is more generally the project of our whole culture, whose natural condition is "obscenity." Ours is a culture of "monstration" and demonstration, of "productive" monstrosity (the "confession" so well analyzed by Foucault is one of its forms). (*Forget Foucault*, 22)

Baudrillard, building on Georges Bataille's reflections on symbolic exchange and conspicuous consumption in *La Part maudite*, often describes the contemporary situation as a double movement of production of refuse and reintegration of those remnants, excesses, and residues in the social process: "The social," he writes, "exists on the double basis of the production of remainders and their eradication" (*In the Shadow of the Silent Majorities*, 78). In this perspective, modernity, by destroying traditional economies and cultures, has contributed to the production of many deterritorialized, deculturated, and/or marginalized individuals and groups. All the "others" of contemporary critical theory (peasants expelled to the city, immigrants, women, sexual, ethnic, and racial minorities, mental patients, criminals, illiterates, the unemployed, etc.) are immediately reinserted in the various agencies of the management of social life: schools, hospitals, government clinics, vocational training centers, and so on, all institutions in charge of recovering the "residues of symbolic disintegration." Baudrillard notes, "Waste and recycling: such would be the social in the image of a production whose cycle has long escaped the 'social' finalities to become a completely described spiral nebula, rotating and expanding with every 'revolution' it makes. Thus one sees the social expanding throughout history as a 'rational' control of residues, and a rational *production* of residues" (*In the Shadow of the Silent Majorities*, 73).

Céline's underground toilets and Duhamel's stockyards are examples of the breathing of modernity, the inhaling and exhaling of refuse. The double movement of production and elimination recycles the residues of production so that nothing will be sacrificed without return. But once all reality has been thus "socialized," then "the social itself is only residue" (72). The production/recycling cycle leads, in Baudrillard's view, to an unchecked "accumulation of death," to "pure excrement. . . . the fantastic congestion of dead labor, of dead and institutionalized relations within terrorist bureaucracies, of dead languages and grammars." The social "is already the accumulation of death" (73). Céline and Duhamel suggest the same discharge and removal of dead organic matter, offal, or meat scraps, and the infinite transformation of the by-products of death that the idiom of modernity calls *food processing* and *waste processing*.

Of Legs and Men

All this is a far cry, indeed, from the enchanted vision that sent Ferdinand Bardamu in a state of raptured amazement as he caught the first glimpse of the New World. At that moment, America looked more like paradise than hell as the fog lifted over New York harbor. It seemed as though his journey to the end of the night had finally brought him to the eve of a new dawn, filled with the wonders of the promised land. "The night before, one fine evening, everything suddenly became calm. I was no longer delirious" (183). Was the New World a symbol of new-found health, then, and a promise of freedom and happiness?

> Next morning when we woke up, we realized on opening the portholes that we had arrived at our destination. What an incredible sight! Talk about a surprise! What we saw suddenly through the fog was so astonishing that at first we wouldn't believe it was true, and then, standing there bang in front of it all, galley slaves that we were, we had to laugh, seeing it jutting right up in front of us like that. (184)

Bardamu's first vision of America instantly became one of the most popular passages of the whole book, judging from the press reviews following its publication in France in 1932. Georges Altman claimed in the newspaper *Le Monde* that the passage compared favorably with anything by Paul Morand (*Œuvres*, 1: 778). Another critic, André Rousseaux, wrote enthusiastically in *Candide:* "If you dare say that the *Journey to the End of the Night* depresses you, or even disgusts you . . . let us throw in your face the arrival in New York. It was mentioned to me twenty times during one afternoon. This passage will quickly become, I think, as famous as the wedding in Normandy in *Madame Bovary*" (792).

Ferdinand had first caught a glimpse of the wonders of the American space while "exploring" the body of Lola, a young nurse he had met in a hospital in Paris during World War I:

> Her body was an endless source of joy to me. I never tired of caressing its American contours . . . Indeed, I came to the very delightful and comforting conclusion that a country capable of producing anatomies of such startling loveliness, and so full of spiritual grace, must have many other revelations of primary importance to offer—biologically speaking of course. My little game with Lola led me to decide that I would sooner or later make a journey, or rather a pilgrimage, to the United States; and certainly just as soon as I could manage it. Nor did I find respite and quiet (throughout a life fated in any case to be difficult and restless) until I was able to bring off this supremely mystical adventure in anatomical research. Thus it was in the neighborhood of Lola's backside that a message from the new world came to me. (49–50)

Lola's evasive answers to her lover's more and more pressing inquiries about America only fuel his desire to pursue his erotic-mystical quest. "It was due to Lola that I became curious about the United States. I immediately asked her a lot of questions about that country, which she hardly answered. When you start out on journeys in this way, you come back as and when you can." (45).

Despite the disappointment of being quarantined offshore for weeks, Bardamu does not lose at first his enthusiasm for the Land of (libidinal) Opportunity, nor his dream of quick physical recovery and soon-to-be sexual and financial gratifications. "I might perhaps have tried, as others had successfully before me, to swim across the harbour and once I was on the quay to start shouting 'Long live the Dollar! Long live the Dollar!' It's one way of doing it. Lots of chaps have landed that way and afterwards made their fortunes" (184–85). Bardamu's companions, who think of America as "their bête noire," try in vain to dissuade him from going ashore, pointing at the illusion of the American Dream and at the economic inequalities prevalent in America. "We'll tell you right now what the Americans are like, if you want to know! They are all either millionaires or scum—nothing in between" (186). The warnings of Bardamu's friends dispute the widespread claim that, in the United States, everybody belongs to the middle class.

Although, once ashore, Bardamu encounters two sailors who debate whether they ought to drown him, and although he later weathers the anger of the chief quarantine officer, who takes him for an anarchist, his hopes are rekindled by the sight of the "fine legs" and "budding young flesh" of Major Mischief's daughter, "an absolute challenge to happiness, an exclamation of promised delight" (190). Once in the city, Bardamu is forced to acknowledge the presence of the "usual poor . . . going to their work, no doubt, with their noses to the ground" (193). Just as he is about to admit the truth of his friends' predictions, he finally grasps what he takes to be the true promise of the American Dream: "Out of this gloom, this jogging, disjointed, mournful crowd, there surged towards noon, a sudden avalanche of absolute lovely women! What a discovery! What an America! What delight! Oh, memory of Lola! As a type, she'd not deceived me. It was *true!* I was getting to the quick of my pilgrimage" (193).

At the sight of all these "unreal office girls," Bardamu slips back into the raptured state of amazement, the intimation of a total transfiguration of self he had felt at the very first sight of New York City. "If I had not at the same time felt frequent pangs of hunger, I should have believed myself to have reached a moment of unearthly aesthetic inspiration. These beauties I was discovering could, with a little confidence and comfort, have ravished me from my trivial condition of humanity." The harmonious delicacy of features of these "blondes, brunettes and red-heads too" make him wonder if Greece has not been reborn in front of his very eyes. The living "masterpieces of face and figure," however, are all the more idealized as they are truly inaccessible, forever removed from Bardamu's reach because of his wretched physical and social condition:

> They appeared to be totally unaware of my presence, my existence, as I sat close beside them on my bench, goggling in the fullness of my erotico-mystical admiration, silly with quinine and also, one must admit, with hunger. . . . They could have carried me off, these unreal office girls, could have sublimated me, with only a gesture, with but one word, and I should have sailed away at once, all of me, into the world of dreams. But no doubt they had other business to attend to. (194)

Later, as he enters the Gay Calvin Hotel in search of a cheap room, Bardamu experiences again the painful inaccessibility of those potentially sublimating young women he sees in the lobby, for they are masked in darkness and protected, as if in a shell, by the deep armchairs in which they sit. Other men, like the narrator himself, are condemned to revolve endlessly around them like silent stars, prevented by an invisible barrier from ever entering the forbidden universe (and, a fortiori, the consciousness) of these distant and haughty goddesses. "Men, silent and attentive, passed around them to and fro, a little way off, timidly and inquisitively, just out of range of crossed legs displaying magnificent heights of silk. . . . Clearly [these young women's] thoughts were not of me. And I in turn passed by, most furtively, before this long and palpable temptation" (196). As he returns from his room a moment later, Bardamu realizes once again that the wretchedness of his situation prevents him from ever fulfilling his "eroticomystical" desire: "I still had to cross the vestibule past more rows of ravishing enigmas with such alluring legs and delicate, severe little faces. . . . One might have come to an understanding with them. But I was afraid of being arrested. . . . Almost every desire a poor man has is a punishable offense" (200).

Bardamu encounters the cruel law of repressed desire in an even more tangible and painful way when he, in a fast-food restaurant, asks one of the waitresses to marry him.[3] He never gets an answer. "A giant of a doorkeeper, he too dressed all in white, came along at that moment and pushed me outside neatly, quietly, without being at all insulting or rough, into the night, like a dog that's forgotten itself" (207). The brutal white knight, who, in such an unemotional and uncharitable way, applied the moral law and defended the purity of white-clad waitresses, had definitely turned the American Dream of desire into a nightmare of yearnings never acknowledged, let alone satisfied.

Bardamu should have known from the start, though, that he had not reached the end of his libidinal night. He should have trusted his first impression indeed, the funny feeling he and his companions had felt at the first sight of New York City. In the French language, cities are feminine, of course, but what a strange sort of woman that was, standing there, in front of their bewildered eyes:

Understand that it went up in the air, quite straight, that town of theirs. New York is a town standing up. . . . At home, dammit, cities lie on their sides along the coast or on a river bank; they lie flat in the landscape, awaiting the traveller—whereas this American one, she didn't relax at all; she stood there very stiff, not languid in the least, but stiff and forbidding. It seemed damn funny to us; we laughed and laughed. It can't help being funny, a town built straight up in the air like that. (184)

The American city does not abandon itself passively to the male visitor's gaze but stands erect, a phallic woman, a threatening sword guarding the garden of desire, "stiff and forbidding" like the goddesses themselves, with their "severe little faces." The Celinian narrative seems to imply that if only Bardamu had understood the full meaning of his companions' (and his own) nervous laughter, everything would have made sense—the indifference between the sexes in the street and in bed, the satellite-like, peripheral behavior of American males, and the haughty aloofness of waitresses and "office girls."

The perception of American women as frigid, frustrated wives and authoritarian, castrating mothers, is a common topos of European descriptions of American gender relations. In an extremely critical account of American life published in *Nouvelle École* (1975), the review of the French intellectual new Right, Robert de Herte and Hans-Jürgen Nigra offer an ideal typical assessment of "American matriarchy." In a country obsessed with the refusal of all power and hierarchy, the father has been deprived of all authority, reduced, in the eyes of his children, to the passive role of benevolent clown and "buddy." The little authority left in the family belongs to his wife. In the authors' view, the "specifically feminine values of 'comfort,' 'love' and 'security,'" have come to dominate American culture because they illustrate and bolster the anti-heroic ideal of bourgeois egalitarianism, which had undermined the father figure in the first place.

As dedicated consumers and the prime target of advertisers, women are seen by some European intellectuals as the most docile perpetrators of the capitalist system. The female domination in the private sphere of sexuality, emotions, and consumption gives rise to the Puritan fear of women, the "unconscious gynophobia" of the American male, who escapes mother's overpowering influence only to fall in the grip of his nagging and domineering lover or wife. Hence the war of the sexes and the suicidal libidinal relations described, for instance, in the American thriller novel. Could it be that American men, Herte and Nigra wonder, are so bent on succeeding in their professional life because they are such losers at home? The reverse is true for women, however: all-powerful in the home, they are systematically excluded from positions of power in the public sphere. We see here at work, by the way, the now-familiar mechanism of what I call "the critical double bind": this is the belief that, while American civilization is far too liberal and too democratic in the domestic sphere, it is also too intolerant and hierarchical in the world of work and politics and equally blamed for both. One way of countering the fear and hatred of women's power is to idealize them and hold them accountable to unreachable standards: unable to be "real" females ("des femmes-femmes"), American women are trapped in the myth of the superwoman. In the words of Herte and Nigra, they are "either castrating 'Moms,' or conditioned little 'housekeepers,' or sophisticated career women" (77).[4]

In some instances, the Right's hatred of American sexual mores takes on hyperbolic misogynous connotations. In *Pourquoi la France* (1975), an anti-American pamphlet, Jean Cau equates democracy with the feminine ("The more democratic a country, the more female it is") and gives the reader the secret of his "relentless diagnosis" of our contemporary disease: "If you wish to know where decadence lies, look for the woman. That's where it is. If you want to know where lies the future, look for the man. . . . Woman is the Great Ungodly One. I am aware of how courageous I am to utter such a cry, in this *fin de siècle* when *everything* is feminine, feminist, feminized, feminoïd and feminizable. Everything: mores, social relations, the height of heels, the length of hair, the Church, politics [and so on]" (130, 126).

In *La Grande prostituée*, meaning egalitarian modernity, America is given first place among industrial nations in the race to decadence: "The USA, that female country where the most hysterical matriarchy of history is triumphant . . . has a dark and most likely desperate future ahead" (54). Cau describes American society as a repulsive female body pregnant with all the evils of consumer capitalism: "How low will this huge body slide down, this fat democracy whose belly is bursting with cars, gadgets, fridges, filthy movies, lousy dollars and mercantile greed, how far will this fatso slide down before falling in the muck, its belly exploding, slit open by the cutting edge of the lowest step?" (112). In another pamphlet, America is seen as the child of Europe indeed, but she is a "rude and horribly misbehaved" brat, and a daughter to boot, half hysterical whore, half castrating mother: "One day, the girl went away, to the other side of the water, and there, she grew large teeth, bedecked herself with jewelry, gelded the males to whom she was giving birth, and finally suffered from fits of nerves she tried to soothe with psychiatrists" (*Pourquoi la France*, 54).

Such characterizations of gender relations in the United States are not confined to the chauvinistic prose of right-wing males, however. In *America Day by Day* (published in France in 1948), Simone de Beauvoir paints a strikingly similar picture of American women, who are torn between conflicting roles and expectations. She seems to agree with most of

Philip Wylie's then well-circulated book, *Generation of Vipers*, which, she said, portrayed the "middle-age woman who subjects America to the rule of the matriarch. Making free of her husband's check book, dominating her children, demanding respect from all men, such is the American woman, and she may be compared to the praying mantis that devours the male species. The comparison is more or less just, but one must understand it" (251). The French visitor recalls how she had believed, before coming to the United States, in the freedom and independence of the American second sex. She soon realized that, behind the myth, lay the reality of deeply unequal relationships. Their obsessive concern with power and equality made American women highly dependent on their male counterparts, and, paradoxically, extremely vulnerable to men's judgments and attitudes. "They despise, often with good reason, the servility of French women, who will always smile at men and bear with their ill-humour; but the tension they show in writhing on their pedestals only masks their feebleness" (251).

At Vassar College, Simone de Beauvoir had been impressed and charmed by the look of health and happiness, ease of manner, wholesomeness and spontaneity of the students, who were comfortably clad in jeans, shorts, and sweaters. Seeing them again the next day in the train to New York City, she barely recognized them, dressed like their mothers and older sisters, in hats, flowers, veils, furs, and high-heeled shoes. American women, Beauvoir remarked, never dress for comfort or for themselves. "Even those women who defend their independence on every occasion, and whose attitude to men so easily becomes aggressive, dress for men: those heels which paralyse the footstep, those fragile plumes, those flowers with wintry hearts and all those furbelows are clearly dazzling effects designed to stress their femininity and attract men's looks. Certainly European women's clothes are altogether less servile" (44).

For Simone de Beauvoir, those women's "inferiority complex" and "inability to prove themselves" stemmed from the limited horizons of their lives (Herte and Nigra's "private sphere") in a culture marked by "the absence of future objectives" and social or political goals. She also indulged in the ritualistic remarks on female frigidity and male impotence, which dozens of French observers have attributed to puritanical taboos and phobias. The apparent objectivity and matter-of-factness with which sexuality is dealt with is presented again as the expression of a profound distrust of, and inability to deal with, physical love, conducive to behavior unthinkable in the eroticized cultures of southern Europe. "You never see loving couples in the streets, no couples intertwined in Central Park, nor lips that meet" (254).

Besides their puritanical attitudes, Beauvoir believes that American women suffer from "a social complex," the result of conflicting drives: "The wish to dominate their men and rule them must seem incompatible with the animal desire for self-immolation which is latent in them. . . . Whether they are really frigid, or whether men just sum up in this accusation all the reproaches with which they saddle women, the fact remains that American women do not look like lovers, girl friends or companions" (254). Like Céline and Duhamel before her, Simone de Beauvoir concludes her observations with a few considerations on the ongoing war of indifference and frustration that the sexes in America wage upon each other: "Men shut themselves up in their clubs, women take refuge in theirs, and their relations consist in endless small vexations, disputes and conquests" (254).

In *Polylogue* (1977), Julia Kristeva voiced similar concerns and reservations, and despite generational differences in vocabulary and philosophical references, both descriptions are strikingly alike in their logic and presuppositions. For both writers, the problem with American women is, quite simply, their Americanness, for they share all the weaknesses and shortcomings of the society in which they live. For Beauvoir, they cannot escape the alienating grip of a civilization lacking worthy collective goals; for Kristeva, they partake of the hysterical character of American culture, a system that "allows and absorbs transgression" by channeling the transgressive expressions of desire (the body, "the substance") through the established forms of "the Law."

The deep affinity between American women and the political culture in which they operate causes the foreign observer to worry over the future of the feminist movement and to question its radicality, its capacity to subvert a society that, ever since Tocqueville, Europeans have viewed as dominated by the successful tyranny of conformity. Kristeva wonders, "Will the hysteric's eternal frustration with discourse force discourse to make itself anew? . . . Or will it remain a scream outside time, akin to great mass movements, breaking old systems, but willing to bow to the demands of some order, as long as it is a new order?" (*Polylogue*, 511). Central to Kristeva's assessment of gender relations in the United States are the now-familiar figures of the dominating mother and dominated son or husband. "What is striking, is that the woman—the mother—is still in the center [as in the medieval tradition], but now she requires it. The servant must bring pleasure and children: she does not ask for words or songs. If he does not, she will ask another man, or woman. Nowhere else did men seem to me so ready to accept such servitude, so skillful in making it come true" (512).

Georges Duhamel also dwelled at length on the dangerous powers of the American woman. Sitting nervously in the passenger's seat of Mrs. Graziella Lytton's six-cylinder convertible and fearing for his life, he fought his growing uneasiness by conjuring up pleasant visions of shapely female legs, obviously one of the French male visitors' favorite American fetishes:

> The pears that like juicy grapeshot, American sends in salvos to the ends of the earth, for I have eaten them even in Egypt,—I can guess where they are grown, and I even know where they are sold. But the legs, the lovely legs with their beautiful contours, obviously mass-produced, that are sheathed in glistening, artificial silk, and that the little knickers clasp with so charming a garter—where are they grown? The knickers—yes—a thousand pardons! I speak only of what I see, of what indeed everyone sees. How do the American ladies all manage to procure those same delectable legs which they display so generously? (64)

Mrs. Lytton, no doubt, is another one of Bardamu's childlike angels, one of these blond stars who live only on the screen, "published in an edition of two or three million copies, through the service of a vigilant industry, as the prize and pride of the American citizen," and whose "clear, full, symmetrical, well modulated laugh" will no doubt, thanks to the talkies, soon conquer the world. Mrs. Lytton, with her foot, "excites the machine"; her wild, careless driving epitomizes the freedom of the modern woman in the eyes of her French guest. She fits, no doubt, the horrified description that André Maurois' friend had offered of those creatures who "leave their homes in the morning and participate in the universal restlessness." Since her youth, Mrs. Lytton "had made these big gulpers of gasoline roar along every road. In this country automobile maturity legally arrives at the age of sixteen. And at that infantile age, rouged and powdered young girls pilot mastodons to and from school" (69). As for her spouse, "an athletic and profoundly silent gentleman," he seems to occupy the same peripheral position vis à vis the goddess behind the wheel as Céline's young men in the hotel lobby: sitting in the back seat, apparently very busy, he is quietly smoking a cigarette, like "men under a death-sentence." He never drives, explains his wife, for he is too busy doing business. Another horrifying vision of things to come, a foreboding of the sexual division of labor in a

Baconian civilization assails the French visitor: "What better symbol of it could there be than this madly rushing machine, turned loose at full speed between two pasteboard landscapes, steered by a charming woman with manicured nails and beautiful legs, who smoked a cigarette while traveling between fifty and sixty miles an hour, while her husband, seated on the cushions of the rear seat, with a set jaw scribbled figures on the back of an envelope" (71).

The world of "epileptic" machines, as Duhamel calls American cars, has for the humanist the uninviting dryness of numbers: like Mr. Lytton himself, it is hard, aloof, tense, hectic, and solitary. Céline's Ferdinand is also sensitive to the metallic indifference of the industrial universe, which is spreading to all domains of human existence: "Everywhere you look now, everything you touch, is hard. And everything you still manage to remember something about has hardened like iron and lost its savour in your thoughts. . . . Life outside you must be put away; it must be turned into steel too, into something useful. . . . It must be made into a thing, into something solid. By Order" (225). Life is not supposed to be hard as a metallic object, but soft, alive, and warm, like the female body Bardamu longs to caress, "a body rosy and alive in real, soft, silent life" (225).

In a "house" of the northern part of town, a sort of counterpuritanical haven, the anti-hero will find an alternative to the Gay Calvin Hotel, the perfect antidote to the dehumanizing stiffness of capitalism and metallic indifference of overstressed city dwellers and unreachable goddesses. The brothel soon becomes Bardamu's new home, a cozy refuge from the vastness and inhumanity of urban life. The cold and dark cave of the hotel, the womb of the evil phallic mother, has turned into a warm kitchen, where Bardamu—who is in love with Molly, archetype of the prostitute with a heart of gold—blissfully writes short stories, savoring at last the delights of literary creation while baseball players "take their joy" on Saturday nights.[5] "It was the first place I'd been in America where I was received without brutality, even kindly, for my five dollars. And they were good-looking young women too there, plump, bursting with health, grace and strength, really *almost* as beautiful as the ones at the Gay Calvin Hotel" (226; emphasis is mine).

The oxymoronic name of the hotel reactivates one of the commonplaces of the European critique of America: Calvin's star pupils have done away, once and for all, with all the fun in the world. Georges Duhamel found tragically lyrical accents to suggest the joylessness of modern times: "I gazed through the window at the nocturnal city, unbridled and shaken with all the furies and with all the lusts that seemed to me to be seeking everywhere, even in the rain-sodden clouds, the phantom of joy, pure human joy driven from the world" (127). These harsh words go beyond the mere condemnation of the systematic violence of the slaughterhouse or of the alienating order of the anthill; beyond technological and political processes, they aim at the ideological and philosophical foundations of the Baconian civilization. Here lies the fundamental difference between the repressive totalitarianism of the Soviet experience and the seductive bourgeois collectivism of the American one. The first one, Duhamel says, is "purely political and ideological," and, besides, it is already compromised by the very despotism of its leaders. But the other is triumphant, seldom questioned, it is the gospel of the future. It overlaps the boundaries of politics, it is, in Gramscian terms, truly hegemonic: both simple and all-encompassing, it describes itself as a mode of living, affecting "every act and every person," it is common sense, self-evident truth, and self-fulfilling prophecy (210). Duhamel anticipates the sixties radicals who would bemoan, thirty years later, the "recuperating" power of the system, its ability to weather all crises and turn oppositional ideas and practices, such as hippie life-styles, drugs, or rock and roll into brand new grist for the consumption mill. In the 1920s, Americanism already seems compatible with every political system, and infant communism itself will not escape its deadly embrace. "It adapts itself to anything, takes charge of everything, and succeeds in everything. It is turning Soviet Russia itself into a colony, purely in virtue, if I dare say so, of its clearly pointing the way" (Duhamel, 211).

The Empire of Signs

While the socio-economic critique of American industrial (or postindustrial) capitalism usually comes from the Left, the theme of cultural decadence has traditionally been high on the conservative or reactionary agenda. For humanists and cultural nationalists alike, the diabolical universe of the slaughterhouse and the anthill is more than just an attack upon nature, whether vegetable, animal or human: it is a direct assault on culture, a sin against the spirit. Georges Duhamel dedicated a whole chapter, "Fireworks or the Extravaganzas of Advertisement," to what was for the European visitor of the 1920s and 1930s the perfect illustration of American modernity. The French word for fireworks is *feux d'artifices*: Madison avenue is ablaze with artificiality, it is pure show, a display of cunning and illusion. Once again, Duhamel's text announces the subsequent, often naturalistic, critique of consumption society which, from Wilhelm Reich to Herbert Marcuse, attempted to rescue the fundamental, authentic, natural aspirations of human beings from the artificial needs created through the skillful manipulation of desire by the professionals of manufactured dreams. These aspirations would be restored to their original purity in a liberated society.

In Duhamel's *America*, the reader encounters advertising at first in the giant posters that border the freeways: they are nothing but a decor, a facade behind which "what they call here the country" has been thoroughly eliminated. The travesty of nature is the necessary outcome of the spread of material civilization: in a different context, Duhamel remarks that the Father of Waters, the mighty Mississipi, is often invisible, "strangled among the docks of New Orleans," after having crossed the dull plains "between immense levees, like a shameful prisoner" (90). In fact, the artificiality of advertising is a disguise of the second degree: while the city conceals nature, the signs themselves conceal the city. Buildings are often "disfigured with blazing signs that cover or crown with the lettering that remains the parasite of modern architecture" (87). The subterfuge of advertisement not only maims the landscape, whether bucolic or urban, it corrodes culture itself, emptying the sign of its signification and, as in the movies, reducing the viewer to a "sedentary mollusk" submitted to a series of flashes, repetitions, explosions, and titillations, "this tickling, this burlesque, a kind of masturbation of the eye" (133).

Beyond its cultural vacuity, "The Kingdom of Darkness" has disquieting political and moral consequences: a "tremendous business of coercion and brutalization. . . . of propaganda and intimidation," it treats human beings as a stupid herd and demoralizes the poor "by pushing them into foolish expenditure and squandering a good part of our common wealth on costly follies" (131). Duhamel suggests that one of his hosts form a "league of protest" to liberate man and nature from the encroachments of consumerism and to save the genteel values, "those holy things now ruined, or in decay—the horizon, quiet, reverie, courtesy, elegance, smiles, free will, the virgin wall, and white paper" (130). Not content with invading and manipulating the everyday life of the masses, the new disease, notes Duhamel, has even spread to *belles-lettres*, to the sacred realm of high culture: books are sold like soap and liquor. Duhamel denounces, with a vehemence that may seem quite naive and overdone to readers in our cynical fin de siècle, the stirrings of the now omnipresent process of the commodification of cultural goods.

If things of the spirit fall prey so easily to the corrupting influence of "literary merchants," it is probably because they were not of the spirit after all. The work of the true artist speaks for itself, and the authentic creator should not tolerate the presence of any intermediary between himself and the public, for he must bare his soul. "Let me alone, then, come to an understanding with those who like me and do me the honor to read me. Above all do not tell them that my latest book 'is perhaps the most astonishing book that has been published in the whole world since the twelfth century'" (137). Duhamel cannot find harsh enough words to condemn the treason of those *clercs* who, "losing all decency and honor," unabashedly pander to the tastes of the masses and try to rival "the manufacturers of chocolate and *apéritifs*" (136). The manipulation of tastes and ideas for profit runs counter to everything a humanistic civilization has always stood for: the autonomy of the individual, the self-determination of reason, the superior value of reflection and the fine arts, the disinterestedness of the quest for truth and beauty. If the ideological power of American civilization lies in its apparent simplicity and its capacity to "present to people elementary, powerful and seductive images," then nowhere is that power more apparent as in the movie theater, the Kingdom of Darkness par excellence.

Lost in the Funhouse

Everything about the "temple of moving images" speaks of its inherent mass democratic character: after paying a uniform price, crowds of hypnotized pilgrims are pushed forward in long liness "like lambs going to slaughter, between two cords that served as handrails" (25) and shoved into the "lair" and "the oesophagus of the monster," that "Gargantuan maw," the slaughterhouse of culture. Sitting in the belly of the beast, utterly lost in the funhouse, Duhamel as educated man goes through the most harrowing experience of his life as he witnesses the deliberate, systematic assassination of the most cherished treasures of the European artistic, musical and literary canon, those very same Great Works whose value is today so fiercefully debated within the American academia:

> And no one cried murder! For great men *were* being murdered. All those works which from our youth we have stammered with our hearts rather than with our lips, all those sublime songs which at the age of passionate enthusiasms were our daily bread, our study, and our glory, all those thoughts which stood for the flesh and blood of our masters, were dismembered, hacked to pieces, and mutilated. They passed by us now like shameful flotsam and jetsam on this wave of warm melted lard. And there was no one to cry murder! (30)

Endowed with a cultural capital that enables him to identify the various excerpts that make up the musical background of the movie, Georges Duhamel singles out with mounting horror, within the barbarian *medley*, the "muddy torrent" of background music, ten measures, not more, of Lohengrin's nuptial march, of Haydn's military symphony, of the first allegro of Beethoven's Symphony in C, and then, while actors are kissing over there, on the huge screen, four measures of *Tristan* and of Schubert's "Unfinished" Symphony. While one listens to Bach or Beethoven, one only hears the ubiquitous, "musical molasses" oozing from American phonographs. One is helplessly invaded by the flow of sounds and images instead of actively re-creating for oneself the masterpieces of old, be it in an imperfect way:

> "Wait a minute," murmured Pitkin, looking hurt. "Wait at least for the music. They're going to play something French. Debussy, I think. They are wonderful disks." "My dear Pitkin, excuse me. I don't care a rap for the music. That thing of Debussy's I'll rattle it out this evening on your piano, and I'll explain what it is. . . ." "What!" cried Pitkin. "The disks are made exclusively by eminent artists. They are perfection." "Pitkin, I don't give a damn for perfection this evening." (Duhamel, 40–41)

The fundamental incompatibity between European civilization and American mass culture disseminates itself throughout the text in a series of binary oppositions: listening versus hearing, active versus passive, but also authentic versus bogus, (real) life versus (unreal) image, awareness versus hypnosis, depth versus surface, and *mesure* versus *démesure*. The European *homme de lettres* takes it as his duty and mission to uphold the standards of reason and taste in the face of the overwhelming tide of meaninglessness and vulgarity and to defend what he calls nonreversible values, "an old dream, ideas, rules, laws and discoveries which would be almost impossible to use against man" (200).

The cardinal sin of mass culture is not that it creates its own forms out of its own needs, but rather that, with the help of modern recording and broadcast technologies, it submits the products of aesthetic creation to a process of decontextualizing/recontextualizing that totally falsifies and denatures them. As in the advertising world, the universe of images in motion is the supreme illusion, the perfect technological artifact of reality. The jumble of musical masterpieces reaches the apex of meaningless, tasteless kitsch, while everywhere in the movie theater, on the walls as well as the floor, Duhamel, the disgusted humanist, identifies "copies after copies of famous, and hideous, pictures . . . a multitude of statues in some plastic and translucent material . . . and imitations of thick Oriental rugs" (24). Everything in the "abyss of forgetfulness" is tainted by the curse of artificiality. False the music, false the sky and the stars and clouds on the ceiling, false "the life of shadows on the screen," false also, perhaps, this slumbering human multitude "that seemed to dream what it saw. . . . I myself was perhaps no longer anything but a simulacrum of a man, an imitation Duhamel" (27). The whole scene, from the princely liveries of the ushers, the plush carpeting, and the spacious empty hallways, smacks of the "luxury of a great bourgeois lupanar."

Just as many artists and writers have fallen for the charms of literary marketing, many fashionable intellectuals have crossed over to the enemy and endowed popular culture with legitimacy by treating jazz and cinema as genuine artistic creations. Surrendering to the lure of the modern, they forfeit their sacred mission of enlightenment. "Tired of being bored stiff in their ivory tower they shamelessly sought their recreation in the common amusements of that mob and of those middle classes whom they had so severely censured" (38). The apologists of mass culture have moved away from the "Romantic morality" that endowed the artist with the privilege and the duty of "passing judgment on the pleasures of the crowd, of condemning them sometimes and, in the name of intelligence, of subjecting them always to severe criticism" (38). Consequently, they are responsible for "having allowed the cinema to become the most powerful instrument of moral, aesthetic and political conformism" (64).

The true measure of art—that is, its capacity to sublimate and transcend ordinary concerns—is singularly lacking, says Duhamel, in the products of mass entertainment: "The cinema has sometimes diverted me and sometimes moved me: it has never required me to rise superior to myself. It is not an art. It is not art" (37). As for jazz, undoubtedly the main American contribution to modern popular music, it has none of the redeeming qualities of film. When one travels by boat from Europe to the New World, one can still hear on the captain's radio, during the first few days of the voyage, a few excerpts from *Carmen*, or some informative lecture. But after the Canary Islands, the "voices of the Old World" become inaudible (Duhamel, 1). After days of silence, one can finally hear America: no more Bizet, no more uplifting talk, but plaintive, almost funereal harmonies, which the officer identifies as "hymns, sung by Negro choruses. . . . There's never anything else but them or jazz," the captain goes on. "Every hour now, you will be more aware of America" (2).

At the end of his essay, "The Work of Art in the Age of Mechanical Reproduction," Walter Benjamin took Georges Duhamel to task for writing that cinema was nothing but "a pastime for slaves, an amusement for the illiterate, for poor creatures stupefied by work and anxiety . . . a spectacle that demands no effort, that does not imply any sequence of ideas . . . that excites no hope, if not the ridiculous one of some day becoming a 'star' at Los Angeles" (*America*, 34). On the contrary, Benjamin argued, the new medium has enriched our field of perception and deepened our critical awareness of reality. By making the work of art an object of scandal, Dadaism had broken the magic spell of bourgeois aestheticism as the serene, passive contemplation of beauty; in like fashion, the moving picture shocked the audience out of its complacency and forced them to participate actively, and critically, in the viewing.

Rejecting the traditional opposition between art as concentration, the highest form of encounter with the world, and popular culture as mere divertissement, Benjamin claimed that distraction did not necessarily mean passivity and that the critical faculty was not equal to consciousness: "The film makes the cult value [of art] recede into the background not only by putting the public in the position of the critic, but also by the fact that at the movies this position requires no attention. The public is an examiner, but an absent-minded one" (243). The German critic saw Duhamel's attacks as yet another instance of the elitist privileging of high culture, the "same ancient lament that the masses seek distraction whereas art demands concentration of the spectator" (241). Deeply influenced at the time by Brechtian aesthetic theories, Benjamin contended that film fulfilled better than any other medium the new function of art in modern times: the political mobilization of the masses for revolutionary change. The politicized aesthetics of socially conscious films, he argued, were the most efficient response to the aesthetic politics of fascism.

The publication of Benjamin's "Work of Art in the Age of Mechanical Reproduction" in France in 1936 sparked a heated debate over the political function of the mass media between Benjamin and his compatriot and fellow critical theorist Theodor Adorno. The latter criticized Benjamin for exhibiting, in the words of Richard Wolin, "a Brechtian uncritical and immediate fetishization of the powers of 'technique' with fatal disregard for the manipulative social employment of that technique in reality" (193). This uncritical celebration of film as a transparent vehicle for political messages was further reinforced, in Adorno's view, by a naive idealization of working-class self-consciousness and a blind faith in the revolutionary inclinations of the masses. Adorno insisted on distinguishing contemporary mass culture, dominated by manipulative technologies, from the endangered popular culture of earlier days, seen as a genuine expression of the working class experience. In his 1938 essay, "On the Fetish-Character of Music and the Regression of Listening," he took a stance somewhat akin to Duhamel's, although his argument rested on a totally different set of political premises, as well as on a modernistic, rather than humanistic, conception of art.

For Adorno, the commodification of music by the record industry and its star system transformed the use value of the work of art as object of an aesthetic experience into an exchange value determined first and foremost by the dictates of the market. In these conditions, art, which for the modernists had meant a distancing from and questioning of ordinary ("alienated") perceptions and evaluations of social and physical reality, was "regressing" to a mere cult, in the totemic sense of the term. The individual work of art had become a "fetish," and its exchange value was embodied in the name and jacket-cover picture of the performer. Adorno was rephrasing in a Freudian and Marxian vocabulary Duhamel's more traditional denunciation of passivity in the commercial consumption of music: commodification makes the listener regress to a mindless, manipulable state, conducive to what would later be called subliminal seduction.

Singing the Country Electric

Not all French intellectuals in the 1920s and 1930s shared Duhamel's (or Adorno's) contempt for American popular culture. Sartre, for one, repeatedly stressed his love of jazz and interwar Hollywood productions. In 1931, during an award distribution ceremony at the Lycée du Havre, where he was teaching philosophy, Sartre shocked the respectable, bourgeois audience of parents, teachers, administrators, and local notables by celebrating film as a form of art and encouraging his students to go to the movies. The Surrealists, following the poet Guillaume Apollinaire (who had prophesized that "the epic poet would express himself with film") and the Dada movement, also perceived the motion picture as a powerful means of liberating the imagination, duplicating the condensation and speed of dream sequences, and subverting the bourgeois codes of taste and representation. The deep affinity the surrealists perceived between moving images and the metaphorical processes of *l'écriture automatique*, prompted Philippe Soupault to write "cinematographic poems," while Salvador Dali collaborated with director Luis Buñuel in pioneering experiments such as *Le Chien Andalou.*

The case of Paul Claudel deserves some attention in this context, if only because the poet-diplomat, unlike most French critics of American society, had extensive professional contacts with the United States. The poet was assistant consul of France in Boston and New York from 1893 to 1895, and French ambassador in Washington from 1927 to 1933. Claudel's perception of the New World underwent a considerable, if somewhat cyclical, evolution in the course of his life. The young diplomat of the mid-1890s felt bored, lonely, and out of place in America. A recent convert to Catholicism, he fell prey to "culture shock" in a Protestant, somewhat provincial culture, which he found to be light years away from the genteel bourgeois Parisian environment he came from. Although he had been sensitive to the beauty of the land ("I will miss America and the exquisite purity of his skies," he wrote to a friend in 1895), the young poet felt exiled in a world he would later describe, in *La jeune fille Violaine*, as "a mixture of the mechanic and the animalistic." The overall negative impression left by his first experience overseas informs his second play, *L'Échange* (1897), which is set in America and which I shall discuss later (see chap. 5).

Judging from several texts he wrote in the 1930s, the picture somewhat changes during Claudel's second stay in the United States. Some of these writings are speeches delivered in the role of ambassador or recollections associated with the performance of his diplomatic duties, and need to be read with caution. His professed admiration for President Roosevelt, the celebration of the energy and resiliency of the American character (*l'élasticité américaine*) may represent in part what was expected of the official representative of an allied nation. After he left Washington, however, Claudel was sufficiently critical of the French government's refusal to come to an agreement with Roosevelt on the issue of war debts to suggest he had a genuine sympathy for the American position. Moreover, the literary texts he wrote at the time leave no doubt as to the fascination he then felt for some aspects of American modernity, even if this fascination was not without serious misgivings. Several passages of *Conversations dans le Loir-et-Cher*, written in 1928 during his tenure in Washington, attest to the ambiguity of his feelings for "the civilization which was thriving as a mixture of smoke and concrete on the other side of the Atlantic in this fabulous year 1929" (from the preface to the 1934 edition). The form of the text itself, made up of exchanges between artists and intellectuals who disagree on the interpretation of the modern is indicative of the contradictory nature of Claudel's perceptions of the United States at the time.

Two words describe American life in *Conversations:* movement and electricity. "Between the swirling America and the painfully congealed Russia, Europe is nothing but a narrow, ragged strip of land. . . . America does not talk, it sings, it purrs, it counts, it turns indefinitely on itself, like a dynamo inserted between the two poles and the two ends of the continent" (788–89). In a 1936 piece entitled "American Elasticity" Claudel indulges in a few Tocquevillean reflections on the American gregariousness and propensity to form associations of all kinds: "The average American has loneliness in horror, probably in reaction to the huge supplies of space and emptiness provided by a continent so rich in deserts." Americans, "those little complicated beings," feel a desire "to escape from nothingness by noise, numbers and automatic movement" (1207). As a consequence, individuals will passionately insert themselves "in one of these big throbbing dynamos, a sport stadium, a popular parade, a banquet, a professional meeting, a dance, a picnic, a collective sightseeing trip" (1206).

Like many artists of the early twentieth century, from Apollinaire to the Italian Futurists, Claudel stresses the role of speed and distance in re-shaping categories of perception in the age of restlessness: "Movement has replaced digestion and the whole of humanity has been submitted to a centrifugal working-out. Movement is everywhere and cities are the power-plants which supply it. . . . The car and the cinema are similar in principle. With one, motionless nature is transformed through our own movement in some kind of colorful wind. With the other, we remain seated and inexhaustible masses of ghosts charge into us. . . . The car enabled us to possess the planet, the airplane allows us to dominate it . . . we are no longer subjected to circumstances, we dominate a text, we take a walk in the cosmos" (*Conversations dans le Loir-et-Cher,* 769).

One of the dialoguing voices in *Conversations* underscores how ordered and orchestrated contemporary collective movement is, as opposed to the disorderly, individualistic chaos of people and things in an earlier stage of the modern: "It seems to me that, in many points of the universe, what I would call a state of liquidity has been substituted to a state of disorder. Take society as described by Balzac or Zola (but what a difference already from the first to the second!), it carried in its wake a quantity of ill-assorted objects, shapeless fragments of the past, untimely attempts to mold the future, all kinds of rudimentary sketches and anarchic imaginations. . . . Go and stand today on the divider strip of the Opera and marvel at the perfect order. Ten rows of homogeneous vehicles stop and automatically resume their course when a single policeman blows his whistle" (690). The plasticity of modern Man is like that of concrete, that most basic constituent of contemporary urban life: it is "semi-liquid" and "lends itself to whatever you want" (692), a symbol of the passivity of humanity in the age of mass conformity.

The synchronic character of modern conformity shows in a great number of rhythmic activities, above all in dancing. "The boredom of modern society," says Furius, the most antimodernist among the friends assembled in Claudel's essay, "is such that people will end up refusing to put up with it. Just look in hotels at the simulacra of men and women dancing for eternity. . . . Such is human happiness! Such is our paradise!" (686). Is dance itself not "the best example of monotony"? It scans the harmonious, but repetitive, tempo of the modern, made up "of regular and easy movements performed on always the same rhythm" (793). Jazz, that most American of contemporary musical forms, is the most obvious expression of the collective orchestration of labor in a mass society: "There is no movement without measure, and the indefinitely repeated measure makes a dance. All of work in America is some kind of formidable jazz" (793).

For all the admiration Claudel the diplomat professed for the United States as a political and economic power and a major new player on the world diplomatic scene, Claudel the poet and the Catholic never reconciled himself to the American way of life. In May 1927, rediscovering the New World after a long Asian parenthesis, he wrote in his journal that America was still for him "the land of exile, of nostalgia" he had described thirty years earlier (*Journal*, 1:768). In 1933, the year he left his post in Washington, he despaired (in his journal again) of a "country where even the dogs no longer bark, as someone wrote. It is, by the way, perfectly true. And the roosters don't crow either" (quoted in Kushner, 246). The emphasis on the loneliness of American individuals, on the emptiness of the land (and by extension, of social relations) announced the negative views Claudel would again express at the end of his life. The second version of *L'Échange*, published in 1952, twisted his earlier dislike of American life toward the pessimistic and the crepuscular. In his 1949 comment on *Winds*, Saint-John Perse's lyrical celebration of the American experience, Claudel took up again the theme of the huge void of America, this time with unprecedented acrimony (see below, chap. 5): "Everywhere around us the immoderate, the Void, the absence of any external justification for the position I occupy, the lethal obsession of this Boredom from which one needs to escape at all costs" (619). In a July 1951 letter to Jean-Louis Barrault, he mentions "the strange feeling of *unreality* which America, the other world, gave me and others, too (Lenau, Stevenson)" (*Œuvres en prose*, 1482).

The twenty-five years which had elapsed since his days as ambassador had only strengthened the old poet's negative impressions of the New World: the mobile unreality of America was no match for the earthen solidity of the ancient civilizations of Asia. In *Conversations dans le Loir-et-Cher*, the often dissenting voices agree in singing the praises of the Chinese mountainous hinterland, with its back turned away from the sea: "How refreshing Asia is when you come in from New York! One is steeped in wholesome humanity! . . . [Asia] has not broken its peduncle. It is in touch with the origin. . . . It knows that salvation will not come from the sea. . . . It looks up at the mountain with obstinate hope. . . . [It is] a pole of gravity and fullness offsetting the pole of movement and void which was created over there in America" (789). In Claudel's reading of *Winds*, the same opposition crops up again, pitting Chinese gravid resiliency against the lightness of the American experience: to understand all of this fully, Claudel writes, "one has to have lived for a long time in the midst of the most authentic people in the world, a people of Epicurean Jobs, basically happy, basically satisfied, basically basic, autochthonous, the Chinese people" (620).

New York! New York!

The poet and critic Paul Morand shared some of Claudel's vision of the modern, but none of his friend's deep cultural pessimism. Among the prominent French writers of the interwar period, Morand stands out for his enthusiastic celebration of American urban life.[6] His essay on New York, published in 1930, hailed the rise of the United States to a central position in Western culture and praised architecture as the finest product of a distinctive American style, a witness to the truth of Emerson's typically American claim that "beauty is only the expression of the efficacious" (35). "Whatever people may say," Morand wrote, "the skyscrapers are in no way indebted to Babylon or the Indian pueblos. If a style is the expression of life at a given moment, America now has every right to say that she has a style" (43). American art was coming into its own: walking through the streets of New York, the visitor felt awed and elated by the new play of emptiness, surface effects, and optical illusions: "The Cunard Building is among the most important monuments of New York decorative art. . . . Beside this stands the Hamburg-Amerika. . . . Its surface shows nothing but glass; the voids have definitely mastered the solids" (46). Seen from the Brooklyn Bridge, "the lines vanish; no more walls, no more solids, no more relief; all the skyscrapers are merged and simplified, looking like a vast, square, checkered conflagration fanned by the wind from the open sea." (74).[7]

Morand tells the story of the genesis of this truly American modernity, of its cultural and political emancipation from the models of the Old World at the turn of the new century. All of a sudden, New York fin de siècle broke out of its colonial isolation and threw its inferiority complex to the winds. It is on the stage that the repercussions of this newfound independence would be felt most strongly. The theater had "leapt from Union Square to Broadway" with English-style musical comedies, music hall, Jewish burlesque, "follies," and the vanguard dramas of Eugene O'Neill: the American stage had "advanced to conquer the world." One finds in Morand's prose a fascination, an excitement, a sense of exhilaration before the inevitability of the American Age, which contrasts sharply with Duhamel, Claudel, and Céline's horrified recoil. Morand takes it all in, the perpetual metamorphosis of a city that is rejuvenated with the passing of time ("The newer it is, the more beautiful does New York appear" [39]), the powerful merging of movement and light, the crowds, the elasticity of space ("Dickens called it an elastic country" [299]), the alternating rhythms of the boom and the crash, the ceaseless experimentations. "The savagery of the Indians," he writes, "the cruelty of Spanish buccaneers, the mysticism of the Quakers, the dreamers of '48, the disruptive spirit of the anarchy of the Irish, the poetry of the German Jews, the nihilism of Slavs— New York, the great laboratory, has essayed them all, good and bad alike" (299).

All the markings of the modern can be found in New York: speed, the obsession for numbers, and, above all, electrical energy. "New York is supercharged with electricity. People undress at night amid sparks crackling on the skin like purple vermin. . . . 'I shake your hand at a distance,' Claudel wrote to me from Washington, 'happy to save you a shock'" (307). Are Samuel Morse, Alexander Graham Bell, and Thomas Edison not the true cultural heroes of the New World? Morand likes to wander and muse, like Baudelaire's *flâneur*, in the Battery: it is an apt name for one of the most vibrant sections of a city whose buildings are described as so many "glass accumulators and condensers of energy" (52). Is it any wonder that one of the plays of O'Neill's raw, primary, "electrical" theater should be titled *Dynamo*? Throughout the hot summer nights, Coney Island shines like "a midnight sun which does not fade till dawn" (77). Manhattan at night, seen from the Brooklyn Bridge, attests to the radical subversion of time and space the foreign traveler experiences in the city: the familiar visual and temporal landmarks are gone and America is adrift, all moorings cut loose, beyond history and reality. "Suddenly the electric lights go on in fifty stories; and lower Manhattan loses all its solidity, is riddled with lights like those optical views behind which a candle is moved. . . . The moon has never a chance. Those cathedral towers, fired surely by the devil, are a mirage from some fantastic world, looking not eternal but astride of time" (74). In the city of light and illusion, night and day are forever abolished, and the rhythms of nature, the times to eat and rest, and the seasons for mating and procreation have been dissolved in the frenetic artificiality of the eternal Now:

> No more shadows; not one tree . . . not one thing placed there by nature has been left untouched. . . . New York's supreme beauty . . . is its violence. . . . The town's violence is in its rhythm. . . . As soon as you set foot on Broadway, taut as a fiddlestring, you yourself obey the vibrations and no longer notice them. I only realized the fullness of that frenzy when I saw a cat. It was the only creature I met during my stay which did not move and preserved its inner life intact. I chased it away like a pang of remorse. Family life no longer exists. . . . There are no small children in the streets. (*New York*, 301, 303–4)

New York, like the Brooklyn Bridge, is a gigantic *échangeur*, a huge accelerator of particles, whether monetary, automotive, or informational; through it, past and future endlessly merge and trade places, for "New York is the grand central [station] of America" (298). Signs of wealth and desire—means of transportation and metaphors of advertising (metaphors, literally, *are* means of transportation, things to carry you further)—circle endlessly, faster and faster, around the heart of modernity, Wall Street and Madison Avenue, as so many satellites orbiting the sun. "New York is the reign of directness" (the French *en direct* translates the American *live*). Everything is fast and straightforward, free of mediations: the rise and fall of stock values, the immediacy of information ("All this energy expended for the luring of this factitious thing to be served hot with tomorrow morning's coffee, the thing we foolishly never grow tired of—News!" [212]), the marvel of the photostat ("[It enables] one to photograph immediately the passages of books or manuscripts that one may want to copy" [140], the accelerated obsolescence of things ("During the first days of January, 1931, I was astonished at the fifty percent cut in the price of a trunk: 'It's a 1928 model,' said the assistant; 'it isn't the right thing at all now'" [177]), the frenetic pace of the black theater.

"New York has been raised in a hundred styles: Washington Square is in the Louis-Philippe style, Fifth Avenue is like the Plaine Monceau, Eighth Avenue is like the Avenue Jean-Jaurès, and lower Broadway is pure Nebuchadnezzar" (300). The cosmopolitanism of races and cultures, the juxtapositions of style and taste, the timeless spatialization of the distinct historical moments of human history (the synchronization of diachrony) announce the postmodern love of kitsch and rococo, the fascination for the gadget and the "thing" that has no use. We are reminded of contemporary descriptions of a totally contingent universe, a world of pure chance and random events. The crisis of 1929 lacked "deep economic causes; it was merely an immense collective panic of Wall Street" (67), thus reflecting the artificial effect of meanings gone mad. Coney Island is part Luna Park, part Cockaigne, a "carnival in bathing suits, where in place of masks and Bergamasks, you have penny-in-the-slot machines, candy peddlers [and] cardboard cows whose stiff udders, without having to be milked, fill you a glass of iced milk" (78). Images are proliferating ad infinitum, mirroring one another from billboards to giant screens, pasted on buildings and landscapes, taking over the most sacred symbols of tradition and history. Trinity Church for example, the oldest ecclesiastical building in New York, once filled with Redcoats and Dutch-speaking ministers, is now the site of the optical illusion of modernity: "Passing in front of the church, you cannot see the altar, but a glazed door reflects the picture of the street, so that by a trick of reflection the choir seems to be full of hurrying people and street-cars" (48).

There is no fear and loathing in Morand's America, only the apprehensive elation of he who witnesses what may well be "mankind's warmest moment" (301). Granted, New York is "the great image of towndom. . . . The malady from which one suffers there is that corruption of the city which St. Francis of Assisi called the Babylonian evil" (295). However, if life in cities is madness, "New York is at least a madness that is worth while" (295). The false promises of urban life are only false on the morrow. There is a sense of inevitability, a feeling that one will never be able to stem the flood of signs on the printed page that is the idiom of modern times: "This unthinking tide rushing from these open locks, this black pool, those tons of daily ink in which the unshaped words still lie sleeping" (14). One has no choice but to learn the alphabet of the brave new world, which is spreading across Broadway and across the globe and has replaced the obsolete language of old world history:

> "Stimulating," "spectacular"—the newspapers keep on shouting; this
> is life at its most spectacular. . . . History is forgotten. Nature, gods,
> the sea, are replaced by new words that must be mastered. . . . The
> electric lamp is no longer a lighting device, it is a machine for fascinating, a machine for obliterating. . . . On 42nd street there are no
> more windows in the building—nothing but letters. It is a kindled
> alphabet, a conspiracy of commerce against night; in the sky, an advertising airplane. (181–82)

For the code of modernity to be truly adequate, letters must give way to sheer numbers, the cyphers of the new age. At the New York Stock Exchange, "that huge suction pump swallowing up the world's capital, draining Europe dry," the walls are covered with immense billboards on which the reference numbers of traders incessantly flicker, while bank representatives on the telephone warn them of orders to buy (64). At Madison Square Garden, the game of ice hockey is an allegory of life in North America, with the flags, the crowd, the shouts, the hot dogs and roasted peanuts, the roughness and toughness of the players, displaying on their chests their totemic animals, and on their backs "immense numbers" that "transform the rink from a distance into a sort of brutal lotto, a sort of swift-moving arithmetic, lightning calculations instantly undone by ever-fresh combinations" (200–201). The idiom of the modern, indeed, all speed, is numbers and electricity.

For Morand, New York has already become the center of the Western world, and no amount of nostalgic yearning for the European age will ever change that: the twentieth century is the American moment. "A sporting instinct," he wrote, "makes the pupils in any history class long to be Spaniards in the sixteenth century, Englishmen in the eighteenth, Frenchmen in the days of Austerlitz. And that same enthusiasm makes us now desire, momentarily at least, to be Americans. Who does not worship victory?" (290). Many reasons, says Morand, prompt foreigners to take a good look at America: no longer the Rousseauian sentimental attachment for its pristine, primitive land, but curiosity, the pull of the dollar (away from Europe, "that debtors' prison"), new art, and above all, freedom from socialism and the state, the opportunity to live for a while "where neither gas nor telegraph nor modes of communication nor education are state or municipal monopolies, and where, therefore, they work" (198).

There was a time when his anticommunism, and the poor quality of French telephones, made Morand wish that Paris were more like New York and claim that France had no alternative but to become American or to give in to bolshevism. Not any more. Like Jean Baudrillard, whom he resembles, Morand argued that Europe ought not imitate America's modernity: "It is better to be a frankly outmoded city, like London, than a poor attempt at New York, like Berlin or Moscow" (291). America appeared to him, however, as the ultimate refuge against the rising threats of totalitarianism and the failures of democracies. Morand saw New York City as the last hope of Western culture, now threatened on its own soil by the rise of the new barbarians: Lenin himself proclaimed "the Party has no need of intellectuals." New York was the place where "our artists will go to seek a haven for that luxury article, thought" (293). Far from being the grave digger of the European tradition, American civilization would shelter the white race behind the walls of what Lenin had called the "great universal fortress of capitalism and reaction," and, in the 1920s and 1930s,

New York was truly the pride and joy of the "Aryan race" (299). According to Morand, "The great city is the sole refuge from intolerance, from the Puritan inquisition" (296). Anticipating the debates of the Cold War, the conservative Morand argued that the sense of impending doom and the threat of communism should caution Europeans against criticizing the United States too harshly. After all, it was industrial England that contaminated a once-rural America with the woes of urban civilization:

> People keep on saying in France that America is merely machinery and materialism and that the spiritual forces of the human race are elsewhere. But where? "In Latin America, in Russia," says Durtain, who is so severe in his condemnation of the North American civilization. I myself believe that the spiritual forces of humanity are not the apanage of one country or of one race, but of certain men of varied origins, sheltering on board a leaking boat; and that part of the hull which seems to me to be still the strongest is the United States. (298)

Paradise Lost

In Duhamel's narrative of America, there are, for sure, humanistic spaces within the fabric of American life, havens of culture where the treasures of civilization have been preserved, sheltered from the debasing tinkering of literary merchants and tasteless tastemakers. Such are colleges, libraries, and museums, havens and relays of eternity:

> I have discovered an oasis. To begin with, there was a small room opening on the "campus" of a big college. A silence that smelt of boxwood unexpectedly evoked the grave peace of the Escurial. A young man was there among his books. "Mind," he said, and his voice had wings, "cannot die. . . . I feel so far removed from the encompassing world, that, without even thinking of the matter, I have restored monastic discipline and the monastic cell. The very excesses of our civilization will produce anchorites. We must never despair." (*America: The Menace*, 188)

This is Montaigne in his library, of course, or Niccolò Machiavelli telling his reader, in what may be the most striking expression of the humanistic ethos, how every night he enters the sanctuary of his study, casting-off his everyday clothes covered with dust and mud, leaving behind the bustle of politics and the debasement of intrigue. Putting on "garments regal and courtly," he finds himself, like Duhamel's American student, in "the ancient courts of ancient men," taking up where he had left it the learned conversation, the sacred picking of great minds, which alone can bring him peace and contentment. "And for four hours of time," Machiavelli wrote, "I feel no boredom, I forget every trouble, I do not fear poverty, death does not terrify me" (quoted in La Capra, 15). Duhamel hastens to add, however, that the college and the museum are only privileged sites, blessed islands in the sea of mediocrity and oblivion, peripheral spaces leaving the rotting core of decadence untouched.

In the New World, high culture has been marginalized, it is but a divertissement for wealthy women, the product of what George Santayana called the "genteel tradition." "This afternoon," Duhamel told a male friend, "I attended the symphony concert, and an excellent concert it was too. There were more than a thousand women there, and I'm almost ashamed to say that there were only six men. I am positive, for I counted." To which his friend responded: "Well, what can you expect, Monsieur Duhamel? Our men like to work" (148). "I was not too proud of myself," quipped the French writer, "I looked like one of those effeminate aesthetes who take unmanly pleasures, while real men, seated in their offices, sell jars of preserves, as becomes the stronger sex." As for the teachers of classical culture, they barely survive on the fringe of affluent society, in the sheltered ghettos of academia. There is one professor of literature in Duhamel's story; he earns less money than conductors on Pullman trains, he does not own a car, and the University where he teaches has more stones than books. His "ironic and sorrowful smile" reminds the narrator of "those intelligent, sensitive people who sometimes appear, no one knows how or why, in some parvenu family, and whose suppliant glances ask for your indulgence" (180).

Upon seeing the goddesses of Manhattan Céline's Ferdinand Bardamu had wondered for an instant if ancient Greece had not been reborn, under his very eyes, on the shores of the Hudson River. For Duhamel, industrial civilization could only at best preserve, and at worst replicate, the realities of the past. In a series of hallucinatory moments, he had mistaken anonymous passersby for the great figures of European culture and politics. Twice Pirandello had asked for his ticket on the Pullman train, the poet Max Jacob cashed his checks, André Gide opened his taxi door, and the French actor Louis Jouvet ran an elevator in the Times Square Hotel. Eduard Benès, the Czechoslovakian statesman, sold orange juice on Sixth Avenue, and Rabindranath Tagore paced the Brooklyn Bridge, while Lenin, whom everyone thought dead, could be seen driving in Manhattan. Of course, these were only ghosts, clones, doubles, deceiving copies of the original, like the replicas of Greek statues in movie theaters.

In America, both time and space render artistic pursuits impossible. "Time is money," says the old proverb, but the demands of quick investment and quick return did not mix well with the unpredictability of the creative act. An émigré sculptor, "an imported talent" from France, who thought that sculpture had a great destiny in the United States, complained to Duhamel that his mentors gave him only three months to complete a composition. Past the deadline, he forfeits a thousand dollars a day. "What artist can accept that bargain, and not become a tradesman? And what artist can live here unless he accepts those terms?" (87). Art aims at eternity, while the American way of life rewards the short-lived and the ephemeral. Duhamel did not share Baudelaire's concept of the modern as the union of the eternal and the transitory, but sided in the matter with Tocqueville, who saw the business of bourgeois society as the very antithesis of the aristocratic leisure demanded by aesthetic pursuits.

Even architecture, "the sole interpreter of the genius of America" (88), the only one of the fine arts to have been successfully transplanted in the New World, had fallen prey to the cardinal sin of modern aesthetics: it lacked the ambition "to defy time" (88). Buildings replaced buildings in a frenzy of innovation and newness, but time is the greatest commodity in the world and Americans never had enough of it to earn the privilege of losing it. The moral atmosphere of modern times had killed that "sublime serenity which art must have if it is to quicken" (89). As for space, the hubris of the American landscape, urban or otherwise, made it totally improper for artistic representation. Chicago is beyond human grasp, it is "no more paintable than the desert"; its "absolute dimensions" defy all the canons of the Apollonian principles of classical humanism. "Everything that for centuries the artists of old Europe have painted has been in scale with man. True greatness is not a matter of absolute dimension: it is the effect of happy proportion" (86). In America, however, everything is too big, "everything discourages Apollo and Minerva" (90).

The Politics of Cultural Despair

Céline's Bardamu, upon arriving on the American soil, had decided that his best chance to find a job in the land of applied science was to display some sort of mathematical ability. Fortunately, he had acquired, during the long voyage across the ocean, a set of highly marketable skills. He reports that he has "become very good on board at counting fleas (not only catching them, but adding them up and subtracting them, in the way of statistics I mean), I wanted to make use of this intricate craft of mine, which you mightn't think amounted to much but which does possess, when all's said and done, a technique of its own. You can say what you like about the Americans, but in these matters of technique they win, hands down.

They'd be crazy about my way of counting fleas, I was positive of that. As I saw it, the thing was a cinch" (185). Having easily convinced the local authorities that the numbering of bugs was "a civilizing factor, because numeration is the basis of statistical data of incalculable value," Bardamu did find a job as official counter of immigrants' fleas in the bathhouse of Ellis Island. Our hero removed the last lingering doubts of his potential employers when he remarked that "a progressive country ought to know the number of its fleas, divided according to sex, subdivided according to age, years and seasons" (189).

During the interwar years, the debate over the place and value of analytical thought, mathematics and the quest for mechanical laws of the universe in "Western" (i.e., for their German critics, Anglo-American) natural and social sciences opposed the apologists of intuition and experience and the defenders of logical positivism (e.g., Heidegger versus Carnap).[8] There is something Faustian about the traditionalists' indictment of American civilization: human beings pay a high price for what they seem to have gained by selling their souls to the technological Prince of Darkness. The discourse on decadence is always deeply reactionary, in the root sense of the term, for it holds the nostalgic celebration of a superior or perfect stage of history, or nature, which will never be retrieved. From Plato and Aristotle to Rousseau and Spengler, most narratives of the degeneration of culture rest on the idealized, naturalistic description of a once unaltered essence of human and social perfection. When applied to modern America, the logic of corruption and decay underscores the *losses* suffered by the ideals of ancient and classical Europe at the hands of materialism. There is not only loss of *quality*, replaced by an obsessive concern for the quantitative, but also loss of *vitality* and *passion*, as expressed in the will to live, creative emotion, and the capacity to withstand suffering. The first theme is more humanistic in approach, while the latter clearly belongs, with its romantic and Nietzschean overtones, to the radical critique of the Enlightenment. In the chapter "Insurance or the Law of Compensation," Georges Duhamel views with irony the bourgeois quest for comfort and security:

> It's a touching business, this taste for security in a species that at the same time shows so strong a taste for risk. Oh, I should like to insure against mosquito bites, against head colds, against seasickness, against laziness, against blue devils, against doubt, against remorse, against grief, against jealousy, against anger, against love, and against friendship. If . . . I were a religious man, I'd take out insurance on the existence of God, and more insurance on the reality of

heaven. And what else besides? Against myself, against everything, and on everything! (170)

The only problem with the quest for absolute protection is that it removes tragedy from human life and subsumes death and suffering under the general categories of economic exchange. Duhamel proceeds to give his American friend, who manufactures and sells spring mattresses for a living, a short lesson in Bergsonian philosophy, emphasizing the difference between qualitative and quantitative views of the universe:

> A French philosopher, Henri Bergson . . . asks in what respect, and for what reason, intensity is comparable to quantity. Listen carefully, Mr. Stone; Bergson is seeking what there can be in common between the extensive, which by definition is something that has extent, and the intensive, which is without extent, and which, consequently, is subject to no measure. Well, Mr. Stone, to that question insurance makes an answer that I find disquieting, but that all the rest of the world is beginning to approve: the common measure between the extensive and the intensive is money. (167)

By taking out insurance policies, one acquiesces in "the commercialization of certain moral values." By doing so, Duhamel goes on, "one is willing to "assign commercial value" to life and death, pain and pleasure; the result is that events and feelings "lose a part of their human . . . or of their divine value, and lose, also, their majesty, their real greatness" (170). The French philosopher Gabriel Marcel used to oppose "problem" and "mystery": only the former could be solved by logical analysis and the application of instrumental reason. In the secularized universe of insurance policies, the mysteries of life and death are turned into problems, and their symbolic, transcendental, "divine" meaning becomes another exchange value in the endless circulation of capital.

The loss of the tragic deprives human existence of its heroic qualities. For there is no pleasure without pain, the wisdom of the moralist teaches us, and no joy without the acceptance of sorrow. In a social universe where risk and suffering have been eliminated, there is nothing left to desire and nothing to overcome, nothing to fight against and nothing to fight for. What America lacks, then, is what the immigrants ran away from, what Europe and the world have had plenty of: wars and epidemics, plagues and revolutions, droughts and inquisitions, invasions and occupations, absolute monarchies and totalitarian states, in short, for Duhamel, the very stuff of history. "What was lacking in this people to keep it from being really great, the bearer of a great message, deserving honor, respect, and admiration? What was lacking to that glory? Great misfortune, doubtless, and great trials, the terrible adventures that ripen a nation, turn it back upon itself, make it cherish its real treasures, squander its finest fruits, and discover its true path" (216).

To reactionary and fascist thinkers in the 1930s, fear of danger and avoidance of risk testified to the debilitating, "feminizing" effects of a materialist civilization on the old master races of Europe. The *Völkisch* ideology of the 1930s exalted the moral superiority of the soldier as well as the aesthetics of war, the virile values of mastery, command, and obedience, the political nihilism of death, blood and annihilation as instances of total mobilization, the will to power as will to the overcoming of self. In the eyes of the European Right, not only did the democratic ethos erase all qualitative differences and collapse all hierarchies, it also negated the height and the distance of the true aristocratic spirit, the heroic overcoming of self, the cult of personal excellence through spiritual asceticism.

Making ample use of interpretive categories elaborated more than half a century ago by the proponents of what Fritz Stern has called "the German ideology of cultural despair," de Herte and Nigra claim that American history displays the unheroic quality of bourgeois ideals: the American Revolution was won even before it started, the myth of the frontier was nothing but a "fable," and the westward movement was the mere "conquest of emptiness" (18), "a kind of stroll toward wealth" (27). Even the slaves were not conquered, they were more prosaically purchased (31) as befits "a nation of dollar worshippers." Since their mechanical civilization has dissolved the organic ties of national cultures and Americans ignore the mystique of tradition and time, their history has no epic qualities. Their country may have had a past, but it never had a destiny. Cosmopolitism prevents America from being a nation, and the melting pot is nothing but "a confusion of peoples and races . . . an aggregate of human elements, free of tradition, of monuments, of history, and with no other ties that their redoutable selves, whose common achievement has begun to reward them" (Duhamel, 89, xiii).

Standardizing the Flowers

Georges Duhamel, for one, never espoused the pessimism of the spirit which prompted Céline to welcome the Nazi occupation of France and to revile, in his wartime pamphlets, the United States as the center of an international Jewish plot. In the preface to *America*, Duhamel wrote that while "others take refuge in despair, which is a 'refuge' in no sense whatever," he had not yet surrendered to that despair. "And if, weak as I am, I am obliged to let events take their course, certain that things will not necessarily end in curing themselves, I want at least to know whither I am being dragged. I do not surrender my right to investigation, knowledge and conjecture" (xi). Neither Cassandra nor Faust, neither prophet of gloom nor servile apologist of the modern, the free spirit must squarely face the "genius of evil" and uphold the honor of the human mind, that flickering light in the growing darkness. It is in Europe, of course, in the wisdom of its age-old culture, that the materials of the resistance to the Baconian civilization are to be found. The narrator takes pride in belonging to "a community of peasants who for centuries have lovingly cultivated fifty different varieties of plum, and who find in each a taste deliciously unlike that of any of the others" (201).

For whoever agrees, with Voltaire's Candide, that the true goal of life is not to conquer the world, but to cultivate one's garden, there cannot possibly be any worse nightmare than the one from which Duhamel awoke, drenched with sweat, in the Pennsylvania Station hotel: "I had dreamed that American gardeners, to simplify their business, reduce labor costs, push sales, and lower prices, had decided to standardize the flowers, and no longer grow any but a single species that was specially profitable, and that lasted well" (187). Lost in the midst of the American inferno, the French traveler invokes the shadows of his ancestors, praying for help in this hour of gloom: "Inspire me, I cried, 'O peasantry of France . . . you whose whole history is patience, reserve, economy and shrewdness, inspire me for I am alone in the midst of this foreign people. My Fathers, save me!'" (187).

The idealization of the past and of the genius of the race goes hand in hand with the celebration of the motherland. Offering his own version of Montesquieu's political theory of climates, Duhamel sees a correspondence between France's varied landscapes and temperate weather and the unclouded wisdom, tempered tolerance, and sunny skepticism of the national intellectual tradition it fostered and nourished: "It is curious to observe that the moral climate of North America imitates in its sharp changes the variable humor of the great valley that extends from Labrador to the Gulf of Mexico. . . . Almost all America works in a draught, now burning, now icy. . . . It is the climate of the 'boom' and the 'crash'. We are far indeed from Touraine with its smiling horizons, from the moderate Seine and from pure and sonorous Provence" (89).

French writers, for the most part, do not travel well. Exiled in the Rome of modern times, Duhamel sounds just like the Renaissance poet du

Bellay, who mourned from Italy the loss of his beloved country, in verses millions of French schoolchildren have memorized over the years: "Blessed is he who, like Ulysses, went on a long voyage," only to come back, full of seasoned wisdom, and spend the rest of his life among his relatives. Back in the old country, reminiscing on the awful sights and smells of America's industrial hell, Duhamel savors the precarious, threatened bliss of living in the heart of genteel Europe and gives free rein to what critics would call today his "Francocentrism." "As I write these lines, I am in my own home, in my garden in Île-de- France, caressed for yet a little time by the smile of a civilization that is ancient, wise, and noble" (85).

There is, somewhere in New Orleans, a Catholic cemetery, "a graveyard of memories" where the French past of America is forever buried and forgotten. Or rather, since the marshy soil is unfit for proper burial, the nameless, forsaken bodies have to "waste away" in boxes built above ground, so far from their native land. And the flowers on the tombs, instead of blooming as they do in the lovely gardens of Touraine and Île-de-France, are left to rot in the damp, sultry heat:

> It is the burial-place of a race and of a civilization. The epitaphs tell in laconic French all sorts of mishaps, trials, epidemics, all sorts of sufferings endured for the conquest of this bitter land. Under one and the same date you read: 'Paul, Lucie, Joseph: Three Angels. And their Mother.' There is no commentary, or even a family name. A fine moss of a brilliant green covered the neighboring stones. Well, even in death, the races must be separated. . . . The Negroes have their own graveyard apart. . . . There is nothing in common among the races, even in dissolution. (144)

Absolute difference, then, solution of continuity. The gap will never be bridged, America is no heir to Europe. The two stand forever apart, like two races in a segregated graveyard, and the triumph of the one will mean the demise of the other. The last lines of Duhamel's narrative share in that paradigm of rupture to which most of the French interwar descriptions of life in the United States subscribed: "If I thought that [American] civilization were the carrying on of that which, in spite of many errors, has for thirty or forty centuries enriched the heritage of the species, how heartily would I not sing its praises? But where others see a continuation, I see a deviation, I find a breach" (216). Paul Claudel, reminiscing on his first visit to the United States in 1893, said in his *Mémoires improvisées* that America and Europe were separated by a world of difference at the time:

"Europe was much more Europe or France much more France, and America much more America than they are now. Relations are much closer today; there are many more contacts between the two countries, while then the feeling of disorientation . . . was extremely painful" (92). As the world shrank, the proud resistance of the European literati became harder to sustain. Soon, the G.I.'s, Marilyn, blue jeans, and rock and roll would make their crusade a lost cause. During the Cold War, Sartre and the intellectual Left would give it another try, to be sure, but the youthful fascination for popular art and music would leave highbrow anti-Americanism in a state of acute schizophrenia: hatred of U.S. hegemony, certainly, but also love of its underground, countercultural forms.

THREE

AMERICAN IDENTITY, AMERICAN DIFFERENCE
The Existentialists and the Objective Spirit of the United States

▼

We have the extraordinary paradox of the descendants of English and Scotch Nonconformists being changed into the narrowest of conformists, and the United States becoming a country where a man who does not fall in line socially and morally runs the risk of not being allowed to express himself freely. *André Siegfried*

The "American way of life" is the negation of what the European intellectual means by the word ideology. Americanism does not formulate itself as a system of concepts or propositions, it knows nothing of the "collective saviour," the end of history . . . or the dogmatic negation of religion. . . . It is learned at school and society enforces it. Conformism if you like, but a conformism which is rarely felt to be tyrannical since it does not forbid free discussion in matters of religion, economics or politics. . . . The individual cannot question the ways of thought and the institutions which are regarded as an integral part of the national idea without becoming suspect of a criminal lack of patriotism. *Raymond Aron*

The texts on American society which Jean-Paul Sartre wrote in the late 1940s have not received much attention from the many critics of Sartrean thought. Neither "philosophy" nor "literature," they have an ambiguous status, somewhat akin to the "philosophical journalism" with which Sartre himself contemptuously identified György Lukàcs's criticism of his own positions (in Lukàcs's *Existentialism or Marxism*). Most of these texts are newspaper articles written during a five-month visit to the United States in the beginning of 1945.[1] Sartre, envoyé spécial of *Combat* and *Le Figaro*, was part of a small group of French journalists invited by the Office of War

Education to report on the American war effort in the last months of the conflict. As Simone de Beauvoir recalled in *Force of Circumstance*, Albert Camus, then editor of *Combat*, had asked an enthusiastic Sartre to represent the formerly underground newspaper on the American tour. Sartre reserved his best written reporting for *Le Figaro*, sending *Combat* mostly technical, laboriously penned, matter-of-fact articles, to the great displeasure of Camus. "According to an agreement made between Camus and Brisson [editor of *Le Figaro*], some of the articles were supposed to be given to the latter; Sartre sent him his impressions, the notes and reflections written in passing, keeping the pages that had cost him most effort and struggle for *Combat*. Camus, having read a sprightly and entertaining description of American cities in *Le Figaro* the day before, was flabbergasted when he received a careful study of the Tennessee Valley Authority" (18).

The interest of the articles published in *Combat*, however, rests in the quality of the day-to-day reporting, full of anecdotes and details on everyday life in wartime America, from the price of cigarettes to the social security system. Upon his arrival in New York City, the French visitor was struck by the level of comfort Americans still enjoyed, a sharp contrast with the hardships Europeans were suffering at the time. "Shoes are of good quality," he wrote, "and the average New Yorker eats two pounds of meat a week, mainly chopped" (2 February 1945). A conscientious ethnographer, Sartre drew up in another article the complete inventory of an American home, noting that "the furniture looks like products of our Galeries Barbès" (June 9). What the philosopher at large discovered in the United States was the universe of objects and signs, of values and behaviors that a fraction of the youth of industrial democracies would reject, a quarter of a century later, as "consumption society." "Already before the war," he informed the reader, "every single household had a fridge, many a car and a telephone. In every kitchen one could find fancy corkscrews and can openers, electric ovens, etc." (2 February 1945). Modernity does not lie in gadgets alone, however; it is also an ethos, a specific economic behavior: the religion of credit. "The American does not like to save. Over and above greed, a genuine economic principle motivates Americans: 'Money is supposed to circulate'" (4–5 February 1945).

Sartre honestly acknowledged that his visit had been too short for him to derive anything more than "personal impressions and interpretations" from it: "This America may be something I've dreamed up. In any case, I will be honest with my dream: I shall set it forth just as it came to me" (*Literary and Philosophical Essays* [*LPE*], 104). Admitting that to write about

135 million Americans, one would have to spend ten years in the United States, Sartre nevertheless tried to share his findings with his readers by drawing comparisons with their own environment. "The South," he wrote in *Combat*, "has been invaded by chain stores which look a little bit like our Uniprix" (4–5 March 1945). In an odd comparison, he remarked that the European visitor who walks through the streets of New York or Chicago for the first time "feels as though he was travelling through a rocky chaos that resembles a city—something like Montpellier-le-Vieux rather than a city" (*LPE*, 122).

To help his compatriots imagine a typical American house, our reporter had to conjure up more familiar images (at least to the upper classes) of French beach resorts such as Trouville, Cabourg or La Baule. "Only those ephemeral seaside chalets with their pretentious architectural style and their fragility can convey to those of my French readers who have never seen the States an idea of the American apartment house" (*LPE*, 120). In the same piece on American cities, Sartre suggests that the reader who wants to picture Los Angeles should try to imagine "not one Côte d'Azur city, but the entire region between Cannes and Menton" (121). One can measure here, by the way, the gap separating the contemporary reader from those not so distant days when a writer had to resort to such comparative strategies to help non-Americans *imagine* Southern California

Most of the articles Sartre wrote in *Combat* did not appear in the third volume of *Situations* (*S III*) published in 1949: only the more "cultural" and more "literary" articles in *Le Figaro* were deemed worthy of publication in a separate volume. These texts aimed at baring "the soul of America": they were mainly philosophical considerations of American culture, which is described as a "monstrous complex of myths and values," or, in more Hegelian fashion, as "the objective spirit of the United States." The Sartrean analysis of Americanism, original when it focused on everyday cultural practices and social relations, gradually gave way, after 1946, to the traditional left-wing description of the United States as the land of the impossible revolution, a highly integrated "system" that undermined all attempts at radical change and demanded conformism and submission from the individuals who lived in it.

Sartre's early essays on the United States display his ability to transform the material of everyday experience (here, impressionistic notes on American life, *choses vues*) into a coherent body of brilliant systematic analysis. In those texts, he transformed the "minor" genres of travel narrative and journalistic essay into philosophical discussions of inauthenticity, alienation, and bad faith, enrolling in turn Descartes, Hegel, Marx, and

Freud in support of his interpretation of the American character. The whole of Sartrean existentialism is mobilized to make sense of the architecture of New York City, the reformist politics of the AFL-CIO, or Hollywood's cultural industry. By referring to Americanism as "the objective spirit of the United States," Sartre gave a philosophical legitimacy to his critique of American culture. The dialectics of the in-itself and the for-itself in *Being and Nothingness* became the tension between the "system" and "the people" which I examine below.

The value of Sartre's remarks on American culture, apart from the fact that they are a brilliant exercise in applied existentialism, lies in their prophetic quality: they anticipate most of the subsequent criticisms of mass consumption as *société du spectacle* (Debord) or "one-dimensional society" (Marcuse), which would focus on the homogenizing, standardizing, and rationalizing tendencies of contemporary social formations. Furthermore, Sartre's emphasis on the diffusion of advertising and the mass media at all levels of American life, his keen perception of the emergence of new forms of "soft" social control, and his reflections on the disappearance of individual characteristics within the totality of the "system of Americanism," offer interesting perspectives on the contemporary debates about the "postmodern condition."

Is Americanism a Humanism?

Simone de Beauvoir recalled in *Force of Circumstance* that, in the fall of 1944, Jean-Paul Sartre was obsessed with one idea: visiting the United States.

> I have never seen Sartre so elated as the day Camus offered him the job of representing *Combat*. To obtain all the necessary papers, as well as the dollars, he had to go through a labyrinth of red tape. He made his way through the whole thing during a freezing December with a joy marred only by a nagging uncertainty. In those days, nothing was ever definite. And in fact, there were two or three days when it looked as though the project had fallen through. Sartre's dismay then told me how much he wanted to go. (17)

Twenty years later, invited by faculty at Cornell University to give a series of lectures on Kant and philosophy, Sartre declined the invitation and discussed the reasons of his refusal in the French press. A dual evolution had taken place between these two dates: America had changed, no doubt, and so had its international image, from the victory over Nazism to the Vietnam War, from the Nuremberg Trials to the Russell Tribunal. Sartre also had changed, moving away from the political soul-searching of the late 1940s and into the revolutionary engagement of the 1960s. While visiting the United States in 1945, like so many other Europeans intellectuals, he had been fascinated by the artistic achievements of cultural icons such as John Dos Passos, King Vidor, William Faulkner, and Louis Armstrong. A few years earlier, he had written enthusiastic reviews of Dos Passos's *1919* and Faulkner's *The Sound and the Fury* in *La Nouvelle Revue Française*. Simone de Beauvoir shared Sartre's passion for the new cultural forms that had developed in the United States during the interwar period. "It meant so many things, America!" she wrote in *Force of Circumstance:*

> To begin with, everything inaccessible; its jazz, cinema and literature had nourished our youth, but it had always been a great myth to us as well; myths do not allow themselves to be handled. . . . America was also the country which had sent our deliverance; it was the future on the march; it was abundance, and infinite horizons; it was a crazy magic lantern of legendary images; the mere thought that they could be seen with one's eyes set one's head whirling. I rejoiced, not only for Sartre's sake, but also for my own, because I knew that one day I was sure to follow him down this new road. (17)

In the months following the liberation of Paris in September 1944, the positive features of this American democracy, which was still basking in the glory of its victory over Nazism, made capitalism and racial segregation (so fiercely anathematized, a few years earlier, by Vladimir Pozner in *Les États désunis*) look like a minor sin, even in the eyes of left-wing intellectuals. In a postwar surge of patriotic fervor, communists, socialists, radicals, Gaullists, and Christian Democrats had temporarily buried the hatchet; gone were the days of the fierce ideological battles of the Popular Front. The political atmosphere was one of *union sacrée* against the enemies of the republic: Petainists and pro-Nazi collaborators. Sartre had undoubtedly been drawn to some aspects of America, such as the poetic beauty of its cities, its open spaces or, as he wrote, "the truly human gentleness pervading class relationships." In those days, he also supported U.S. domestic and international policy. Seduced by Roosevelt, whom he described as a profoundly human and intelligent leader, the philosopher was also favorable to the president's economic policies, praising the Tennessee Valley Authority as an alternative to both liberal capitalism and socialist planned economy, a convincing version of what was then called *la troisième voie*.

Sartre was also extremely forgiving regarding race relations, finding many excuses for the "imperfections" of American society. "The Negroes of Chicago," he wrote in August 1946 in *The Atlantic Monthly*, "are housed in hovels. That is neither just nor democratic. But many of our white workmen live in hovels that are even more miserable. These injustices have never seemed to us a defect of American society but rather a sign of the imperfections of our time." This is a far cry, needless to say, from the subsequent extremely critical positions of the man who would preside over the Russell Tribunal in 1965, an international court of justice set up by a group of world-renowned intellectuals to judge American war crimes in Indochina. Two decades after his enthusiastic reporting for *Combat* and *Le Figaro*, Sartre told the *Nouvel Observateur* that the bombings of North Vietnam clearly showed "that the structures of American society are based on imperialism" (1 April 1965, 3). How did such a radical change come about? The Cold War, the failure of the Rassemblement Démocratique Révolutionnaire—a party he had helped create in 1948—and his (re)reading of Marx had brought him closer and closer to the French communists. But his critical reassessment of American society does not stem only from events that occurred after his first visit to the United States. Simone de Beauvoir shrewdly perceived the mixture of fascination and uneasiness, attraction and repulsion, that constituted Sartre's reaction to American culture as early as 1945:

> Sartre came back to Paris and told me about his trip. . . . Apart from the economic system, segregation and racism, there were many things in the civilization of the Western hemisphere that shocked him. The Americans' conformism, their scale of values, their myths, their optimism, their avoidance of anything tragic; but he had felt a great deal of sympathy for most of the people he had come in contact with; he had been greatly moved by the crowds of New York and felt that the people were worth more than the system. (33)

Sartre himself made much of this contrast between "the people," attractive and complex, and the abstract and alienating "system" in which they had to live. In his introduction to a special 1946 issue of *Les Temps Modernes* devoted to the United States, he described the system as "a huge external apparatus, a relentless machinery which one might call the objective spirit of the United States and which is called Americanism over there. . . . [It is] a monstrous complex of myths, values, recipes, slogans, numbers and rites" (in *S III*, 126). In Sartrean terms, Americanism is a species of the *practico-inert*, the objectified social world. Sartre's dualistic ontology, however, required a counterprinciple to the system. This principle of difference, freedom, or negativity (the American equivalent of the for-itself) resides in the people, who desperately tried to escape the ideological machinery of Americanism:

> When we are confronted in Europe with a carefully designed arrangement of notions such as melting-pot, puritanism, realism, optimism, etc. which, we are told, are keys to the American character, we are intellectually satisfied and we think that, indeed, it must be so. But when we walk along the streets of New York City . . . we understand that the finest intellectual constructions will be of no avail: they will allow us to understand the system but not the people. (*S III*, 126)

The tension between the interpretation of human actions and the description of the objective structures of society goes beyond Sartre's ambiguous perception of America. It is part and parcel of his philosophic appropriation of the world. It rises from the paradoxical thinking of a man who was, at the same time, a dramatist, eager to stick to human reality, a philosopher of the concrete, hostile to the systematic (*l'esprit de système*), and a prose writer, torn between the demands of analytical rigor and a desire, in Sartre's own words, to "express ideas only in a beautiful form—i.e., in a work of art, novel or short story." Francis Jeanson said that Sartre was experiencing "at any moment two contradictory passions, one for the explanation of facts (at the level of their objective rationality), the other for the understanding of men (at the level of their subjective intentionality)" (284). In his reflections on America, Sartre tried to harmonize his two passions, to reconcile objectivism and hermeneutics, to better understand, through the analysis of the system, "those who are in it" and, beyond, perhaps, the equivocal feeling of attraction and uneasiness, the fascinated repulsion, that he had himself experienced during his first visit.

It is fair to say that Sartre *did* see elements of freedom, or "negativity," within the totality of American culture. The foreign visitor, as he called himself, felt attracted to "the temporary look" of American cities, which revealed "the other side of the United States: its freedom. Here everyone is free, not to criticize or to reform their customs, but to flee them, to leave for the desert or another city" (*LPE*, 124–25). The celebration of the American space and of the rootlessness and mobility of those who dwell in it, is a recurring theme in European descriptions of the New World. Although Sartre, faithful to his militant intellectual anticonformism, had set out to disprove in his articles some of the most pervasive French myths about America, "the contradictory slogans that are current in Paris" (*LPE*, 104), he occasionally gave in to the Manichean views he was trying to avoid. In the opening pages of *La France colonisée*, Jacques Thibau made out a long list of binary oppositions which turn "France" and "America" into incompatible entities: on the one hand, archaism, centralization, bureaucracy, Cartesianism, ideology and elitism; on the other, modernity, private initiative, pragmatism, spontaneity, and a democratic culture. Sartre himself seemed to have lapsed from time to time into a similar form of dichotomized thinking, as when he compared French and American cities, but it was, as usually, to make a philosophical point:

> We Europeans change within changeless cities, and our houses and neighborhoods outlive us; American cities change faster than their inhabitants do, and it is the inhabitants who outlive the cities (*LPE*, 118).
>
> For us a city is above all a past; for them it is mainly a future. . . . And ultimately one comes to like their common element, their temporary look. Our beautiful cities, full as eggs, are a bit stifling. . . . Frail and temporary, formless and unfinished, [American cities] are haunted by the presence of the immense geographical space surrounding them (*LPE*, 119).
>
> [They] are open, open to the world, and to the future. This is what gives them their adventurous look and, even in their ugliness and disorder, a touching beauty. (*LPE*, 125)

The Parisian philosopher par excellence, whose natural environment, as he claimed in *The Words*, was "a sixth-floor apartment in Paris with a view on the rooftops," could not resist the appeal of wanderlust and the charm of the American space: "What fascinated us really—petty bourgeois that we were, sons of peasants securely attached to the earth of our farms, intellectuals entrenched in Paris for life—was the constant flow of men across a whole continent, the exodus of an entire village to the orchards of California, the hopeless wanderings of the hero of [Faulkner's] *Light in August*, and the uprooted people who drifted along at the mercy of the storms in [Dos Passos's] *42nd Parallel* " (5). With the categories of *Being and Nothingness* in mind, the mobility of the American people appears as a species of Sartrean freedom, a denial of contingency, a way of escaping from *being-in-itself*, an instance of that *neantization of facticity* which was part of the liberating *pro-ject* of the *for-itself*.[2] The American people, he wrote in *Combat*, "instead of having the suffocating feeling of being drowned in a collective destiny, have acquired a sort of individualistic sense of their personal dignity because they know . . . that they crossed the ocean to find a fate for which they feel responsible" (7 June 1945). Did the author of *Nausea* recognize in the children and grandchildren of immigrants the same relentless desire to elude the grasp of the past and to escape from the kinds of conditioning, whether familial, social, cultural, or existential, which had driven his own philosophical quest? The "suffocating feeling of being drowned in a collective destiny" reminds us of the anxiety that Roquentin, in *Nausea*, feels at the sight of the oppressive thickness of things, the muddy stickiness of being. Feeling responsible for one's fate—was that not the ultimate goal of the phenomenological consciousness, condemned to choose itself in time, projected as it was toward a future that it must constantly create anew? American cities are a continual building site and America itself is a Sartrean being: its existence precedes its essence, for it is always in the making.

> And there is nothing more immediately striking than the contrast between the formidable power, the inexhaustible abundance of what is called the "American Colossus" and the puny insignificance of those little houses that line the widest roads in the world. But on second thought, there is no clearer indication that America is not *done*, that her ideas and plans, her social structure and her cities have only a strictly temporal reality. (*LPE*, 120)

This view of freedom as mobility, however, is only a negative one. The very possibility of moving West to escape harsh living conditions on the East Coast acted as a safety valve for American capitalism rather than as a true principle of its negation. What is lacking is the moment of synthesis and creativity, when the Sartrean consciousness turns around and squarely, decisively, faces the sticky materiality of "facticity" to make it into the very stuff of its experience. The reader derives an overwhelming feeling of powerlessness from Sartre's description of the apparatus of Americanism. Its hold on minds and attitudes seems so tight that one can hardly see how freedom, as the power of annihilating the given, could make a difference in any successful way.

The system of American culture was the object of the first public lecture Sartre gave upon his return from the United States. Entitled "The Americans as I Saw Them," the talk was entirely devoted to *l'américanisme*, "this strange phenomenon in the eyes of a European," which Sartre described as a complex web of interrelated ideological traits arranged in a system. Rationalism, "optimism à la Rousseau," Puritanism, pragmatism, positivism and anti-intellectualism were presented as the roots of America's "naive and passionate faith in the virtues of Reason" (*LPE*, 108). The systematic character of Americanism leaves no room for contradiction and difference, and individuals within its fold fall prey to alienation and the anxiety to conform. Sartre tried to show, phenomenologically, how the cultural totality embodied itself in a concrete, singular existence that directed representations and practices, motivated each and every act, and permeated the whole of life:

> An American told me in Bern: "The truth is that each one of us is inhabited by the fear of being less American than our neighbor. . . . Being confronted with Americanism creates anxiety in each American; such an anxiety is ambivalent, as though he was wondering at the same time: "Am I sufficiently American?" and "How can I escape from Americanism?" A human being, in America, is a simultaneous answer to both of these questions; and each human being must find the answers alone. (*S III*, 130)

The Dialectics of Alienation: Individualism versus Conformity

When transferred to the political and social spheres, the dialectic of identity (in-itself) and difference (for-itself) becomes that of conformism and individuality and is reminiscent of Tocqueville's views on public opinion: "The public has . . . among a democratic people a singular power, of which aristocratic nations could never so much as conceive an idea; for it does not persuade to certain opinions, but it enforces them, and infuses them into the faculties by a sort of enormous pressure of the minds of all upon the reason of each. In the United States the majority undertakes to supply a multitude of ready-made opinions for the use of individuals, who are thus relieved from the necessity of forming opinions of their own" (*Democracy in America*, 2:11–12).

Tocqueville saw this "enormous pressure of the minds of all" as the main threat to individual freedom in modern democracies, an opinion voiced by Simone de Beauvoir, a hundred years later, in *America Day by Day*. She claimed to have seen the perverse logic of what she called, after Lord Brice, "the fatalism of the multitude" at work in the country of rugged individualism: "In America, the individual is nothing. He is the object of an abstract cult; convince him of his individual value and you arrest in him the awakening of the collective spirit. . . . Without collective hope or personal audacity, what can he do? He can be submissive or, if by some rare chance this submission becomes too odious, he can leave the country" (78). Beauvoir explicitly links the helplessness of the individual with the triumph of material civilization; this is construed in Heideggerian terms as the undue preoccupation with "utensils," the products of instrumental reason. "Heidegger says that 'the world appears on the horizon of instruments gone crazy,' but here the instruments are not at all crazy; the world, global and confusing, does not unmask, nor for that matter does the subject correlated with it. The individual is too much taken up with use of the telephone, elevators and ice-boxes, and too much occupied with this and that utensil to look beyond or around him" (239)

Sartre also thought that the "factors of universalization" (namely technology) at work in American society, were depriving modern men and women of their individuality: "Thus, when the American puts a nickel into the slot in the tram or in the underground, he feels just like everyone else. Not like an anonymous unit, but like a man who has divested himself of his individuality and raised himself to the impersonality of the Universal" (*LPE*, 109). Yet, the disappearance of the individual within the universal does not imply that he or she is simply negated by society or by the state, as in the European liberal and existentialist traditions (Kierkegaard's "unauthentic existence" or Heidegger's "world of the one"). Americanism, far from opposing individual freedom to conformism, welds them together in a higher synthesis, which is, "perhaps, what a Frenchman will have most difficulty in understanding." The French, Sartre argued, can only conceive of individuality as a struggle against society, they can only imagine freedom, like the author of *Being and Nothingness* himself, as a negation of the facticity of things. Not so in America: only when completely subjected to the objective spirit are the individuals totally reconciled with themselves:

> I have said enough, I hope, to give some idea of how the American is subjected, from the cradle to the grave, to an intense drive to organize and Americanize him, of how he is first depersonalized by means of a constant appeal to his reason, civic sense and freedom, and how, once he has been duly fitted into the national life by professional organizations and educational and other edifying organizations, he suddenly regains consciousness of himself and his personal autonomy. He is then free to escape into an almost Nietzschean individualism, the kind symbolized by the skyscrapers in the bright sky of New York. (*LPE*, 113)

In a sense, Sartre erased the tension between (individual) freedom and (tyrannical) equality that was central to Tocqueville's perception of the democratic age. In the Sartrean version of Tocqueville's dilemma, it is only at the end of the process of homogenization of thought and behavior that the new definition of individual autonomy can appear. Far from conflicting with the objective spirit and the forces of Americanization, individual identity presupposes them: "The citizen must, first of all, fit himself into a framework and protect himself; he must enter into a social contract with other citizens of his own kind. And it is this small community which confers upon him his individual function and personal worth" (*LPE*, 113). To help his French readers grasp such a paradox, Sartre used, of course, an urban metaphor: the American city is the symbol of individualism within conformity. "Seen flat on the ground from the point of view of length and width, New York is the most conformist city in the world." The nameless avenues and streets all look alike and intersect at right angles. "But if you look up, everything changes. Seen in its height, New York is the triumph of individualism" (110). Each building has its own personality, eluding all regulations "from the top.... Thus, at first, American individualism seemed like a third dimension. It is not incompatible with conformism, but, on the contrary, implies it. It represents, however, a new direction, both in height and depth, within conformism.... There are individuals in America, just as there are skyscrapers. There are Ford and Rockefeller, Hemingway and Roosevelt. They are models and examples" (110–11).

Just as each skyscraper blends into the skyline of the city, the human individual exists only as a dimension of conformity. The multiplicity of individuals is not a negation of totality, let alone a threat to the universal system of Americanism; it is not even a necessary moment in a dialectical process of totalization. This multiplicity is simply a by-product of the system itself. Individualism is the only escape route available to the American for-itself. But is the way *up* the skyscraper really a way *out?* Is the autonomy of the individual a mere illusion, since it is confined, and defined, within the boundaries of conformism?

Sartre mobilized all the resources of his own philosophy to clarify the relations between the abstraction of the system and the reality of the concrete individual. What remained to be explained was the principle underlying the articulation of ideology and practice, the process through which abstract representations become concrete actions. By then, the travel narrative had turned into political philosophy, anticipating Sartre's later historical and political works, and the renewned dialogue with Marxism that would produce the *Critique de la raison dialectique (Critique of Dialectical Reason)* as a theory of revolutionary practice. In his 1945 analysis of the American character, Sartre refused both idealism and the Marxist definition of ideology as mere superstructural effect of the social and economic infrastructure. The preservation of existential freedom implied the denial of mechanistic determinism as well as of innatism, the idea of a divine, that is, external origin of thought, as in Cartesianism. The for-itself of the New World, confronted with the forces of Americanization, had to be able to choose freely between conformism or revolt:

But one should not believe that the system has been deposited in the mind of each American as the god of Descartes deposited the primary notions in the mind of man; one should not think that the system is "refracted" in the minds and hearts to determine at every moment emotions or thoughts which would constitute its exact expression. In fact, it is outside; it is presented to the citizens; the most clever propaganda keeps presenting it to them over and over again: it is not in them, they are in it; they struggle against it or accept it, they suffocate in it or they go beyond it, they submit to it or create it anew each time, they give in to it or make violent efforts to escape from it; in any case it remains external to them, it transcends them because they are people and it is a thing. (*S III*, 126)

In the Sartrean view of social reality, the "monstrous complex of myths and values," although it is a set of representations, weighs heavily on human beings. It exists like a thing, beside the individuals and around them; it is a threatening entity that surrounds them on all parts and can engulf them unexpectedly, just as the in-itself submerges the consciousness, which then renounces its freedom and opts for bad faith. The psychological realm mediates between the two contending forces, it is the domain of human reality by which the external is internalized. The world of representations embodies itself in individuals by means of their obsessions, their phobias, and their dreams. The system, first written in the mind, soon takes hold of the body, inscribing itself in the most commonplace gestures and attitudes. The tension between Sartre's two dominant passions—the explanation of fact and the understanding of behavior—thus finds a measure of resolution: the order of things is an ordering of the mind.

The extraordinary power that Sartre attributed to the system could not but have a disquieting effect on the philosopher of freedom, the nonconformist professor who, in the 1930s, taught sans tie, in shirtsleeves and sport jacket, the intellectual ever so busy "thinking against himself" and eager not to alienate his independence to any group, organization, or party. Sartre remarked at one point how "mild and persuasive" the forces of Americanization were, as opposed to the brutal enforcement of totalitarian regimes. They drew their power from the fact that they appealed to reason and freedom rather than to the acceptance of an external rule. These forces did not give orders; they suggested the obvious. America was for Sartre the land of the "directed dream," a classroom the size of an entire nation. With the help of radio stations, newspapers, and associations, the social energy was channeled into an all-pervading process of "soft" socialization. It would be a mistake, though, to envision the reasonable use of propaganda as "an oppressive tactic on the part of the government or the big American capitalists" (*LPE*, 107). Sartre warns the reader against any simplistic and Manichean vision; he does not offer a deterministic theory of the manipulation of minds by the invisible hand of an all-powerful, all-knowing conductor. "This educative tendency springs from the heart of the community. Every American is educated by other Americans and educates others in turn" (107). The process of Americanization is all the more efficient since it is not in the hands of a particular group of specialists of coercive education, whether ideologues, pedagogues, or psychiatrists. It is the collective responsibility of the whole community: each individual internalizes the common values and influences others to do the same.

In America, Sartre encountered a new form of social control based on manipulation rather than violence, on persuasion rather than brute force. Many sociologists and political scientists would later describe this milder form of authority as a distinct feature of postindustrial societies. One of the most frequently quoted examples of this new social definition of education and social control is the best-selling success of Dr. Benjamin Spock's brand of pediatrics. In the 1950s, Western Europe witnessed, after the United States, the rise of public relations, group dynamics, group therapy, and other ways of managing individual and group conflicts; twenty years after Sartre's visit, the 1960s radicals emphasized the remarkable power of integration and recuperation of what they also would call "the system." Sartre saw this new pedagogy, based on the constant recourse to reason in interpersonal relations of power, as a sign of modernity: "I have known modern mothers who never ordered their children to do anything without first persuading them to obey. In this way they acquired a more complete and perhaps more formidable authority over their children than if they had threatened or beaten them" (*LPE*, 108).

"And perhaps more formidable": these few words are critical to an understanding of Sartre's subsequent ideological evolution. For if those who are subject to authority willingly accept their own subjugation, do they not surrender their freedom in a more durable way? Far from being only in the realm of things or utensils, the constraining order of what Sartre would later call the *practico-inert* may well reside in the heart of subjectivity itself. The social and cultural uniformity of a whole nation became a political issue when considered from the point of view of those who already represented for Sartre, in the 1940s, the future of a world liberated from alienation and bad faith. For what is true of children could also very well apply to the working class. While Simone de Beauvoir admitted, in the preface of *America Day by Day*, of having "crossed this great industrial country without visiting its factories, without seeing for myself its technical achievements, and without making contact with its working classes" (7), Jean-Paul Sartre wrote several articles on the American labor community.

Obviously, it would have been difficult to investigate the American war effort while only visiting universities, editorial rooms, and libraries. Beyond the constraints of his journalistic activities, however, one can see Sartre's interest in the ideology and professional organizations of the American working class as a sign of his evolution toward socialism. The analysis of the objective spirit of the United States was a transition between Sartre's somewhat mythical vision of America in the 1930s, which was based on his fascination for the movies and for the novels of Steinbeck, Caldwell, and Dos Passos, and the anti-imperialistic stand he would adopt in the 1960s. Sartre's texts on the American labor movement in 1945 represented the United States as the land of the impossible revolution. Prosperity played a critical role in integrating American workers into the economic system of the country. Here, as Sartre wrote in *Combat*, they could find "high wages, comfortable housing, freedom and equality. . . . And, since [the worker] perceives the link between his high wages and the general prosperity of the United States, he feels a solidarity with capitalism. He wants to improve his situation within the framework of capitalism. . . . The workers' ideal remains to establish permanent harmony between employers and employees, between Labor and Capital" (22 June 1945). The bourgeoisie, for its part, did everything it could to "encourage a familiarity [between the classes] that is nowhere to be found in Europe. It serves them because it hides the profound inequality in social conditions; but the upper classes are sincerely proud of American 'equality.' They may even be more mystified than the others" (10–11 June 1945).

Beyond reasons of immediate material interest, American workers favor cooperation over revolution because they are, like everyone else, "filled with the optimistic rationalism which is one of the characteristics of Americanism and which says that there is no problem which cannot be solved with common sense, good will and mutual concessions" (*Combat*, 22 June 1945). Instead of attributing its material well-being to an exceptional economic situation resulting from the wealth of the land and the chronic shortage of labor, the working class sees it as a consequence of public spirit and political constitution. Although their country is far from being a worker's paradise, their individualism and faith in a possible rationality of human relations mean that most American blue-collar workers do not consider themselves engaged in a struggle with the very structure of society; rather, they believe problems arise from the ill-will of some individuals.

"What workers fear above all," Sartre concluded, "is that socialistic measures will lower their standard of living and endanger American prosperity. Their professional individualism alienates them from communism. . . . And so the American worker ignores the poverty-based internationalism which united European proletarians before the war. The famous slogan 'Workers of the world, unite!' leaves him cold. He is first and foremost an American" (22 June 1945).

Sartre's vision of the American working-class movement is at best partial, for it seemed to overlook the most violent and most radical episodes of an extremely confrontational labor history, from Haymarket Square to the Wobblies. It is true that the most progressive elements of the labor movement had been eliminated by the late 1930s, but the emphasis on the reformist and class-collaborationist tendencies within labor unions confirmed Sartre's picture of the overwhelming ideological consensus of Americanism. Even the communist members of the CIO, he wrote, although sympathetic to the Soviet regime, did not "contemplate the possibility of transplanting it to the United States" (*Combat*, 12 June 1945). In Sartre's narrative, the practical anticommunism of the working class was only matched by the rejection of Marxist thought in progressive intellectual circles. "Marxism," Sartre told his readers in *Combat*, "is the American pet peeve. A hundred times during my visit, in all walks of life, I have been asked with genuine concern: 'Is France going to turn communist?'" This widespread anticommunism was largely responsible for Simone de Beauvoir's strong disillusionment upon arriving in the United States: "I was prepared to love America. . . . The reality was a great shock to me. There flourished among almost all the intellectuals, even those who claimed to be on the left, an Americanism worthy of the chauvinism of my father. . . . Their anti-communism verged on neurosis. . . . It was explained to me that in order to defend freedom it was becoming necessary to suppress it: the witch-hunt was under way" (*Force of Circumstance*, 123).

In the realm of ideology, everyone cherishes illusions about reality. Americanism was, for Sartre and Simone de Beauvoir, the opiate of the people, regardless of their class distinctions. The author of the yet-to-be-written *Critique of Dialectical Reason* was already quite close to the Marxist conception of ideology as mystified consciousness and misconstruction of social relations:

> There are the great myths, of happiness, of freedom, of triumphant motherhood, there is realism, optimism—and then, there are the Americans who are nothing at first, who grow up among these colossal statues and who get by as they can in their midst. . . . There is the

myth of equality and there is "segregation"; . . . the myth of freedom and the dictatorship of public opinion. . . . There is the smiling belief in progress and the pessimism of those intellectuals who think that action is impossible. . . . There are pretty and clean little houses, whitewashed apartments with a radio, a rocking-chair, a pipe in its case, little heavens, and then there are the occupants of those apartments who, after dinner, leave rocking-chair, radio, wife, pipe and children behind and get drunk all by themselves in the bar next door. Nowhere maybe will one find such a gap between people and myths, between life and the collective representation of life. (*S III*, 127–30)

The opposition between the people and their myths is here perfectly static, an absolute difference, never to be superseded or reconciled in a higher synthesis. In the most pessimistic version of Sartre's Americanism (reminiscent of Horkheimer and Adorno's *Dialectic of Enlightenment*,), there is no cultural or political *Aufhebung*, no dialectical liberation from illusion and myth. The historical failure of socialism in the United States points to the main characteristic of the system of Americanism: it makes no room for authentic, successful, liberating negativity. The apparent impossibility of collective revolution echoes the powerlessness of the individual to "negate the given" of alienation and escape from myths and social control. Sartre's pessimistic diagnosis announces Marcuse's repressive desublimation, and today's debates over the political nature, progressive or reactionary, of postmodern culture. In Sartre's vision, American culture was radically anti-Hegelian, hopelessly nondialectical.

The quasi-magical power of illusion that the system held over the people, the dissemination of bad faith and alienation at all levels of society, could only put off the prewar existentialist Sartre still was at the time and the postwar Marxist he was fast becoming. As early as June 1946, upon returning from his second visit to the United States, Sartre had already made up his mind about America. His determination can be seen in a conversation that took place as the original editorial committee of *Les Temps Modernes* was starting to split:

Aron's anti-communism was becoming more pronounced. At about that time, or a little later, we had lunch at the Golfe-Juan with Aron and Pia, who was also being attracted to Gaullism. Aron said that he had no great affection for either the U.S.A. or the U.S.S.R., but that if there were a war he would be on the side of the West; Sartre replied that he himself had no relish for either Stalinism or America, but that if the war broke out he would be found in the ranks of the Communists. (*Force of Circumstance*, 93–94)

The Return of the Tragic

Sartre never ceased to ponder the moral question. Michel Contat and Michel Rybalka consider it his "basic concern" (229), and Francis Jeanson wrote that "in reality, the most constant of Sartre's preoccupations has been to deal with the moral problem" (230). Sartre's postwar position is best expressed in the conclusion of his *Saint-Genet* (1951): "the moral 'problem' stems from the fact that for us Ethics is both inevitable and impossible. Action must create its own ethical norms in such a climate of indepassable impossibility. It is in this perspective that, for example, we ought to view the problem of violence or that of the relationship between means and end" (quoted in Contat and Rybalka, 251). Sartre wrote two thousand pages on questions of morals in the late 1940s, as a projected sequel to *Being and Nothingness*. Parts of these reflections were published posthumously as *Cahiers pour une morale*. His growing political concerns led him to give up the project of a sequel, which he later viewed as cast in purely idealistic terms. It is nevetheless remarkable that the only fragments of this project ever published in his lifetime (in *Combat* in 1949) were entitled "Le noir et le blanc aux États-Unis" [Blacks and whites in the United States]: the philosopher used racial relations in the United States as a departure point for his analysis of the ideological aspects of racism.

Sartre resumed his project of a moral treatise in the 1960s, this time focusing on the theoretical basis of the *Critique of Dialectical Reason*. He was forced to postpone the project again to finish his *Flaubert*. Some of his reflections on ethics and history can be found in the notes for the lecture he read at the 1964 conference on morals and society sponsored by the Gramsci Institute. As mentioned above, Sartre never finished *Cahiers pour une morale*, although he told Contat and Rybalka in 1969 that "its dialectical ethics . . . was entirely composed in [my] mind" (449). The question of the political significance of morals, even if it was never given a definite philosophical form in Sartre's work, was central to the plays he wrote in the late 1940s and early 1950s (e.g., *Dirty Hands*, 1948, and *The Devil and the Good Lord*, 1951). It also informs some of the philosophical essays he wrote at the time, notably those on the United States. The political specificity of America, namely its imperviousness to revolutionary practice, has its counterpart in the realm of theory: American culture is radically foreign to the tradition of European transcendental metaphysics. The denial of negativity, expressed historically as the impossibility of a radical questioning and transformation of the social order, translates in the realm of ethics as a fundamental inability to believe in evil:

An American said to me one evening: "After all, if international politics were in the hands of well-balanced and reasonable men, wouldn't
war be abolished for ever?" Some French people present said that
this did not necessarily follow, and he got angry. "All right," he said
in scornful indignation, "go and build cemeteries!" I, for my part,
said nothing; discussion between us was impossible. I believe in the
existence of evil and he does not. (*LPE*, 108)

Three years later, in a public lecture entitled Defense of French Culture
through European Culture, Sartre took up again the issue of evil to underscore the philosophical difference between the two cultures:

The evil in the world is inexpiable, and European culture is certainly
a reflection on the problem of evil, on the thought, What can a man
do, what can he be, what can he succeed at if we grant that evil is
inherent in the world? Now, generally speaking, evil is not an American concept. Americans are not pessimistic about human nature and
social organization. (Quoted in Contat and Rybalka, 227)

He also emphasized the dialectical character of the relationship between
good and evil in the conclusion of his *Saint-Genet:* "Either morality is stuff-
and-nonsense or it is a concrete totality which achieves a synthesis of Good
and Evil. For Good without Evil is Parmenidian Being, that is Death, and
Evil without Good is pure Nonbeing" (251).

The denial of evil is a commonplace of most French accounts of the
United States. In his book tellingly entitled *Le Mal Américain* (the English
translation, *The Trouble with America*, does little justice to the double meaning of the French *mal*, both disease and evil), sociologist Michel Crozier
struck a similar chord:

Americans have simply decided not to believe in evil. Their ideal
world could be depicted as an eighteenth century pastoral scene,
where everyone wears a modest little wig—no extravagant papists
here—making sure to appear neat, properly powdered, smiling, the
perfectly social creature. . . . When all is said and done, what is missing in American culture? I venture to say, it is evil, or more precisely
the acknowledgment that evil exists. (120, 136)

In *America Day by Day*, Simone de Beauvoir recalls an evening spent
with Nelson Algren in a seedy bar of Chicago's West Madison Avenue. On
the dance floor two people described as a drunk and a "fat floosie" start
dancing with "madness and ecstacy, so old, so ugly, so miserable . . . lost
for a moment and . . . happy." The French writer's reaction to the scene

triggers another instance of crosscultural misunderstanding: "I felt bewildered, stared and said: 'It's beautiful.' N.A. was astounded; it seemed to him very French. 'With us,' he said, 'ugliness and beauty, the grotesque and the tragic, and even good and evil, go their separate ways: Americans do not like to think that such extremes can mingle" (81).

Crozier sees this absolutist dichotomy between good and evil, and its corollary, the avoidance and denial of evil, as one of the main weaknesses of American culture, hindering its ability to deal with the growing complexity of worldwide economic and political relations:

> Americans will not be able to rediscover the sense of community and public enterprise, they will not be able to rediscover any depth in their lives, unless they are willing to stretch their thoughts beyond the single dimension of law, virtue, and the consensus, because thought deals with evil differently from the way it deals with good. The problems of sin, punishment, or deterrence are in sharp contrast with those of choosing what is best, the pursuit of happiness, or respect for juridical forms. . . . American logic—based on simple good-and-evil formulas and on simple patterns of adjustments and resource allocations that cannot easily deal with complex systems and do not allow for longer learning processes—is especially ill fit for such a world. (136, 141)

The streak of skepticism (Sartre called it "pessimistic rationalism") that runs through French thought, from Montaigne to the seventeenth-century moralists, and beyond to Tocqueville and Alain, was often construed as a healthy antidote to the stern dogmatism of the Reformation or the idealistic rationalism of the German Enlightenment. Crozier thus opposes Calvinist Manicheanism to the more flexible, "inventive" casuistry of the Jesuits: "For the casuist good and evil, exist naturally, but they always have to be viewed in context . . . and every condemnation of an individual must be measured against the social consequences it will have" (124). In the French view, Americans pay a high price for the expulsion of negativity, the denial of evil, and the active forgetting of "the tragic sense of life." America, far from being a contented utopia, is secretly haunted by the return of the repressed. Evil is bound to come back as an acute sense of guilt and sin, or, like Captain Ahab's white whale, as vengeful punishment. "When you live by the assumption that goodness is supreme," Crozier writes, "you are obliged to suppress evil, to deny its existence. . . . But hypocrisy helps evil prosper and, though suppressed, from time to time it comes back. Then you have a scandal, and there is no way to restore the status quo except by recourse to the God of wrath" (122).

The French judgment on America is almost always that of the skeptical moralist, as in Tocqueville's remarks on American restlessness:

> In America I saw the freest and most enlightened men placed in the happiest circumstances that the world affords; it seemed to me as if a cloud habitually hung upon their brow, and I thought them serious and almost sad, even in their pleasures. . . . It is strange to see with what feverish ardor the Americans pursue their own welfare, and to watch the vague dread that constantly torments them lest they should not have chosen the shortest path which may lead to it. (*Democracy in America*, 2: 144)

Sartre, coming after Freud, described the American tragedy in terms of repressed libido and subconscious resistances and denials, applying the principles of his "existential psychoanalysis" to the American way of life:

> One finds, on the one hand, happy-ends and movies which every night show the exhausted crowds a rosy picture of life. On the other hand, one has people who are tragic for fear of being so, because of the total absence of the tragic in them and around them. . . . There are thousands of taboos forbidding love outside marriage, and then there are all these condoms strewn all over the backyards of co-ed colleges. . . . There are all these men and women who drink before making love, in order to sin and forget in a drunken stupor. (*S III*, 127)

Evil, then, returns with a vengeance as self-destruction, and the noble savage gives in to bad faith. This tragic picture of an absolute and unfulfilled need in the heart of abundance and of the desperate quest for meaning within a materialistic utopia is, of course, not specific to non-American imagination alone. Henry Miller in *The Air-conditioned Nightmare*, the writers of the Beat Generation and, later, the 1960s counterculture, have all voiced the romantic protest against a rationalized and standardized social reality. What is peculiar to many French descriptions of American culture is the critical *hauteur* from which they engage their subject matter. From the perspective of an old skeptical wisdom only one diagnosis is possible: Americans are condemned to deal unsatisfactorily with the eternal recurrence of the tragic because they will not conceptualize it.

The Philosophical Method of the Americans

I have quoted enough passages from *Democracy in America* alongside excerpts from Sartre's account of the United States to suggest a strong similarity between the two authors. Tocqueville's works display a variety of judgments on the United States, some very favorable (like his celebration of the American political system in vol. 1), others extremely critical (e.g., his attacks on democratic mass culture in vol. 2). Sartre does not quote Tocqueville, let alone claim any sort of (af)filiation with the liberal thinker, but their respective visions of American culture are often very similar despite the differences in their social origins, ideological views, or political trajectories. Tocqueville, the grandson of Malesherbes on his mother's side, the scion of an old Norman legitimist family going back to the days of William the Conqueror, witnessed, with a good dose of nostalgia, the collapse of his forefathers' social world and observed, with unsurpassed critical acumen, the convulsive birth of a new era, fearing its excesses and poking fun at its shortcomings. Sartre was born, as he said, "in a milieu of petty bourgeois intellectuals," and he took part in all the progressivist battles of the 1950s and 1960s, true to his belief that "the revolutionary act is the free act par excellence."

What can there possibly be in common between the two men? Tocqueville was a skeptical analyst of the French Revolution, a magistrate who rallied around the Bourbons during the Restoration, became a liberal representative in the French Assembly under the July Monarchy, and briefly served as a moderate minister of the Second Republic; Sartre, a member of the French Academy and the iconoclastic radical firebrand who refused the Nobel Prize, enjoyed for a quarter of a century an undisputed worldwide reputation as *the* quintessential critical intellectual. He was welcomed in Moscow and revered at Cornell, and he preached the revolutionary gospel to workers outside the gates of the Renault factory in Boulogne-Billancourt. Yet, they followed parallel paths in their analyses of American culture and society, perhaps because freedom was at the core of their respective intellectual enterprises. Despite their differences, the aristocratic Tocqueville and the individualistic Sartre (attributes considered synonymous by many intellectuals) were equally hostile to the cultural and moral homogeneity of American society.

"I think," Tocqueville remarks at the beginning of the second volume of his *Democracy in America*, "that in no country in the civilized world is less attention paid to philosophy as in the United States. The Americans have no philosophical school of their own; and they care but little for all the schools into which Europe is divided, the very names of which are scarcely known to them" (20). Still, one should not conclude too hastily that Americans do not have a "philosophical method." In fact, "almost all the inhabitants of the United States conduct their understanding in the same manner, and govern it by the same rules"; the truth is that they

125

simply "have not been required to extract [it] from books," for they have "found it in themselves" (3). Tocqueville then proceeds to describe what this philosophical method is like:

> To evade the bondage of system and habit, of family maxims, class opinions, and, in some degree, of national prejudices; to accept tradition only as a means of information, and existing facts only as a lesson used in doing otherwise, and doing better; to seek the reason of things for one's self, and in one's self alone; to tend to results without being bound to means, and to aim at the substance through the form; such are the principal characteristics of what I shall call the philosophical method of the Americans. . . . America is therefore one of the countries of the world where philosophy is least studied, and where the precepts of Descartes are best applied. . . . The Americans do not read the works of Descartes, because their social condition deters them from speculative studies; but they follow his maxims because this very social condition naturally disposes their understanding to adopt them. (2:3)

The citizens of the new republic, like Molière's Monsieur Jourdain, write in (Cartesian) prose without being aware of it, for they are natural disciples of the Enlightenment. Sartre was of the opinion that their positivistic rationalism precluded authentic concern for what he called metaphysical problems: "For [the Americans], the main problem is to adapt man to society and one sees here the social character of their rationalism which never looks for metaphysical problems. . . . The tragic sense of life, the sense of the human destiny are questions an American mind never asks itself" (*L'Ordre*, 4). Philosophy as Socratic maieutics, Cartesian doubt, Kantian critique, or Hegelian dialectic is, to use Sartrean language, an expression of the power to *nihilate* that which constitutes human existence at its most authentic. The philosophical activity, as departure from common sense, rested for Sartre on the dualism of consciousness and being, on the possibility to challenge the positivity of *what is* by conceiving the thought of *what ought to be*. The system of Americanism, because it implied an optimistic, practical form of rationalism, precluded the liberating moment of critique, thereby preventing the rise of authentic philosophy:

> If I were to compare French rationalism to American rationalism, I would say that American rationalism is white, in the sense of white magic, and that French rationalism is a black rationalism: . . . French rationalism is, as a matter of fact, always pessimistic. . . . Reason is that struggle against a universal which escapes us everywhere and which we keep trying to overtake; it's a sort of limited confidence in

human freedom seen as being [a] more or less desperate situation. . . .
American reason is above all technical, practical, and scientific.
(Quoted in Contat and Rybalka, 227)

These cultural differences extend beyond the realm of epistemology or
political philosophy, however, bearing on literary and artistic endeavors as
well. "It must be acknowledged," Tocqueville wrote, "that amongst few of
the civilized nations of our time have the higher sciences made less progress than in the United States; and in few have great artists, fine poets, or
celebrated writers been more rare" (*Democracy in America*, 2:37). The
French historian drew a direct line between the overriding concern of
bourgeois society for the immediate results of action and the absence of a
high critical culture. American civilization, dominated as it was by utilitarian values, implied that no time should be wasted in vain metaphysical and
aesthetic speculations, once the preserve of aristocratic intellectual elites.
The traditional figures of the speculative scholar, whether lay philosopher
or theologian, and of the creative genius were bound to disappear, for they
owed their existence to the protection of the prince and to the siphoning
away of resources from economic production. "The general mediocrity of
fortune, the absence of superfluous wealth, the universal desire of comfort,
and the constant efforts by which everyone attempts to procure it, make
the taste for the useful predominate over the love of the beautiful in the
heart of man" (2:50).

It is not that citizens of modern, egalitarian societies are indifferent to
science or literature; they simply do not make learning sacred as a disinterested calling and leisurely activity (*otium, scholè*). In fact, great numbers of
individuals will engage in intellectual pursuits once they see them as
profitable endeavors by which to advance their social conditions: mass education and mass information are bound to develop in a democratic universe. Not only is knowledge in the democratic United States less elitist
and less selective, and, so, less likely to perform at the individual level (that
of the Romantics' genius), but it is also, since it is American, less theoretical, and of course oriented toward concrete results and useful applications:

> In America the purely practical part of science is admirably under-
> stood, and careful attention is paid to the theoretical portion which
> is immediately requisite to application. . . . But hardly anyone in the
> United States devotes himself to the essentially theoretical and ab-
> stract portion of human knowledge. . . . Permanent inequality of
> conditions leads men to confine themselves to the arrogant and ster-
> ile research of abstract truths; whilst the social condition and the in-

stitutions of democracy prepare them to seek the immediate and useful practical results of the sciences. (*Democracy in America*, 2:43, 47)

The opposition between theory and practice, pure and applied science, academic and vulgarized knowledge, is loaded with value judgments in French high culture, which was (and still is, in many respects) dominated by a taste for abstraction and rhetorical effects, the cult of art for art's sake, and a model of intellectual excellence based on the celebration of the humanities and *culture générale*. Tocqueville, despite his sympathy for democratic achievements, remained faithful to his own patrician upbringing when it came to comparing European taste for theory and American concern for practice, the quest for truth on the one hand and the pursuit of comfort on the other: "But at the very time when the Americans were naturally inclined to require nothing of science but its special applications to the useful arts and the means of rendering life comfortable, learned and literary Europe was engaged in exploring the common sources of truth, and in improving at the same time all that can minister to the pleasures or satisfy the wants of man" (2:37).

In most cultures, spatial metaphors signify social hierarchies: the activities of the elites are elevated and uplifting, while the humble, obscure practices of the people are "down to earth." One sign that the period of the High Roman Empire is over is when people resort to such vernaculars as low Latin. So it is with the ancients and the moderns. When equality and utility win the day, the life of the mind is inevitably debased:

> All men who live in democratic ages more or less contract the ways of thinking of the manufacturing and trading classes; their minds take a serious, deliberate, and positive turn; they are apt to relinquish the ideal, in order to pursue some visible and proximate object, which appears to be the natural and necessary aim of their desires. Thus the principle of equality does not destroy the imagination, but lowers its flight to the level of the earth. No men are less addicted to reverie than the citizens of a democracy; and few of them are ever known to give way to those idle and solitary meditations which commonly precede and produce the great emotions of the heart. (2:218)

Studies in American Literature (and Art)

If the democratic age curtails imagination and smothers the ideals and passions of the heart, it is no wonder that it cannot produce any literature of quality. The tyranny of the majority can only cause the decline of *belles lettres*, and there is no country, says Tocqueville, in which there is as little independence of mind and freedom of discussion as in America, for "the majority raises very formidable barriers to the liberty of opinion: within these barriers an author may write whatever he pleases, but he will repent it if he ever steps beyond them" (*Democracy in America*, 1:269). There have not been any great American writers because "literary genius needs freedom of opinion to flourish." While the Spanish Inquisition has never been able to suppress the circulation of anti-religious books, "the empire of the majority succeeds much better in the United States, since it actually removes the wish of publishing them" (1:269). Many commentators have pointed out, with good reason, that the judgment was unfair, even at a time (1840) when American literature was still in infancy.

What about Washington Irving or James Fenimore Cooper? True, Tocqueville could not have met them in the United States, since both of them were living in Europe at the time, where their works were widely circulated among literary circles. Cooper had finished *The Prairie* (1827) in Lyon, where he was consul of the United States. The author of *The Sketch Book* enjoyed a solid reputation in European academic and intellectual salons: he had been elected a member of the Spanish Royal Academy in 1829 and had received an honorary law degree from Oxford University the following year. It may be that neither Cooper nor Irving would have qualified as "literary geniuses" in Tocqueville's eyes. But consider these works, all published during the decade preceding the publication of *Democracy in America*: Emerson's *Nature* (1836), Longfellow's *Voices of the Night* (1837), or Poe's *Adventures of Arthur Gordon Pym* (1837). Poe, in fact, would later be hailed by Baudelaire as one of the masters of modernism.

Tocqueville, whose foresight has often been rightly celebrated, should not, perhaps, be held accountable for having overlooked the quality of a national literature still in its nascent stage. His perception of a prosaic America, devoid of any literary genius and of any taste for art or speculation does not withstand the judgment of time, however, and certainly does not apply today. Nobody would be arrogant enough, the argument goes, to maintain in this century such a reductive opposition between the "learned and literary Europe" and the land of bourgeois philistinism, where imagination "lowers its flight to the level of the earth." Is this so sure?

Sartre was extremely attracted to the American literature of the 1920s and 1930s, perhaps more so than any other French writer of his generation, with the exception of Simone de Beauvoir. He was too much of a *provocateur* not to have enjoyed the pained expression he often brought upon American faces when he mentioned the admiration of the French for Hemingway and Caldwell.

An American lady who knew Europe very well asked me one day what American writers I preferred. When I mentioned Faulkner, the other people present started to laugh. . . . Later I met a young liberal writer. . . . I told him I had been asked . . . to get in touch with literary agents of several writers who were particularly admired in France. . . . When I mentioned Caldwell, his friendly smile vanished suddenly; at the name of Steinbeck he raised his eyebrows; and at the mention of Faulkner he cried indignantly, "You French! Can't you ever relish anything but filth?" (*Atlantic Monthly* [*AM*], 114).

Sartre praised Faulkner's *Sartoris* and Dos Passos's *1919* in no uncertain terms before the war, when their authors were virtually unknown in Europe. In a lecture given at Princeton in 1946, he acknowledged the debt a whole generation of young French writers owed to the writings of Hemingway, Steinbeck, and Dos Passos: "It seemed to us suddenly that we had just learned something and that our literature was about to pull itself out of its old ruts. At once, for thousands of young intellectuals, the American novel took its place, with jazz and the movies, among the best imports from the United States" (*AM*, 114). Does this mean that the masters of the American novel had managed to escape from the "objective spirit of the United States" and did not suffer the damaging consequences of their culture's incapacity to think in metaphysical terms? After all, Malraux had written that "the novels of Faulkner were eruptions of Greek tragedy in the detective story," and Sartre himself had said that the passion and violence of *The Sound and the Fury* and *Sanctuary* showed the French "the face of the United States—a face tragic, cruel, and sublime" (*AM*, 114).

In fact, the ultimate value of American writing, Sartre proceeded to tell his American audience, lay precisely in its pragmatic, action-oriented nature, in its depthlessness and one-dimensionality. Faulkner or Steinbeck could not care less about "intellectual analysis," and that is why the French enjoyed them so much: "The heroes of Hemingway and Caldwell never explain themselves. . . . They live because they spurt suddenly as from a deep well. To analyze them would be to kill them" (*AM*, 115). This "unconscious spontaneity" does not apply to the characters only: it is symptomatic of the writers themselves. American novelists are original and fascinating precisely because of the basic anti-intellectualism of their literary endeavor. No more psychological novel, no more introspection, no more omniscient creator à la Flaubert, but a synthetic approach and unconscious motivations.

Intellect versus life energy and primitive power, aestheticism and refinement versus "barbaric brutality": literary redemption had to come from the other side of the Atlantic, from the land of the creative innocence that precedes thought and theory, as in the romantic opposition between the corruption of the old continent and the virginal purity of the Americas. Once again, Old World effete aristocrats of the mind are left to admire and envy the muscular body of the Whitmanesque woodsman. The distinctive style of the Lost Generation, Sartre argued, is anything but a conscious strategy: it is rather the natural, unreflective novelistic version of the Americans' philosophical method, in their concern with getting things done. Even if they tried, none of these writers could cast off the mould of pragmatism: "When Hemingway writes his short, disjointed sentences, he is only obeying his temperament. He writes what he sees. . . . If Faulkner breaks the chronological order of his story, it is because he cannot do otherwise. He sees time jumping about in disordered leaps" (*AM*, 118).

But there is more. What is good for America is not necessarily good for Europe. The naïveté of the American novelist may be a recipe for success: it cannot serve as a model. The fundamental difference between the literary traditions precludes direct borrowing and uncritical adoption by French writers of these innovative techniques. Nowhere is the incompatibility between the two ways of writing more obvious than in Sartre's contrast between Hemingway and Camus:

> We were weighed down, without being aware of it, by our traditions and our culture. These American novelists, without such traditions, without help, have forged, with barbaric brutality, tools of inestimable value. We collected these tools, but we lack the naiveté of their creators. We thought about them, we took them apart and put them together again, we theorized about them. . . . We have treated consciously and intellectually what was the fruit of a talented and unconscious spontaneity. But when Camus uses Hemingway's technique, he is conscious and deliberate, because it seems to him upon reflection the best way to express his philosophical experience of the absurdity of the world. . . . Soon the first French novels written during the occupation will appear in the United States. We shall give back to you these techniques which you have lent us. We shall return them digested, intellectualized, less effective, and less brutal—consciously adapted to French taste. (*AM*, 118)

Despite the genuine admiration which he felt for the American novelists of his time, Sartre still thought that they suffered from the same cultural limitations as the rest of their compatriots. They too were prisoners of Americanism, unable to attain the (self)consciousness of their art and to practice it, like Camus, in a deliberate manner. Although he felt his own incapacity to write "naively" as a shortcoming, Sartre could no more than Tocqueville renounce the philosophical stance and the analytic approach that, in his eyes, epitomized French taste; he recognized that American novelists wrote the way they did because they could not do otherwise. Tocqueville's learned and literary Europe retained the privilege of intellectuality in Sartre's view. "French culture" and "American culture," hypostatised as immutable entities, face each other for eternity: theory versus practice, thought versus substance, spirit versus body, contemplation versus action, consciousness versus the unconscious, abstract versus concrete, sedentary versus nomadic, old versus new, cunning versus naive, refined versus primitive.

The opposition surfaced again some thirty years later in a special issue on the United States of the avant-garde literary review *Tel Quel.* Many French newsweeklies and intellectual journals celebrated the bicentennial of the Declaration of Independence by devoting one of several issues to the United States. *Tel Quel*, for its part, faithful to its vanguardist theoretical and literary calling, offered a mixed bag of interviews with prominent French and American artists and writers, as well as essays on the latest developments in American aesthetic, political, and academic life. The volume was prefaced by a debate between Julia Kristeva, Marcellin Pleynet, and Philippe Sollers, entitled "Pourquoi les États-Unis?" (Why the United States?) in which the participants exposed their views on such varied topics as the art scene in Greenwich Village, Noam Chomsky's critique of U.S. foreign policy,[3] or the matriarchal components of American culture. At one point in the discussion, Julia Kristeva emphasized the diversity of American art forms, which she described as nonverbal:

> The other striking feature of the United States . . . is the place of artistic practices. It is a place that is by definition marginal, as in every society. But it concerns a marginality that is also *polyvalent:* "aesthetic" experiments are more frequent and more varied than in Europe . . . [and] they are *non-verbal.* The Americans today seem to me to excel in any research into gesture, colour and sound, which they pursue in great depth and scope and much more radically than is done in Europe. . . . For in the beginning is not the word, at any rate not at this particular beginning. They do not know what they do; they don't have a verbal, that is to say, conscious and analytical (in the naive sense of analysis) connection to what they are doing. When they do say something in these performances, it does not correspond to what is done in gesture, color and sound. (*The Kristeva Reader*, 275)

Such a characterization of American aesthetic achievements strikes a familiar chord and is quite similar to Sartre's opposition between American (ab)original, unmediated spontaneity and European elaborate reflectiveness in novel writing. Just as Faulkner or Hemingway wrote the way they wrote because "they could not do otherwise," the artists and intellectuals of the seventies "do not know what they are doing," which is why they need the help of European theorists. There seemed to exist, according to Kristeva, a spontaneous preverbal understanding between her and her American students, which in turn explained their enthusiastic reception of her ability to verbalize, and accounted for the success in the United States of European literary theory:

> I sometimes felt, especially in my classes, that even though I was using a specialized language, I was speaking to people who knew what it was about, even if they found it difficult. It corresponded to a lived experience, whether pictorial, gestual or sexual. Thus, despite the naïveté, the American audience gives the European intellectual the impression that there is something he can do on the other side of the Atlantic, namely that he can speak in a place where it [ça] doesn't speak. (*The Kristeva Reader*, 275)

American art is practice without a theory, or, in Kristeva's words, "a void which returns little more than a dim presence and the punctuation of sounds, colours and gestures" (275). The enigma of America lies in this speechless presence: a silent body. In a chapter of *Polylogue*, reflecting on her experiences as a traveler and lecturer in the United States, Kristeva elaborated further on the characteristic aphasia of American culture. "It is unnamed, unnamable and fascinating. An entire culture, new, alive, which produces itself without speaking itself" (500). When it does speak, however, it is through the body, "the hysterical substance . . . the pulsion, a *jouissance* that imagines itself without the Word, and rebels against the Law" (510). But the insurgent body cannot produce a discourse equal to its radical novelty; it falls back on the preexisting "consecrated forms of official culture" and traditional literary aesthetics, "the old sentimental discourse of the everyday," espousing a traditional positivist and scientist rationality or "resuscitating archaic forms of paganism or matriarchy" and spiritualism (500, 510).

In the same way, Freudian theories have lost their radicalism in the United States. They have been reduced to a vulgar form of scientism and have become "normative." Kristeva wonders if psychoanalysis did not meet such a fate not only because of Protestantism, but also because of the fact that "Americans have no language," American English being more like a "code," a simplified linguistic system that reduces the user's capacity for complex symbolization or verbalization. Is it possible, she wonders, to implant psychoanalysis in a code? (*The Kristeva Reader*, 279). In "From Ithaca to New York," Kristeva writes that she brought back with her "a whole lot of feminist reviews, leaflets and sheets: confessions, critiques, demands, poems, drawings, uteri, sexual organs, photos, children, drafts of cycles, of pregnancy" (511), which she finds "naive and ugly." The reason for this negative impression is that this material is not trying to "say something one did not know," but that it simply "shows itself . . . revealing the underside of the skyscrapers, Rockefeller Center, and Watergate." The silent opacity of these statements needs to be deciphered, interpreted, like so many symptoms of a neurotic disorder: "I cannot quote from them: nothing is written there, it simply speaks, without any regard for style. They are symptoms: their truth lies elsewhere. Where? Who knows? What if their function was not to know, but simply to show that which does not find its way in the discourse (of man or woman)?" (*Polylogue*, 511).

This in turn explains, in Kristeva's eyes, why the American avant-garde craves European intellectual products; they help them articulate what Americans can only express through the hysterical projections of the body. European theories give them an interpretive tool that can match, in its radicality, their own nonverbal innovative prowess. But they are, of course, ill-equipped to deal with imported theories, and they tend to borrow them without sufficient discernment, much like colonized people indiscriminately aping the colonizers' ways. Kristeva's considerations on the business of theoretical import-export, in the way that seems to lament the natives' inability to make the most of Western interpretive technology, did indeed sound a lot like patronizing neocolonialist rhetoric to some American readers.[4] American intellectuals, dependent as they are on imported models of interpretation, "may be getting bogged down today now they take anything and everything from Parisian intellectual cuisine." But in fact "there's no mainstream in their choice" (*The Kristeva Reader*, 281). "Obviously, in so far as there are institutions, they're tempted to choose what is valued in French institutions, and it then goes out of fashion in the analoguous American institution. A philosopher who's in fashion at the rue d'Ulm will be in fashion at Yale for two years, and that will upset his colleagues. But these phenomena get lost in such a variety that in the end they don't involve the same diktat of styles as they do in Paris" (281). The aglossic hysterical machine ends up swallowing Old World rhetorical subtleties; this permanent aesthetic and ideological revolution transforms them into something totally Other—and distinctly American, as a kind of ideological melting pot. "And then they borrow from intellectual masters to make ideologies as ephemeral as they are unrecognizable. It is an immense machine turning Western discourse into refuse" (281).

For the *Tel Quel* theoreticians, the incapacity of the American mind to come to terms with the symbolic order and to adequately articulate its own visions in words explains that the influence of European modernity is felt in music and the plastic arts rather than in literature. Echoing Tocqueville, Kristeva contends that "strictly speaking, there is no contemporary American literature, in the sense of literature as 'an experience of limits': their avant-garde novelists are Cage and Bob Wilson, music and theater" (*Polylogue*, 500). Commenting on Sollers's remark that American art is the result of the "grafting" of the European avant-garde in America during World War II, Kristeva acknowledges that the graft unquestionably took place, but resulted in something totally different from what was to be expected. "They took Artaud and Duchamp but produced Pollock, which couldn't have happened in either France or Moscow" (281).

Sollers's own genealogy of American modernity is another instance of the (self)privileging of European culture that is so characteristic of many French intellectuals' views on American aesthetics. While acknowledging that modernity did not originate in Europe alone and that it was present on American soil in the early nineteenth century (he cites the obvious example of Edgar Allan Poe as paradigmatic of early American modernity), Sollers nevertheless refers the latest developments in American art (Cage, Wilson, Pollock) to the influence of European emigré artists and intellectuals in the 1930s and 1940s, "the draining of marginalized European personalities into an American exile" (280). "This grafting, it seems to me, is at the source of what we call American art. Like it or not, the very rapid development of an American art dates from this point, whether we're talking about painting or gesture, or the creation of an atmosphere bordering on something like the materialization of an unconscious which might have been experienced in Europe" (280).

Sollers, in a sense, is saying the opposite of Kristeva, who underscored the radical originality of American culture (its nonverbalization). In any case, he reduces the scope of that originality by stressing its European origins and components. The difference in American artistic expressions, far from being indigenous, is construed as the result of a translation on American soil, and in the American aesthetic idiom (or code), of a difference that already existed in Europe in the marginalized communitities of avant-garde cultural producers. The recognition, and even the celebration, of the value of American art by French intellectuals who, in the case of the *Tel Quel* group, are particularly open to contemporary developments in the US, still implies that American creators are culturally indebted to their European counterparts.

This is no denying the obvious influences of surrealism, futurism, and other European modernist movements on American twentieth-century aesthetic practices. In cultural and intellectual matters, influences or affinities are complex processes and usually work both ways (Poe came before Baudelaire and Emerson before Nietzsche, and the latter both acknowledged their debts to the former). Philippe Sollers's genealogy of transatlantic modernity fits in what I have called a paradigm of cultural continuity. By privileging the European origin and stressing the "supplementarity" of American art, his narrative falls prey to the canonical set of oppositions that informs most French discussions of American high (and a fortiori mass) culture.

FOUR

CULTURE IN SODA CANS
The Cold War of the French Intellectuals

▼

I can already hear the suspicious ones, complete with moustaches and starched collars: American trade will submerge us. . . . They will buy our souls with refrigerators. *Denis de Rougemont, 1947*

American ideology and culture will necessarily come to us with screws, manufactured goods, and canned fruit juices. *Jean-Paul Sartre, 1949*

The intellectuals are more pained than simple mortals by the hegemony of the United States. Persecution is more bearable to the intelligentsia than indifference. *Raymond Aron, 1955*

It is always difficult to be on the left and to be interested in American culture; one becomes suspect. The 'cold war' of the superstructures is not over. *Julia Kristeva, 1976*

Between World War II and Vietnam the perception of American culture and society in French intellectual circles changed considerably. During the moment of euphoria following the liberation of France, a period marked by the political alliance of the various ideological streams (communists, socialists, Christian Democrats, Gaullists, and liberals) that had resisted fascism, the United States appeared as a nation of liberators who had made the key contribution to the victory over Nazi barbarity. The onset of the Cold War, on the other hand, rekindled the anti-Americanism of many in the French intelligentsia, regardless of their political persuasion. The United States had become, with no serious rival, the largest industrial nation (producing half the world's manufactured goods), the self-appointed "leader of the free world," and the police officer of the planet. At the same time, Marxism was attaining a dominant position within the intellectual Left. It had become for many, in one of Sartre's most famous phrases, "the unsurpassable philosophy of the times." The new criticism was more political and added the denunciation of economic and military imperialism to the essentially cultural and often humanistic anti-Americanism of the 1920s and 1930s.

The Cold War of the Intellectuals

In 1945, most prominent French intellectuals were once again extremely critical of the American way of life. This prompted ideological cross-fertilization, unexpected agreements, and startling "objective" alliances, as one used to say in those days. One could very easily apply to Cold War France the ironical judgment that N. Tucci, an Italian then living in the United States, passed on the intellectual climate prevalent elsewhere in Europe: Italian communists, he wrote at the time in the Atlanticist review *Preuves*, accuse "America of being excessively conformist and lacking in freedom [while] the monarcho-fascists [think] it lacks conformism and suffers from an excess of freedom" (54). In France, the moral condemnation of "American decadence" reconciled the communists and the progressive Christians of the review *Esprit*. In their daily *L'Humanité*, Stalinists railed against the revolting obscenities of bourgeois art and the barbarity of jazz in terms the prewar Maurassian Catholic Right would not have disowned, while *Les Temps Modernes* denounced the hysterical moralism of the McCarthyite witch-hunters.

Besides the strict Stalinist orthodoxy, one can distinguish three major positions regarding the United States during the Cold War: fellow traveling, neutralism, and Atlanticism. The first option entailed both an unconditional opposition to American civilization and foreign policy (the latter being a natural consequence of the former) and overall support of the Soviet Union, at times with reservations (adherents include Sartre, Merleau-Ponty). Neutralism, on the other hand, rejected *la logique des blocs* and refused to choose between the two "superpowers," or, as the French say, between the plague and cholera. The Atlanticist camp, far from unreservedly admiring the American way of life, thought that the only chance for weakened European countries to regain their rank among leading nations and to preserve freedom and humanism was to rebuild their strength under the American "umbrella." In *Le Spectateur engagé*, a collection of interviews given a short time before he died, Raymond Aron recalled the all-or-nothing logic that characterized the ideological climate of the times, which turned every political argument into a corollary of the fundamental question of the relative merits of the Soviet or American "blocks": "The diplomatic discussion: 'Shall we accept to be part of the Atlantic entity with the United States?' became inevitably entangled with the other issue:

'Which of the two countries, the Soviet Union or the United States, is preferable?'" (175).

Choosing one side, far from being determined by the positive, enthusiastic support of one societal model, was dictated by the refusal of the other; in the case of neutralism, it was by the rejection of both. The fellow travelers of the French Communist party were often more anti-American than pro-Soviet, and their Atlanticist opponents more anticommunist than pro-American. All in all, little in what the two competing superpowers had to offer attracted Western European intellectuals—with the exception of the hard-line Stalinists and a few unconditional apologists of America, whom Raymond Aron called the "new collaborators." They had resigned themselves, he said, to the fatality of American hegemony just as they had accepted, a few years before, the domination of the Third Reich. It is useful to recall Simone de Beauvoir's account of the feelings of the prominent members of the editorial board of *Les Temps Modernes* in the summer of 1946. "Aron ... had no great affection for either the U.S.A. or the U.S.S.R, but ... if there were a war he would be on the side of the West; Sartre ... had no relish for either Stalinism or America, but if the war broke out he would be found in the ranks of the Communists" (*Force of Circumstance*, 94; see also chap. 3 above).

The ideological division of the intellectual field was institutionalized: each group had its review or weekly magazine, while prominent journalists collaborated with famous writers and philosophers. *Les Temps Modernes* and *Esprit* supported the communist movement, critically at times; the neutralists gathered around Claude Bourdet and his *Observateur;* and the Atlanticists wrote for *Preuves*, a review directed by the Swiss critic Denis de Rougemont, known for his studies of courtly love in the Western tradition. *Preuves* was published "under the auspices" of the Congress for the Liberty of Culture, a gathering of intellectuals "determined to resist totalitarian moves against free thinking."[1] Founded in 1950 in West Berlin with the financial help of the American government and the AFL-CIO, the congress prided itself for having among its honorary presidents the most respected members of the non-Marxist European intelligentsia, from Benedetto Croce and Bertrand Russell to Karl Jaspers and Jacques Maritain. *Preuves* published on a regular basis articles by the likes of Arthur Koestler or Ignazio Silone and brought together contributors of various political and ideological persuasions, from the far Right (Thierry Maulnier) to the reformist Left (André Philip), including liberals (Aron) and Christian Democrats, in a kind of anti-Stalinist *union sacrée.*

Reading the first issues of *Preuves* today, one is struck by the fact that most of the contributors, although favorable to North Atlantic solidarity, were far from being unconditional apologists of America. Devoted as they were to the rebirth and preservation of "the European spiritual community," they often were pragmatic Atlanticists, the pro-American side appearing to them, in the current state of international power relations, as the only real barrier against totalitarianism. The United States, however, was nevertheless a disquieting "big brother" to most of them. The Atlanticists' emphasis on the common political tradition of Europe and North America, that is, parliamentarian democracy, human rights, and the balance of powers—in no way implied a blind acceptance of the American way of life, which produced "cultural standards" rather than "rooted diversities," in the words of Denis de Rougemont: "Since the Stalinist threat loses its urgency in the cultural domain, an issue of a different order arises . . . namely the problem of American influence" (*Preuves*, 69).[2]

Most of the commentators in *Preuves* kept on repeating that Europe had to guard against playing, for the United States, the ancillary role devolved to Greece in the Roman Empire: "Let us not become somebody else's 'graeculi.'" As Raymond Aron, whom *Pravda* called (as it did Sartre, for that matter) a "neofascist" and a "U.S. agent," repeatedly stressed in those days, France needed to see itself not as the satellite or the client of the United States, but as its ally. The growing concern with the anticommunist hysteria that was developing on the other side of the Atlantic could not but strengthen the intellectuals' natural suspicion of any kind of ideological consensus manufactured and manipulated by the media. The European intelligentsia was not alone in this: during the McCarthy period, *Preuves* documented the ideological divisions of the public opinion in the United States and published several articles from prominent critics of the red scare, from Norman Mailer to Mary McCarthy. Reinhold Niebuhr was undoubtedly voicing the concerns of his European counterparts when he explicitly linked political conformism and technical civilization: "The mental hygiene of America is not only threatened by the mixture of power and insecurity which has become our destiny. Our culture is also threatened from the inside by our exclusive concern for technique" (*Preuves*, 50–51).[3]

The reader is hard pressed to find, even in the reviews most favorable to the Atlantic alliance, an unqualified endorsement of life in "outre-occident," as Georges Duhamel called prewar America. One can imagine, a fortiori, the feelings of the intellectual Left. In fact, 1950s anti-Americanism, far from breaking away from that of the 1920s and 1930s, took up most of the themes of the former period, adding as its own distinct contribution a political critique of American hegemony. The same individual could occupy, simultaneously or in succession, the various positions constitutive of standard Americanophobia: cultural criticism, neutralism, or oppositional Marxism. Such was the case of Sartre, who personified, in this area as in many others, the ideal of the left-wing intellectual.

America against the Intellectuals

I will focus my discussion of the postwar intellectuals' anti-Americanism on three of its major themes, which are closely interrelated in most of the texts of the period: (1) the manipulation of consciences by the mass media and the advertising industry, (2) the submission of creative activity to the demands of capitalistic competition and profitability, and (3) the issue of the radical difference between American civilization and European culture.

These motifs were far from being either new or especially French, even though the Cold War gave them a particular slant. Raised to the dignity of philosophical objects in Horkheimer and Adorno's *Dialectic of Enlightenment*, published in 1947 but written during the war, they were already present, as we saw, in prewar narrative constructions of America. The theme of the infection of Europe with the American virus in the writings of the physicians Céline and Duhamel surfaced again after the war, as in the following excerpts from the June 1952 issue of *Esprit:* "From the very beginning, we have denounced here ... the threats to the health of our country coming from American culture, which attacks at the root the originality and the mental and moral cohesion of European peoples" (quoted in Rougemont, *Preuves*, 69). Ironically enough, at the same time, American conservatives were trying to establish, via a redefinition of immigration visas, a kind of *cordon sanitaire* against the communist epidemic.

Most of the postwar writers were extremely critical of the cultural conformism that Tocqueville had called "the tyranny of public opinion," even if they were, like Camus, sensitive to the poetic quality of nights in New York City or, like Sartre, sympathetic to the openness of the American space or to "the truly humane kindness which characterizes class relations" in the United States. This awareness of the growing standardization and homogenization of styles of life and thought shows in the countless studies of advertising and the mass media, and the anxious examination of the *Kulturindustrie* anathematized by the Frankfurt school philosophers. In this sense, the 1950s continued and deepened the prewar concerns with the new status of signs and communication in Walter Benjamin's age of the technical reproduction of the work of art. The seminal role played by mass propaganda in Hitler's collective mobilization for war also explains the postwar sensitivity to the "authoritarian personality" and the spectacular manipulation of crowds.

During his first trip to the United States in 1946, Camus was surprised by the overwhelming presence of advertisements in American life: "Even the Salvation Army advertises. And in those commercials Army women have red cheeks and shiny smiles" (*Journaux de voyage*, 47). Sartre had also been struck by the power of advertising slogans and by the collective orchestration of consumptive behavior on a national scale. The United States had appeared to him as the land of the directed dream: In America . . . you are never alone in the street. The walls talk to you. To [the] left and right of you there are advertisement hoardings, illuminated signs and immense display windows . . . The nation walks about with you, giving you advice and orders" (*Literary and Philosophical Essays* [*LPE*], 105). This commercial pedagogy semed to Sartre to be all the more efficient as, unlike Nazi propaganda, it was "mild and persuasive. You encountered it everywhere, in the streets, in shops and on the radio, you felt everywhere "their effect upon you, like a warm breath." The ever-present image never does violence to the beholder, for "he *must* draw the conclusion *himself*. . . . There is no pressure put on him. On the contrary, the cartoon is an appeal to his intelligence. He is obliged to interpret and understand it. . . . It requires his cooperation in order to be deciphered. Once he has understood, it is as though he himself had conceived the idea. He is more than half convinced" (*LPE*, 106).

In 1954, André Siegfried, who had introduced French readers to the economic power of the United States a quarter of a century earlier, devoted a new volume, *America at Mid-Century*, to life in the New World. Siegfried wrote many pages on the modern manipulation and mystification of public opinion. The mass media, the main agencies of the production of conformism, were the perfect example of the double character of the American threat, both technical and ideological. Television shows and commercials were said to be essentially aimed at women and children, thus reinforcing the feminine, that is, sentimental and emotional, character of American culture and rewarding passivity and mental laziness and discouraging original thought. As for the technical ideology, it was a mixture of Prussian efficiency and Anglo-Saxon pragmatism:

> In this the American appears to us as Germany's star pupil. He has inherited from Germany, in addition to efficiency in organization, an almost fanatical respect for method, for objectivity, for Science and

everything which may claim kinship with it. The conscience (*Gründ-lichkeit*) and the objective spirit (*Sachlichkeit*) of the Germans are found in America, but with modification due to Anglo-Saxon common sense which German lack of proportion has never possessed. (354)

In his famous Pleyel address delivered on 5 March 1948, André Malraux contended that "European values are threatened from the inside by techniques born of the means of appealing to collective passions: newspaper, cinema, radio, advertising—in short the "means of propaganda," which are called, in nobler terms, "psychological techniques" (*Romans*, 171). When a journalist asked him in 1954 if the development of communications and the widespread diffusion of the written word was not a sign of cultural enrichment, Camus answered that "these mass media, as you say, go hand in hand with a degrading of values" (*Essais*, 1837). The values threatened by decadence were not only moral and political, but intellectual and aesthetic as well, and thus close to the professional interests and practices of artists and writers. Many of them agreed with Horkheimer and Adorno's view that "the spirit cannot survive when it is defined as a cultural good and distributed for consumption."

A similar pairing of the media and behavioral psychology as twin evils of Americanism occurs in Jean-Marie Benoist's *Pavane pour une Europe défunte*, a much more recent account of U.S. cultural hegemony. Picking up again the traditional theme of the similarities between the two superpowers, the author writes that

> the police brutality of the "Gulag," whose operation has been laid bare by Solzhenytsin in his explanation of how the cancer spreads throughout the social organism (a process prophesied Cassandra-fashion by Orwell in *1984*) is the counterpart, albeit assymetrical, of course, of the way the media and opinion polls are used as channels of propaganda by Atlantic imperialism in order to condition the people of Western Europe and the Mediterranean basin. (69)

Benoist goes so far as to equate "opinion polls and moronization through television" with the "physical aggression of napalm" in Southeast Asia as "terminal states of a Manichean logic" (105). Africa is next on the list, says Benoist, as witnessed by the way "African peoples during the recent Accra conference have tried to rebel against the pollution of American television and of its westerns, cultural models that ended up disorganizing the symbolic space of African cultures, focusing on the impossible television legend, a dissolved multitude of uprooted, disoriented viewers" (106).

Mass media and opinion polls, in their forms as well as in their contents, help to legitimize and popularize the "tyranny of normality" implied in the "midatlantic ideology," defined as "a strange mixture of an a priori and quasi religious definition of what is *proper*, suitable, and of an empirical determination of what is adapted" (107).

Two specters haunt the texts of the Cold War: the best-seller and the rewriter, both evil consequences of the disastrous influence that mass consumption has on the independence and quality of literary production. Capitalistic profit making and technical rationality, placed at the very heart of cultural practice, undermine the classical principles of the individual creation of a genuine piece of art: originality, stylistic concerns, constant reference to the tradition, whether one embraces or rejects it. The best-seller, unlike the original and personal chef-d'œuvre, which is written for the centuries, is tied to the market: it is content with following the recipes that have worked, it sacrifices form to communicability, and it is so absolutely new today only because it will be forgotten tomorrow. The rewriter, required by the publisher or the editor to adapt intellectually demanding texts to the "practical" tastes of the readers, calls into question the independence and the sacred character of the learned calling, while running roughshod over the private property rights of literary production.

Sartre vehemently protested the American version of his play *Les Mains sales*, staged in New York City as *Red Gloves*. "They're performing one of my plays in America in a version I have never read," he complained in *Combat* (27–28 November 1948). A few months later, given the negative reviews of the play in the United States, Sartre claimed that the American adapter had changed 90 percent of the original text. Among other momentous revisions, the new script had turned Hoederer, the forceful Lenin-like character who gets murdered in the play, into an elegant, refined politician who at some point in the play gives a long speech on Abraham Lincoln.

Denis de Rougemont, who certainly did not share Sartre's allergy to American culture, also denounced the arbitrary and sacrilegeous practice of rewriting. After one of his articles appeared in modified form in an American journal, Rougemont wrote the editors an indignant letter: "Dear Sirs, please consider the following sentence: reed, the weakest in nature, but it is a reed. The words are from Pascal, undoubtedly. But I strongly doubt that he would have agreed to sign them, the two significant elements of his sentence, man and thinking, having been deleted by the same 'editor,' obviously, who took such good care of my article" (86). Let us note in passing that the phrase Rougemont chose to make his point is borrowed from the most revered tradition. Writers in America seemed to be faced with a dilemma that ruled out the traditional role of the free creative spirit: either they agreed to conform their prose to the demands of the market, sacrificing at the same time the aesthetic criteria of *le bien-dire*, or they refused to compromise style and content and were sure never to reach a large audience.

In this respect, the 1950s witnessed a transition from what, in *Teachers, Writers, Celebrities*, Régis Debray has called, in a French context, the "publishing cycle" (where intellectual consecration took place within a somewhat restricted field, made up of literary salons, reviews, and prizes) to the "era of the media," which enlarged the cultural market and submitted it to different principles of selection, legitimation, and competitiveness. If a great number of today's artists and writers readily accept the logic of the production and diffusion of the best-seller, and obligingly play the game of media stardom, it was not yet the case thirty years ago: many prominent intellectuals considered with concern and reprobation the growing imposition of commercial and advertising norms upon aesthetic creation.

The political and economic struggles that took place between the communists and their fellow travelers, the Gaullists, and the Atlanticists around the issues of the North Atlantic Treaty Organization (NATO) and the Marshall Plan took, in the cultural sphere, the more philosophical form of a debate on whether American civilization did or did not belong to the Western tradition. André Malraux, Raymond Aron, and the Atlanticists of *Preuves* stressed the continuity between Europe and America, claiming that above and beyond their historical specificities, both worldviews shared a respect for individual liberties and human rights, an attachment to parliamentary democracy, and a reference to Judaeo-Christian ethics and value systems. At the onset of the Cold War, Malraux emerged as one of the most ardent proponents of the paradigm of cultural continuity. Consider the following remarks from his Pleyel address:

> In fact, America never conceived of itself, in the cultural realm, as a part of the world; it always conceived of itself as part of OUR world. There is not so much an American art as there are American artists. We share the same values; they do not have all that is essential to the European past, but everything essential they have is linked to Europe. Let me say it again: American culture, as distinct from ours as it is from Chinese culture, is a pure and simple invention of the Europeans. (*Romans*, 167)

André Siegfried, on the other hand, argued that ancient Greek culture and its European heritage (Renaissance and classicism) had had very little influence in the United States: "[America] needed a Montaigne, and all it had was an Emerson" (*America at Mid-Century*, 342). In American universities, the subordination of the humanities to scientific and technical disciplines, the cult of quantitative procedures (statistics, multiple-choice exams), and the obsession for method had led to the eclipse of European humanism: consequently, the United States needed "a strong diet of Classicism," and could not be compared to France, Poland, or Denmark. For Siegfried, America belonged to a distinct civilization, another stage of human development, characterized by the dominance of the collective over the individual, of consensus over critical consciousness, standardized output and method over unique and original creation, quantity over quality, the tool over its function, action over thought. Both the French and the Americans value savoir faire, but the former cherish the knowledge part of the compound, while the latter emphasize the practical half of it, eager as they are to put blueprints in action. Taylorization versus craftsmanship ("It takes some craft to make a book," La Bruyère used to say, "just as to make a clock"), expert versus *honnête homme*, homo faber against homo sapiens: if France was the paradise of the literati, the United States, then, must be their hell on earth.

In the scientific field, "pure" research (in mathematics, theoretical physics, or biology) is subordinated to its technical applications (electronics, computer science, or biotechnology). The French intellectuals' refusal to submit the activities of the mind to the demands of mass production and consumption explains why their anti-Americanism so often took the form of a critique of American professionalism. The French intelligentsia was all the more attached to its learned tradition—even when pretending to subvert or renounce it—since that tradition endowed its members with power and prestige. The hierachy of social and cognitive functions legitimized by the intelligentsia's value system asserted the superiority of "disinterested" creation over "application" and "vulgarization," of literary culture over scientific and technical knowledge. In America, on the contrary, the technician and the researcher were valorized at the expense of the contemplative virtues of the artist and scholar.

Denis de Rougemont thought that "the writer in the United States lives in a kind of social vacuum. He moves between everyday reality which puts him off, ignores him, makes no room for him, but from which he borrows his subject matter—and the commercial machine of publishing. Nothing sustains him. Everything attacks him—or pays him" (78).[4] Even Malraux had remarked in his afterword to *Les Conquérants* that "in the United States, the man of culture is not the artist, it is the academician; an

American writer—Hemingway, Faulkner—is not at all the counterpart of Gide or Valéry. . . . They are brilliant specialists, within a given culture: they are neither historical figures nor ideologues (169). Reduced by technical civilization to the organic function of the expert or the specialist, American intellectuals can never reach the same level of prophetic universality or of historical efficiency as their European counterparts.

The reign of the experts is never more pernicious than when they are called to reform the school system that has for centuries produced the elites of French high culture. In *Pavane pour une Europe défunte*, Jean-Marie Benoist denounces the fact that "American experts who know our country well but are bearers of a rationality which has nothing to do with our institutional oddities, laden with history and symbol" are charged with "pronouncing oracles on the prospects and tools of scientific research in France. . . . Used to a pragmatic and one-dimensional logic, incapable, with their brand-new intelligence, of assessing the value of our institutional archaisms," the experts, he goes on, "are proposing a functional redistribution that parcels out and distorts the baroque quality or monstrosity vital to intellectual life and aesthetic pleasure alike" (115). The same subservience to the "planning, programming, and budgeting system" religion worshipped at the Harvard Business School, Benoist argues, explains, together with economic competition, American hostility to the European supersonic transport (SST), "a challenge to one-dimensional profitability and productivism. . . . The arrogant *Le Concorde* is comparable to the towers built during the Quattrocento by the aristocracy of San Geminiano, [towers] vying in height and of no other use than to highlight the importance of the values of luxury, unproductive *dépense*, heraldic challenge of pure show, display of one's own motto over that of the others. There is no more room for such a thing in a world in which waste is only vulgar and ostentatious, and not, like Le Concorde, haughty and superb" (118).

The perception of the difference in status and power implied in the two definitions of intellectual practice could, in its most acute phases, become condescension for the social marginality and political helplessness of progressive intellectuals in the United States, as in Sartre's assessment of the plight of the American Left during the Vietnam war: "An American Leftist who sees his situation clearly, who sees himself isolated in a country completely conditioned by the myths of imperialism and anticommunism, I think this man, to whom I offer my respect, is one of the wretched of the earth. He totally disapproves of the policy being carried out in his name, yet his action, at least in the short run, is completely ineffectual" (quoted in Contat and Rykbalka, 463).

Simone de Beauvoir devoted many pages of *America Day by Day* to the plight of writers and artists in a professionalized and anti-intellectualist culture. She may not have met many blue-collar workers or Southern farmers during her trip to America, but she became acquainted with quite a few writers and critics, thanks to Ellen and Richard Wright, to whom she dedicated her book, and to Nelson Algren, with whom she eventually fell in love. She went to many parties in small apartments in Greenwich Village, discussing until the wee hours of the night the situation of labor unions or the stylistic value of the American thriller novel with renowned scholars and aspiring young poets and painters. What struck her above all was the American writer's "intellectual solitude" (85), from which the only escape is music, "essential like bread, the sole antidote to American conformity and boredom, the one outlet to life. . . . To grasp what jazz means for a young American writer one must understand the stifling routine and the despairing solitude of his days" (203).

The material and social environment in which intellectuals found themselves, the absence of networks of sociability and the atomizing effects of life in a huge metropolis, made it almost impossible for them to overcome their spatial and psychological isolation:

> In France, in Italy, in Spain, in Central Europe, the life of the café offers intellectuals and artists, after the day's work, the relaxation of companionship, the emulation and fever of conversation: there is nothing like that here. . . . In Paris literary life sometimes ends by giving a lead to literature itself (not a good thing); but the absence of literary life is altogether wrong and far more of a handicap. . . . Under these conditions, creative effort is very hard, when one is without friends or rivals. An unknown painter arouses interest neither in other painters, who are ignorant of his existence, nor in the enlightened public, since this public does not exist. (*America Day by Day*, 203)

Besides being marginalized by the pervasive anti-intellectualism of American life and isolated from each other by the sheer size of the country, creators are also exploited by a ruthless, profit-driven entertainment and advertising industry. Most publishers and newspaper managers share a deep scorn for both their product and their consumers; they arrogantly view the writer's gift in the same manner an impresario views the legs of a female dancer. Articles are paid by the word, like groceries by the pound, and one has the choice between writing good books in starvation or selling one's soul to Hollywood. "One can understand why Hollywood, with its mirage of easy success, is a dangerous temptation for the gifted writer. One must be very ascetic, and determined, to stay the pace. And this explains a phenomenon that worried me for some time: I mean that so many gifted writers, after producing a good book . . . are then silent for ever. One can cite a whole list of these infant prodigies. They are one of the most striking proofs of the possibilities to be found among individuals . . . and of the way in which American civilization has strangled them" (*American Day by Day*, 203).

Simone de Beauvoir's short and tense meeting with the editor-in-chief of a prominent newspaper puts in a nutshell the plight of the critical mind in the land of capitalism:

> The great man sat on the edge of his swivel chair; from the height of his power and the power of America he threw me an ironical look; so France amused itself with Existentialism? Of course he knew nothing of that, his scorn was aimed at philosophy in general, and even more at the audacity of a country that is economically poor and pretends to think. Is it not derisory to wish to think if one has not the advantage of being at the head of a great American newspaper, which in itself absolves one from having to think? . . . "Ah yes!" he said. "In France you ask questions, but you do not answer them. We do not ask them: we answer them. (38)

A conversation with famous columnist Elsa Maxwell did nothing to dispel the author's feeling that "America is hard on intellectuals." Upon seeing the series of "nasty stupid things" the editorialist had recently written on intellectual life in France, Simone de Beauvoir asked Maxwell if she had read any of the books she had so mercilessly torn apart. "In America," she said, "no one needs to read, for no one thinks. That's right. When you think you waste your time, it's anarchy. We do not think, and we don't need to because we have our instinct. Look at Truman: it is not that he thinks, but he has instinct. His policy is wholly successful because he has the right instinct" (*America Day by Day*, 136). Novelists themselves often share the general distrust for abstraction and speculative thought; hence the divorce between artists and their more theory-oriented counterparts, critics, scholars and academicians, which amounts to a sort of "class quarrel. . . . Most writers started as newspaper vendors or shoeshine boys, and got their culture in the course of life with all its ups and downs; conversely it is very rare for cultured men to write, at least to write books that appeal" to a large public (48). France, on the contrary, has enough intellectuals as it is, and the American writers' efforts to "integrate life in its crudest form in literature" is precisely what endears them to French readers.

Simone de Beauvoir had gone to the United States to give lectures on French philosophy. Her short visits to Vassar, Oberlin, Mills, Berkeley, UCLA, Rice, Smith, Wellesley, Yale, Princeton, the University of Pennsylvania, and Harvard prompted her to write ethnographic vignettes on American academia. In her eyes, the isolation of faculty members in the gilded ghettoes of elite institutions reduced them to the same state of powerlessness as writers and artists in New York or Chicago. Liberal students and professors alike watched with equal fatalism the assaults of Congress against the labor movement and the gradual spread of the Cold War mentality (*America Day by Day*, 78). The specialization of the curriculum widened the gap between the world of academia and society at large. Nothing could be farther from the existentialists' notion of *littérature engagée* than the genteel conception of humanistic pursuits as art for art's sake:

> To specialize in literature is something suspect: literary people are considered aesthetes, they themselves derive a certain glory from this name, and isolate themselves; nothing worries them more than the idea of literature "made to order," they loathe it. The realm of art, poetry and the word is cut off from the rest of the world in their opinion. (*America Day by Day*, 234)
>
> The result from this—at least in literature—is a precise divorce between university people and intellectuals. The reverse is true of my country, where they complain that too many writers are, or have been, professors. (235)[5]

The visitor also perceived that the American intelligentsia was not only divided according to practices, aesthetic or theoretical, but also along geographical lines, following a pattern of "intellectual regionalism. . . . Henry Miller has little importance in New York, but on the West Coast where he lives he is taken for a genius" (*America Day by Day*, 114). These differences made for a more complex picture of intellectual life than Europeans usually allowed; the countless discussions she took part in convinced Simone de Beauvoir that "American literature was a living reality, crossed by various currents which often conflict" (48). What American cultural producers, whether sculptors or philosophy professors, had in common, however, was their "intellectual defeatism," their inability to fulfill the symbolic function that Sartre, Camus, Malraux, or Simone de Beauvoir herself had recently claimed for themselves: that of spiritual guide and prophet *engagé*, following a national tradition that harks back to Voltaire, Hugo, and Zola. The historical specificity of the French literati, whether as counsels to the prince or as self-appointed representatives of the people, allowed them to have an impact on politics and culture than no American could ever dream of.

The postexistentialist generation of French intellectuals coming of age in the 1960s was also very aware of this crucial difference in the social roles of the intellectuals, even though some of them were starting to question the superiority of their national model. In the course of their discussion on political and cultural developments in the United States, which I examined in chapter 3, Philippe Sollers and Julia Kristeva also waxed eloquent on the purely technical role of the American intelligentsia. Isolated in its ivory towers and gilded ghettoes, its only involvement in politics consists in (merely) providing positivistic expertise as special counsel to the powers that be. In the words of Julia Kristeva:

> The role of the intellectual is defined differently in each case. The intellectual you describe is the technician, the specialist in foreign affairs, the sinologist or economist, etc. That does exist [in France] and, in fact that sort of collaboration between the government and the intellectuals would be the actual equivalent of a graduate of the Ecole Nationale d'Administration or of the Ecole Polytechnique working for the French government. But in the United States the intellectual doesn't cook up ideas, or act as a go-between for the masses, the media, the political parties and learning, as in Europe. (*The Kristeva Reader,* 278)

In the course of her debate with Sollers and Pleynet, Kristeva repeatedly stresses how sensitive she has been to the problem of the intellectuals during her stay in the United States. She comments time and again on the absence of an intellectual position comparable to the one that "probably derives from a kind of clergy, if we go back very far, but . . . essentially comes from the French Revolution's idea of the intellectual as mediator between the different political parties and thought" (*The Kristeva Reader,* 277). The gap between the critical intelligentsia and the political caste implies that "the intellectuals (apart from the Marxists) don't have ideas that can be politicized," since "positivism is the prerogative of the academic intellectual." The latter "does not see himself as entrusted with a political mission or when he does, it's under the auspices of Marxism, which is a recent trend, a return of everything McCarthyism repressed" (277).

Kristeva seems to espouse here the traditional antiprofessionalism of the universal intellectuals, characteristic of both the humanistic, conservative viewpoint and the critical revolutionary persuasion, that I have discussed at length. Her position, however, is not thoroughly and unquestionably dismissive, for it registers the emergence of new paradigms heralding the end of the Cold War of the intellectuals. In Kristeva's view, the ghettoization of American artists and intellectuals, their confinement in academic departments and bohemian sections of major metropolitan areas, is not entirely negative. Granted, the hemming in of critical and transgressive practices within specific enclaves has successfully prevented the rise of what she calls a specific intellectual caste, "heir to the bourgeois revolution and, perhaps, beyond that, to what is most corrosive in the spirit of monotheism (Judaism, Christianity)." By this she means the European secularized clerisy, whose function was to "introduce unrest, if not straightforward dissent, at all levels of the social structure" (*Polylogue*, 501).

Still, the marginalized, apolitical stance of both the experts and the creators does not mean for Kristeva that American society is a monolith, hermetically sealed from protest and change. Resistance to "the law" simply takes on another form: instead of being a direct assault on state power and its ideological instances, as in Europe, resistance disseminates itself within the various "areas reserved for transgression." If the notions of truth, law, and universality have been more weakened in America than in Europe, it is not "because they're attacked head-on and pursued in depth as, for example, would be done by any French intellectual shaken up by May 68. It's because they are multiplied" (*The Kristeva Reader*, 279). The result may not be as "radical in terms of thought," but it is "more efficient in terms of society as a whole." Besides, American academic life "even accords a place to European intellectuals, including all their radicalism," which is not the slightest of its advantages (279). Could postwar America then, have become the paradise of the (radical, continental) intellectuals? Not so, but it serves at least to highlight how European intellectual prophets have reached a historical stalemate: "The limitations of the intellectual's role in the United States, which I incidentally consider unsatisfactory, therefore serves to foreground some of the problems in the overexpansion of the 'intellectual vocation' of the Europeans which now is sinking its own ship, as it were" (278).

The Intellectuals against America

The specific form that the debate on the virtues and vices of American society took in French intellectual quarters, after World War II, acquires added meaning when related to the position French (and European) intellectuals occupied and to the set of interests they defended within the new international division of cultural production and consumption. The painful realization of the decline of European nations as dominant world powers colored the political and ideological atmosphere of the 1950s. The feeling was particularly prevalent among the cultivated elites, in part because of their deep scorn for mass culture made in the USA, and in part because they felt threatened by the growing influence and competition of the English language and of American cultural and literary products. In Raymond Aron's words, the intellectuals, as self-appointed legitimate advocates of the dignity of critical thought, "are more pained than simpler mortals by the hegemony of the United States" (*The Opium of the Intellectuals*, 217).

Cultural nationalism and elitism were at the core of the intellectuals' anti-Americanism after the war: both components explain the support the learned community gave the communist campaigns against America as a threat to the political and cultural identity of the French nation. As Pascal Ory and Jean-François Sirinelli aptly remark, "The American theme is . . . one the communist intelligentsia is sure will be met with the largest consensus since it is treated in a similarly negative manner, albeit in a more moderate form and with different arguments, by some members of the RPF [Gaullists]" (182), and, one might add, by many intellectuals of the non-Gaullist Right. In 1949, the Soviet exile Viktor Kravchenko filed a libel suit against the communist review *Les Lettres Françaises* for intimating that his best-selling autobiography *I Chose Freedom* was a pack of lies manufactured by American propaganda offices.

The passionate debates that followed, and the support given to *Les Lettres Françaises* by a large part of the noncommunist intellectual Left show that a slogan such as "Kravchenko against France" was sure to strike the corporatist and nationalist nerve of an embattled intellectual community beset by self-doubt. Ory and Sirinelli note that the Communist party appealed to old intellectual reflexes: (1) the "Dreyfus effect," associated with the apparently strictly ethical and humanitarian defense of a victim of the judicial system (here *Les Lettres Françaises*), and 2) the "sacred union effect," exemplified by the "constitution of a wide national front on the basis of the defense . . . of the cultural identity of the country" (182). Similarly, the 1946 Blum-Byrnes agreement, which made it easier to import American movies into France, was decried as a form of colonization and, because Hollywood productions were viewed as constituting unfair competition, as a threat to France's international role in matters of culture.

The United States, beyond its economic and technical predominance, was criticized for its claim to replace Europe as the center of democratic values and to be the legitimate political and ideological leader of the "free world." Immediately after the execution of Julius and Ethel Rosenberg, Sartre wrote an open letter to the American people in the left-wing daily *Libération* (22 June 1953). The title of the piece, "Les Animaux malades de la rage" (The animals infected with rabies), was patterned after La Fontaine's well-known fable, "Les animaux malades de la peste" (The animals struck by plague.) In his scathing attack, Sartre declared that "the execution of the Rosenbergs . . . is a legal lynching which has covered a whole nation with blood and proclaimed once and for all your utter incapacity to assume the leadership of the Western world" (quoted in *The Opium of the Intellectuals*, 224).

The editorial of the July 1953 issue of *Les Temps Modernes* struck a similar chord, calling the execution a "cold-blooded murder perpetrated by the Good and Just Ones, supported by the entire apparatus of law and morality," which helped one to "measure the breadth of the ignoble American self-righteousness." The editorial went on to challenge the American establishment to "go on, now, and speak in your own jargon of 'American leadership.' *Your* free world is not *ours*" (5).

A decade later, having caused quite a stir by refusing to speak at an American university, Sartre still denied the United States any legitimate claim to occupy a central position in international affairs:

> One should not consider America as the center of the world. It is the largest world power? Granted. But be careful. It is far from being its center. As a European, one has a duty not to consider it as the center, one needs to carry one's gaze, to manifest one's interest, to prove one's solidarity with all the Vietnamese, Cubans and Africans, all our friends in the Third World who are gaining their independence and freedom" (*Le Nouvel Observateur*, 1 April 1965).

Taking up in his own way the Maoist theme of the United States as a paper tiger, or the more classical one of the colossus with feet of clay, Sartre saw Third World anti-imperialist struggles as evidence that "the greatest world power is unable to impose its laws, that it is the most vulnerable one, and that the world did not choose it as its center of gravity." The man whom the world's progressive intelligentsia considered then as the universal consciousness of his times, as Marcuse used to say, undoubtedly found in this uncomprising stance, beyond the political and humanitarian motivations of his *prise de parole*, purely intellectual profit and gratification in fulfilling once again the prophetic function of the David of critical thought against the Goliath of philistinism and barbarity.

From Roosevelt to Castro: A Paradigmatic Trajectory

I devoted a good part of chapter 3 to Sartre's perception of the United States at the end of World War II. In the following years, his interpretation of American culture and society underwent a considerable evolution in relation to changes in domestic French politics and the international role of the United States. I quoted from texts published in the third volume of *Situations*, writings inspired by Sartre's two visits to America in 1945 and 1946. As we saw, these works constitute a kind of philosophical reporting, that is almost entirely focused on a critique of everyday Americanism. The philosopher had proposed an analysis of what he had called, in Hegelian terms, "the objective spirit of the United States," described as "a huge external apparatus, [a] pitiless machine, . . . [a] monstrous configuration of myths, values, recipes, slogans, numbers and rites" (*S III*, 126), a mixture of rationalism, "optimism à la Rousseau," puritanism, pragmatism and anti-intellectualism. Echoing in his own way Tocqueville's reflections on the tyranny of the majority in cultural matters, Sartre denounced the alienating effects of the ideological consensus that reigned unchallenged in the United States. He described it as an oppressive universe based on the manipulation of consciences by techniques of mass psychology and the control of the working class by means of a dense network of trade unions and civic organizations. The American tragedy (a motif one could find also in Albert Camus or Simone de Beauvoir's writings on the United States)[6] lay for Sartre in the desperate efforts of the American pour-soi's to wrench themselves free from the "system," efforts that resulted in a quasi-schizophrenic alienation, on which the new method of existential psychoanalysis could throw some interesting light.

In spite of this excessively dark picture of the American tragedy and of the psychopathological aspects of Americanism, Sartre always refuted the charges of anti-Americanism repeatedly brought against him. When *The Respectful Prostitute*, a drama inspired by the true story of nine African-Americans sentenced to death for having raped two white prostitutes, was first performed in Paris, his political opponents accused him of tarnishing the name of an allied nation which had just liberated France from the Nazis. The conservative writer Thierry Maulnier wrote in *Le Spectateur* (19 November 1946) that "this play in which, only two years after the liberation of Paris, we are shown Americans displaying the most repulsive ferocity, imposture, and hypocrisy, produces an almost intolerable discomfort. . . . If there had been an American soldier in the theater," Maulnier went on, "I would not have dared to look at him" (quoted in Contat and Rybalka, 138). To a reader of the *New York Herald Tribune* who also accused him of being anti-American, Sartre gave the following reply: "I am not anti-American. I don't even know what the word means. . . . It is true that if I had shown only the unsavory aspects of your civilization, it could have been said that I was against it. But I haven't. I have just devoted two whole issues of my review, *Les Temps Modernes*, to the United States" (139).

Sartre's relationship to the United States, however, quickly soured under the double influence of international developments and of his own re-reading of Marx. His cultural critique of the system of Americanism gave way to an increasingly violent denunciation of capitalist social relations and cultural, economic, and military imperialism. At the end of the 1940s, Sartre still believed in the virtues of neutralism and in the possibility of a third way, neither capitalist nor Stalinist, toward a "socialism of freedom." Those were the days (1950) when articles by the philosopher Maurice Merleau-Ponty, then still very close to Sartre politically, revealed in *Les Temps Modernes* the long-kept secret of Soviet labor camps. Those were also the days (1948–49) when Sartre actively supported the Rassemblement Démocratique Révolutionnaire, a political organization almost entirely made up, he said, of intellectuals committed to the triumph of "revolutionary democracy" and determined to avoid "the corruptions of capitalist democracy, the flaws and weaknesses of a certain sort of social democracy, and the limitations of Stalinist communism" (quoted in Contat and Rybalka, 208).

During this period, Sartre was particularly sensitive to the cultural effects of American hegemony, since his militant neutralism and his growing intellectual notoriety naturally led him to privilege the necessary preservation of the political and cultural integrity of Europe. In a 1949 lecture entitled "A Defense of French Culture by Means of European Culture," the philosopher insisted on the dangerous intellectual consequences of American technological penetration: "American ideology and culture will necessarily come to us with screws, manufactured goods, and canned fruit juice" (quoted in Contat and Rybalka, 226).

Before World War II, Sartre had enthusiastically welcomed the products of American popular culture, such as jazz, thrillers, and movies, which he contrasted with the academic and fossilized forms of the bourgeois humanistic culture of old Europe. In his 1945 articles on Hollywood, however, he contended that the quality of the American cinematographic production between the wars was largely due to the existence of a cultivated European audience, who had imposed a high standard of cultural demands on American moviemakers. The breakdown of this restricted elitist foreign market during the war, Sartre went on to argue, had ruined American cinema, now entirely dominated by the constraints of a domestic mass market and condemned to mediocrity and demagoguery: "The existence of a European audience . . . had called for the selection . . . and preservation . . of a high quality industry. Since the war broke out, the American public absorbs everything. Hence the growing temptation of facility rather than quality" (*Combat*, 27 March 1945). Now deprived of the quality standards demanded by sophisticated European audiences, American movies were once again making their way into the old continent, but this time they were targeting a totally different audience, namely the popular classes, which they would brainwash, stultify, and depoliticize.

If one wished to save French culture threatened with "Marshalliza-tion," the only solution was to seek its integration within a greater Euro-pean cultural ensemble and to turn a socialist and unified Europe into "an autonomous power which [would] not let itself be torn between American optimism and Russian scientism" (Sartre, quoted in Contat and Rybalka, 228). In fact, Sartre would quickly give up all hope in the viability of a third party outside Gaullism and Stalinism; in October 1949 he broke with the Rassemblement Démocratique Révolutionnaire, in part, it seems, be-cause of the financial ties that bound the organization to the AFL-CIO, compromising it with the anti-Soviet activities of the American labor movement of the day.

After a period of intense ideological disarray, during which, as Simone de Beauvoir noted in *Force of Circumstance*, he had "practically given up all political activity . . . [and] worked mainly in the fields of history and economics" (199), Sartre drew his own conclusions from the failure of *la troisième voie*. Giving in to the all-or-nothing logic of the times, which compelled everyone to choose sides (the Cold War, like Pascal's nature, held the void in horror), Sartre gradually grew closer to the French com-munists while reasserting his independence at every occasion. From 1952 until the Soviet repression of the Hungarian uprising of 1956, he danced an interesting, and convoluted, pas de deux with the Communist party, trying to define and fill out the uncomfortable space of what he called his *ralliement critique* (critical rallying). He was careful not to alienate Boul-ogne-Billancourt (the communist working-class stronghold in the recently nationalized Renault factories outside Paris). At the same time, he was bent on underlining the philosophical differences that separated him from the many versions of what has since been called "vulgar" or "positivistic" Marxism (economism, the cult of personality, Zhdanovism, socialist real-ism, proletcult, *diamat* orthodoxy, etc.).

On the home front, Sartre repeatedly embraced the communist cause during the frequent crises and conflicts that made of 1952 one of the hot-test years of the Cold War. He rallied to the defence of Henri Martin, a young soldier sentenced to five years in prison for giving out leaflets against the war in Indochina, and "l'affaire Henri Martin" became to him what "l'affaire Callas" had been to Voltaire, who had denounced as an injustice the condemnation of a young Protestant falsely accused of having killed his father. Sartre actively supported the communist leader Jacques Duclos, who had also been jailed following a demonstration against the visit to Paris of General Ridgway, Eisenhower's successor as head of the allied forces in Europe. Meanwhile, on the international front, fellow traveling had led Sartre to an increasingly critical view of American foreign policy, from the Marshall Plan to the Korean War. As already mentioned, he also rose to the defense of the Rosenbergs, calling all Europeans to withdraw from the influence of the United States, for fear of being contaminated by the virus of American culture. "Do not be surprised," he told the American public, "if you hear us shouting from one end of Europe to the other: 'Watch out, America has got rabies.' We must cut ourselves off from her or else we'll be bitten and infected ourselves" (quoted in *The Opium of the Intellectuals*, 225).

During the following years, Sartre persisted in his opposition to the United States as an economic and military power and to America as an alienating and demobilizing civilization that strangled freedom and revolutionary praxis. His opposition to the Marshall Plan, fellow traveling with the French communists, participation in the Soviet-backed Peace Movement and the Peoples' Congress in Vienna, support of Algerian Independence and of the Cuban Revolution, and his frequent, highly publicized trips to Moscow, Beijing, and Havana, all marked Sartre's growing involvement in anti-imperialist struggles. In 1965, in a conversation with Greek musician Mikis Theodorakis, Sartre took up again the issue of the three sides of imperialism (economic, cultural, and political) that had been so popular in the early years of the Cold War. "To permit the imposition of an alien culture," he said, "is to agree to live someone else's life," that is, to experience alienation, in the root sense of the term. France, he went on, suffers like Greece from the Americanization of culture and from depersonalization (quoted in Contat and Rybalka, 474). In consequence, the French and the Greeks "share a common struggle" to advance the three objectives of the progressive agenda in the age of pax Americana: economic democracy, political sovereignty, and the preservation of national cultures. By the mid-1960s, Sartre would have been hard pressed, despite his denials, to find anything positive in the United States. Even the vocal minority of liberal and radical opponents to the Vietnam War did not seem to him to offer any credible challenge to the overwhelming power of Americanism as ideology.

The year 1965 seems to have been a turning point in Sartre's political journey. As Francis Jeanson noted, it marked the end of his "many efforts to 'do the splits' between the two super-powers" (224): he would from now on refuse to visit either the Soviet Union or the United States. Sartre may have come to grips with the ultimate consequences of his rejection of the "logic of the blocks" during the Cold War period. That same year, he emerged as one of the staunchest opponents to the United States' policy in the Far East. In 1966, the British philosopher Bertrand Russell decided to set up an International War Crimes Tribunal specially directed against the American military involvement in Southeast Asia. Sartre took part in the project from the onset and was soon elected executive president. In this capacity, he was asked in 1967 to find enough evidence to back up claims by the Tribunal that the United States government and armed forces were committing genocide in Vietnam. Sartre's report, entitled "Vietnam: Imperialism and Genocide" first appeared in English in the *New Left Review* (vol. 48, 1968).

Also in 1965, Sartre refused, as a protest to the war in Vietnam, to give a series of lectures on Flaubert and on philosophical topics at Cornell University. Responding to David Grossvogel, a Cornell professor who had criticized him for ignoring American reality and for substituting hatred for understanding, Sartre denied once again, in his typically sarcastic manner, being an unconditional foe of the United States: "It is easy, but absurd, to say that hatred explains my refusal [to go to Cornell]: I feel no hatred for anybody; and especially not for two hundred million people: that would exhaust me" (*S VIII*, 26). The philosopher justified his post-1945 change of mind in the following manner: "I did go to the United States in the past. I had friends there, but it was different. America was coming out of the war and even if I did not approve of everything I saw, it was not the same. Today we are talking about a clear, cynical, deliberate act of aggression [against North Vietnam]" (*S VIII*, 18).

"It was not the same": the myth had failed to deliver its promises. In 1945, the United States had been a progressive nation. Despite all its shortcomings, Americanism meant the victory over Nazism and the hope of a new democratic world order. Twenty years later, the tables were turned: as Sartre pointed out, in the eyes of "any intellectual on the side of the Third World," U.S. policy in Southeast Asia represented an attack on the rights of nations to determine freely their own fate and a desperate effort to reverse the march of history. The Monroe Doctrine, Sartre quipped, used to mean that America belonged to the Americans. Now, it meant that Latin America belonged to North Americans. The philosopher, of course, did not deny the existence of strong progressive forces within the United States; he even praised the civil rights movement for the courage of its members and its considerable gains. What was true of domestic issues did not apply to foreign policy, however. The more liberal the Johnson administration appeared on the home front, the more reactionary were its policies in Southeast Asia, and Sartre was highly skeptical of the impact of the emerging antiwar movement. As already mentioned, he wrote in *Le Nouvel Observateur* that "an American leftist who clearly sees his situation, who sees himself isolated in a country entirely conditioned by the myths of imperialism and anticommunism . . . is one of the wretched of the earth" (quoted in Contat and Rybalka, 463).

These pessimistic and somewhat derogatory comments caused quite a stir, as one can imagine, in American liberal and progressive intellectual circles. In April 1965, *The Nation* printed an English version of the *Nouvel Observateur* interview, prefaced by an editorial blaming the French thinker, labeled "Europe's most tough-minded critic of America," for having misjudged public opinion in the United States and having undervalued the power of the antiwar movement. A few weeks later, in May 1965, Sartre, who must have assessed by then the damaging impact of his statements, released some of the tension by sending a cable to the organizers of a teach-in on Vietnam at Boston University. He expressed his sympathy for their struggle and hoped that they would be more successful than the French intellectuals who had opposed the war in Algeria: "As for us, in spite of our efforts, we did not succeed in mobilizing our public opinion. . . . I wish you better luck than we had and ardently hope that you succeed. . . . But even if you do not succeed, your demonstrations will not be in vain. They are occuring at a time in history when irresponsible men are presenting an odious image of your country to the world, and they help us see that this image is false and that the coming generation is determined to disassociate itself from it completely" (quoted in Contat and Rybalka, 467). Sartre ended his message on a more hopeful note: "When your youth, formed by courageous teachers, is of age to take over the management of affairs, there will be every reason to hope that a profound change will take place in the United States and in the world" (*The Nation*, 31 May 1965:574).

Pointing out that "countries as well as men can be ostracized," *The Nation*'s commentator called Sartre's telegram "the most cordial statement he had made of late on the United States." It would have been perhaps more accurate to say "in the past twenty years." Sartre's refusal to set foot in America was more than a simple case of unfair generalization, of confusing the American people as a whole with the government or the armed forces of their country. *The Nation*'s editorialist had been right to call Sartre the toughest-minded critic, not only of the Johnson administration, or even of big business, but of American civilization as a whole. As I have already argued, he had made up his mind as early as 1946 that the "system of Americanism" was much more efficient than European, Latin American, and Asian societies in defusing criticism, reducing difference (of color, gender, opinion, or praxis) into another dimension of the same, and cornering oppositional forces into a hopeless and wretched state of political helplessness. The moralistic conformism of Americanism was to him the antithesis of his own intellectual project as a model of critical consciousness. In 1968, Sartre had come all the way around, back to his criticism of both superpowers in the early days of the Cold War. In a letter called "On Spheres of Influence," written with Bertrand Russell and other prominent intellectuals, he denounced both the United States and the Soviet Union as equally threatening to freedom and sovereignty everywhere: "It is essential that this identity of interest between American capitalism and the Soviet bureaucracy be clearly understood and fought" (quoted in Contat and Rybalka, 534).

The anti-intellectualism of a large portion of the political establishment and of public opinion in the United States during the Cold War (campaigns against Adlai Stevenson and his fellow "eggheads," witchhunts in academic and artistic circles, etc.) could only fuel the traditional resentment of the French intelligentsia against the bourgeois philistinism and Puritan crusading spirit to which they often reduced American culture. The anti-Americanism of the 1950s and early 1960s appears in this regard as one of the many forms taken by the ceaseless war waged by modernist French writers, from Diderot and Baudelaire to Céline and Sartre, against bourgeois moralism and clerical traditionalism. To criticize the America of Joe McCarthy and "Ridgway la peste" (the Ridgway plague), of Hollywood and Coca-Cola, was a way for the intellectuals to have it both ways. They reaped the benefits attached to the legitimate support of oppressed nations and classes in the eyes of progressive public opinion, *and* they secured the symbolic rewards bestowed by the enlightened public upon the scornful indictment of mass (non) culture. Raymond Aron, who, as self-appointed critic of the intellectual Left during the "Sartrean years" enjoyed an unobstructed view on the aporias of the opposing camp, could easily lampoon the contradictions and acute case of Sartrean bad faith displayed by the *double langage* (doublespeak), both populist *and* elitist, of the intelligentsia: "But why do the intellectuals not admit to themselves that they are less interested in the standard of living of the working class than in the refinements of art and life? Why do they cling to democratic jargon when in fact they are trying to defend authentically aristocratic values against the invasion of mass-produced human beings and mass-produced commodities?" (*The Opium of the Intellectuals*, 228)

At the time, the combined indictment of American economic imperialism and cultural hegemony enabled one to keep together Marx and Flaubert, Baudelaire and Flora Tristan (or Artaud and Aragon), to weave for a little while longer the two major, but not always compatible (as evidenced by the communist rejection of modern art as the expression of "petty bourgeois intellectual decadence"), strands of modernity: the political and economic critique of capitalism, on the one hand, and the philosophical and aesthetic attacks on bourgeois moralism and philistinism, on the other. We may be witnessing today (and that could be one of the meanings of *postmodern*), the fateful coming apart of these two historical trends, the uneasy alliance of which has shaped the European critical tradition. Today, art no longer claims to change the world, and politics has definitely lost its romantic aura.

FIVE

POETICS OF SPACE
The Body of America

▼

Isn't the west the home, the true homeland of men of desire? *Paul Claudel*

When one arrives in the United States one drifts around very easily, with a liberty found absolutely nowhere else, simply because there are so many discourses and their subjects are multiple. You can always leave a milieu, abandon a discourse to enter another. *Marcelin Pleynet*

To its European settlers, however, America did not connote society, or history, but indeed in its natural parameters, geography. America was an avatar of the world prior to feudalism, and, in the sense that it still awaited its primal molding, it was anterior to the world's divisions. *Myra Jehlen*

I am glad on the whole that my lot is cast in a land where life doesn't wait upon death, and where consequently no natural but only artificial picturesque is possible. *Henry James, Sr.*

My own quarrel with America, of course, was that the geography is sublime, but the men are not. *Ralph Waldo Emerson*

While America's industrial, urban civilization found few supporters among the French intelligentsia up to the 1960s, the unsoiled, unspoiled beauty of the land has always inflamed the French imagination, prompting a host of impassioned, lyrical celebrations of unlimited space and exhilarating vistas. Not that many of these texts, mostly the work of poets, did not retain a fundamental ambiguity toward the New World. The exaltation of the land often derived its evocative force from the contrast between the pristine stretches of wilderness and the mechanical and commercial civilization always threatening to destroy them for ever. The canonical opposition between nature and culture indeed structures most of the texts I consider here, but, all in all, the enthusiasm generated by the raw energy and boundless generosity with which their authors endow the body of America makes for a much more positive, at times almost Whitmanian, description of the New World. The sad story of the domestication and commodification of the American wilderness is not enough to dampen the romantic spirit of awe and thanksgiving that seizes the French traveler at the sight of a continent so vast and so inhuman. The redemptive and liberating power of the land is so great that even cities may, in privileged moments of epiphany, become wild again, and display some of the poetic magic of the virgin spaces.

Natural Simulacra

Michel Butor's *Mobile: Study for a Representation of the United States,* published in France in 1962, is an interesting attempt to match the written text of the poem with the overpowering diversity and boundlessness of the American landscape. The book is an ambitious collage, a patchwork of America made up of the alphabetical litany of the fifty states and containing a hodgepodge of seemingly unrelated notations on topics such as flora, fauna, meteorological conditions, flavors of Howard Johnson's ice cream, geological formations, colorful individuals met on the way, cars, gas stations, narratives of Indian folklore and history, extensive quotes from Franklin's autobiography, and even excerpts from a mail order catalog. The temporal distribution of the text (in typical *nouveau roman* manner) matches its spatial structure, since each state, or chapter, corresponds to a particular hour, from midnight in Alabama to midnight again, mountain time, in Wyoming two days or some fifty hours later.

Since one of the many narrative voices obviously belongs to the driver of a car (hence the constant allusions to other drivers and names of gas stations such as "Caltex" or "Flying Service," where motorists, we are told, will have to stop to fill up) and since the reader herself is on the road, crossing one state line after another, the most obvious form of relationship to space in *Mobile* is that of tourism. Parts of the poem do indeed sound like the slick brochures printed by state or local agencies to tout the merits of their region's climate and historic landmarks. Apprehended through the tourist's viewpoint, the American space often appears domesticated, dominated, and sterilized by the demands of consumerism and commercialism. The wonders of nature are made into a spectacle, turned into commodities, endlessly reproduced and serialized in the form of simulacra. Through the Sears and Roebuck mail-order catalog, which symbolizes the imperatives of advertising and commercialization, one can acquire various signs of the natural order, monkeys or guinea pigs, an eighteen-month-old Mexican burro, (*Mobile*, 55), huge posters of "idyllic American landscapes" such as the Grand Tetons or Florida's Cypress Gardens "to transform your wall into a window open onto the world," or even a lamp with a revolving action scene depicting Niagara Falls (103–4).

In *America Day by Day*, Simone de Beauvoir resents the way that the staging of the Grand Canyon for the tourist's gaze dwarfs its majestic beauty, as if its inhuman proportions were too awesome to bear:

> Here I find the same climate as at Niagara: they have made most ingenious efforts to change the marvels of nature into a kind of Luna Park. . . . In a circular room on the ground floor the windows are so arranged as to reflect the scenery; I do not know just how they absorb the light, already over-tense: in place of direct vision, so crude and violent, they have substituted a "conditioned" view with filtered colours. (141)
>
> The tourist is offered every means of assimilating by various devices, this scene which is in itself almost too natural; in the same way they get "conditioned" air, frozen meat and vegetables. . . . Americans are nature-lovers: but they only admit of nature proofed and corrected by man. (142)

Similarly, Hollywood has forever robbed the most photographed scenery in the world of its capacity to generate wonder. The European visitor has seen so many western movies with mesas and canyons in the background, so many thrillers set in the sun-drenched foothills of California that she cannot prevent those images from superimposing themselves on reality, the copy spoiling what is no longer the original. Furthermore, the California landscape has served to depict other parts of the world, in a further twist of duplicitous duplication:

> The Whitney chain provides Hollywood with likenesses of Switzerland, the Himalayas and the Caucasus. A little further on there is Africa with its sandhills, and the Australian bush. The miracle is that this same Tibet, this illusory Switzerland, are authentic bits of the planet. (123).
>
> Beyond the oasis the valley dips below sea level. It is there that Von Stroheim shot the last scenes of one of his films. Just as one sees Holland through the eyes of her painters, . . . so one discovers California through the screen. (125)

As for Williamsburg, it looks "like second-rate scenery built of cardboard" (195), devoid of any poetry or authenticity, Rockefeller having decided to destroy all the remnants of the past which could not find a place in the reconstructed site. The true past has to make room for the effects of truth generated by its unauthentic replica.

In a New York restaurant overlooking Central Park, huge mirrors allow the patrons who could not sit by the window to enjoy the reflection of the breathtaking view as trompe l'œil, for want of the real thing (197). After a few days spent with her friend in an artists' community in New Mexico, the narrator remarks how the former city dwellers try to imitate and reproduce Indian lore in their dress and art, without, however, going beyond the mere aesthetization of ancient civilizations (157). In another passage, she lists all the exotic Others of the American way of life, all these dead or marginalized cultures displayed in the innumerable curio shops that are strategically placed along the main tourist routes. In the East, the other is the Californian Eden, in California, it is Mexico, in the Southwest, Indian folklore, in Louisiana, the remnants of the French influence. But these quixotic others are never confronted in their radical and unsettling difference, they are always tamed, reappropriated through the reassuring staging of the tourist industry.

There is indeed some charm in this humanization of nature, for everything is filtered through the eyes of traveling companions. In a sense, since the American space has never really been settled and colonized, at least to the extent that it has in Europe or Asia, there is no humanized, historicized middle-ground between the sacred grandeur of the wilderness and its reduction by the mobile gaze of the uprooted tourist passing through. In the absence of any stable, enduring historical referent, America is always already its own representation: "Tourism in America is something privileged, it does not cut you off from the country it would show you. On the contrary, it is a means of access. . . . This Far West country which we were exploring has a definite tourist existence. Hardly anyone lives there, and they derive their sole human significance from those who pass through them without stopping" (*America Day by Day,* 131).

In Butor's *Mobile,* the commodification of time and space obeys a similar logic of representation. Indian cultures are turned into shows (82), the Richmond, Vermont, Museum of Natural History has a "splendid full-size wax replica of a blooming magnolia" (298), and in Los Angeles' Brookdale Cafeteria the visitor can admire a "diorama of a sequoia forest" and a faithful representation of the Garden of Gethsemane (299). Freedomland, an entertainment park in New York City, symbolizes the compulsive attempt to bring together in one single space the multiplicity of past events and distant lands. "Excitement! Adventure! Education! Cross the centuries from Colonial New England to the pioneer West, from Mexican border towns to Great Lakes ports, from Cape Canaveral to the Northwest Passage. . . . Over forty authentic themes to make history live again at Freedomland!" (192).

In a sense, Butor's narrative itself vies with Freedomland in this effort to totalize reality past and present, to exhaust, through the encyclopedic accumulation of details, anecdotes, trivia and the display of erudition, the multiplicity of being. The poem itself, in its very structure (each chapter covers a state of the union) encompasses the whole of American space and tries to account for the totality of the prehistory, history, and even future of the American continent. The book itself, then, becomes the diorama of America, a 360-degree grand spectacle in 3D. In *Mobile*, just as in Freedomland, one can hear the cries of the seagulls, the crash of the surf, the rumbling of thunder, the war chant of the Sioux, and even the earnest advice of Benjamin Franklin. The total poetics of America delivers what is promised in the Freedomland brochure: "Among the more exotic plants are buffalo grass and rare water lilies, palm trees, birds of paradise, New Zealand flax, orchids and banana plants—all blossoming in their 'natural habitats.' The duplicated Kansas farm area has a full-size corn field, complete with ears of corn on the stalks" (*Mobile*, 191).

Umberto Eco has offered, in *Travels in Hyperreality*, his own brilliant account of the various iconic landscapes of the American hyperreal, from holographic images to wax museums, from Disneyland to haunted houses to Marine World. Althougy Eco, admittedly, is not French, his vision, like Butor's and Beauvoir's, is one of a culture obsessed with realism, iconic representation, perfect likeness, and all-consuming syncretism. The Lyndon B. Johnson Library, the Hearst Castle, or the Getty Museum are all expressions of the "reconstructive neurosis" that holds parts of the American taste and imagination in its grip, and shows in the excessive attention to details, the overriding concern for authenticity and "the real thing," and the obsession for the total disclosure of meaning through the extermination of ambiguity.[1]

In reference to the Hearst Castle in San Simeon, California, Eco remarks that "the striking aspect of the whole is not the quantity of antique pieces plundered from half of Europe, or the nonchalance with which the artificial tissue seamlessly connects fake and genuine, but rather the sense of fullness, the obsessive determination not to leave a single space that doesn't suggest something, and hence the masterpiece of bricolage, haunted by *horror vacui*, that is here achieved" (23). The visual, theatrical character of the popular representations of distant lands and times suggests that in America "knowledge is only iconic," pointing to a philosophy of immortality as duplication, of history as reincarnation. The fact that a private home seventy years old is already archaeology, or that 1970s songs are already oldies but goldies tells us a lot, says Eco, "about the ravenous consumption of the present and about the constant 'past-izing' process carried out by American civilization" (9).

In the Museum of the City of New York, like in Butor's Freedomland, the reverence for kitsch and the "authentic" reproductions of historical documents gives the visitor the impression of "entering and leaving time in a spatial-temporal haze" (Eco, 11), where the centuries are confused. The obsessive concern for accurate replication (the diorama as substitute for reality) and the collapse of the distance implied by aesthetic or historical knowledge are products of the democratic ethos: everything and everyone has a right to be reproduced, regardless of their ontological status, of their belonging in real or possible worlds. "Another characteristic of the wax museum is that the notion of historical reality is absolutely democratized: Marie Antoinette's boudoir is recreated with fastidious attention to detail, but Alice's encounter with the Mad Hatter is done just as carefully" (Eco, 14). The principle of epistemological tolerance and ontological equality that guarantees the fundamental right to be replicated to Hop O'My Thumb and Fidel Castro alike distinguishes the American pop museum from its European counterparts, and especially from its possible models in German and Flemish baroque religious art (America's exacerbated realism, Eco suggests, may reflect the Middle European taste of various waves of immigrants).

In a sense, then, the obsession for detail and the desire for the exact reconstitution of the past, in its temporal and spatial dimensions, could be construed as a desperate response to the emptiness of the American space, as an effort to counter the erasure of memory and meaning that the archaic, primeval land always threatens to render absolute. In fact, most European narratives of America tell us that the domestication of the primeval, although it may parallel the dissolution of the self, does *not* counter or reverse its effects by magically restoring the historical consciousness that had been previously erased. For the "authentic" sense of the past—equated by European writers with being European, of course—can never be retrieved in America. The crossing of the Atlantic, like the passage of a modern Lethe, means forgetting the Old World, which cannot be remembered, let alone conjured up or resurrected, but only simulated.

The iconic knowledge embodied in posthistorical landscapes such as amusement parks or living history museums dominates, in Eco's words, "the relation with the self, with the past, not infrequently with the present . . . and even, with the European tradition" (6). Eco very perceptively remarks that there are, in our contemporary iconic culture, "subtle links between the worship of Nature and the worship of Art and History" (53). Indeed, the process of derealization through hyperrealization does not apply only to the past, to distance in time, but also to remoteness in space and to the threatening difference of nature:

> Not only far-off Africa but even the Mississipi must be re-experienced, at Disneyland, as a reconstruction of the Mississipi. It is as if in Rome there were a park that reproduced in smaller scale the hills of the Chianti region. But the parallel is unfair. For the distance between Los Angeles and New Orleans is equal to that between Rome and Khartoum, and it is the spatial, as well as the temporal, distance that drives this country to construct not only imitations of the past and exotic land but also imitations of itself. (53)[2]

Earth, Winds, and Fire

The dominant mood of Butor's or Beauvoir's account is not merely the detached irony of Eco's narrative. A strong romantic current runs through most French celebrations of the American land. There is often more at stake here than mere fascination for the mobility of signs, images, and surface effects: there is genuine awe and a keen sense of the sacred character of an indomitable power. For the paradox of Europe's America, and the source of its fascinating spell on the imagination of the Old World, is that the relentless efforts of the people to tame the energy of the land and reduce its threatening diversity to the comfort of conformity are perceived to have failed, again and again. The American way of life, which most French authors reject for its monotony and ennui, is also constantly threatened by that sublime power, nature, which the poets will harness to their own endeavors and which will, in turn, vindicate them. Below the surface networks of interstate highways and Howard Johnson's restaurants, of yesterday's telegraphs and the fax machines of today, the formidable, relentless resistance of nature to the veneer of civilization is at work, as in the hyperealistic painting that shows tropical plants and wild animals claiming their own, taking over the broken, useless freeways of a deserted city in the wake of what must have been a nuclear catastrophe. "The Europeans," Butor wrote, "have covered the plains with a thin film like a layer of paint, in which the reservations make snags" (Mobile, 59).

169

Lyrical celebrations of the land as generous, fertile, prolific good mother abound in twentieth-century French accounts of the American landscape, echoing, without the moralistic tone, eighteenth-century primitivistic mythologies of the New World. In these tales, the redeeming virgin land is a place where degenerate and evil Europeans could be cleansed of their sins and reborn in wisdom and virtue, as new Adams, through frequent contacts and exchanges with noble savages. In a famous passage of *Atala*, for example, Chateaubriand mobilized all the resources of his craft to match the sublime, edenic majesty of the shores of the Meschacebe:

> Savannahs spread out as far as the eye can see, and their verdant swells, receding in the distance, seem to rise into the blue of the sky where they fade from view. In these endless prairies herds of three or four thousand wild buffaloes wander about aimlessly. . . . Down avenues of trees, bears may be seen drunk with grapes. . . . Green parrots with yellow heads, crimson-tinged woodpeckers and fire-bright cardinals spiral up to the tops of the cypresses. . . . Should any breeze happen to stir up these solitudes . . . then there emerge from the depths of the forest such sounds, and the eyes behold such sights, that it would be futile for me to attempt their description to those who have never themselves passed through these primeval fields of nature. (18–19)

A large part of Butor's *Mobile* also evokes America's luscious flora and wondrous fauna. One of the recurrent motifs of the poem is a reference to Audubon's portraits of native American birds. The objective, purely descriptive tone of the vignettes underscores the mysterious and awe-inspiring remoteness, the dignified and unsullied aloofness of the birds, pure of any human presence, save that of the painter himself. "John James Audubon painted the hooded warbler twice, calling it by different names, first alone on a stem of pheasant's eye, then with its mate on a plant with blue flowers and large seed-pods" (58).

Saint-John Perse, for his part, was particularly sensitive to the paradisiacal profusion of plants and flowers that bloomed in the hothouse of the Deep South, inspiring some of his most beautiful versets, as in the opening lines of "Rains":

> The banyan of the rain takes hold of the City,
> A hasty polip rises to its coral wedding in all this milk of living water
> . . .

Hatching of golden ovules in the tawny night of the slime
And my bed made, O fraud! on the edge of such a dream,
Where the poem, obscene rose, livens and grows and curls

(Exile and Other Poems, 55)

Perse was also an expert on birds, and his poetry constantly draws on his wide ornithological knowledge, wide enough to challenge Audubon on his own turf: "And all your painted birds are not enough, O Audubon, but I must still add to them some species now extinct: the Passenger-Pigeon, the Northern Curlew, and the Great Auk" *(Winds,* 149).

The American space derives its sacred, sublime character from the fact that its elemental grandeur leaves no room for the autonomy of the human. What distinguishes the Indians is that they never set themselves apart and against the natural order, while the European settlers indulged in the gesture of hubris and defiance known as civilization. It is through the gigantic, superhuman interplay of minerals, waters, and winds that the continent reaches its true cosmic dimension. While the aerial and aquatic elements testify to the mobility of America, the mineral realm will serve to symbolize, through the recurrent motif of the desert, the disorienting and purifying effect of the American experience on the foreigner's mind.

I have already mentioned the importance of the elements and of climactic considerations in Butor's *Mobile.* It is in Saint-John Perse's work, however, that the elemental mobility of America acquires an epic dimension. The first three poems Perse wrote after his forced exile to the United States (following France's occupation by the Nazis), are suffused with images of natural phenomena as symbols of metaphysical concerns. *Exile,* written in 1941, while the poet lived in a beach house on Long Beach Island, makes ample use of the imagery of sea and sand to explore the various aspects of his separation from his homeland. Particularly significant in this respect is the theme of the beach as threshold, or passage, between two worlds, and of the ocean as both separating and uniting the two shores of the poem's (and the poet's) transatlantic space. Paradoxically, "the shore of exile" is also the "native shore" to which the poet is "restored," since, born in the Guadeloupe in the French West Indies, he grew up in the New World before experiencing his first displacement and relocation on the old continent.

The age-old break of the surf becomes the all-encompassing element of the experience of exile, which is at once heart rending and fulfilling, since it gives rise to an unexpected burst of creative energy (Perse had not published any poetry since 1924): "There has always been this clamour, there has always been this grandeur, / This thing wandering about the world, this high trance about the world, and on all the shores of the world, by the same breath uttered, the same wave uttering / One long phrase without pause forever unintelligible" (*Exile and Other Poems* [*EOP*], 15). In his introduction to the 1973 edition of *Exile*, Roger Little points out that "the versets are felt to break with the rhythmic regularity of waves. No two waves break in exactly the same way; no two lines of the poem have the same rhythmic effect. The interplay of incoming waves and receding wavelets has a fascinating complexity within a clear general pattern" (15). Perse himself referred in a letter to Archibald MacLeish to his poem's "alliterations, assonances and incantations, constrained by the rhythm of the waves" (quoted in Little, 15).

"Rains," written during a 1943 trip to Georgia, also stresses the affinities between the liquid element, which was to become one of the main elements of Perse's private mythology of America, and the cleansing, liberating power of poetic writing. Like a torrential shower of summer rain, the forces of language are let loose onto the world, bringing both destruction and fecundity, "foam on the lips of the poem like milk of coral rocks!" (*EOP*, 57). *Snows*, written in New York City in 1943, confirms the cosmic dimension of the poet's experience of America and explores more subtle and aerial modes of inspiration, such as the unexpected, unforeseen deluge of words, immaterial as snowflakes, coming upon the world—as Nietzsche said of worthy ideas—on little doves' feet. "None has surprised, none has known, at the highest stone frontal, the first alighting of this silken hour, the first light touch of this thing, fragile and so trifling, like a fluttering of eyelashes" (81).

It is in *Winds*, Saint-John Perse's best known poem of America (written off the coast of Maine in 1945), that the liberating mobility of the New World as cosmos finds its most powerful expression and its clearest relation to poetic language as *souffle*, breath or spirit: "And there are messages on every wire, marvels on every wave. And in this same movement, to all this movement joined, my poem, continuing in the wind, from city to city and river to river, flows onward with the highest wave of the earth, themselves wives and daughters of other waves" (150). Jean-Paul Sartre together with a generation of young French novelists discovering Faulkner and Hemingway, Dos Passos and Caldwell, had been fascinated by "the constant flow of men across a whole continent, the exodus of an entire village to the orchards of California, the hopeless wanderings of the hero of *Light in August*, and the uprooted people who drifted along at the mercy of the storms in the *42nd Parallel*" (*Atlantic Monthly*, 5). In *Winds*, not only immigrants and pioneers on horseback and Indians in their canoes are drifting across the continent, but typhoons and tornadoes, clouds and thunderstorms, rivers and cascades, trains, plains, timber, and ice, mud, silt, and alluvium, "flights of insects going off in clouds," whistling swarms of bees and digger wasps, "insects migrating over the seas like the fumes of fugitive things" (126), flocks of migratory birds, petrels, seagulls, and "violent swans," crabs, eels, and morays, algae and water plants, wild horses and buffalo, cattle and sheep, all intertwined and pell mell, carried away in the whirlwind of their westward movement, together with the poet himself. "Thither were we going, westward-faced, to the roaring of new waters. . . . Thither were we going, from swell to swell, along the western degrees" (149).

The geography of the land matches the history of the people, wave after wave of wandering newcomers driven by the winds and stubbornly trying to hold out against all odds, tenaciously striving to get a foothold on the windswept surface of the prairies. "Men, in Time, have had this way of confronting the wind" (*Winds*, 171). "Men again have found, in the wind, this way of living and climbing" (174). All of them are called in turn on the poetic stage, "Commentators of charters and bulls, Captains of corvée and Legates of adventure . . . the great Itinerants of action and dream" (171), story tellers and assemblers of images, radiologists and sponge fishermen, great reformers and great protesters, "they wandered at peace under assumed names in the great Titles of Absence" (176). "Chivalries wandering the world on our stone borders" (178), they inexorably rose westward, headed for the aridity of high country, since the epic of humanity always takes the wanderers "on the verge of another age" (148), "at the threshold of a great new country without title or device, at the green threshold of a great bronze country without dedication or date" (154). The poet stands at the threshold of this immense void deprived of name and time, and his quest ends up, once again, in silence, as in the hallucinatory voyage across the white lands in *Snows:* "You I question, O plenitude! / And there is such a silence" (154). The flight across the dry lands does not even stop at the sea, for beyond the sea, there are more spaces yet, further to the west, forever calling on,

Further down, further down, and westward-faced!
. . .
To this other mass of unreality, to this high layer of pallor, in the West,

Wherein abides the grace of a great name—Pacific Sea . . .
. . .
The one that must never be named . . .
. . . Farther on, farther on, where the first solitary islands are . . .
and beyond, and beyond, what is there other than yourself.

And Man at sea comes to his death.

(*Winds*, 202)

Here the poet echoes another voice celebrating the open-ended, un-bounded character and prospective quality of the American experience: "Suffice it for the joy of the universe, that we have not arrived at a wall, but at interminable oceans. Our life seems not present, so much as pro-spective; not for the affairs on which it is wasted, but as a hint of this vast-flowing vigor" (Emerson in "Experience," 341). Freely moving across space toward the realization of nothingness, at each step the poet becomes lighter, leaner, shedding excess fat and flesh: "Our rough roads are to the West, where stone runs to its afflux. Emaciation, emaciation to the bone!" (*Winds*, 164). Perse's American experience is one of gradual emptying, the jettisoning of past lives and identities. On the "shore of exile," the wan-derer has lost all sense of origins, he has been stripped of all the garments of his former self and stands naked on the threshold of the unknown, born again: "You shall not cease, O clamour, until, upon the sands, I shall have sloughed off every human allegeance (Who knows his birthplace still?) (*EOP*, 19). "Like him who strips at sight of the sea / . . . My hands are more naked than at birth, and lips more free, ear to the coral reef that sounds the lament of another age" (23).

In "Rains," the steady downpour, which at last overcomes a grateful world, erases the traces of men and cleanses human history of all the debris and alluvia of the past, blowing out the candle of consciousness and mem-ory and bringing to the tormented the relief of oblivion and the blessing of sleep. "Widow clay under virgin water, earth washed clean of the steps of sleepless men / And, smelled close-to like wine, does it not truly bring on loss of memory? (*EOP*, 55). "And the warm rain on our roofs did just as well to quench the lamps in our hand" (59). The flow is both destruction and renewal, the coolness of the rains a sign of rebirth and the promise of poetic fecundity, while the power of the purifying stream sounds the toll of famous deeds and sinful acts, washing away monuments and learned cultures, all the landmarks of civilization: "Each stone washed clean of street-signs, each leaf washed clean of the signs of latria, we shall read you at last, earth cleansed of the copyists' inks . . ." (69). "Wash, wash the peoples' history from the tall tables of memory. . . . Wash, wash, O Rains! the most beautiful gifts of men . . . from the hearts of men most gifted for the great works of reason" (73).

In *Winds*, Perse says that the new land brings forth new scriptures and new ways of writing. In fact, the poem becomes immaterial, labile, divested and naked, emptied of the secure, motionless certainty of meaning. The poet himself is homeless, a "stranger, on all the shores of the world. . . . [A] precarious guest on the outskirts of our cities" (*EOP*, 33). His words share the laughable weakness of foam, froth, snowflakes, and raindrops, the elusive lightness of memories and dreams. "Dedicated to no shores, imparted to no pages," poetic discourse is truly utopian, standing nowhere, lacking both origin and destination, beginning or end. "I have chosen a place glaring and null as the bone-heap of the seasons" (11).

The whirlwind of snowflakes that surprises New York City with the first snowstorm of the year brings the poet's disorientation and drift to its culmination. The white mantle erases all traces and all landmarks, blurs all distinctions and differences, robs the city of all its density and transfigures it into a weightless ship which soars upward into the clouds: "And all night long, unknown to us, under this lofty feat of feathers . . . the lofty pumice stone cities bored through by luminous insects had not ceased growing, transcendent, forgetful of their weight" (*EOP*, 81). From "the height of his corner room surrounded by an Ocean of snows," the poet takes his leave, traveling northward to the wintry immensities of the Great Lakes, westward to the High Plains and the Rocky Mountains, the words of the poem stretching across the continent, encompassing the totality of the land. "I know of strange alliances between sky and water at the waterfalls of the great rivers. . . . And there is also that siren from the factories . . . above there in the great lake country. . . . It is snowing, out there, there, out towards the West, on the silos and the ranches of the vast, unstoried plains marched over by pylons." (85).

At the end of his adventurous journey, Edgar Allan Poe's Arthur Gordon Pym reached a land of pure whiteness, bathed in "a luminous glare." "Nearly overwhelmed by a white ashy shower," he and his companions found themselves surrounded by "many gigantic and pallidly white birds" flying low over the milky waters of the ocean. Before being engulfed by the cataract that rushes toward him, the narrator caught a glimpse of a "shrouded human figure, very far larger in its proportions than any dweller among men" (250). The tale ends with these ominous words: "And the hue of the skin of the figure was of the perfect whiteness of the snow" (250). Adrift on the "ocean of snows," lost in the blinding whiteness of the storm, the French poet also embarks on a quest for the origin of languages that will only bring him to the end of all language, to the white page "on which no more is written," to a nowhere of peace, absence, and silence, "a beautiful country without hatred or meanness, a place of grace and mercy for the ascension of the unfailing presages of the mind; and like a great *Ave* of grace on our path, the great white rose-garden of all the snows all around" (*EOP*, 93).

Desire and the Desert

The last verses of *Snows* bring the poet's linguistic ascesis to completion: there is a gradual emancipation from the constraints of past identities, a growing awareness of the rootlessness and paradoxically absent presence of the source of poetic language, which is clearly associated in Perse's work to the elemental power of America. Myra Jehlen has argued that "to its European settlers . . . America did not connote society, or history, but indeed in its natural parameters, geography. America was an avatar of the world prior to feudalism, and, in the sense that it still awaited its primal molding, it was anterior to the world's divisions" (5). I would like to emphasize three points in Jehlen's quote: (1) her emphasis on the ancient, primal, prehistorical character of the American landscape, (2) the explicit attribution of this vision of the American space to the *European* mind in the New World, and (3) the opposition she draws between (European) history and (American) geography. The prehistorical character of America's geography, however, is only one way in which the United States can be said to escape, or dissolve, the Europeans' sense of historical belonging. Today, descriptions of America as posthistory, such as the one found in Umberto Eco's *Travels in Hyperreality*, relay older, more traditional romantic depictions of the New World as a pristine, uncontaminated tract of wild expanses.

In another type of reading, which often makes use of the Hegelian notion of the "end of history," America ends up leaving the orbit of historical consciousness not as the land before time, but as a universe in which the traditional categories of European culture, especially in their Enlightenment forms, have no purchase whatsoever. I will explore the postmodern vision in more detail in chapter 6. The two versions of American timelessness, prehistory and posthistory, are often grounded, as it were, in descriptions of the physical space of America. In the case of the New World as prehistory, the references are usually to the *natural* space and scope of the continent, while the examples used to illustrate the posthistorical character of the United States are drawn from *artificially* constructed sites, such as Disneyland or the Getty Museum.

The southwestern deserts are often used by European travelers as the paradigmatic sites of America as prehistory. Two major events, particularly appealing to the romantic imagination, overcome the European consciousness in the American desert: the encounter with a primeval, archaic, repressed power that no amount of civilization has ever been able to domesticate or eradicate, and its corollary, the experience of the disappearance of all human signs, of being lost in the sacred, awe-inspiring void of timelessness. In the majestic setting of the California sierras and deserts, Simone de Beauvoir was struck by the inhuman, humiliating indifference of the American space: "At each bend of the road the country changed, yet it was always the same. We were crossing a single desert, and it could be seen in its entirety in each vision. We were even more lost than on the coast where the sea at least put limits to the land. Here, all around, the landscape disappeared into the infinite, the horizon was so vast it made one giddy. There was no sign of man" (*America Day by Day*, 121).

This experience of disorientation, in the root sense of the word, of having lost one's bearings in losing the orient, is shared by many Easterners in the West, whether they come from Europe or not. Consider the New-Englander Kerouac on his first trip across the nation, waking up on a strange bed in a strange hotel of a strange midwestern town, suddenly lost in the heart of the heart of the country, bereft of all moorings and of all certainty, robbed of his very own familiar self:

> I woke up as the sun was reddening; and that was the one distinct time in my life, the strangest moment of all, when I didn't know who I was—I was far away from home, haunted and tired with travel, in a cheap hotel room I'd never seen . . . and I looked at the cracked high ceiling and really didn't know who I was for about fifteen strange seconds. I wasn't scared; I was just somebody else, some stranger, and my whole life was a haunted life, the life of a ghost (*On the Road*, 17).

Kerouac's eerie experience of absolute exile recalls that of Saint-John Perse, down to the imagery of the threshold, of being poised between two equally unreachable worlds: "I was half-way across America, at the dividing line between the East of my youth and the West of my future, and maybe that's why it happened right there and then, that strange red afternoon" (17).

One finds similar events in Simone de Beauvoir's *America Day by Day*. Her first impression of New York City triggers a series of discomforting reactions. She feels as though she is about to embark on the "extraordinary adventure of becoming someone else" (9) and soon realizes that she will never be able to get a grip on New York with mere words, for she is in "a state of dissolution" (15). Lost in the whirlwind of city life, she becomes merely a detached, wandering consciousness, reduced to the pure presence of an impersonal gaze, without memories, without tradition, "cut off from the future and the past" (12). New York and Paris, she writes, are not co-existent, they are not "linked together like two elements belonging to the same system; each one existed in its own time not coinciding with that of the other" (12). Everything seems unreal, which throws her into a trance-like state; she experiences a mystical feeling that she is "but a charmed conscience to which the sovereign Object would soon reveal itself" (18).

Like Kerouac in Des Moines, Simone de Beauvoir has been turned into a pure spirit, a disembodied zombie: "Mine was the incognito of a phantom. Should I be able to reincarnate myself?" (*America Day by Day*, 13). Sitting on a bench overlooking New York City, she is granted a revelation of a realm beyond the limits of her ordinary life, beyond the boundaries of her own identity. "So Brooklyn existed, Manhattan, with all its skyscrapers, and all America beyond the horizon; but I no longer existed. . . . Now Paris had lost its power" (17). A few days later, walking at night in the empty streets of Buffalo, New York, the narrator once again finds herself lost in empty space, having lost all her bearings: "I am no longer in Paris or New York, and not yet in Chicago: I was nowhere and I had escaped from the laws of space" (76).

More than the ocean or the snowscape, the desert is the ideal setting for such a magical moment, an epiphany of liberation and loss, when all codes are abolished and all coordinates suddenly dissolve. For water and falling snow retain some of the gentle, fetal associations of rhythmic movements that rock the mind to a peaceful sleep. Besides, the dynamic flow of waters and winds, as in Perse's writings, point to the exhilarating, transgressory side of self-abandon; they overcome obstacles, they are mobile energy, excess, and illimitation. Rocks and craters, by contrast, do not move; their silent threat brings the wanderer to a halt. The harsh desert leaves no room for consolation, no escape from the total dessication of self. Saint-John Perse wrote of the high country, in *Winds*, that "it is up there one must look for the last chances of an ascetic rule, with our faces bare to the bone" (*EOP*, 165), echoing Paul Morand in El Paso: "I desire nothing, neither house, nor ice-cream, nor bath, nothing but the desert that no bor-

der can stop. I like to return with a sad face, having harvested nothing"
(*U.S.A.—1927*, 24).

Encountering time and again the monumental indifference of the desert (in this case the Grand Canyon), Simone de Beauvoir humbly acknowledges, in a poignant passage, that neither she nor the frenetic effort at domestication of the tourist industry, are a match for the sacred eternity of the land:

> I looked at the cyclopean walls in front of me. Cut in two, just like you cut a cake that is stuffed with cream and jam, here was the earth with its strata placed on top of one another, its shells, its fishes and its ferns embedded in the rocks of succeeding ages. . . . The sun was setting and the rocks were now blood red, this mineral red seemed to liquefy before evaporating. I looked and I understood the point of the mirrors that reflected the images upside down, the moving panes of glass and all the rest of their clumsy efforts to grasp the scenery and turn it into good account. It was here and I was here: I wanted something to happen. I looked and that was all. Nothing happened. . . . The sand, the rocks, the moon, the setting sun; these things were there and I was there, we confronted one another. But it is always I who get up and move away. (*America Day by Day*, 142)

The desert is wilderness par excellence, absolute absence, pure abstraction, pointing, before history and before humankind, to an immemorial past, more past than the past, where meaning has no meaning, and where morality and civilized social intercourse no longer obtain. The inhumanity of a time and space before us and without us, which fills the mind with terror, is always there, lurking below the thin crust of civilization—Butor's "thin film like a layer of paint." In the twinkling of an eye, New York City reverts to the prehistoric, stellar state it never really left behind:

> The landscape changes. The word landscape is appropriate to this city abandoned by men and invaded by the sky—the sky that soars above the skyscrapers . . . and is too vast for the city to annex it. . . . I walk between high cliffs in the depths of a canyon where the sun never strikes; there is the tang of salt in the air. The history of man is not inscribed on these buildings. . . . they are nearer to prehistoric caverns than the houses of Paris or Rome. In Paris, in Rome, history has percolated to the very roots of the soil. Beneath the underground railways, the drains and heating plants, the rock is virgin, not touched by man. Between this rock and the open sky, Wall Street and Broadway, deep in the shadows of their gigantic buildings, belong to nature. (*America Day by Day*, 14)

But, on the other hand, the desert also points beyond history and beyond mankind, to a posthistorical time when man will no longer inhabit
the earth. "A day will come," Paul Morand predicts, "when amateurs of
archaeological digs will look for the location of New York City. A whole
forest of these great oiled steel trees, which are the backbone of elevators,
will be found. Scientists will try to guess whether these remnants date from
the 20th century or the Aztec period" (*U.S.A.—1927*, 118).

O Land of Exile!

The experience of the desert, like the mystics' night of the soul, is
both an exhilarating and terrorizing event, for the rebirth into a new Adam
implies the death of the old man, the undoing of former identities, a process often described as painful agony. It is striking in this respect to compare the opposite uses Perse and Claudel make of the relationship between
wilderness and mobility. The former sees the desert in a positive light, as
the empty space in which to deploy the poetics of liberation as movement,
speed, and drift; the latter dreads the American geographical void as the
symbol, and matrix, of a meaningless, despairing civilization. In a way,
these contrasting views duplicate the commonplace opposition most histories of religious philosophies draw between the Western conception of
emptiness as lack and the Eastern appreciation of it as plenitude, as a fullness of energy.

One finds in Claudel's early play *L'Échange*, written in 1893–95, a powerful, if not entirely original, celebration of the American land coupled
with a violent denunciation of money as the deity of modern society. The
play (at least in its original version) has been considered by many Claudel
scholars as a minor piece, the creation of an inexperienced dramatist. The
poet, however, deemed it important enough to write a second version in
1952 and to talk about it at length in his *Mémoires Improvisées*. He describes
the drama as a concerto or a quartet, in which each one of the protagonists
finds meaning and value in his or her actions in relation to the other three,
"as in a concerto [in which] the value of the violin or of the alto is en-
hanced, brought to its full potential, by the dialogue with the other violin
or cello" (100). *L'Échange* is a role play, "a system in which each role, and
the passion which it represents" (108) is defined in interaction with the
others. America is both the setting and the engine of the play, "the back-
drop" and the "common reactive" of the four protagonists (105), whom
Claudel considered as "parts of the same soul," (103) as "different faculties
of the same individual . . . like . . . an idol who has four faces turned toward
the four cardinal points" (quoted in Blucher, 111).

In this highly symbolized and somewhat overly didactic universe, Marthe, a French woman who has come to the New World to follow her love, Louis Laine, represents reason, virtue, and salvation. Her young husband, on the contrary, exemplifies the raw, untamed energy of the wild. With Indian blood in his veins, he is in Claudel's own words "the last representative of a condemned race in whom gradually rises the call of the horizon and of death" (*Théâtre*, 729). Laine is undoubtedly a Rimbaudian figure, a dreamer and a rebel, a brother, Claudel says, to the modern savages of our cities, those "irredentists" who keep voicing "the protests of the individual against the rule." In one of Rimbaud's best-known poems ("Ma bohème") a young bohemian rebel walks around with his fists in pockets full of holes: the spendthrift Laine, for his part, does not have any pockets. His adventurous spirit draws him away from the stifling prison of Marthe's stable, sedentary world into the arms of Lechy Elbernon, an aging, alcoholic actress, who, as living symbol of imagination and the unknown, bewitches the young man with the diabolical powers of her nihilistic, self-destructive drive.

Lechy's puritanical husband, Thomas Pollock Nageoire, is a staunch and astute stockbroker, who claims that "everything is equal," and who goes around glorifying the lord for having "given the dollar to man." As an *agent de change* (stockbroker), he is the operator of capitalism as an exchange of values and cash flow, the vector of the endless circulation of liquidities and commodities. Through him, money plays its fundamental function, that of providing people with "something other." In the stereotyped modern American couple formed by Lechy (from lecherous?) and Thomas, one recognizes Georges Duhamel's Mrs. Lytton, the neurotic bourgeois praying mantis, and her oblivious workaholic businessman of a husband.

L'Échange's Racinian plot, in which everybody loves someone who does not return his or her love, presents four characters in search of America who are both attracted and repelled by opposite sides of the same individual. Marthe loves Laine, the dreamer, but she also admires Pollock's dedication and realism, his thriftiness and utilitarianism. "You know the value of things," she tells him, "you don't deal in the currency of dreams . . . and you trade in real things, and through you good things do not remain useless" (*Théâtre*, 790). Louis Laine recognizes the value of Marthe's saintly, all-enduring love but is unable to sacrifice his freedom for it. As for Pollock, he is attracted to Marthe, precisely because she embodies the virtues of humility and acceptance which, Claudel implies, he has been looking for all along. Each character then, typifies a facet of America's complexity:

181

Pollock is materialism and the love of money, Lechy, the neurotic quest for excitement and artificial pleasures, Laine the rootless paganism of a "poorly baptized land," and Marthe, the wisdom of (the European) tradition, a mix of peasant down-to-earth endurance and Roman Catholic love for the real world. Pollock is capitalism, Lechy aesthetic modernity and narcissistic individualism, Marthe tradition, and Laine primitive nature.

The differences between his characters' perceptions of the American space reflect Claudel's own ambivalence toward the United States. Louis Laine's Indian blood accounts for the privileged relationship he enjoys with the wild. He appears naked at the beginning of the play, coming out of the ocean in the dawn of a summer day, one with his surroundings, praising his own intimate knowledge of nature's ways:

> And I was walking all naked, and from the pines drops were falling on me between the ear and the shoulder. And all of a sudden I threw myself, head first in the sea. . . . And now I was swimming, and now, near the shore, standing, I was running my hands all over my body, from top to bottom, like a man casting off his clothes. (*Théâtre*, 660) We know each other well, the sea and I, we love each other. (730)

Many critics have noted the obvious Whitmanesque echoes of these lines; one is indeed reminded of the opening verses of "Song of Myself": "The atmospere is not a perfume, it has no taste of the distillation, it is odorless, It is for my mouth forever, I am in love with it, I will go to the bank by the wood and become undisguised and naked, I am mad for it to be in contact with me" (27).

Laine takes pride in having not been raised in cities (*Théâtre*, 732), in knowing "ants according to their nations." His Native American ancestry (Marthe calls him "my redskin from the other side of common sense" [735]) explains his knowledge of birds and animals and his familiarity with the zootheist mythologies of Amerindian cultures. In a central passage of the play, he recalls a dream, a pilgrimage to the land of his ancestors' souls, where he meets his great grandfather, the sachem of the Raton tribe. In another passage, he stands spreadeagled in front of his wife, shamelessly exhibiting his nudity (which later on will shock Pollock's sense of propriety), claiming to be a bird of prey, akin to Whitman's spotted hawk which "swoops by and accuses me [and] complains of my gab and my loitering" (Whitman, 87). Louis pretends to be flying in the air like a buzzard, "like a gliding Jean-le-blanc. . . . And I see the earth appear under the flames of the sun and I hear the creaking of the il-lu-mi-na-tion spread all over" (*Théâtre*, 731).

Marthe refers to Louis on several occasions as a wild beast, doomed to die of this very wildness. For Lechy, he is a rare and most interesting specimen, "a man in the pure state, in his native state [*à l'état natif*], in his virgin state, if I may say so" (*Théâtre*, 779). To which his wife replies that he is "like this country, something from ancient, very ancient times, a *native*, as you say, which has been preserved" (779). Laine himself admits to being the prey of a wild spirit: "A terrestrial spirit is in me and reason cannot do anything about it" (760). In his final effort to break away from marital life, he claims to be the "prey of the gods" (764) who never cease to call him.

Marthe's resistance to Laine's adventurous spirit fuels her hostility toward her natural environment, which she holds responsible for the dangerous course of her lover's destiny. She feels exiled in the midst of hostile surroundings, and her nostalgic words often echo those of Saint-John Perse, down to the all-encompassing presence of rain, without, however, the positive connotation of liberation and hope one also finds in *Exile*. She, too, stands on the beach, on the threshold of the new land, but she turns her back on the immensity of the continent, looking longingly toward the old country: "I salute you, solitude! . . . I salute you, distance! Here I stand, barefoot, on the hard sand where the wave has sculpted strange figures. Here I stand on this land of the West. O land which has been found beyond the rain. . . . O land of exile, your countryside bores me and your rivers seem dull to me!" (702).

Although she speaks of the New World as a land of exile and solitude, Marthe, like Claudel himself (in his 1893 letters to M. Pottecher), has been sensitive to its beauty. She admires its open skies and its exotic flora, its azaleas and Spanish moss. She finds lyrical accents to relate her first impressions of the land during her transoceanic crossing. Her dominant impression of America, however, is one of destructive power. One night, she has to withstand alone the violence of a storm, since Laine has left their home to sleep with Lechy. All by herself in the little cottage, like a frail skiff at sea, she takes the full measure of America's mighty "pagan" winds: "And I listened on the other side of the door to the laborious, unbridled sea, and all along the distant coast the waves thundering in the cracks of the stones . . . and always the power of the passing wind, flattening the forest like a corn field. You don't not know what it is; but it blows" (753). She then recalls an earlier storm that had broke out during her transatlantic passage, and her vision blends various liquid elements: "From the door we could see like a field where there was some snow left, and the sea in disorder in the rain, and the funereal space. Who knows why the wind blows?" (*Théâtre*, 753).

Gradually, Marthe comes to see her tug of war with Louis as an expression of the incompatibility between East and West, of the rift between Europe and America: she calls the latter "the land of exile, the land of death on which the rain comes down, towards which all creatures bow down" (669). Laine, on the contrary, does not care much for the Old World, for there are no deserts there, and one can never get lost: "I don't like this old country. It has an old musty smell like the bottom of a vase. There are too many roads and one always knows where one is, and people stare at you like at a dog without a collar" (665). If Lechy Elbernon, who told Laine to love her because she is freedom (770), is the embodiment of the American spirit, the young French peasant is the antithesis of freedom, a woman, Lechy says, "who is a little country, a hell of a piece of tiny country with a pole in the middle for the man" (769).

Marthe will come to see America as the enemy she must eventually overcome, for its spirit fills Laine's and Lechy's death wishes. "Do you think I am afraid of your America?" She tells Laine, "I am not afraid of it, for I am stronger than it is!" (739). Her deepening resentment at Laine's romantic fascination for the lure of the open road stems for her own belief in the virtues of achievement and closure, in the security she calls her share, for it is "the woman's share" (667). "To flee! Where to? To run away! To hide away! You savage!" she scolds him. "To run away! Run away as you can! You vagrant, you coward! Isn't it a beautiful invention, all the same, to end up? To end up somewhere" (764). The symbolism of the tree, of course, aptly illustrates Marthe's commitment to time and place, for if the tree "does not keep in itself an appetite for the earth below, it will not grow toward the sun, branches and all, if it does not secure itself where it stands" (668). Marthe opposes the final victory of the earth, "which always ends up catching up with [water] and making mud out of it" (763) to her lover's celebration of the power and strength of running streams. To her, Laine is less a buzzard than an eel, or a "broken eagle" for which a resting place at last had been found, albeit temporarily (764).

What Claudel clearly rejects here is the idea of an open-ended cultural process, of an unlimited, undirected quest for freedom, in which the young woman sees only cowardice and self-deception. Laine's ancestors are of unknown origin; where they came from remains a mystery; he himself is an orphan who boasts to have been born alone (*Théâtre*, 732). Marthe's deep-seated suspicion of the nomadic, uprooted paganism of Indian cultures echoes Claudel's remark in his *Mémoires improvisées* that "Christian civilization comes from somewhere and goes somewhere," that the myths of creation and of the final judgment, intent as they are upon establishing an origin of times, as well as prophesying an end to history, are the sign of Christianity's superiority over pagan mythologies. Laine's conversion to Christ, to "the One who is perfect and motionless" (*Théâtre*, 711) is, in Marthe's eyes, the only way out of the deadly course his existence has taken. Conversion alone can transform his pagan wedding with the sea into the renewal and salvation of baptism, through acceptance of incarnation and finitude. "Isn't it interesting," she says, "to come into the world . . . instead of running away?" (739). There lies the promised land, there the true voyage of discovery: "You dove into the sea this morning and you wanted to go all the way down to the bottom; that salted water won't purify you, the [tears] coming from your eyes will. O Laine, you are still alive. Give me your hands" (711).

In Perse's epic poetry, the empty space is the invisible engine of human (and poetic) renewal and self-creation, the missing hub in the wheel of time that revolves forever toward death and rebirth, from beginnings to new beginnings. Not so with Claudel: although he was a diplomat, a self-described "professional exile," the poet was at the same time too much of a *terrien*, a product of the European soil and its millenary tradition, to succumb to the temptation of open, uncharted spaces, and the cyclical recurrence of the same. To Claudel, the song of the desert smacked of romantic nihilism, of mystical hubris; he chose to see in it less a liberation from attachments and defilements than the stubborn denial of all anchoring, the frightful, and sinful, rejection of roots, established beliefs, and perennial values.

Claudel's own reading of *Winds*, although it is full of perceptive and laudatory comments on Perse's "monumental testimony," provides the reader with a final (1949) judgment on the United States. He is quick to point out what sets him apart from the author of *Winds:* Perse wished to divine, in the root sense of the word, the meaning of America, while Claudel claims to have more plainly understood the New World. Perse's apophantic approach may have been an exercise in negative theology; Claudel's own vision of the New World is simply negative in a more prosaic way:

A continent altogether poorly tamed [*apprivoisé*] by man, a land more violated than wedded, that one feels under the bruising knee still wild, rebellious, indomitable. Another world, not wholly authentic, torn between the double nostalgic yearning for memory in the East and for curiosity in the West. An atmosphere of suspense, like the end of the day, permeated with puritan melancholy in the North . . . and with a stagnant, funereal, mortuary stupor in the South. (*Œuvres en prose*, 619)

The poets he calls to the witness stand, Robert Louis Stevenson and Nikolaus Lenau, are notorious for their dislike of life in America. Lenau, a German romantic, attributed the absence of vineyards and nightingales in the United States to the crass materialism of its civilization: "Brother, these Americans have souls of shopkeepers, dead, absolutely dead to any intellectual life. The nightingale is right not to come and dwell among such people" (quoted in Bucher, 74). In a letter to Jean-Louis Barrault dated July 1951, Claudel mentioned again "the strange feeling of *unreality* which America, the other world, gave me and others, too" (Lenau, Stevenson; *Œuvres en prose*, 1482). Like Sartre and Duhamel, he saw the much-touted energy of the New World, so central to Perse's song of the West, as the expression of a dangerous cultural manic depression, "the continuous, pervasive, penetrating presence of a fluid which finds there its native domain, electricity: which now sets you up, saturates you, overexcites you to hysteria, and now leaves you weak, dead-beat, annihilated, and then, quick! a little drink, the knob of the radio set" (*Œuvres en prose*, 619). The blind, inhuman violence of nature matches the cultural and psychological emptiness of what Sartre called "the American tragedy." In Claudel's words, "From time to time, one gets Nature's own kind of despairing crisis, the frantic gallop of tornadoes and blizzards, as if to test the limits of this huge Void in which we are immersed" (619).

The American void is beyond measure, robbing individual existence of justification and salvation, producing "the lethal obsession of this boredom from which one needs to escape at all costs" through alcohol, politics, dancing, the movies, the automobile, and above all, the radio antenna. But the void is also deeply spiritual, of course. What one is trying to escape is "the persistence of that look around us that looks at us" (*Œuvres en prose*, 619), the eye which in the tomb mercilessly stared at Cain. In the end of *L'Échange*, the four protagonists have to face the blinding light of their consciences in the final consummation of Pollock's house by fire: "The door is closed and bolted; the windows are closed . . . and the shutters are fastened from inside with locks and bars. But all of a sudden like a man in whom dismal madness has flared up, one can see through the openings and the holes in the door and windows the blaze of the dreadful inner sun" (791).

That Pollock is a Calvinist ("He found his salvation ready-made," Lechy sneers, "that's why he made a fortune, for one has to do something," 754) is of course central to Claudel's deeply Roman Catholic view of America's secularized religious culture. Anglo-Saxon Protestantism has traded God for comfort and material progress just as Pollock convinces Laine to trade his wife for a handful of dollars. In such a world, as Lechy reminds the other three, even the dead, in their tombs, talk money (684). It is the mobility, the speed of American life, seen here in the French *moraliste* tradition as a hopeless flight from guilt and spiritual despair, that repulses Claudel's moral sense. One would be hard-pressed to find in his later writings the enthusiasm for the electric quality of modernity shared by some of the voices in his 1928 *Conversations dans le Loir-et-Cher.*

In his commentary on *Winds,* Claudel contrasts the frenzied civilization of the New World with the wisest, happiest, most sedentary of all cultures, that of the Chinese. Note the repetition of the adverb *foncièrement,* which means basically, *fundamentally* but also refers to *foncier,* that is, "landed, pertaining to the land," and the intended coupling of the two terms in *foncièrement foncier.* This vocabulary attests to the fact that, in Claudel's eyes, the superiority of Chinese culture (and of rural Catholicism as well) rests in its landed, grounded, *rooted* character: "To understand all this, one has to have lived for a long time among the most authentic people of the world, a people of epicurean Jobs, basically happy, basically satisfied, basically landed [*foncièrement foncier*], indigenous, the Chinese people" (*Œuvres en prose,* 619–20).

The Body of America

In his *Dialogues* with Claire Parnet (published in France in 1977), Gilles Deleuze attributes the "superiority of Anglo-American literature" over the French literary tradition to its constant use of mobility, flight, and exile, an endless process of uprooting or "deterritorialization. . . . To fly is to trace a line, lines, a whole cartography. One only discovers worlds through a long, broken flight. Anglo-American literature constantly shows these ruptures, these characters who create their line of flight, who create through a line of flight" (36). The spatial, geographical character of American literature rests on this specific practice of writing as (in Deleuze's terms) nomadic thought, deterritorialization, and becoming-other: "American literature operates according to geographical lines: the flight towards the West, the discovery that the true East is in the West, the sense of the frontiers as something to cross, to push back, to go beyond. The becoming is geographical" (37).

187

French literature, by contrast, is the product of a culture obsessed with real estate, with the possession of land as a source of wealth, power, and status. French history is marked by the politics of "land, of inheritance, of marriages, of lawsuits, of ruses and cheating." While the British rulers unleashed the flood of capitalism, the French invented "the bourgeois apparatus of power capable of blocking [it]" (37). "The French," continues Deleuze, "are too human, too historical, too concerned with the future and the past. They spend their time in in-depth analysis. They do not know how to become, they think in term of historical past and future. Even with the revolution, they think about a 'future of the revolution' rather than a revolutionary-becoming" (37). In such a perspective, Paul Claudel, with his concern for trees, roots, and spatial inscription becomes an eminent representative of everything Deleuze loathes in the French tradition. But it is this aspect of tradition that causes the French to have a hard time understanding Anglo-American literature, based as it is on lines of flight and deterritorialization. "They think that fleeing means making an exit from the world, mysticism or art, or else that it is something rather sloppy because we avoid our commitments and responsibilities. But to flee is not to renounce action; nothing is more active than a flight" (36).

In *A Thousand Plateaus*, written with Félix Guattari, Deleuze returns to the theme of the fundamental role of geography in American literature and mythology. "Every great American author creates a cartography, even in his or her style; in contrast to what is done in Europe, each makes a map that is directly connected to the real social movements crossing America. An example is the indexing of geographical directions throughout the work of Fitzgerald" (520, n. 18). The authors reconstruct the opposition between Europe and America in light of their own terminology; they especially outline the difference between cultures dominated by the vertical figure of the tree and those informed by the horizontal structure of the rhizome. The latter exhibit specific principles of connection, heterogeneity, and multiplicity: "The rhizome connects any point to any other point, and its traits are not necessarily linked to traits of the same nature" (21). This is unlike trees and their roots, which "plot a point and fix and order." Western reality, and all of Western (and, prominently, French) thought are said to be dominated by the tree image, "from botany to biology and anatomy, but also gnosiology, theology, ontology, all of philosophy. . . the root-foundation, *Grund, racine, fondement*" (18). The East, on the other hand, seems to "offer something like a rhizomatic model opposed in every respect to the Western model of the tree."

In this international division of figurative labor, the United States occupies a special place, somewhere between East and West, bridging worlds, mixing static rootedness and mobile rhizomatic connections:

> America is a special case. Of course it is not immune from domination by trees or the search for special roots. This is evident even in the literature, in the quest for a national identity and even for a European ancestry or genealogy (Kerouac going off in search of his ancestors). Nevertheless, everything important that has happened or is happening takes the route of the American rhizome: the beatniks, the underground, bands and gangs, successive lateral offshoots in immediate connection with an outside. American books are different from European books, even when the American sets off in pursuit of trees. The conception of the book is different. *Leaves of Grass*. (*A Thousand Plateaus*, 19)

Literary differences are ascribed to linguistic specificities. Among major European languages, English is the only rhizomatic one, the only one not patterned after the tree-root structure: "German is dogged by the primacy of being, the nostalgia for being, . . . the cult of the *Grund*, of the tree and roots, of the Inside. English, on the other hand, creates composite words whose only link is an implied AND, relationship with the Outside, cult of the road which never plunges down, which has no foundations, which shoots on the surface, rhizome" (*Dialogues*, 59). The contradictory movements constituting the dynamics of American culture, the quest for roots and the flight away from them, are not only symbolic or social; they are inscribed spatially in the geography of the land:

> And directions in America are different: the search for arborescence and the return to the Old World occur in the East. But there is the rhizomatic West, with its Indians without ancestry, its ever-receding limit, its shifting and displaced frontiers. . . . America reversed the directions: it put its Orient in the West, as if it were precisely in America that the earth came full circle; its West is the edge of the East. (India is not the intermediary between the Occident and the Orient: America is the pivot point and mechanism of reversal.) The American singer Patti Smith sings the bible of the American dentist: Don't go for the roots, follow the canal. (*A Thousand Plateaus*, 19)

Deleuze and Guattari read Leslie Fiedler's *Return of the Vanishing American* along the same lines; the various regions of the United States harbor different processes of "coding" and "decoding," of settlement and

uprooting, whereby the exceptional destiny of American culture and literature plays itself. "In the East, there was the search for a specifically American code and for a recoding with Europe (Henry James, Eliot, Pound,
etc.); in the South, there was the overcoding of the slave system, with its
ruins and the ruin of the plantations during the Civil War (Faulkner, Caldwell); from the North came capitalist decoding (Dos Passos, Dreiser); the
West, however, played the role of a line of flight combining travel, hallucination, madness, the Indians, perceptive and mental experimentation, the
shifting of frontiers, the rhizome (Ken Kesey and his "fog machine," the
beat generation, etc.) (520, n. 18).

Capitalism plays a prominent role in the entire decoding and deterritorialization process which is at the heart of the American experience as
mobility, lability, liquidity: "America . . . proceeds both by internal exter-
minations and liquidations (not only the Indians but also the farmers, etc.),
and by successive waves of immigration from the outside. The flow of capital produces an immense channel . . . where each person profits from the
passage of the money flow in his or her own way (hence the reality-myth
of the poor man who strikes it rich and then falls into poverty again): in
America everything comes together, tree and channel, root and rhizome"
(20).

Deleuze's nomadic processes find in the wilderness, of course, one of
their preferred spaces. The whole westward movement is in fact described
as a "becoming-wild" of stable, rooted European ways of life and thought.
What the desert suggests (in a threatening way) is that the power of the
land will never be tamed, that its mobile, unsettled space will never be
securely contained by the traditions of ancient religious civilization or the
networks of modern communication, that its elusive essence will never
submit for long to the constraints of history and the demands of social
order. It is no wonder that the California deserts appealed so much to the
narrator of Jean-François Lyotard's *Le Mur du Pacifique* (The wall of the
Pacific): Merlin Vachez is caught up in the dialectics of power and desire—
the one ceaselessly subverting and canceling the other—which we have
come to associate with the philosophical mood of the 1960s and 1970s.
Nowhere perhaps more than in Lyotard's narrative is the capacity of the
American space to resist human domination and to elude the grasp of
meaning affirmed and celebrated:

Reaching or expecting to reach L.A. by car, coming from the North-
east or the South, you find on Interstate 5 or on Highway 395, in the
middle of a steppe or desert, exit signs like Kennedy Boulevard, 48th

Street, Laurel Ave. These are ejected organs of a city busy turning itself inside out. The Western deserts are strewn with these unassignable members . . . Ghost towns by desertion or by anticipation, they all belong to the white space that one cannot occupy. They show that there is in the heart of the whiteness an excess of desire over time and space, an outgrowth of power which renders any point in the continuum undecidable, which in itself constitutes an insult to any construction of coordinates. (*Le Mur du Pacifique*, 48)

What Deleuze and Guattari would call America's "body without organs" is made up,[3] in Lyotard's text, of an all-encompassing stretch of uninterrupted white skin that leaves no room for the ruptures, growths, and value differences of human cultures: "From the whiteness of the skin results the fact that it does not contain any shadow or any value: made up of a tissue equal to itself in all its points, the skin shows more than anything else . . . that bodies are not volumes, that there are only surfaces" (*Le Mur du Pacifique*, 31). On the blank surface of America run the labyrinths of cities and the grid maps of empires, freeways, and waterways, the networks of supermarket chains and TV stations and cable connections, the systematic checkerboard (*quadrillage*) of road signs and names of towns, rivers, and counties; this is assignation by designation. But this immense "effort to contain the central mobility [of the white skin] . . . to localize places which should be inhabited and attribute names which should become countries, [all] this domestication leaves the mad belly untamed (maybe)" (49).

The white body of America, like that of Melville's great whale, which in the end destroyed its pursuer and would-be conqueror, is a frightful sight to behold, for "it is not a center but the undulation of ungraspable articulations, the labyrinths of vain routes, it is unaccountable joy" (*Le Mur du Pacifique*, 64). More than any other city in the United States, Los Angeles, because of its rhizomatic, labyrinthine structure, its sprawling, tentacular growth of suburbs and roadways, exemplifies the decentralized and unlimited character of spatial America. According to Lyotard, "L.A. shows that a capital location cannot be found, that there is no center, that in the heart of the empire there lives a white nomadic belly . . . an agitated basin" (45). Things fall apart, the center cannot hold. The very movement of American history is patterned after these undulatory dynamics; the westward migration is an ellipsoidal motion, "the center always decentered on its western edge" (66).

The dialectics of the westward movement illustrate the subversive dynamics of desire that move the whole narrative onward. A relentless undoing of established patterns and combinations, the shifting frontier perpetually calls into question familiar, unexamined sets of rules and regulations: it is Frederick Jackson Turner revisited by post-Freudian critical radicalism. The settlers' communities are only islands on the prairie, temporary montages, precarious products of cultural bricolage soon to be swept away by the formidable attractive energy radiating from the western edge. "As soon as a culture starts to coagulate . . . this island then ceases to be the West, its population becomes wild, peasant-like, rooted, European. One waits for a fragment to detach itself once again and to push further West, in order to reconstitute surfaces devoid of any pathos, of all assignation" (*Le Mur du Pacifique*, 43). The settlers, like so many existential heroes, are "condemned to be free," bound to reenact again and again their original break from the rootedness of Europe, at least until they reach the edge, which the narrator calls the absolute West, "an island of forgetfulness . . . where everything that is imported from the mother cultures gathers itself in order to better emancipate itself from them" (42). Just as the settlers' trails, mail routes, and transcontinental railroads used to converge in California, so do all the metaphorical paths of Vachez's American mythology.

The state's true capital, Los Angeles, is also "the capital of the world because it is not a city in the European or East Coast manner, an appearance of unity clustered around its ecclesiastical, administrative, economic navel" (45). It is not either, then, a capital in the European manner, "for in the impossible center of the Empire (a center which is not in the center, but on one of the foci of an ellipse always stretching toward the West), there is no supreme instance, but a patchwork of white, ephemeral, labyrinthine, useless surfaces" (44). Los Angeles, and California as a whole, are the most accomplished expressions of Vachez's indivisible "white skin": "The white skin of Western women . . . is the absolute West. Today, I call California the situation of this skin" (17). Vachez's America, like Saint-John Perse's, is a gendered being, a man's woman, a male version of femininity, endowed, like mother nature herself, with the only genuine power, "which is to receive" (54), and to enjoy a "pleasure and a power of self [*puissance de soi*], prior to any virile sexuality" (57).

Paradoxically, the mother's very weakness and subordination is said to be the source of all power, for hers is the only genuine knowledge, that of the "profound imbrication of dependency and power" (55). "When this imbrication (which is the fascinating skin I am talking about) is occulted," Vachez contends, "then everything is ready for the staging of politics" (55), that most masculine of games. This sounds, of course, like the old strategy of domination by which the master celebrates the slave's passivity, congratulating her on her being deprived of power, for power corrupts all, and assuring her that that very passivity is mastery of a higher order (your time will come, or rather, has always-already come). Vachez's Los Angeles (L.A. or *LA*, the French feminine) is woman par excellence, for her highways and boulevards are like a checkerboard layout, in French *un jeu de dames* (a ladies' game) which is not, however, as in Renaissance poetry, "the *blason* of a feminine body (which has holes), but . . . a rigorous and aleatory joining up of parts" (45).

This elusiveness of America's body, however, for all its ambiguous idealization and marginalization of female power, also echoes descriptions of femininity by women. In *This Sex Which Is not One*, Luce Irigaray, suspecting the existence of "an old complicity between rationality and a mechanic of solids only," contrasts them both with the fluidity of feminine desire, which relentlessly exceeds and overcomes the most enduring constructs of philosophical and scientific discursive logic. "*The object of desire itself* for psychoanalysts," she writes, "*would be the transformation of fluid to solid* . . . which seals—this is well worth repeating—*the triumph of rationality. . . .* Woman never speaks the same way. What she emits is flowing, fluctuating. *Blurring.* . . . Whence the resistance to that voice that overflows the 'subject.' Which the 'subject' then congeals, freezes, in its categories until it paralyzes the voice in its flow" (112–13).

Is the elusive skin of America, the surface of an organless body, not an apt metaphor for that fluidity of desire that strives to escape the congealing grasp of the one and the same, the deadly squeeze of the subject's power, of history, politics, and technology? In a chapter of *Polylogue* relating her impressions of America, Julia Kristeva also reflects on the disarticulating and dissolving effects of the American space: "When you fly four times a week, seeing schedules, faces, landscapes drift, deprived of loneliness, speaking /listening, ceaselessly changing addresses . . . then the ensuing whirlwind ends up breaking not only your language, syntax, lexicon and syllables, but your body itself. Space gets broken, carried up by violent waves, high-low-oblique, acute oppositions, which resonate like Webern's music" (496). Her experience, all in all, is very close to Simone de Beauvoir's loss of self and language in the prehistoric landscape of Manhattan. Breaking up code and body substitutes the fluidity of the American experience for the solidity of meaning and self, liberates discourse and desire, frees up the wanderlust of woman as traveler, or speaker, or writer:

One probably has to be a woman—to assume her posture—in order neither to identify oneself with the break which guarantees the be-

193

ginning again of the journey, nor to experience oneself as hanging over the route, nor to play at being the boss always at home or the actor always looking for recognition. . . . Which means that, contrary to received opinion, the traveler is in quest of no native home, no proper land, no familial harbor. No return, each arrival is a departure, a wandering, over and over again, through the territories of land, sea and air. (*Polylogue*, 495)

The traveler is also, if not above all, this: impossible speech, words that can't be heard, strangled in libido and/or repression, for which she tries, anyway, to open up a trail. (513)

Although in this "era of the woman," Ulysses looks female, the wanderer does not, like the Greek hero or Saint-John Perse's male conquerors, come back home, but rather, like a female Abraham, embarks upon a journey without end. "The trick of the traveler, as opposed to the Hellenistic ruse, consists in not having any 'home' [*chez-soi*], in considering any 'home' as the Other's place, and, exasperated by its fixity, to refuse it, to escape from it in order to test it, before settling again somewhere else, i.e. within herself, and, without delay, to attempt again to dissolve it" (495). The wandering of the traveler in quest of freedom and desire finds in America its metaphorical space. "To interrogate this fascinating place: first to acknowledge its difference from Europe (New York is as far from Paris as Paris is from Moscow), then to find it in what, here, everywhere, allows us to go around in circles. To start on the journey again, endlessly, as soon as possible. To do it again on the spot, without a spot" (515).

The place is fascinating because it evokes an ambivalent response: the exhilaration of freedom and boundlessness implies the deep anxiety of the loss of identity, the fear of collapsing into what psychoanalytic theory calls the symbiosis of primary narcissism, the dread of the undifferentiated identification with the mother. Julia Kristeva calls "abjection" this contested boundary space where "'subject' and 'object' push each other away, confront each other, collapse, and start again" (*Powers of Horror*, 18). As Diana Fuss puts it, "Primary narcissism, by erasing the borders between subject and object and immersing both mother and child in abjection, 'threatens' the ego and 'menaces' subjective identity" (727).[4] America is this no man's land, where the price to pay for the regression to the archaic, prelinguistic "body" is psychosis, a state that Kristeva herself defines as "the panicking at the loss of all reference." Something of the sort was clearly happening to Jack Kerouac and Simone de Beauvoir, adrift in the heart of the heart of the country, turned into ghosts, specters. The abject quality of America as the bad, engulfing mother also accounts for the revulsing descriptions of massacre, dismemberment, mutilation, expurgation, and refuse found earlier in Céline and Duhamel's descriptions of life in the urban jungle. In America, the European (i.e., civilized, or, in psychoanalytical terms, "œdipeanized") traveler is violently stripped of his unified self, thus he regresses to the terrorizing "imagos of the fragmented body" that Jacques Lacan associates with the presymbolic state of absorption in and with the mother.

There is, finally, another way in which America embodies principles of womanhood: its prehistoric landscapes escape the linearity attributed to masculine (historical) time. In an article entitled "Women's Time," Julia Kristeva, drawing on the Nietzschean distinction of types of time, argues that female subjectivity is linked to both cyclical time, or repetition, and monumental time, or eternity, "at least in so far as both are ways of conceptualizing time from the perspective of motherhood and reproduction," as Toril Moi puts it (*The Kristeva Reader*, 187). The body of America, in the eternal grandeur of its southwestern deserts (after all, one of the most spectacular of these geological formations is called Monument Valley) exhibits traits of female subjectivity as viewed by Kristeva: it is related both to cosmic eternity and monumental temporality, it stands outside human history, outside the symbolic realm. The American wilderness (in Beauvoir's texts, for example) exists both in "an extra-subjective or cosmic time," occasioning "vertiginous visions and unnameable jouissance," and in "the massive presence of a monumental temporality . . . which has so little to do with linear time (which passes) that the very word 'temporality' hardly fits: [the wilderness is] all-encompassing and infinite like imaginary space" (*The Kristeva Reader*, 191).

In Lyotard's tale, the whiteness of the skin is the result of the fusion (or liquefaction) of all colors, or cultures, in the absolute West, the resting place where all history comes to an end, where all the once-solidified traditions of the past come to be dissolved and blended into the smooth, unbroken surface of America's epidermis. California is "the means of American capitalism, i.e., Roman power; the beauty of bodies running on the beach . . . and the confidence given to discussion and honored by the sun, i.e., the Greece of stadiums and schools; urban gardens and deserts, namely Phoenicia; Anglo-Saxon freedom of enterprise and travel" (*Le Mur du Pacifique*, 42).

The library of the University of California at San Diego (where Vachez is a visiting librarian) is the ultimate postmodern utopia, since it is, like the white skin of the West, a circle whose center is nowhere and circumference everywhere. "A transparent jewel," it gives free access, indoors, "to all the points of culture . . . thanks to the wealth of the collections" and, outside, to "everything Californian nature has to offer in the way of elements, minerals, flora, and living mobiles." But precisely because it is such an open vehicle of informational and perceptual flow, the library is a prison from which, since there is no entry, there is no escape. "There is no inside or outside, no space to take, and even no space for taking" (12). It is pure utopia, then, taken in the etymological sense of the word.

The Absolute West

Lyotard's narrative, because of its obvious philosophical and psychoanalytical implications, is undoubtedly one of the most radical and intriguing of all the utopian mythologies of California produced by the anti-institutional mood of the late 1960s. One finds strikingly similar images and metaphors in other books of the period, however. In Edgar Morin's *Journal de Californie* (California diary), for example, the Salk Institute, where the author is doing some research, plays the same role as Lyotard's library as a symbol of the status of information and knowledge in a post-industrial society: it has the same prisonlike structure (the building is compared to a blockhaus, with its "two wings of concrete apparently closed in on a kind of inner courtyard" [39], and the same architectural tension between inside and outside, closure and openness. "[A] blockhaus closed in the East on the land, the road, the social 'world,' it opens up, on the West side, with all its windows, on the ocean and the cosmos" (156).

Could anyone dream of a better metaphor of America, torn between Europe and the Pacific, between its past and its future? The scientific activity that goes on at the institute displays the same tension between inside and outside, since it aims at advancing pure science as well as solving humanity's most pressing problems. The building stands in the midst of a desolate plateau, away from the "California Riviera of gardens, tropical plants, lawns and bungalows" (39). The center of the institute, its inner courtyard, which Morin repeatedly calls "agora" or "austere Acropolis," is always empty, arousing a feeling of malaise in the visitor (191). Morin's San Diego is another version of Lyotard's Los Angeles. With the same absence of center, the same endless proliferation of nodes, connections and networks, the city is "a gigantic urban protoplasm," a "seemingly undifferentiated surface," a "polycentric and automobilistic structure" (49). The true center of the city is "circulatory, rotative, spinning: it is the traffic on freeways 5, 8, 395, 94, the meeting of which forms a gigantic pump, breathing in and out, sucking life in and pushing it out in a thirty-mile radius" (50).

196

Within this strange biocybernetic organism, one feels like "a corpuscle in a blood vessel" (70).

While New York, Chicago, and the Deep South were the favorite objects of French interpretations in the 1920s and 1930s, the West Coast became the new locus of American mythologies after World War II. Once again, the physical environment seemed to possess a perfect symbiosis with the cultural and historical processes under scrutiny. While the Chicago stockyards or the underground toilets of New York City epitomized the demonic side of industrial civilization in the eyes of traditional humanists and right-wing nationalists alike, the edenic beauty of California, America's America, appeared as the natural, obvious locus of the new postindustrial utopia. In Morin's words, California was the extasis of history, a paradisiacal oasis, an enchanted place, an exotic Eden, a new Eldorado.

Journal de Californie appeared in 1970. That same year, Jean-François Revel, faithful to his already well-established reputation of intellectual nonconformism, claimed that the revolution of the twentieth century would in fact take place in the United States. In *Without Marx or Jesus*, Revel granted that this revolution was not inevitable (and most revolutions, he warned, do not succeed), but if it did not take place in America, it would not occur anywhere else. As Mary McCarthy humorously remarked in her afterword to the American edition of Revel's book, one had to be French to get the full impact of what amounted to a declaration of war. "Ever since you could count up to ten or spell c—h—a—t," she wrote, "you have been secure in the thought that the U.S. is the citadel of imperialism, racism, vulgarity, conformism, and now a Frenchman returns from a voyage of discovery to say it is a hotbed of revolution" (243).

Although the enthusiasm of Morin, Revel, and many others for the "new American Revolution" may seem a little misguided today (now that Jerry Rubin is a Wall Street broker and Jann Wenner, the founder of *Rolling Stone Magazine*, shuttles from coast to coast in his Lear jet), all these books signaled an important change in French intellectual politics. And it is fair to say that most observers of the countercultural scene, Revel and Morin among them, took pains to underline the equivocal character of the new cultural revolution: its basic vulnerability in the face of repression, its lack of cohesiveness and long-term perspective, the possibility of it being short-lived. No matter, suddenly Berkeley and Venice Beach replaced Beijing and Havana as symbolic sites of revolutionary change.

In a way, all these new readings of American culture prepared the ground for the painful *aggiornamento* of the French intellectual Left in the mid-1970s and for the subsequent waning of Marxism. What facilitated the transfer to the new celebratory mood in the French intelligentsia's perception of the United States was that the phenomena taking place on the shores of the Pacific did not contradict in any way the prevalent opinion among French literati that American culture was unacceptable. The hippies and yippies and the Students for a Democratic Society were violently rejecting, in campus demonstrations all across the nation, precisely what most French and European writers, poets, painters, essayists, and philosophers had opposed for over a century, were they not? In the name of aesthetic modernity, political vanguardism, cultural chauvinism, or traditional humanism, all had decried the cult of the mighty dollar, the worship of technological progress, the standardization of thought and behavior, the puritanical phobia of the body, the scorn for art and *belles-lettres,* the racist and sexist contempt for difference, as well as U.S. military and economic imperialism.

The shift in the interpretive paradigms of American culture was far from being unproblematic for those in the progressive intelligentsia who felt puzzled, questioned by, and attracted to the counterculture. It was hard to let go of the old familiar critical frameworks, categories of understanding, and neat sets of binary oppositions that had prevailed in the Cold War period. Nowhere is the difficulty of the transition from a modernist (derogatory) to a postmodernist (celebratory) vision of American culture more apparent than in the texts written in the mid-1970s by the leading theoreticians of *Tel Quel,* as they rapidly jettisoned all the markings and trappings of their Maoist past. In the discussion we examined earlier of the relevance of America for the European avant-garde, Philippe Sollers, Julia Kristeva, and Marcelin Pleynet emphasized both the vitality and the marginality of American artistic and academic communities and saw in this peripheral position the reason for the very success, and limitations, of these aesthetic and critical practices.

The relative insulation of the artistic elites from mainstream American culture, while giving them enough social space to innovate and "do their own thing," also accounted for their inability to have any significant impact on capitalism. The United States appeared simultaneously as a loose, polyvalent or polytopic social formation, which allowed the working out of various political agendas, *and* as a system of permanent "recuperation," which constantly plastered over the cracks of its endemic crises. Kristeva saw American culture as dominated by what she called "the law," in the legal, economic, and psychoanalytical (as in Jacques Lacan's symbolic law imposed by the instance of the father) senses of the term. The permanent revolution that ran along the networks of aesthetic, racial, sexual, and political minorities, however, showed that they had found ways of "dealing with the Law, with more and more stringent economic and political constraints" (*The Kristeva Reader*, 4).

In Kristeva's view, the resistance to the law ended up in France in a dual configuration of "antinomic systems which nevertheless internalize each other and mirror each other's qualities," that is, the Gaullist regime and the traditional Left, respectively described as "a government, a System, established and conservative," and "an opposition which ultimately shares the same statist . . . and totalitarian flaws." In the United States, on the other hand, "it seems that the opposition to constraints is not alone, unique and centralized; it is polyvalent, there is a polyvalence which fritters away at the Law but does not attack it frontally" (4).

This polyvalence in turn prevents the "paranoization of the system" and the rise of fascism. "The logic of the American system, as a space which welcomes pluralities," Kristeva acknowledges, is an "antidote to totalitarianism" (*Polylogue*, 514). But this is not to conclude, of course, that the United States is a truly free society. Just as geographic space and the westward movement provided American capitalism with a safety valve, preventing the exacerbation of labor conflicts into an all-out class war and the triumph of socialism, the space of polytopic America allows for the satisfaction of localized transgressive desires without ever undermining the hegemonic rule of the law. An "abyss" separates this law from what Kristeva calls substance, by which she means "an opaque body which can indulge in all the variations of perversion, even to absences induced by drugs, not to mention the small pleasures of consumption society, but who, as soon as it speaks, believes in the social order and in subjective integrity" (501).

One recognizes in this body/discourse split Sartre's characterization of America's cultural schizophrenia, discussed in chapter 3, or the traditional leftist critique of the ambiguities of the libidinal aspects of fascist ideologies. In the eyes of the cultural Left, not yet ready in the mid-1970s to embrace the all-out neoliberalism of some recent postmodernist discourses, the successful separation of substance from law prevents their "dialectization," namely the *generalized*, and authentic, liberation of desire in language:

> This separation (substance/law) seems to me to be the mechanism which allows the constitution of small areas preserved for transgression. [It is] an efficient way of neutralizing the effect of all practices in the social whole: negativity is limited to the domain of which the

discourse (as far as there is such a thing) has no purchase on the social structure as a represented, spoken, symbolized whole. For the social whole, and, by way of consequence, its discourse—its superstructure, if you will—closes up on the ignorance and censorship of negativity. (*Polylogue*, 501)

In other words, the liberated areas of counterculture, far from implying a gradual subversion of the social order, in fact help reproduce the separation between substance (narcissistic pleasure) and law (repressive social order) and benefit from it. The impossibility for "liberated" desire to find a "represented, spoken, and symbolized" expression at the level of society at large, accounts for the nonverbality which stands, as we saw in chapter 3, at the core of Kristeva's perception of American aesthetic transgressions. The American counterculture, caught as it is in the "substance" of libidinal drives, is unable to articulate its desires in a politically efficient critical theory. On the one hand, the fluidity of American society allows the permanent questioning and refashioning of cultural and moral norms (the "do your own thing" and "question authority" slogans of the 1960s, replaced by the more sophisticated "subvert the dominant paradigm" of the following decade); on the other hand this permanent revolution leaves economic structures, the sphere of capitalist production, untouched.

This paradoxical nature of American society finds its metaphorical expression in yet another description of the American space, seen from the top of that "Notre Dame of money," the twin towers of the World Trade Center:

The unconscious shock, i.e. the beauty effect, is certain: you can draw squares, cut up, number, accumulate cubes, set them up in the sky, light fires as you please, it's free; but it is impossible to do otherwise than what this freedom allows, because it is the law. Don't be afraid of the dice throw, the dice throw is not here to crush you, the dice throw is your dream, you are the dice throw, you are the law, uphold the law. The unconscious requires some sublime to make up with the superego: in the heart of Manhattan, it's done; from now on, everything is free, but nothing is possible. This architectural message of Manhattan will reveal itself to me, later, in each and every bit of my overview of America. (*Polylogue*, 498)

"Everything is free, but nothing is possible." There is the dilemma of the contemporary critical intellectual, who is forced to come to terms with the failure of the *political* program of the 1960s: it is impossible to successfully reconcile Marx with Freud. Caught in an ironical double bind, she celebrates the plasticity and flexibility of a capitalist society, which allows for innovative and oppositional aesthetics and cultural politics, while deploring at the same time the inability of these same "ghettoized" practices to undermine the hegemony of capitalism and bring about any substantial change. While welcoming decentralized, post-Leninist, anti-essentialist challenges to the status quo, the disenchanted radical finds it hard to abandon the romantic hope in a complete overthrow of the same status quo which the same anti-objectivist worldview she has come to espouse renders illusory; now, there is no point outside the system from which to conceive, and effectuate, its radical subversion.

In the mid-1970s, many old New Left intellectuals were halfway across the ford, already convinced of the 'undecidability' and/or anachronicity of emancipatory metanarratives. They were still clinging for dear life to the old familiar beliefs in the epistemological superiority of critical theory as the privileged road to intellectual liberation and the sole legitimate ground for collective revolutionary practice. The tension would be resolved later by those postmodernists who did away with the abstract separation between the cultural realm (Kristeva's substance, in permanent revolution) and the economic sphere (Kristeva's law, impossible to subvert). They would argue, on the one hand, that changes in aesthetic and intellectual practices were both conditions and effects of the transformation of capitalist production and exchange (computerization, transnational corporations, market integration, etc.), and on the other, that the adoption of a pragmatic or antifoundationalist stance implied the demise of theory, seen as having no effect whatsoever on practice, save as yet another form of rhetorical strategy.

In the 1960s, the revolution of dissent, which had risen in the midst of unprecedented wealth and extreme moral disorientation, represented in the eyes of an increasing number of anarchists and neoliberals alike the radical erasure of all that the European nineteenth century had worshipped: the state, revolution as the seizure of central power, and the gradual domestication of minds and bodies under the imperatives of instrumental reason. California represented, both in a geographical and chronological sense, the ultimate resting place of the Western adventure, the paradise where all the demons of Western culture, the accumulated evils of Christianity, the Enlightenment, and the Industrial Revolution would finally be exorcized. In Lyotard's narrative, history stopped at the foot of the wall of the Pacific; there the wandering souls of Saint-John Perse's epic poetry could finally come to rest and enjoy the fruit of the earth.

California was the theater and the museum of historical times. It endlessly recycled all the cultural products of humankind, as in the following laundry list of terms from Morin's California diary: neo-paganism, neo-Christianity, neo-mysticism, neo-orientalism, neo-Buddhism, neo-archa-ism, neo-puritanism, neo-naturalism, neo-Rousseauism, neo-communism, neo-kibbutzism, neo-tribalism, and so on. One can find them all in the cultural hodgepodge of "postbourgeois civilization" (Morin), but in the form of *neo-* precisely, as innocuous simulacra, cleansed of their violent, intolerant past, rendered compatible with each other in the very moment they have become useless, since history is over.

The revolution is like Vachez's white skin: it combines all colors, and on its surface borders are constantly crossed and rules ceaselessly trans-gressed. The community of dissenters is not a homogeneous vanguard party or a disciplined secret society but a loose rainbow coalition of now united, now conflicting ethnic, sexual, and cultural groups: "The image of a series of superimposed circles," Jean-François Revel writes, "rather than of stratified social levels describes the nature of this community" (152). "The movement," as they called the radical coalition in the 1960s, is the epitome of modernity in that it combines its most crucial elements, speed and mobility: "The stuff of revolution . . . must be the ability to innovate. It must be mobility with respect to the past and speed with respect to cre-ation. In that sense, there is more revolutionary spirit in the United States today, even on the right, than there is on the left anywhere else" (*Without Marx or Jesus*, 123). Edgar Morin, for his part, saw in the California free press the perfect illustration of this "seething movement, both with and without a thousand forms, which shifts from the psychedelic to the politi-cal, from the sexual to the mystical . . . goes from the hippie to the leftist militant of the campuses" (21). The movement had the fluidity and adapt-ability of experimentation, its ideological flexibility matched the complex-ity of the society it strove to reform, a society in which power is dissemin-ated and does not "fall into the hands of anyone who succeeds in mounting an attack on the Capitol" (*Withouth Marx or Jesus*, 224).

It was necessary, then, to jettison the old certainties of post-Hegelian political philosophy, the old revolutionary strategies of the conquest of central power by a determined minority of ideological professionals. Euro-pean intellectuals needed to sail across a whole ocean of beliefs and anti-quated dogmas—they had to rediscover America. Once again, the United States had become Claudel's "other world," the flip side of the western coin, but in a positive way this time, as the only alternative to the political and intellectual decline of Europe: "The most common error concerning the United States is to try to interpret that nation in terms of the revolutionary guidelines with which we are familiar, and which are usually purely theoretical. Then, when we see that those guidelines are not applicable to the American situation, we conclude that America is a reactionary country" (*Withouth Marx or Jesus*, 148). Morin saw in the various social movements he discovered in California a call to give up an "alternative thought" based on the old dichotomies between "intellectualism and existentialism, empirism and rationalism, objectivity and subjectivity, etc." (82), in favor of a more open, pragmatic, inclusive, "dialectical" vision of social and biological processes. The counterculture was seen as a denial of this binary way of thinking, a refusal to choose between two equally unsatisfactory paths, and a prompting not to defer the quest for a new, *third* term out of the contradictory tension itself (83).

What the new American revolution showed to its neoliberal or libertarian apologists, was that bourgeois democracy with its "constitutional benevolence," far from being an obstacle to the rise of the homo novus, could alone bring about the necessary changes facing humanity: "We may therefore say that revolutionary action is most profound, varied, fertile, and creative when it takes place within the classic liberal system" (*Without Marx or Jesus*, 185). The celebration of what a decade earlier had been anathema to the intellectual Left provided a meeting ground for writers from such diverse philosophical and political horizons as Morin, Lyotard, or Jean-François Revel. Revel's insistence on political freedoms and constitutional rights signals the profound change in intellectual attitudes that was to culminate, after 1975, in the loud, highly visible, media-orchestrated rallying of many a former Maoist or Sartrean revolutionary to the homelier and more prosaic cause of the defense of human rights.

In a way, all three authors traced the exceptional and exemplary nature of the countercultural revolution in America back to the vitality of what the liberal tradition used to call "civil society," while all the evils of Europe and the Third World came from the centralizing tradition of statism. Revel, close to the reformist republicanism of the French Parti Radical, favored a modern version of Montesquieu's separation of powers, which would ensure the independence of political and social processes from the constraints of capitalism. For Morin, a former communist who had rejected his Stalinist past in *Autocritique* (1951), the countercultural break was due largely to "the under-policed or under-politicized character of American society" (*Journal de Californie*, 136), itself a function of the physical and social *spaciousness* of the country:

In the vast geo-sociological spaces which, from the origin, are constitutive of America, the meshes in the net of the *polis*, and of the police,
are wider and looser than in the old and dense Western societies. . . .
Such an under-politicization allows us to understand the double tolerance [of American society], on the one hand a tolerance for doses
of violence, crime and jungle-like disorders which, elsewhere, would
shake the whole social structure, and, on the other hand, a tolerance
for anomie, difference, innovation, as long as they develop in the
margins of the *polis* or between the meshes of the net. To this we
need to add the fact that freedom, within those areas of tolerance,
has been protected and warranted by the most liberal constitution
any individual could hope for. (*Journal de Californie*, 137)

Near the end of *Le Mur du Pacifique*, Jean-François Lyotard introduces
another narrative voice, which engages in a short discussion of Vachez's
version of America. This unnamed narrator, who claims to have found Vachez's manuscript in the library of the University of California is sending
his comments on the story, along with the text itself, to a friend named
Michel Vachey. (Vachez himself?) After having criticized most of the opinions contained in the manuscript, including the notion of the "white skin,"
the narrator imagines the kinds of objections his correspondent would undoubtedly raise in defense of Vachez's ideas. From there a debate ensues on
the meaning of the strange events occurring at the foot of the Pacific wall.

For Michel Vachey, the dissolving and disorienting effects described
in the narrative, far from subverting American capitalism from the outside,
are in fact the product of the system itself: given all the information coming from all the corners of the "homogeneous cross-ruled space" of
America, anybody should assume, on the left as well as on the right, that
there exist "traces" of Vachez's unchartable space. "Positioned in such a
space," concludes Michel Vachey, "all the categories and all the ends of
politics, even of the most 'revolutionary' of politics, are mere imposture"
(81). The commentator (who, of course, will have the last word) disagrees
with this cynical and pessimistic view of the contemporary United States,
a view generally found in conservative and reactionary quarters ("decadence . . . corrupts the Empire more than any revolution could ever subvert it"). He proposes a more sympathetic assessment of postindustrial
America, insisting, in a purely neoliberal manner, on the "vitality of civil
society" and on the contractual character of the American social fabric:

If there is one thing American by which Europeans should let themselves be struck, and which certainly strikes them, although they resist its shock with all their might, it is not "decadence," but how little

state power there is [*le peu d'Etat*], and the vitality of civil society. For American society did make itself with the help of additions, annexations and pieces of legislation hatched from a center; it owed its existence, at first, from a pact among free wills, and it owes its permanence to the sole conjunction of interests. The absorption of Indians, blacks and Mexicans in the Union was obviously achieved without their consent: this imperial trait is not enough, however, to make Washington into a new Rome. The American is a citizen, while almost all continental Europeans are subjects. (*Le Mur du Pacifique*, 82)

For the narrative voice (could this be Lyotard speaking?), the main flaw in Vachez's vision lies in a blindness to the fundamental difference between Europe and America. As most "European provincials" who have spent some time in the United States, Vachez refused to acknowledge that he had gone through a change of time and space, that he was witnessing the birth of another history, "in which the solution to the problems of the social fabric are not to be found in the central authority of the state, but in the accessibility and competitive reversibility of informational channels" (82). "What should have struck [Vachez]," continues his critic, "is what we used to call civil society, [is] today a population ready for the postindustrial era" (83).

Vachez's bad faith is all the more inexcusable as he lived in Southern California, where "the combination of geographical, historical, cultural distances, the accumulation of influences, the beauty of sites and skies, and wealth, by freeing more than anywhere else Americans from their European past, prompts them to offer an already pagan version of capitalism, relieved of the worries of legitimation" (83). For what did the image of the wall mean, if not that the age-old procession of mankind comes to an end and that history dissolves into utopia on the shores of the absolute West?

> The golden dream is over and one enjoys it. The social consensus is not sought for any longer in the authority of a capital, it cannot be differed any longer in its westward displacements. The history of the States is over. Another bustle is heard in the silence of the accomplished. What is at stake is no longer the occupation of lands and much less the exploitation of their resources. It is the conquest of knowledge: its storage in memories, its availability, its use for new machineries. The time-space where they dwell, and where this game is going to be played, isn't that your "unchartable space," wasn't it Vachez's "white skin"? (*Le Mur du Pacifique*, 85)

Le Mur du Pacifique ends where *The Postmodern Condition*, published the same year (1979), begins: in his controversial and widely criticized study of the effects of computerization on contemporary culture, Jean-François Lyotard argued that the information revolution, like Revel's counterculture, had rendered obsolete all the previous "metanarratives" through which Westerners had tried to make sense of their history. At the same time, Philippe Sollers claimed that the United States was "on the edge of the new reason" (*The Kristeva Reader,* 16), and Julia Kristeva wondered whether American society was not "the perfect closure . . . , social finality reached" once and for all: "Is completed capitalism," she asked in *Polylogue,* "opening up a new historical cycle?" (514). Postmodernism, the name for the new frontier, the new reason, the new time-space of the conquest of knowledge, was to become, in the eyes of many French intellectuals, a synonym of America just as modernity and its discontents had been in a previous era.

SIX

(RUNNING) OUT OF HISTORY

Our age—whether through logic or epistemology, whether through Marx or through Nietzsche—is attempting to flee Hegel. But truly to escape Hegel . . . assumes that we are aware of the extent to which Hegel, insidiously perhaps, is close to us. We have to determine the extent to which our anti-Hegelianism is possibly one of his tricks directed against us, at the end of which he stands, motionless, waiting for us.   *Michel Foucault*

Santayana was entirely free of the instinctive American conviction that the westering of the spirit ends here—that whatever the ages have labored to bring forth will emerge between Massachussetts and California, that our philosophers have only to express our national genius for the human spirit to fulfill itself . . . Santayana saw us as one more great empire in the long parade.   *Richard Rorty*

Rather than ask why Americans lack a "sense of history," we can now as well ask why Europeans have the particular sense of it that they do.   *Myra Jehlen*

The changes in aesthetic and political mood now labeled "postmodernism" have led to a renewed interest in American culture, once again seen, in a much more positive light this time, as the herald of things to come. In the early 1960s, the few voices from the French liberal Right or from Christian Democratic quarters that rose in defense of American democracy, voices such as Raymond Aron's, were drowned in the concert of violent protests and demonstrations against U.S. imperialism. Within a few years, however, one witnessed political realignments and ideological reversals of stunning magnitude and perplexing character. The diffusion of the American counterculture and the waning of "dogmatic" Marxism as *the* legitimate theoretical horizon of the intellectual Left gave rise, almost overnight, to a new brand of pro-Americanism, often within the same *cénacles* that had so vehemently criticized the "system" and its alienating mass culture a few years earlier. Favorable accounts of American society, such as those I discussed in the previous chapter, celebrated the social and cultural diversity of the United States, especially in California, and described it as the only alternative to bureaucratic socialism and Western European decadence.

Meanwhile, the growing skepticism of the cultural Left for *le socialisme réel* in Paris and Stockholm as well as in Moscow and Beijing, made room for the return of previously repressed, or silenced, ideologies and intellectual traditions: pre-Marxist and anti-Marxist discourses surfaced again in fashionable Parisian intellectual reviews. Kant, Tocqueville, and Aron replaced Marx, Nietzsche, and Sartre as legitimate *maîtres-penseurs*. While some praised economic liberalism and "the Reagan revolution" in neoconservative rhetoric, others took another long look at the Tocquevillean paradigm, adapting it to the new social and cultural developments in Western democracies.[1]

These ideological developments were accompanied by dramatic changes in aesthetics and theories of representation. As Fredric Jameson pointed out, postmodernism is characterized by a form of aesthetic populism, based on an intense fascination for the very forms of mass culture that were so vehemently rejected twenty years ago as *société du spectacle* or *one-dimensional society.* Jean Baudrillard's recent book on the United States (*America*), as well as Gilles Lipovetsky's celebration of consumerism, the media, advertising, and fashion as truly democratic phenomena, underscore the new status of mass consumption for some contemporay French theorists. Lipovetsky contends that "the process of personalization constantly reinforces the demand for freedom, choice, pluralism and creates an individual who is relaxed, tolerant and open to differences" (*L'Ere du vide*, 145). The development of narcissism goes hand in hand with democracy, the two processes harmoniously reinforcing each other: "As narcissism develops, democratic legitimacy wins over, even if it is in a cool mode; democratic regimes with their plurality of parties, their elections, their right to opposition and information are more and more closely linked to the personalized society of self-service, testing and combinatory freedom" (145).

Numerous recent French interpretations of contemporary America have been marked by what Jameson has described as "an inverted millenarianism in which premonitions of the future, catastrophic or redemptive, have been replaced by senses of the end of this or that (the end of ideology, art, or social class; the 'crisis' of Leninism, social democracy, or the welfare state, etc.)" (53). In that respect, the notion of the "end of history," central to many French philosophical and literary versions of our present cultural situation, from Kojève and Blanchot to Bataille and Klossowski, seems a very useful tool for the understanding of postmodern readings of American culture.[2] Maurice Blanchot, commenting on George Bataille's work, wondered in *L'Entretien infini:*

> Should not we say that, as of now, history is coming to an end? Which does not mean that nothing will ever happen, or that man will not have to bear the pain and ignorance of the future; but man as universal has already mastered all the categories of knowledge, he can do everything and has an answer for everything. For everyone, in one form or another, history is running out (in all but the outcome). (quoted in Descombes, 113)

Similar considerations on the end of history can be found in many French studies of contemporary life in the United States, although these interpretations often disagree over the moral or political evaluation of America's alleged flight from history.

Neo-Hegelianism: The Animalization of Man

In his influential commentary on Hegel's *Phenomenology of Spirit*, Alexandre Kojève referred to the United States as a posthistorical society. Recent studies of the *Introduction to the Reading of Hegel* stress the importance of the notion of the end of history in Kojève's interpretation of Hegel. For Vincent Descombes, "The 'end of history' is none other than the translation into figural and narrative language of what in the language of philosophy is known as absolute knowledge" (27). Absolute knowledge, understood as the "science of the *identity* of subject and object" (Descombes, 27) is possible only because history, the temporal process through which the Hegelian idea gradually became conscious of itself, has reached an end. "The historical condition for writing the System of science," as the Hegel scholar Barry Cooper remarks, "was that all human potentialities had been fulfilled, that history was over" (77). The reconciliation of spirit and history gives rise to a posthistorical regime, the "universal and homogeneous state," which Hegel, as we know, identified with the Napoleonic state. In such a regime, the contradictions and the conflicts that were the engine of European history are forever overcome. To quote Descombes again, "The end of history would be the end of adversity, the term which adequately translates Hegel's *Gegenständlichkeit*" (28).

In Kojève's view, the contradiction between man and nature as well as the opposition between man and man are overcome in the posthistorical regime. Absolute knowledge, according to Kojève, "is possible only (1) within a *homogeneous* and *universal* State where no man is *exterior* to another, where there is no social *opposition* which is not suppressed, and (2) in the midst of a Nature that has been *tamed* by the labour of Man, and which, no longer *opposing* Man, ceases to be alien to him" (quoted in Descombes 28). "Man," deprived of his purely human, that is, historical, characteristics, which have now become useless, returns to animality, to the organic eternity of the state of nature. The disappearance of man at the end of history, however, constitutes neither a "cosmic catastrophe" (since "the natural world remains what it has been from all eternity") nor a biological one ("Man remains alive as animal in *harmony* with Nature or given Being"). Kojève remarks that "what disappears is Man properly so-called—that is, Action negating the given, and Error, or in general, the subject *opposed* to the object. Practically, this means: the disappearance of . . . *Philosophy;* for since Man himself no longer changes essentially, there is no longer any reason to change the (true) principles which are at the basis of his understanding of the world and of himself. But all the rest can be preserved indefinitely; art, love, play, etc., etc.; in short, everything that makes man *happy*" (*Introduction to the Reading of Hegel,* 158–59). In the end of history, then, there is nothing left to do. Man as negativity, negation of the given by way of thought (philosophy) and action, has lost his raison d'être, since there is nothing left to negate. Only the positive reconciliation of being with itself remains, an eternity of play, desire, and, as in the Declaration of Independence, the pursuit of happiness. "Nature survives time" (Kojève, 158).

Is there any concrete, empirical evidence of the death of man as subject of history and of the coming of the rational state? Which social formations, political regimes, or economic systems can be said to actualize the end of history? The *Introduction to the Reading of Hegel,* although a meditation *on* history, is obviously not a work *of* history. Even if Kojève's purpose was to define the essence and "self-understanding" of modernity (Cooper), he gave us very little in the way of empirical evidence of the posthistorical regime. In a footnote to the second edition of the *Introduction,* written in the early 1960s, Kojève alluded to the return to animality in the end of history. He self-critically questioned his previous assertion that "art, love, play, etc." will survive the annihilation of the historical (i.e., cultural) subject. "Such a view," he acknowledged, "is self-contradictory," since these practices and behaviors are themselves products of human culture:

> If Man becomes an animal again, his arts, his loves, and his play must also become purely "natural" again. Hence it would have to be admitted that after the end of History, men would construct their edifices and works of art as birds build their nests and spiders spin their

webs, would perform musical concerts after the fashion of frogs and cicadas, would play like young animals, and would indulge in love like adult beasts. But one cannot say that all this "makes Man happy." One would have to say that post-historical animals of the species *Homo sapiens* (which will live amidst abundance and complete security) will be *content* as a result of their artistic, erotic and playful behavior, inasmuch as, by definition, they will be contented with it. (159)

The return to animality also implies the disappearance of "discourse" or "logos," that is, of human language and signification, which will be replaced by a system of "vocal signals or sign language" similar to the "language of bees." Such a possibility, far from being the construct of pure philosophical speculation, already existed, for Kojève, in contemporary America. This note from the second edition shows the evolution of Kojève's thought on the universal and homogeneous state. In 1946 the return to animality appeared only as "a prospect for the future (more or less near)." Kojève understood soon after (in 1948) that "the Hegelian-Marxist end of History was not yet to come, but was already present, here and now . . . in the North American extensions of Europe. One can even say that, from a certain point of view, the United States has already attained the final stage of Marxist 'communism,' seeing that, practically, all the members of a 'classless society' can from now on appropriate for themselves everything that seems good to them, without thereby working any more than their heart dictates" (*Introduction to the Reading of Hegel*, 160). These considerations of America as the true embodiment of Marx's classless society are a forerunner of subsequent French writings on the "affluent society" or its counterculture as the only revolutionary alternatives to communism (Revel, Morin).

In Kojève's understanding, communist and Third World societies no longer constitute viable alternatives to the "animalization" of the human world. They are only "backward civilizations of the peripheral provinces" and "anachronistic sequels of a pre-revolutionary past," on their way to the unavoidable end of history. "If the Americans give the appearance of rich Sino-Soviets, it is because the Russians and the Chinese are only Americans who are still poor but are rapidly proceeding to get richer" (160). Having traveled extensively in America and the Soviet Union during the 1950s, Kojève had come to the conclusion that the "American way of life" is "the type of life specific to the post-historical period, the actual presence of the United States in the World prefiguring the 'eternal present' future of all humanity. Thus, Man's return to animality appeared no longer as a possibility that was yet to come, but as a certainty that was already present" (161).

As late as 1958, Kojève thought that American society was the striking confirmation of the truth of Hegelian philosophy. The observation of contemporary social formations and the study of history had led him to believe that the battle of Jena (1806), which marked for Hegel the beginning of the end, was indeed the turning point of human history and the founding event of our modernity. "In and by this battle the vanguard of humanity virtually attained the limit and the aim, that is, the *end*, of Man's historical evolution. What has happened since then was but an extension in space of the universal revolutionary force actualized in France by Robespierre-Napoleon" (160). In such a perspective, the various events of modernity—world wars and revolutions, communism or national socialism—cannot make up a *history*. They are not oriented toward any future, they do not create anything new. They are nothing but the unfolding of absolute knowledge, the enactment of the necessary "elimination of the numerous more or less anachronistic sequels of [Europe's] pre-revolutionary past" (160). Thus, the time-space of (post)modernity is duration without becoming, allowing archaic societies and cultures to catch up with America, conceived as the paradigm of posthistorical regimes.[3]

Kojève did not say much about the empirical conditions of the death of man as signifying historical subject. What sort of relations, certainly no longer "social," exist between "the post-historical animals of the species *Homo Sapiens*"? What are the consequences of the disappearance of "any discursive understanding of the World and of self"? If the utopia of a world rid of meaning and war already exists, what are the concrete signs of its existence? What is the moral and philosophical status of the becoming-animal of humanity? Are we to revel in it and celebrate, armed with such a "gay science," the advent of nihilism and the end of belief? Or are we to lament it and consider the type of society where people can "appropriate for themselves everything that seems good to them" as the supreme alienation of humanity, a nightmare akin to that of "repressive desublimation"? Kojève never answered these questions and eventually renounced his original perception of American society as the unfolding of the end of history.

After a trip to Japan in 1959, he had, he wrote, "a radical change of opinion on this point" (161). The Japanese "post-historical way" based on the institutionalization of *snobbery*, far from being, like the American way, a return to animality, struck him on the contrary as a particular form of the negation of nature, although devoid of any meaningful content. Japanese snobbery, by way of "disciplines negating the 'natural' or 'animal' given," such as the No theater, the tea ceremony, or the "gratuitous" suicide of the samurai, were said to generate "totally *formalized* values," devoid of any "human," namely historical, content. The human being of the Japanese posthistory is neither the for-itself of prerevolutionary history nor the "animal of the species *Homo Sapiens*" of the American version of the end of history: the snob remains human, that is, a negating freedom, but his/her negativity only creates empty, meaningless, morally indifferent forms, which can receive any value and accept any content:

> As I said in the above Note, an "animal that is in *harmony* with Nature or given Being" is a *living* being that is in no way human. To remain human, Man must remain a "Subject *opposed* to the Object," even if "Action negating the given and Error" disappear. This means that, while henceforth speaking in an *adequate* fashion of everything that is given to him, post-historical Man must continue to *detach* "form" from "content," doing so no longer in order actively to transform the latter, but so that he may *oppose* himself as a pure "form" to himself and to others taken as "content" of any sort. (*Introduction to the Reading of Hegel*, 162)

Such an extreme aesthetic formalization of self, pure (gratuitous) opposition to the "given," is, in the Kojevian perception of postmodernity, the only cultural practice now available to human beings, since history, as transformation of the world and moral activity, is totally finished. "Detachment" (of form and content) is the last chance to save man as subject of history, the only alternative to the (American) return to animality, now seen as negative, undesirable, and barbaric, when opposed to the Japanese model of posthistoricity. Luckily, we are headed in that direction. The duration without becoming, which constitutes our present, will make posthistorical human beings out of us, snobs saved by aestheticism. "The recently begun interaction between Japan and the Western World will finally lead not to a rebarbarization of the Japanese but to a "japanization" of the Westerners, including the Russians" (162).

The end of history, whether it is a becoming-snob or a becoming-animal of the human species is, in any case, an ambiguous event. Kojève's conception of America as a classless affluent society should not be confused with the apology of the "free world" or of "the end of ideologies" by contemporary liberal heirs to the optimistic, rationalistic side of Hegelianism. The Kojevian version of the end of history is more reminiscent of the apocalypse. It is a strange tribute to Western (and Christian) history to say that it finds its final meaning and salvation in the most aestheticized of all the cultures of the Orient. Is not the "Japanized" Westerner's aristocratic

213

formalism a paradoxical outcome of the unfolding of absolute reason through history? Kojève's reading leads to a disenchanted and ambiguous Hegelianism, at odds with the triumphant, prophetic vision of the sage (himself the incarnation of the spirit), who wrote of the universal and homogeneous state that "it is the march of God through the world, its ground is the power of reason realizing itself as will. . . . The state must be regarded as a great architectonic edifice, a hieroglyph of reason, manifesting itself in reality" (Hegel, *Selections*, 443, 450). Michel Foucault once observed that "our age—whether through logic or epistemology, whether through Marx or Nietzsche—is attempting to flee Hegel" ("Orders of Discourse," 28). One thing is certain: we cannot read Hegel today as his contemporaries read him, after Schopenhauer and Nietzsche, two world wars, Stalin's state socialism, and the Third Reich. As Vincent Descombes has remarked, the notion of the end of history leads to two antagonistic and incompatible interpretations of our present situation:

> The end of history is indeed the triumph of meaning, as Hegelians believe. It may be final reconciliation, universal recognition or even, in certain versions, a generalized embrace (or simply the embrace of the real by the thinker alone); in any case, a higher synthesis, the annihilation of the negative in a victorious negation of the negation, the presence of truth and the truth of presence. However, it is also the apogee of non-meaning. For there is nothing left to be done (therefore all action is absurd), nor anything left to be said (therefore all speech is insignificant). At the end of history, the human species enters into an irremediable idleness, an aimlessness without end. (*Modern French Philosophy*, 21)

The second interpretation leads to nihilism, to the disappearance of philosophy and of human culture, replaced by something like "the language of bees" or by the value-free formalism of aesthetic snobbery. Hence the influence of Kojève's philosophy on Nietzsche's French readers, from Bataille and Blanchot to Klossowski.[4] Because of its ambivalence, Kojève's reading of the *Phenomenology of the Spirit*, after contributing to the Hegelian turn of French philosophy in the 1950s (Sartre, Merleau-Ponty, Hyppolite), outlived the anti-Hegelian stance of the 1960s and inspired the subsequent debates on the "death of man" and the "postmodern condition." In his preface to the English edition of the *Introduction to the Reading of Hegel*, Allan Bloom, remarking on the decidedly Nietzschean flavor of Kojève's posthistorical universe, wrote that "one wonders whether the citizen of the universal homogeneous state is not identical to Nietzsche's Last Man, and whether Hegel's historicism does not by an inevitable dialectic force us to a more somber and more radical historicism which rejects reason. . . . We are led to a confrontation between Hegel and Nietzsche" (xi–xii).

Zarathustra Revisited: The Land of the Last Man

The reference to Nietzsche, and especially to Zarathustra's "last man" as the ultimate product of nihilism, is a constant in the Right's depiction of the United States. For example, in their essay on America published in *Nouvelle École*, Herte and Nigra refer to the often quoted passage from the prologue of *Thus Spake Zarathustra* as an illustration of America's materialistic, egalitarian, and antiauthoritarian culture:

> "We have discovered happiness"—say the last men, and blink thereby. They have left the regions where it is hard to live; for they need warmth. . . . One still worketh, for work is a pastime. But one is careful lest the pastime should hurt one. One no longer becometh poor or rich; both are too burdensome. Who still wanteth to rule? Who still wanteth to obey? Both are too burdensome. No shepherd, and one herd! Everyone wanteth the same; everyone is equal: he who hath other sentiments goeth voluntarily into the madhouse. . . . "We have discovered happiness," say the last men, and blink thereby. (Herte and Nigra, 12)

European right-wing critics of American democracy have never had difficulty with the paradoxical nature of post-Hegelian philosophy. That the optimistic rationalism of the Enlightenment has given way to the nihilism of the "one-dimensional" society is no wonder to them. What they see as the present decadence of American society is the normal consequence of the precedence of bourgeois utilitarian values over the aristocratic ideals of predemocratic times. They are naturally led to emphasize the differences between the cultures of Europe and America, the latter being seen as a radical departure from aristocratic values and representations. "America was born out of the refusal of Europe, the hatred of Europe, a desire for revenge over Europe" (Herte and Nigra, 10). Ironically, the French radical Right's emphasis on discontinuity and distance between Europe and America mirrors the American national ideology expressed at the time of the American Revolution. In his *First Inaugural Address* (1801), Jefferson congratulated the citizens of the new nation for "having banished from our land the religious intolerance under which mankind so long bled and suffered" and for being "kindly separated by nature and a wide ocean from the exterminating havoc of one quarter of the globe" (333). Philip Freneau expressed the same relief in a more poetic manner:

By persecution wronged,
And sacerdotal rage, our fathers came
From Europe's hostile shores to these abodes,
Here to enjoy a liberty and faith,
Secure from tyranny and base control.
For this they left their country and their friends
And dared the Atlantic wave in quest of peace. (61)

In total agreement as to the essential difference between both cultures, the two nationalistic discourses differ absolutely, of course, as to their evaluation. While the American patriots applied the diagnosis of corruption and inhumanity to the feudal tyranny of Europe, the right-wing ideologues, heirs to an antidemocratic tradition that extends, in France, from Bossuet and Maistre to Charles Maurras, attribute all the symptoms of decadence to the egalitarianism of the children of the "Rousseauean and Jeffersonian rabble." The reference is, here again, to Nietzsche, and specifically to his contemptuous criticism of English culture and philosophy in *Beyond Good and Evil*:

> They are not a philosophical race—the English: Bacon represents an *attack* on the philosophical spirit generally, Hobbes, Hume, and Locke, an abasement, and a depreciation of the idea of a "philosopher" for more than a century. It was *against* Hume that Kant uprose and raised himself; it was Locke of whom Schelling *rightly* said, "*Je méprise Locke*"; in the struggle against the English mechanical stultification of the world, Hegel and Schopenhauer (along with Goethe) were of one accord. . . . What is lacking in England, and has always been lacking, that half-actor and rhetorician knew well enough, the absurd muddle-head, Carlyle, who sought to conceal under passionate grimaces what he knew about himself: namely what was *lacking* in Carlyle—real *power* of intellect, real *depth* of intellectual perception, in short, philosophy. (188)

One of the most common European perceptions of American society is that "Americans do not have a past." The story of the millionaire who bought a bridge in London and had it rebuilt stone by stone in the Arizona desert is often quoted as evidence of the Americans' yearning for history, as well as of their capitalistic ability to turn the most sacred monuments of the past into mere commodities. The relationship of American culture to time and history is one of its most distinctive elements. In the European conservative tradition, the aristocratic ethos, based on an acute awareness of continuity in time, rests on the superiority of tradition over progress, values old age, experience, and the sacred, and sees race, ethnicity (*Volk*), and community as the foundation of social order: quality is what endures. On the contrary, American positivistic materialism favors quantity over quality, idealizes youth and novelty, and equates freedom with the rejection of the past.

This set of values is precisely what distinguishes a mere *culture* from a genuine *civilization:* "Optimism and the belief in progress give rise to the idea of *instant consumption.* Since yesterday can never be as good as today, and today never as good as tomorrow, the American is *indifferent to the past,* for the past, with its traditions, its culture, its roots, etc., has no meaning for him; it is wordless. (To admit that the past could be superior to the present is contradictory to the idea of progress. . . . The predilection for instant consumption, without any regard for the perspective which in-cludes it (for the heritage one has received, for example, and that one is in charge of transmitting), explains why historicist modes of thought have never taken hold in the United States" (Herte and Nigra, 65). American culture is unable to put time in perspective, reducing, for Alain de Benoist, the tri-dimensionality of time to one-dimensionality, "making all men co-incide as best as possible within the same dimension of simultaneity. . . . The American unconscious . . . rests on a mystique of space (the idea that, behind *the frontier,* there always is more space to *exploit*), as opposed to a mystique of time" (*Vu de droite,* 398).

The inability to think in historical terms (and to produce philosophies of history) is here clearly related to the materialistic ethos of a capitalist society based on the instant gratification of mass consumption. The Amer-ican denial of the past as history is also perceived as a refusal of history as future, as time to come:

> The Americans do not want to have a past. . . . They do not want either to give the future any *form* which could create for them some-thing like a *destiny.* They only want a present, a succession of present instants, which they can enjoy now, in accordance with the Declara-tion of Independence which guarantees their "right" to the "pursuit of happiness." Hence this idea of horizontal happiness which Nietzsche attributes to the "last men." (Herte and Nigra, 65).
>
> Friedrich Sieburg used to say: "Politics is destiny." America does not want to have a destiny. It does not have any will to power, it only has a will to end history. (45)

The inability to think in historical terms is also an incapacity to act in history, to pursue a historical project. At first glance, such a claim seems to run counter to most European criticisms of American imperialism and the doctrine of Manifest Destiny. For the essayists of *Nouvelle École*, however, the American mission, because it is conceived in *moral* terms, is the exact opposite of realpolitik and, therefore, doomed to failure: "Since *historical politics* of any kind require a project, the United States, having no such project, aspire to be (and already are) the *least historical* nation in the world" (84). To support their argument, our authors quote André Malraux, de Gaulle's minister of culture, thereby refering to another important component of French nationalism, namely the Gaullist tradition:

> During an interview published in *L'Appel* (January–February 1975), M. André Malraux . . . could not help but comment on such an "absence of American historical politics." "If America had a political project," he said, "it should normally be to conquer the world. In fact, this is not the case. The United States find themselves in the strange situation of a country which has become the most powerful in the world without having really wanted to be so. All in all, they wanted to sell sewing machines. . . . Historical willpower in the old sense of the word, would be, for the Americans, to think the American problem in terms of the whole world. Alexander the Great, Richelieu, Frederic II did just that, although confronted with much smaller worlds. The difference is obvious. (84)

In *Discours de la décadence* (1978), his most violently anti-American pamphlet, the French writer and polemicist Jean Cau, who was Sartre's secretary in the 1950s before espousing more conservative views, also relies on Gaullist principles to denounce America's exile from history: "The United States has no sense of History. No vision haunts this huge soft young body, no mission capable of entering the souls of the other peoples of the West, scarred by the past, by miseries, hopes, memories and—in a word—by History. The United States [is] a 'thing' without a past and hence without a future, a mass floating above the 20th century" (156–157). Ironically enough, the only "white" nation still capable of reversing the decadence of the West and of remaining, through an act of political will, "master of history," is the Soviet Union, protected by socialism from the fatal contamination of liberal capitalism: "Here is the fundamental question: what is [the Americans'] vision of the world? The answer is that, if they have any, it leads to a form of *mondialisme* [globalism] which will destroy us all while Russian *mondialisme* does not exclude *what seems to me to be essential for our salvation:* a form of nationalism. . . . Europe no longer makes history. . . . Russian nationalism is the last barrier against American *mondialisme*" (176).

The outcome of the Vietnam War was for Alain de Benoist (in 1975) the latest illustration of America's lack of historical willpower. "America never wanted to win . . . and what would have been the *meaning* of a victory, when there was no goal? The Russians, today, know what they want. The Chinese, today, know what they want. The Europeans barely know what they do not want. The Americans do not want anything" (*Les Idées à l'endroit*, 264). The problem is not that the United States is imperialistic (as left-wing critics of American foreign policy would argue) but that theirs is the wrong kind of imperialism, economic rather than political (and ideological). Always fond of references to ancient times, Alain de Benoist sees the United States not as the new Rome, but as the new Carthage: "They talk a lot about 'imperialism' these days. But there are no longer any empires. *Imperium* is will, first and foremost. The Soviet Union, most of all America, derive their strength less from any kind of will as from their sheer *weight*. To be the distant subjects—even the mercenaries—of a new Rome, that would not be so bad. But America is not a new Rome. It is a new Carthage. As for us, *Graeculi* that we are, for want of a European Fichte, we are expecting a Cato" (271).

The internationalization of capitalistic modes of production and exchange facilitates the worldwide diffusion of American material culture and hastens the death of genuine Western (i.e., European) civilization. *Mondialisme*, as a process of relentless standardization of all cultures and traditions, is the latest version of the *philosophes*' ideals of universality. The inevitable outcome of the internationalization of American ways is the end of history: Cau says, "*Mondialisme*—in which our highest achievement . . . i.e., History affirmed and lived as will, would perish—is the only horizon conceivable for the United States. Not as History (by definition *mondialisme* is antihistorical) but as fatality" (*Discours de la décadence*, 165). The Nietzschean overtones of this gloomy prophecy, centered on the definition of history as will, are obvious. But the antidemocratic interpretation of American decadence can also lead to a Hegelian reading of postmodernity in many ways similar to Kojève's posthistorical universe.

The homogenization of thoughts, tastes, and behaviors by mass production and mass consumption leads to a systematic erasure of all differences between individuals and cultures: *mondialisme* becomes a form of totality by way of the reduction of multiplicity to the one. "The Americans do not consider their country as a nation similar to the other nations (in fact it is not even a nation at all), but as the model of a universal and cosmopolitan republic, called to *actualize*, in the spirit of the biblical virtues of 'justice' and 'peace' and according to the pattern of the American way of life, *the reduction of the world to unity*" (Herte and Nigra, 94). The combined ideals of the melting pot and of Manifest Destiny are seen as aiming at the gradual expulsion of the Other, of forms of thought or behavior which stand outside (or beyond) universal rationality, in the same way as Kojève's Hegelian universal and homogeneous state reconciled, by overcoming them, all differences and all contradictions in the atemporal truth of absolute knowledge. According to Herte and Nigra, "At the same time as he professes his isolationism, the American feels compelled to propagate in the world the great principles of the *American way of life*. The society in which he lives seems so excellent to him that he cannot conceive one could go *beyond*. He does not only believe in universal judgment, he also believes in paradise on earth. Without knowing it, he is somewhat Hegelian: to him, *stars and stripes* America is the completion, the 'splendid' end of history" (44).

The fact that it is not a nation (that is "not the country of any people," as Alain de Benoist puts it) constitutes the major flaw of the United States in the eyes of French nationalists. The French are often characterized by their ability to perceive a historical continuity in the political and cultural expressions of their national identity, continuity ensured primarily through the time-honored odyssey of the French (literary) language. National politics are inseparable from a politics of the language (*une politique de la langue*) embodied in institutions such as the Académie Française, the Panthéon (where prominent literary prophets are buried alongside with heads of state), or the Ministry of Culture. In Alain de Benoist's words "a nation sanctions a people's homogeneity. America, cosmopolitan by *calling*, is the living negation of *all* specificities, insofar as it aspired from the start to prefigure the future universal Republic" (*Les Idées à l'endroit*, 268).

We are reminded here of the distinction Norbert Elias makes between (French and English) civilization and (German) culture in *The Civilizing Process:* "The notion of civilization expresses the self-assurance of peoples whose national boundaries and national identity have been so fully established that they have ceased to be the subject of any particular discussion, peoples who have long expanded outside their borders and colonized beyond them. . . The concept of *Kultur* mirrors the self-consciousness of a nation which had constantly to seek out and constitute its boundaries anew, in a political as well as in a spiritual sense, and again and again to ask itself: 'What is our real identity?'" (6). What is true of Germany is a fortiori true of the United States—it is a federal republic made up of historically rival regional entities and peopled by races and ethnic groups from every corner of the globe.

For the right-wing critics, American intellectual and political elites, contrary to their French or British counterparts, cannot turn to an ancestral, homogeneous cultural tradition to assert their national identity. Nothing, Alain de Benoist argues, can unify Americans "in the superior sense" of the term, since they have nothing in common other than a deep contempt for the historical European nations they chose to secede from. The lowest common denominator of American identity can only be reached in the material level, in the form of a "technomorphy" which destroys the diversity of the world. "What can the *newcomers* of the American nation have in common besides the Bible, the Constitution, a taste for the dollar and the worship of *standing*? (264). "In a country where the Constitution sets as a goal for society 'the pursuit of happiness,' the people can only long for the end of history through the coming of 'prosperous communism'" (268).

The cosmopolitanism of American society (which in the writings of the new Right, conjures up memories of another culture reviled for its alleged cosmopolitanism, the Jewish one) can also work as a *positive* trait in the eyes of all the modernist admirers of a country that they insist in still viewing as a successful melting pot, open to worldwide diversity and the spearhead of a multinational liberal revolution. Not all French critics of the United States, however, buy into this idea of the fundamental cosmopolitan character of American culture, whether viewed positively or not. They are quick to point out, as does Régis Debray, for example, the difficulty in stressing the lack of "nationalism" of a country in which "every morning, schoolchildren swear allegiance to the stars-and-stripes while singing God Bless America, with one hand on their hearts," a country which "at the slightest opportunity bedecks its streets and houses with giant flags, and turns a parodic ethnocentricism into the measure of everything" (*Les Empires contre L'Europe*, 130). Debray goes on to qualify American patriotism as "the most powerful national egotism which the world has ever known" (130).

The divergent views of the French intelligentsia on the question of the national or transnational character of American society stems, once again, from the paradoxical, and highly specific, relationship Americans have with their past. Almost forty years ago, Daniel Boorstin argued in *The Genius of American Politics* that Americans tend to view their beliefs and values as always already "given" to them by their physical circumstances and history and, accordingly, in no need of justification or correction by theoretical and ideological abstractions. This explains both the pragmatism with which the culture regards its achievements (viewed as the product of "experience") and the high idealism with which it worships its sacred political and geographical origins, that is, the Constitution and "the land" (seen as unchallengeable and transhistorical). At the same time, however, Americans are acutely aware of the fact that, unlike Asians or Europeans, whose civilizations go back to the dawn of time, their national "experience" starts at a specific historical, and not mythical, moment in duration.

The paradox is that history is only important inasmuch as it serves to highlight the ahistorical, transcendent value of the first principles of political and social life, as "codified" by the Pilgrims and the Founding Fathers. "While the temper of much of our thought has been antihistorical," Boorstin remarks,"it is nevertheless true that we have leaned heavily on history to clarify our image of ourselves" (11). Boorstin challenges the European perception that Americans have no tradition of cultural continuity. On the contrary, he claims, they share a strong belief in the homogeneity of their history. "It is the quality of our experience which makes us see our national past as an uninterrupted continuum of similar events, so that our past merges undistinguishably with our present" (10). That is why Americans insist of seeing the Founding Fathers as their contemporaries, thereby collapsing historicity into the very "simultaneity" Alain de Benoist finds so offending. This also explains why they see no wrong with recreating life in the seventeenth or eighteenth centuries in perfect replicas of the past sold in theme parks and "historic" villages for tourists.

Turning the tables on the Europeans, Boorstin counters that it is *their* history which is profoundly *dis*continuous, made up of a succession of social arrangements and political regimes born of revolution and conquest. Nationalism in European countries is always the product of a political decision, of an ideological fiat, which constructs the succession of differences and foreign influences into a commonly assumed past, read through traditionalist or progressivist lenses. Europeans, consequently, fail to perceive that American patriotism, unable to root itself in the nonexistent common cultural past of immigrant groups from all continents of the globe, rests on the commonality of space, the sharing of the "givenness" of the blessings of the land. Aldous Huxley shrewdly perceived this fundamental difference between the two types of national identification when he wrote that "the greatest charm of foreign travel is the very high ratio of European history to European geography. Conversely, for the European, who has come to feel the oppressive weight of a doubtless splendid, but often fatal past, the greatest charm of travel in the New World is the high ratio of its geography to its history" (quoted in Boorstin, 31).

American national identity is rooted in the American way of life, which, in turn, can be interpreted as the domination of religion (over historically specific religions), or of materialism, as in Alain de Benoist's view, or conformity, or whatever. Boorstin's point, however, is that this way of life is seen as springing from the very soil, the physical environment where the historical unfolding took place. In truth, both elements are inseparable: the nation is both land and law, united by lived experience. "If American ideals are not in books or in the blood but in the air," the reasoning goes, "then they are readily acquired; actually, it is almost impossible for an immigrant to avoid acquiring them. He is not required to learn a philosophy so much as to rid his lungs of the air of Europe" (*The Genius of American Politics*, 28).

In the ideologically charged period of the mid-1950s, when hunting down un-American activities at home and exporting the American model of democracy abroad were the talk of the day, Boorstin claimed that the specifity of the American experience explained both why it had worked in the New World and why it was impossible to adapt it, as such, to the rest of the planet. Manifest Destiny was a one-time accomplishment, linked to a particular place, and a specific set of historical circumstances. Accordingly, Americans should not try to "show that we are the perfect embodiment of the European ideal of political institutions and culture. That we certainly are not. The European concept of a political community is of a group oriented toward fulfilling an explicit philosophy; political life there is the world of ends and absolutes" (184). Rather than accept the terms of an intellectual debate posed by Russia or Europe that Americans are sure to lose, says Boorstin, Americans should "discover that our virtues like our ills, are actually peculiar to ourselves; that what seem to be inadequacies of our culture, if measured by European standards, are nothing but our differences and may even be virtues" (184).

Richard Rorty has remarked, in a totally different context, on the Hegelian overtones of the doctrine of Manifest Destiny. In an essay devoted in part to George Santayana's views on philosophy in the United States, Rorty praises the Spanish-born philosopher for having been "entirely free of the instinctive American conviction that the westering of the spirit ends here—that whatever the ages have labored to bring forth will emerge between Massachussetts and California, that our philosophers have only to express our national genius for the human spirit to fulfill itself" (*Consequences of Pragmatism*, 60). Near the end of his essay, Rorty turns back to Santayana again, stressing his ability to avoid what he calls the mild chauvinism according to which America "is what history has been leading up to" (69). Refusing for his part to identify American society with the final resting place of the spirit, Rorty remarks that "there is no reason to think that the promise of American democracy will find its final fulfillment in America any more than Roman law reached its fulfillment in the Roman Empire or literary culture its fulfillment in Alexandria" (70).

The ideologues of the French *nouvelle droite*, of course, do not share Rorty's positive vision of the promise of America and offer a different version of its flight from history. Since, in a materialistic culture, they contend, all differences are only quantitative and can, by definition, be reduced to a common denominator, time itself is subject to the same process of unification and totalization. As mentioned earlier, the difference between past and future gives way to the eternity of the present moment. American society, standing as it does outside history, is nothing but "the crystallization of a moment of European history, the moment of prerevolutionary *Aufklärung* which is the source of the revolutions of 1776 and 1789" (Herte and Nigra, 92).

Here, the model of continuity with Europe takes precedence over the paradigm of absolute difference, which the same authors used earlier to stress the cultural rift between the two continents. America is indeed heir to Europe, but heir only to its most aberrant cultural product, the radical negation of genuine European values: the Enlightenment. The political and religious elites of the new nation took the worst elements of European culture and proceeded to make them the founding principles of the American Republic. American society is then doomed to gravitate endlessly in the orbit of *Aufklärung*, subject to the eternal recurrence of the same, that is, the universal rational values of Lockean liberalism.

The American concept of time is closer to the cyclical recurrence of primitive cultures than to the linear unfolding of historical time. The end of history is seen once again as a return to a prehistorical, prepolitical order reminiscent of Kojève's return to animality: America as Eden and utopia, a world before Europe. In the words of Herte and Nigra, "as a member of a 'cold society' (anti-historical) *par excellence*, the American is the Lévi-Straussian Bororo of modern times. Maybe this is the reason why American anthropology studies with such voluptuous predilection the most archaic of Indian civilizations: it finds in these fixed societies, all things considered, the cultural pattern of American society, the model it wishes to emulate" (93).

Escape from History: How Can One Be European?

Jean Baudrillard also characterizes the United States as "the only remaining primitive society" (*America*, 7). Although his interpretation of postmodern America reaches opposite conclusions, one may find in it many themes common to the neo-Hegelian and antidemocratic traditions.

As a matter of fact, as one examines recent French readings of contemporary America, a common pattern of interpretations and representations begins to emerge. While they generally agree on the description of the United States today, these analyses differ greatly on the evaluation of contemporary American culture.

In a way, Baudrillard addresses some of the questions Kojève, who died in June 1968, left unanswered: the question of the concrete unfolding of what Kojève described as a becoming-animal (or, on the other hand, becoming-snob) of humanity, the question of the value and meaning (or lack thereof) of the posthistorical condition, the question of the evaluation of the disappearance of meaning. Baudrillard's answers, however, based as they are on a critique of Hegelianism and, generally, of European philosophies of history, differ greatly from Kojève's interpretation of posthistorical times. Baudrillard's America has indeed gone out of history (or run out of history, as a car runs out of gas), just like Kojève's, but this did not occur during the French Revolution or after the battle of Jena. The exile from history happened earlier, with the crossing of the Atlantic ocean, a symbol of the ever-widening cultural gap between the two continents:

> Whereas [European societies] were caught up in the revolutions of the nineteenth century, the Americans kept intact—preserved as it was by a breadth of ocean that created something akin to temporal insularity—the utopian and moral perspective of the men of the eighteenth century, or even of the Puritan sects of the seventeenth, transplanted and kept alive, safely sheltered from the vicissitudes of history. This Puritan and moral hysteresis is that of exile, that of utopia. (*America*, 90)

It is no longer the post-Napoleonic rational state that survives overseas in the eternity of the end of time, but an earlier utopia, closer to Rousseau's views than it is to Hegel's. "The spatial and mental break of the migration" across the Atlantic prevented America from being contaminated by the European "transcendental and historical *Weltanschauung*" which, according to Baudrillard, will always baffle the American mind. "The social and philosophical nineteenth century did not cross the Atlantic" (90).

This perception of the absolute difference of American history (and of the American conception of history) is far from being limited to Baudrillard's writings. Philippe Sollers, for one, has expressed similar views on the subject, in the course of a debate on American history published in *Tel Quel* in 1976 to commemorate the bicentennial of the American Revolution:

"The United States is 1776, something that doesn't belong to the Jacobin model of the French revolution" (*The Kristeva Reader,* 279). European intellectuals, because they are fascinated by the Jacobin model, and because they have defined themselves politically as either in favor of or in opposition to it, have "lost a great deal of time considering problems about world revolution, the unification of thought relative to this revolution, and in our interminable debates on socialism," have been unable to conceive that "a completely different planet can exist on the basis of the underground, non-philosophic, non-Greek history which was grafted there" (284). Earlier in the discussion in *Tel Quel,* Julia Kristeva had described this nonspeculative, nonmetaphysical history as a questioning of the "linearity of our contemporary history":

> European societies obviously have an evolutionary perspective. . . . We've had the bourgeoisie, now it's the turn of "socialism" and "progress." . . . Well, I think that American time short-circuits this evolutionist vision because it entails a *split history:* on the one hand, there is in fact the evolutionism dictated by the development of the links between production and reproduction; but on the other hand, this evolutionism has as its underlying base a conjunction of several temporalities. Since this country is made up of emigrants (Jews, English, French, Central Europeans, Blacks, Indians, etc.), various individual ways of experiencing time and history intersect. (*The Kristeva Reader,* 276)

For Kristeva, the plural and pluralistic character of American history successfully holds in check the teleological versions that many radical intellectuals in the United States have inherited from Hegelian and Marxist influences: "This linear rationality, with its over-dogmatic Marxism, is confined to a limited context, thanks to the split American temporality I have mentioned. The cultural, technical and religious base is so riotous and multi-faceted that the non-truth that may obtain in a linearizing evolutionism or in the gratifying populism of dogmatic Marxism doesn't seem to be able to increase its influence" (277). The political implications of such a redescription of American difference are obvious, and candidly stated by the *Tel Quel* theoreticians at a time when they were abandoning their former Marxist-Leninist credo. Their insistence on the divorce between two visions of history is reminiscent, once again, of American cultural nationalism in the first decades of the new nation's existence, which led to what Oliver Wendell Holmes called a "declaration of intellectual independence." At the time, Emerson wrote in "The American Scholar" that his fellow Americans had "listened too long to the courtly muses of Europe."

In both cases, the emphasis on discontinuity between the two cultures clearly fulfills an ideological function: the literary and philosophical nationalism of the transcendentalists, an essential part of their strategy for recognition as legitimate intellectuals by their countrymen *and* their peers abroad, implied a distancing from the European tradition in spite of their acknowledged debt to Carlyle or Swedenborg. The same strategy, all things considered, allows Baudrillard, in a statement congruent with Sollers and Kristeva, to disqualify and delegitimize "the issue of history, of the State and the disappearance of the State which America never addresses," that is, Hegelian thought, and beyond, Marxism:

> Many American intellectuals envy us and would like to fashion a set of ideal values and a history for themselves, and relive the philosophical or Marxist delights of old Europe. . . . When I see Americans, particularly American intellectuals, casting a nostalgic eye towards Europe, its history, its metaphysics, its cuisine, I tell myself that this is just a case of unhappy transference. History and Marxism are like fine wines and haute cuisine: they do not really cross the ocean, in spite of the many impressive attempts that have been made to adapt them to new surroundings. (*America*, 79)

European categories of thought do not only prevent many foreign analysts from understanding American reality, they also condemn Europeans to "miss" the true meaning of modernity, which is the outcome of an irreducible difference. In that sense, it is as meaningless to fear the modernization of French society as it is to wish for it: "The confrontation between America and Europe reveals not so much a coming together as a distortion, an unbridgeable rift. There is not just a gap between us, but a whole chasm of modernity. You are born modern, you do not become so. And we have never become so" (*America*, 73). Let us note in passing that this (traditionally American) perception of America as absolute utopia, dawn of a new world, radical beginning of an other history, forever cleansed of European violence and contradictions, is in total opposition to models of continuity that describe American society as the most elaborate form of European rationalism or nihilism, as Cau writes, "the rude, horrendously *misbehaved* offspring of Europe, an overblown former colony of Europe" (*Pourquoi la France*, 53–54).

For Baudrillard, however, the American utopia is not the realm of absolute good. The loneliness and inhumanity of American inner cities reveals "a world completely rotten with wealth, power, senility, indifference, puritanism and mental hygiene, poverty and waste, technological futility and aimless violence" (*America*, 23). The horrified fascination for American hubris is, after all, a characteristic feature of most European, and especially French, accounts of the United States.

What sets Baudrillard's analysis apart from those of Sartre, Georges Duhamel, or Jean Cau, is his refusal to condemn: fascination wins in the end. "And yet I cannot help but feel [America] has about it something of the dawning of the universe. Perhaps because the entire world continues to dream of New York, even as New York dominates and exploits it" (23). Neither absolute good nor evil decadence, the "American utopia" is beyond good and evil, as it were, beyond the *concepts* of decadence or nihilism, since the end of history means precisely the disappearance of meaning and concept. In the same way, the traditional opposition between nature and culture, the material world and human activity, upon which the Enlightenment's idea of civilization rested, does not make any sense in the postmodern universe. There is no such thing as a raw, elemental reality out of which humanity could carve a meaningful destiny. There is no "nature," physical or mental, to be overcome and transfigured through history, just as there is no longer, in the "hyperreal" simulation of the media, a referent of signs and discourses.

As in Herte and Nigra's analysis, via the same reference to Lévi-Strauss, contemporary American culture is said to be closer to primitive thought than to the historical *Weltanschauung* of Europe. "In 'the savage mind,' too, there is no natural universe, no transcendence of either man and nature, or of history. Culture is everything, or nothing, depending on how you look at it" (*America*, 100). We are back, in a way, to Kojève's vision of posthistory as return to animality. For Baudrillard also, man's renaturalization brings about a world in which there is nothing left to do, because there is nothing left to desire. The Californian Eden is an eternity of pleasure to which death has already come:

> On the aromatic hillsides of Santa Barbara, the villas are all like funeral homes. Between the gardenias and the eucalyptus trees, among the profusion of plant genuses and the monotony of the human species, lies the tragedy of a utopian dream made reality. In the very heartland of wealth and liberation, you always hear the same question: "What are you doing after the orgy?" What do you do when everything is available—sex, flowers, the stereotypes of life and death? This is America's problem and, through America, it has become the whole world's problem. (*America*, 30)

No referentiality, no moral depth, no representation, no critique, not the shadow of a thought, everything is there, immediately given: "The United States is the only primitive society remaining."

Fredric Jameson, in one of his essays on postmodernism, finds at the heart of contemporary culture "the emergence of a new kind of flatness or depthlessness, a new kind of superficiality in the most literal sense" (60). In the world of theory, this means the disappearance of the "critical distance" that was the hallmark of the modernist movement. Jameson lists five of the "depth models" that contemporary culture has caused to collapse: the hermeneutic model of inside and outside, the dialectical [model] of essence and appearance, the Freudian model of latent and manifest or of repression, the existential model of authenticity and inauthenticity and, finally, the great semiotic opposition between signifier and signified. These various "depth models" have been replaced "for the most part by a new conception of practices, discourses and textual play. . . . Depth is replaced by surface, or by multiple surfaces (what is often called intertextuality is in that sense no longer a matter of depth)" (62). For Jameson the cult of depthlessness "finds its prolongation . . . in a whole new culture of the image or the simulacrum," defined, in Plato's sense, as "the identical copy for which no original has ever existed."[5] The proliferation of images (through, e.g., "the transformation of older realities into television images") weakens postmodern man's sense of historicity: this is one of the meanings of the end of history. Conversely, we live in a culture "increasingly dominated by space" and "the spatial logic of the simulacrum." In the new space of contemporary urban architecture, "we are submerged in its henceforth filled and suffused volumes to the point where our now postmodern bodies are bereft of spatial coordinates and practically (let alone theoretically) incapable of distanciation" (Jameson, 81).

Baudrillard's celebration of American superficiality illustrates Jameson's interplay between ahistoricity, depthlessness, and the spatial logic of the simulacrum. For Baudrillard, American culture, having stepped out of history, stands outside time. The timeless spatiality of contemporary America finds its most powerful symbol in the desolation of the great southwestern desert. For in the desert, as within Jameson's Bonaventura Hotel (80–83), there are no more bearings, no more "spatial coordinates," no more cultural landmarks on which to rest our gaze and anchor our collective memories. In the desert, one is adrift in the space of meaninglessness. "Everything here still bears the marks of a primitive society: technologies, the media, total simulation (bio-, socio-, stereo-, video-) are developing in a wild state, in their original state. Insignificance exists on a grand scale and the desert remains the primal scene, even in the big cities. Inordinate space, a simplicity of language and character" (*America*, 63).

The consummation of meaning brings humanity back to its origin, to a world before history and language, to the timeless silence of the wilderness:

> Why is L.A., why are the deserts so fascinating? It is because you are delivered from all depth there—a brilliant, mobile, superficial neutrality, a challenge to meaning and profundity, a challenge to nature and culture, an outer hyperspace, with no origin, no reference-points.... American culture is heir to the deserts, but the deserts here are not part of a Nature by contrast with the town. Rather they denote the emptiness, the radical nudity that is the background to every human institution. At the same time, they designate human institutions as a metaphor of that emptiness and the work of man as the continuity of the desert, culture as a mirage and as the perpetuity of the simulacrum.... In California ... culture itself is a desert. (*America*, 124, 63, 126)

The "stellar indifference" of the American desert becomes the spatial metaphor of the cultural barrenness of a nonnaturalistic, posthistorical universe, which Europeans find so hard to comprehend and accept. "What is new in America is the clash of the first level (primitive and wild) and the 'third kind' (the absolute simulacrum). There is no second level. This is a situation we find hard to grasp, since this is the one we have always privileged: the self-reflexive, self-mirroring level, the level of unhappy consciousness" (*America*, 104). The "extermination" of nature, meaning, and culture, the omnipresence of simulacra, the generalized diffusion of signs without referents (forms without contents) mirror Kojève's second version of posthistory, that is, snobbery and the aesthetics of meaninglessness. "The mirror phase has given way to the video phase.... What develops around the video and stereo culture is not a narcissistic imaginary, but an effect of frantic self-referentiality, a short-circuit which immediately hooks up like with like.... This is the special effect of our times. America is a giant hologram, in the sense that information concerning the whole is contained in each of its elements" (37, 29).

American culture is described elsewhere as pure fiction, which is not to say, warns Baudrillard, that it is imaginary. Here again, the visitor from Europe is in danger of projecting on contemporary America the categories of his own cultural tradition, and the classic opposition between real and imaginary. To do so would be to miss the radical originality of the American utopia, its fictional character. "Now, fiction is not imagination. It is what anticipates imagination by giving it the form of reality. This is quite opposite to our own natural tendency which is to anticipate reality by imagining it, or to flee from it by idealizing it. That is why we shall never inhabit true fiction; we are condemned to the imaginary and to nostalgia for the future" (*America*, 95).

Baudrillard's analysis submits both the Hegelian and Nietzschean readings of America to a double twist. He agrees with the neo-Hegelians that postmodern America is the consummation of historical time through the resolution of the contradictions between nature and man (technology) as well as between man and man (the disappearance of all meaningful conflicts, the end of ideologies). But the universal expansion of techniques and the standardization of life-styles generate new class differences and new social exclusions. The "universal and homogeneous state" is not a classless society. The end of history does not mean the erasure of difference, but rather the generalization of indifference. "The world is almost entirely liberated; there is nothing left to fight for. And yet at the same time entire social groups are being laid waste from the inside (individuals too). Society has forgotten them, and now they are forgetting themselves. . . . This is the Fourth World" (*America*, 112).

As for the Nietzscheans, Baudrillard would agree with them that contemporary America is the apex of nihilism, the realm of insignificance rather than absolute knowledge. The end of history as the coming of reason has turned into the end of time, the apocalyptic empire of irrationality, immorality, and monstrosity:

> The microwave, the waste disposal, the orgasmic elasticity of the carpets: this soft, resort-style civilization irresistibly evokes the end of the world. . . . Nothing evokes the end of the world more than a man running straight ahead on a beach, swathed in the sounds of his walkman, cocooned in the solitary sacrifice of his energy. . . . The thousands of lone men, each running on their own account, with no thought for others, with a stereophonic fluid in their heads that oozes through into their eyes, that is the world of *Blade Runner*, the post-catastrophe world. (*America*, 31, 38)

But for all the prophecies of doom that fill his narrative of America, Baudrillard departs from the desperate pessimism of those who lament the decadence of the West. Fredric Jameson detects in the postmodern sensibility the emergence of a "new type of emotional ground tone," based on "the high, the intoxicatory or hallucinogenic intensity," and in total opposition to the angst of the modern artist (146). Baudrillard seems to share "the peculiar kind of euphoria"; the endless proliferation of simulacra and the growing equivalency of values and lifestyles leads to a form of *gay science*, and gives rise to a sort of postnihilistic, or supernihilistic, exhilaration: "We fanatics of aesthetics and meaning, of culture, of flavor and seduction . . . We who are unfailingly attached to the wonders of critical sense and transcendence find it a mental shock and a unique release to discover the fascination of nonsense. . . . To discover that one can exult in the liquidation of all culture and rejoice in the consecration of in-difference" (*America*, 123).

Are we witnessing here a postmodern form of Nietzsche's *amor fati*, another joyful "yes saying" to the inevitable? Perhaps, although Baudrillard's acceptance of our fin de siècle does not imply the advent of the Superman or the ultimate triumph of Gilles Deleuze's "active forces." For today's Eternal Return is not "the exaltation of a will, nor the sovereign affirmation of an event, nor its consecration by an immutable sign, such as Nietzsche sought, but the viral recurrence of microprocesses" (72). It is both a more modest and more disturbing process, the reoccurence of "the infinitely small, the fractal, the obsessive repetition of things on a microscopic and inhuman scale" (72). Baudrillard's double (dialectical?) *dépassement* of neo-Hegelian and neo-Nietzschean readings of postmodernity reaches here its final stage. In the end, Hegel refutes Nietzsche (American culture is not decadence, it is overcoming the contradictions of European history and thought) and Nietzsche forever disproves Hegelianism (this overcoming is the triumph of insignificance, not of rationality).

It is precisely because they owe too much to the nineteenth century and "its approach of history, the State and the disappearance of the State" that most European, all too European, readings of America cannot grasp its radical "eccentricity." In order to understand, one must displace oneself and go beyond the boundaries of European philosophical and political thought in the same way Americans stepped out of history when they left the Old World. But does not such a model of absolute discontinuity rob all European discourses on America, including Baudrillard's, of any credibility? For if American reality is unthinkable in terms of European categories, what is the point of trying to account for the absolute Other? In truth, the paradigm of absolute difference is untenable. Baudrillard's account of American postmodernity first and foremost criticizes French and European fin de siècle, just as Voltaire's *Philosophical Letters* celebrated English freedom in order to better undermine the ideological underpinnings of French absolutism. Baudrillard's analysis of America's inconceivable modernity, enables him to stress, on the contrary, what he perceives to be the cultural archaism of Europe, hopelessly mired in the nineteenth century:

"We shall never be able to excentre or decentre ourselves in the same way [as the Americans]. We shall therefore never be modern in the proper sense of the term. And we shall never enjoy the same freedom" (*America*, 81).

Paradoxically, not only does the analysis of America enable Europeans to better understand Europe, but Europeans may be the only ones who can truly grasp its significance, precisely because they will never reach American modernity. It is possible therefore, that "the truth of America can only be seen by a European, since he alone will discover here the perfect simulacrum—that of the immanence and material transcription of all values" (*America*, 28). Americans, on the other hand, are necessarily blind to the truth of their own culture. Not only are they totally immersed in it, but they are deprived of the very conceptual tools that would enable them to transcend the "immanence of all values." In fact, the natives have "no sense of simulation. They are themselves simulation in its most developed state, but they have no language in which to describe it, since they themselves are the model. As a result, they are the ideal material for an analysis of all the possible variants of the modern world" (28).

Fascinated as he is by the death of his own culture, which is occuring *somewhere else*, the European observer is endowed with the paradoxical power to speak of the silence of the desert and to produce meaningful sentences on what is deprived of any meaning. Baudrillard himself cannot resist the "prestige of criticism and transcendence" which are in his eyes the hallmark (and the disease) of European culture. The European critic becomes a postmodern version of Pascal's thinking reed: he alone can make sense of a world in which his own culture has no place.

The postulate of the absolute difference of American culture gives way to another narrative, which says that America has achieved what Europe, after having conceived of its possibility, proved unable to do. This achievement is not the dream of the Enlightenment, as in the liberal tradition, but its very opposite, the nightmare of an irrational and nihilistic anti-utopia. America has actualized the theoretical program of the 1960s. The death of man, of philosophy, and of the subject took place on the very shores of the Pacific Ocean. Europeans have been content with conceptualizing the end of history; Americans experience it everyday:

Everything we have dreamed in the radical name of anticulture, the subversion of meaning, the destruction of reason and the end of representation, that whole anti-utopia which unleashed so many theoretical and political, aesthetic and social convulsions in Europe, without ever actually becoming a reality (May '68 is one of the last

233

examples), all has been achieved here in America, in the simplest, most radical way. *Utopia has been achieved here and anti-utopia is being achieved:* the anti-utopia of unreason, of deterritorialization, of the indeterminacy of the subject and of language, of the neutralization of all values, of the death of culture. . . . We philosophize on the end of lots of things, but it is here that they actually come to an end. It is here, therefore, that we should look for the ideal type of the end of our culture. (*America*, 97–98)

In that sense, contemporary America is no longer the absolute Other, but rather the unrepeatable, and fascinating, occurrence of the disappearance of the Same.

Postmodern Tocqueville

I wrote that Baudrillard's variations on postmodern themes were in many respects a way of settling an account with European historicism. But his take on the United States is not only a negative critique of European social and political thought: its explicit reference to and agreement with Tocqueville's analysis of the dialectics of freedom and equality places it within what I have called the tradition of French interpretations of American reality. The central tenet of Tocqueville's argument is well known: American society is the ideal object for a study of the democratic age, because the trend toward equality (the driving force behind the transformation of European societies) has unfolded practically without check in America in the absence of feudal structures. Tocqueville noted that America had "attained the consequences of the democratic revolution which we are undergoing without having experienced the revolution itself" (*Democracy in America*, 1:13). American culture and society are therefore radically different from their European counterparts.

Hannah Arendt's opposition between the French and American revolutions owes much to Tocqueville's model of the "exceptionalism" of American political culture. As we know, Arendt saw in the "prerevolutionary prosperity" of the United States the unique complex of historical conditions having made possible the realization of the dream of the Enlightenment, that is, the eradication of poverty and famine. In *On Revolution*, Arendt writes, "America had become the symbol of a society without poverty long before the modern age in its unique technological development had actually discovered the means to abolish that abject misery of sheer want which had always been held to be eternal." Furthermore, the representation of America as the first "affluent society" in human history "made it possible for the social question and the rebellion of the poor . . . to play a truly revolutionary role" in Europe (15). Although American prosperity spurred the revolutionary fervor of the European poor, the American model played little role in European politics after 1789. The American specificity, first perceived as a difference from the ancien régime, had now become alien to the new regime as well, in a process of rupture within the rupture that further accentuated the gap between the two continents: "If there was a single event that shattered the bonds between the New World and the countries of the old Continent, it was the French Revolution" (*On Revolution*, 217).

Tocqueville's paradigm of rupture, so central to Arendt's thought, also influenced most of the subsequent French analyses of American society, whether sympathetic (the liberal tradition) or hostile (the Marxist and Sartrean interpretations). As for Baudrillard's view of contemporary America as the non-Hegelian society par excellence, it is clearly cast in a Tocquevillean mold:

> We criticize [the Americans] for this: why did the revolution not take place here, in this new country, this land of freedom and advanced bastion of capitalism? Why do the "social" and the "political," our favored categories, have such little purchase here? The answer is that the social and philosophical 19th century did not cross the Atlantic and here the driving forces are utopia and morality, the concrete idea of happiness and mores, all of which political ideology, with Marx at its head, liquidated in Europe in favor of an "objective" conception of historical transformation. (*America*, 90)

Despite his admiration for the American political system, Tocqueville was wary of the oppressive conformism that inevitably followed the generalization of equality. He saw the institutional protection of individual liberties and properties as the only way to prevent egalitarianism from turning liberal democracy into the tyranny of public opinion. "The nations of our time," he warned at the end of *Democracy in America*, "cannot prevent the conditions of men from becoming equal; but it depends upon themselves whether the principle of equality is to lead them to servitude or freedom, to knowledge or barbarism, to prosperity or to wretchedness" (2:348). Re-examining Tocqueville's analysis of the tension between freedom and equality in the light of a century and a half of democratic developments, Baudrillard concedes the final victory to the latter:

> Freedom understood as public action, as the collective discourse of a society on its own undertakings and values, has in fact disappeared in the individual liberation of mores and in agitation (agitation, as is

well known, is one of the Americans' main activities). It is, therefore, equality and its consequences that have been more instrumental in the creation of power. . . . It is this equality, the modern equalization of statuses and values, the uniformity of features and characters, which gives birth to power. (*America*, 89)

The question of the dynamics of equality, of the passage from a liberal (and ascetic) definition of individualism based on the necessary subordination of individual rights to the common good of the body politic (the individual's duties towards the collectivity) to the contemporary hedonistic conception of individualism as the absolute and unrestrained satisfaction of individual psychic and physical needs, is central to the present debate on the cultural evolution of Western democracies. Even the harshest critics of contemporary relativism acknowledge that it did not spring from the subversive minds of a few Nietzschean nihilists. Allan Bloom concedes that "from the earliest beginnings of liberal thought there was a tendency in the direction of indiscriminate freedom" (28). The growth of this "radicalized democratic theory" has led to the establishment of a form of "liberalism without natural rights" (J. S. Mill, Dewey), and finally to the present degeneration of freedom into licentiousness.

Daniel Bell also acknowledges that the various consequences of individualism, such as liberalism, libertinism, and libertarianism, were already present within Enlightenment culture. Bell's thesis is that capitalism itself has undermined, through the development of consumption, its own puritanical value system. Bourgeois society has a double source, and a "double fate." The contradiction within American culture between a Puritan, Whig capitalism "in which the emphasis was not just on economic activity but on the formation of *character* [and] a secular Hobbesianism, a radical individualism . . . which was restrained in politics by a sovereign but ran free in economics and culture" (80) led to the gradual undermining of the Protestant ethic, "not by modernism but by capitalism itself" (21). In this perspective "the greatest single engine in the destruction of the Protestant ethic was the invention of the installment plan, or instant credit," which demonstrated the capacity of the system to create "new wants and new ways of gratifying those wants" (21).

Ultimately, Bell reaches the same conclusions as Bloom: radical individualism undermines the very foundation of Western democracy. Ironically enough, the Frankfurt school Marxists had also come to similar conclusions; Horkheimer and Adorno told us a now-familiar story in their *Dialectic of Enlightenment*: the process of rationalization implicit in eighteenth century social thought has undermined the beliefs in rationality, natural rights, and human nature that has been central to Enlightenment philosophy. "Ultimately," they wrote, "the Enlightenment consumed not just the symbols [of social union] but their successors, universal concepts, and spared no remnant of metaphysics. . . . The situation of concepts in the face of the Enlightenment is like that of men of private means in regard to industrial trusts: none can feel safe" (quoted in Rorty, *Contingency, Irony, and Solidarity*, 56). For the German philosophers, the most perfected (and hence frightening) outcome of this dialectical process of self-destruction was the American mass culture of their day.

Bell's and Adorno's positions coincide with Hannah Arendt's moralistic views on the corruption of the ideals of the Founding Fathers by the materialistic greed of the (European) immigrant masses. For Arendt, the quest for "abundance and endless consumption" (the American dream) is incompatible with the ethical asceticism that is the only true foundation of a free society, for it turns the "citizen" of the Enlightenment into the "individual" of contemporary consumer society:

> The trouble was that the struggle to abolish poverty, under the impact of a continual mass immigration from Europe, fell more and more under the sway of the poor themselves, and hence came under the guidance of the ideals born out of poverty, as distinguished from those principles which had inspired the foundation of freedom. . . . The hidden wish of poor men is not "To each according to his needs," but "To each according to his desires." And while it is true that freedom can come only to those whose needs have been fulfilled, it is equally true that it will escape those who are bent upon living for their desires. (*On Revolution*, 135–36)

The question of the moral and political consequences of radical individualism has also divided French intellectual circles for the past few years. Alain Finkielkraut's *La Défaite de la pensée* (The surrender of thought) is an attack on contemporary cultural relativism and a passionate advocation of the universalist values of the Enlightenment tradition. In Finkielkraut's eyes, the postmodern apologists of "anything goes" individualism confuse the fundamental concept of liberalism, that is, the autonomy of the subject, with the egotistic quest for total self-gratification. The denunciation of totalitarian regimes and of the use and abuse of monological reason "would deserve unreserved applause if . . . it did not confuse egoism (or, to use a phrase totally devoid of any moral connotation: the pursuit by everyone of one's private interests) with autonomy" (164). This fateful confusion has led the apologists of postmodern freedom to assume that "the limitation of authority" guarantees "the autonomy of judgment and will." In fact,

Finkielkraut contends, "the disappearance of constraints inherited from the past is not enough to insure freedom of the spirit: one needs also to be enlightened, as they used to say in the eighteenth century" (165).

In other words, what is happening to "Western civilization" is, to quote French political philosophers Luc Ferry and Alain Renault, that the (Kantian) autonomous subject "is dying with the advent of the individual" (*La Pensée 68*, 100). Finkielkraut agrees with Condorcet, who wrote that "as long as there will be men who do not obey reason alone, who will receive their opinions from an outside opinion, all the chains will have been broken in vain" (165). He also contends, like Jürgen Habermas, that the project of the Enlightenment has been left incomplete:

> The *Philosophes* fought in the same breath for the extension of culture to everyone and for the removal of the individual sphere from the power of the state or the hold of collectivity. They wanted men to be at once free to reach their particular goals and able to carry their thoughts beyond this narrow domain. One can clearly see today that they have won half of the fight: despotism was vanquished, but not obscurantism. (Finkielkraut, 165)

Jean-Marie Benoist devotes a good part of his criticism of American influence in contemporary European culture to the contradiction between economic and political liberalisms, a contradiction summed up in the opposition between the freedom of human beings and that of the market. In Benoist's views, American culture has inherited from the Hobbesian side of the British Enlightenment a propensity to emphasize the nature of things (the objective mechanisms of the market) to the detriment of the Rousseauian conception of the nature of men. The intellectual, and political, conflict between the two worldviews stems from "the major difference between the two types of social contract on which these two ideologies rest. The first, which exalts the notion of competition, derives from the Hobbesian state of war. . . . The second, on the other hand, is akin to the pluralist ideas of a Montesquieu, a Locke, with his theory of the brotherhood and harmony in the state of nature" (139).

In America, the Hobbesian side of British culture is seen has having overwhelmed the Lockean one, opening the door to the absolute domination of economic principles over political considerations. Benoist's own brand of Gaullism attracts him to "continental" theories of the political which, like those of Rousseau or Machiavelli, oppose the power of the sovereign, or of the state, to the "liberal" hegemony of market forces. Benoist sees the gradual ascendency of the media and technocracy over parliamentary democracy and party politics as a passage from "a society structured by Rousseau's social contract to a society to which Locke's social contract is the key" (145).

Jean Baudrillard, as I have already pointed out, does not share the moralistic pessimism of the advocates of ancient or Enlightenment conceptions of the *polis*. He believes that the absolute specificity of American culture removes it from the ideological categories in which such debates are framed. For there is a radical difference in the *meaning* of freedom and equality in Europe and the United States. American equality, as a historical given, cannot be equated with egalitarianism, which is the product of decadence. The specifity of American democracy lies for Baudrillard in the fact that equality was already present at the birth of the republic: "That is the difference between egalitarianism and democracy: democracy presupposes equality at the outset, egalitarianism presupposes it at the end" (*America*, 94).

"The shock of the [French] Revolution," the French historian Pierre Moreau wrote, "by opening a gap between two neighboring centuries, by making nineteenth century people feel foreign to eighteenth century men, gave the former a genuine sense of history" (quoted in d'Hondt, 12). Baudrillard would probably agree with such a view of European intellectual history. But his point, precisely, is that the American people did not develop "a genuine sense of history," simply because, as Tocqueville remarked, they did not experience the "shock of the Revolution."

Thirty five years ago, in his *Liberal Tradition in America*, Louis Hartz picked up where Tocqueville had left off and showed how the absence of feudalism and revolution made liberalism the natural ideology of American society. Hartz also emphasized the egalitarian character of American society at the onset: "One of the central characteristics of a nonfeudal society is that it lacks a genuine revolutionary tradition, the tradition which in Europe has been linked with the Puritan and French revolutions—it is 'born equal,' as Tocqueville said." The "tyrannical force of Lockean sentiment," as Hartz puts it, in American culture made it impossible for Marxism and the socialist movement to really gain foot in the New World. "It is not accidental that America which has uniquely lacked a feudal tradition has uniquely lacked also a socialist tradition. The hidden origin of socialist thought everywhere in the West is to be found in the feudal ethos. The *ancien régime* inspires Rousseau; both inspire Marx" (Hartz, 6).

Baudrillard undoubtedly shares the same perception of an absolute break between cultural developments in continental Europe and (Britain and) America in the nineteenth and early twentieth centuries. He nevertheless seems to hesitate over the moment when the two cultures radically parted ways: "The Americans kept intact—preserved as it was by a breadth of ocean that created something akin to temporal insularity—the utopian and moral perspective of the men of the eighteenth century, *or even* of the Puritan sects of the seventeenth, transplanted and kept alive, safely sheltered from the vicissitudes of history" (*America*, 90; emphasis added). Baudrillard's hesitation as to the true "historical" origins of American specificity, that is, the moment in (European) history when America is supposed to have stepped out of history, may be another instance of the postmodernist's derealized and problematic relationship to the past. The question of the occurrence of such an event is, in this respect, a moot one. It involves more than historical scholarship or epistemology, though: it points to different modes of cultural (self-)perceptions. While most Americans usually perceive themselves as reasonable heirs to the English Revolution and to Lockean liberalism, many Europeans (and specifically the French) tend to see them as still sharing the naively optimistic faith in the essential goodness of human nature characteristic of the Rousseauian side of the French Enlightenment.

The meaning of "or even," the linguistic marker of Baudrillard's indecisiveness, is in itself ambiguous. It cannot have here, I am certain, a connotation of equivalency, as if the referents of "eighteenth-century men" and "seventeenth-century sects" were interchangeable. For if ideological forces in both "centuries" did indeed prepare the advent of the democratic age, distinctions must be made between the pessimistic austerity of the age of Jansenism, *moralisme*, and the Puritan Revolution ("the seventeenth century") and the careless and refined brilliance of the enlightened courts of Europe where Voltaire and Diderot prophesied a world forever free of superstition, ignorance, and bigotry ("the eighteenth century"). Let it suffice to remark that Baudrillard does not make the distinction. Glossing over the difference between puritanism and liberalism as competing cultural forces in American history, a difference which points to the complexity of what we call "the modern times," he is content with stressing the specificity of American culture vis-à-vis Europe, regardless of the complex historical genesis of this specificity.

The emphasis on the radical difference of American culture, however, raises another important question that is critical to the understanding of our historical moment. So far, American culture has been described negatively, in terms of what it does *not* imply (the European metaphysical tradition, Hegel, modernist criticism, socialism, etc.). Assuming that all this is a valid characterization of America, assuming that it did step out of the

European nineteenth century, then what happened to *its* nineteenth century? If the absence of feudalism and the overwhelming influence of Lockean ideas made an American version of Hegel and Robespierre, Goethe and Jaurès, Marx and de Maistre, the Jacobins, the Fabians, and the Bolsheviks, historically impossible, then what type of social and political philosophy did America produce during all those years when Europeans were busy fighting over the type of culture and society with which to replace the ancien régime?

The Pragmatization of the West

Pragmatism, to quote Louis Hartz, is "interestingly enough America's great contribution to the philosophic tradition." In his *Liberal Tradition in America*, Hartz demonstrated how this most American of philosophies was inextricably linked to what he called "the irrational, mass Lockeanism" of the larger culture: "It is only when you take your ethics for granted that all problems emerge as problems of technique" (10). In *The Cultural Contradictions of Capitalism*, Daniel Bell also equated pragmatism with what he called "the liberal temper, which redefines all existential questions into 'problems' and looks for 'solutions' to problems" (28). Sidney Hook, one of Dewey's most prominent disciples, has called pragmatism the first "distinctively American philosophy" (3) and, more recently, Richard Rorty, while remarking that it is "a vague, ambiguous and overworked word," nevertheless sees in pragmatism "the chief glory of our country's intellectual tradition" (*Consequences of Pragmatism*, 160).

As a narrative of Western intellectual history and as a program for social progress, the pragmatic project, beyond its narrower, more technical aspects, appears indeed as *the* philosophical version of the American liberal-democratic ethos, that unreflective, spontaneous mass Lockeanism that Louis Hartz saw as the underlying matrix of political culture in the United States. The American appropriation of British liberalism and empiricism implied that political ideals should be divorced from useless and cumbersome metaphysical claims. Freedom, as Rorty recently put it, *must* come before truth: "When we look for regulative ideals, we [should] stick to freedom and forget about truth and rationality. . . . If we take care of political and cultural freedom, truth and rationality will take care of themselves" ("On Truth, Freedom, and Politics," 634). John Dewey's own brand of cultural history stresses the intellectual and political filiation between pragmatism and the tradition of Baconian practical experimentalism. Consider, for example, the following passage from *Reconstruction in Philosophy*: "When Henry James called Pragmatism a New Name for an Old Way of

Thinking, I do not know that he was thinking expressly of Francis Bacon, but so far as concerns the spirit and atmosphere of the pursuit of knowledge, Bacon may be taken as the prophet of a pragmatic conception of knowledge" (38).

The pragmatists' critique of metaphysics often takes the form of an attack of the political and institutional consequences of pre-Enlightenment scholasticism. According to Dewey, "The effect of the objective theological idealism that had developed out of classic metaphysical idealism was to make the mind submissive and acquiescent" (50). Indeed, "the metaphysical doctrine of the superiority of the species to the individual, of the permanent universal to the changing particular, was the philosophic support of political and ecclesiastical institutionalism" (45).

More recently, in *The American Evasion of Philosophy: A Genealogy of Pragmatism*, Cornel West has taken up again the case of the political progressivism of the pragmatic stance: "American pragmatism is a diverse and heterogeneous tradition. But its common denominator consists of a future-oriented instrumentalism that tries to deploy thought as a weapon to enable more effective action. Its basic impulse is a plebeian radicalism that fuels an antipatrician rebelliousness for the moral aim of enriching individuals and expanding democracy" (5). In West's view, pragmatism is the finest expression of the new "American religion," an Emersonian paean to nature, cosmic consciousness, and unlimited space, the apology of individual self-reliance and untrammeled creativity. After all, Dewey himself said that "the coming century may well make evident what is just now dawning, that Emerson is not only a philosopher, but that he is the Philosopher of Democracy" (quoted in West, 76). The founding father of New World philosophy, as a form of ongoing "cultural criticism" as West puts it, wrote in "The American Scholar" that he did not care much for "the great, the remote, the romantic. . . Greek art, or Provençal minstrelsy," but unshamedly embraced the common, and proudly sat "at the feet of the familiar and the low" (*Selected Writings*, 238).

West goes on to argue that the pragmatic conception of truth can be viewed as "a kind of Americanization of the notion of truth, an Emersonian effort at democratization and plebeianization of the idea of truth that renders it 'various and flexible,' 'rich and endless' in resources, and it is hoped 'friendly' in its conclusion" (100). Dewey, for his part, becomes, "first and foremost an Emersonian evangelist of democracy who views the expansion of critical intelligence as requisite for the more full development of human individuality and personality" (100). Just as the revolutionary masses had chafed under British rule and revolted against the doctrinaire orthodoxies of European monarchies and theocracies, their intellectual heirs and political continuators, the pragmatists, have rejected speculative philosophy as "a remake of medieval scholasticism," debunked the metaphysical concept of reality as another form of authority imposed on the creative efforts of humanity, and criticized epistemology as a secular form of faith, "standing in the way of American and world progress" (West, 93). In that sense, pragmatism is an instance of "class struggle in theory." What the republican patriots did to the Tories and the Redcoats, Emerson and his disciples did to the elitist, priestly, and patrician metaphysics of the Old World: they declared themselves wholly independent from it.

No wonder, then, that pragmatism, the self-described philosophic legitimation of democratic secularism, would appear, to European critics of American capitalism and bourgeois democracy, right-wing and left-wing alike, as the quintessential expression of American naive optimism and unrepentent materialism. Sidney Hook has noted how the emphasis on action that was so central to early forms of American pragmatism quickly degenerated, in its vulgarized versions, in an identification of action with practice, and of practice with usefulness, opening the doors to the traditional contempt of continental Europeans for Anglo-Saxon self-serving utilitarianism:

> Since Americans were considered a practical people with a highly developed sense of the concrete and useful, pragmatism was played up abroad as the American philosophy par excellence . . . And since the chief practice of Americans seemed to be, in the eyes of their poorer neighbors, the making of money, pragmatism was cried down as the typical philosophy of a parvenu people, insensitive to tradition and culture, and devoted only to the invention of machines to make more machines by human beings who acted as if they were themselves only complicated machines. (*Pragmatism and the Tragic Sense of Life*, 4)

Most European observers of the American scene did indeed link the success of pragmatism in the United States to what they saw as a deep antitheoretical current in American culture. Lecturing on the American character after a six-month visit to the United States, Jean-Paul Sartre saw the need to "adapt man to society, which shows the social character of their rationalism which never looks for metaphysical problems" as the main concern of the American mind. As a consequence, "the tragic sense of life, the sense of human destiny are questions an American mind never asks itself" (*L'Ordre*, 4). In her essay *On Revolution*, Hannah Arendt commented on the historical consequences of what she called "the 'American' aversion from conceptual thought":

> However, if it is indisputable that book-learning and thinking in concepts, indeed of a very high caliber, erected the framework of the American republic, it is no less true that this interest in political thought dried up almost immediately after the task had been achieved. As I indicated earlier, I think this loss of an allegedly purely theoretical interest in political issues has not been the "genius" of American history but, on the contrary, the chief reason the American Revolution has remained sterile in terms of world politics. (46)

These various judgments on American pragmatism replicate the canonical opposition between "Anglo-American" empiricism and "Continental" metaphysics which has structured the field of post-Cartesian European philosophy, an institutional and theoretical dualism which the pragmatists have repeatedly tried to leave behind by showing that it is pointless.

Jacques Maritain, despite his admiration for the American experience, warned in his *Reflections on America* of the dangers of empiricism gone awry. He praised what he called the American "modesty before life and reality," a humility rooted in "a sense of the complexity of things, of the fluidity of life which escapes our concepts" (96). This is the "experiential approach, in which it is necessary to get all factual data, all points of view and all possible opinions before making a judgment—itself tentative" (97). This healthy suspicion of ideologies nevertheless runs the risk of turning into an outright "general and systematic Fear of ideas" and intellectual intuition, which would, in turn, damage intellectual creativity. This kind of nativistic know-nothingism could open the gate to a no-holds-barred form of relativism, thereby undermining the rational basis of democratic consensus:

> The deep-rooted intellectual convictions, rationally founded, which man needs for the conduct of his life . . . in particular, the moral tenets of a free people—justice; freedom; equality; human rights— would risk becoming a matter of feeling and national tradition, or adjustment to the environment, instead of being held as objective values, justifiable in reason. Then, on the one hand, these moral tenets would lose their inner vigor in each individual. They would become more or less relativized, subjectivized. And on the other hand, they would lose their intelligible universality, and communicability,

their impacts on the minds of other peoples, that persuasive, illuminating, *apostolic* power which is peculiar to ideas. (*Reflections on America*, 98)

Recent pessimistic accounts of contemporary culture by American critics such as Christopher Lasch, Robert Bellah, or Allan Bloom imply that the present situation has largely born out Maritain's forebodings. Although they differ in many respects, these analyses agree on the devastating effects of contemporary relativism and subjectivism on the Americans' sense of belonging to a historical tradition. Radical historicism has ironically dissolved all sense of historical continuity. In his *Culture of Narcissism*, Lasch contends that the failure of American liberalism is particularly visible in the contemporary "collapse of the historical faith, which formerly surrounded the record of public events with an aura of moral dignity, patriotism and political optimism" (19). Bloom, for his part, argues in *The Closing of the American Mind* that the belief in the relativity of truth has become for most American students "a moral postulate, the condition of a free society . . . the only virtue . . . the great insight of our times" (25–26). A proper historical attitude, on the other hand, Bloom says, "would lead one to doubt the truth of historicism (the view that all thought is essentially related to and cannot transcend its own time) and treat it as a peculiarity of contemporary history" (40). The authors of *Habits of the Heart* also stress the connection between the hedonistic individualism of our times and the dissolution of all links with the past. They see the main antidote to the dehistoricizing effects of radical liberalism in what they call "communities of memory," that is, groups of socially committed individuals (often political activists or civic-minded volunteers) involved in retelling a constitutive narrative, the stories of "the men and women who have embodied and exemplified the meaning of the community" through time (153).

Another possible consequence of pragmatism for Jacques Maritain is a kind of philosophical and political isolationism, a rejection of the universalist claims that have made America one of the beacons of freedom and democracy throughout the world, and the adoption of the kind of ethnocentrism advocated by Richard Rorty, who describes himself and his colleagues as "bourgeois liberals who have gone postmodern." "The citizens of my liberal utopia would be people who had a sense of the contingency of their language of moral deliberation, and thus of their conscience, and thus of their community" (*Contingency, Irony and Solidarity*, 61).[6] Anticipating some of the criticisms presently leveled at the resurgence of antifoundationalism in American philosophical and literary circles, Maritain warned that "the distrust of ideas, the too great ideological modesty of which I am speaking, involves a serious risk: the risk of intellectual isolation, the risk of making American reality, and the greatest human and social achievements of the American people, noncommunicable to other nations . . . as long as ideology or philosophy remains far behind real and actual behavior" (*Reflections on America*, 99). Maritain also linked America's ideological modesty with the rise of the experts, the ascendency of "the notion (imported from Germany) that only specialists have a right to think—and that each one of them . . . is all the more competent in his own field, and all the more reliable, as he shuns knowing anything outside the field in question" (99).

In this context, Jean-François Lyotard's celebration of "social pragmatics" appears to be in total opposition to the French intellectuals' traditional criticism of the practical and empirical ethos of American culture. Lyotard sees the proliferation of autonomous and heterogeneous universes of discourse and behavior separated, and protected, by incommensurable differences as the social and political counterpart to the generalized disbelief in what he calls the "grand narratives" of eighteenth- and nineteenth-century European philosophy. This heterogeneity of discourses and practices is said to be the only alternative to the "terror" of computerized society and technocratic consensus and the only basis for a new conception of justice: "We must thus arrive at an idea and practice of justice that is not linked to that of consensus. A recognition of the heteromorphous nature of language-games is a first step in that direction. This obviously implies a renunciation of terror, which assumes that they are isomorphic and tries to make them so" (*The Postmodern Condition*, 66).

Lyotard cites changes in social relations as empirical evidence of such an evolution toward "social pragmatics" in postmodern society. "The temporary contract is in practice supplanting permanent institutions in the professional, emotional, sexual, cultural, family and international domains, as well as in political affairs" (66). A pragmatic culture demands pragmatic politics, namely, the establishment of local, autonomous types of political and social consensus ("temporary contracts"), aimed at solving local, autonomous, temporary types of social and political problems. Lyotard contends that "any consensus on the rules defining a game and the "moves" playable within it *must* be local, in other words, agreed on it by its present players and subject to eventual cancellation" (66).

The insistence on (ever-changing) contexts rather than intrinsic properties of things or events is central to the pragmatic approach. Lyotard's conception of social pragmatics is presented as the only way to escape the reign of terror which all cultures based on the quest for unity and totality inevitably impose on human beings. Which brings us back, of course, to Hegel, whose "transcendental illusion," says Lyotard, hoped to "totalize [language games] into a real unity" (81). Having established the obsoleteness of the grand narratives and, consequently, of their authors, Lyotard cannot help but reappropriate in the end, even in his characteristically minimalist fashion, the traditional voice of the prophetic thinker, as if it were the one identity that intellectuals, as professionals of speech and thought, cannot renounce without renouncing themselves:

> But Kant also knew that the price to pay for such an illusion is terror. The nineteenth and twentieth centuries have given us as much terror as we can take. We have paid a high enough price for the nostalgia of the whole and the one, for the reconciliation of the concept and the sensible, of the transparent and the communicable experience. . . . The answer is: Let us wage a war on totality; let us be witnesses to the unpresentable; let us activate the differences and save the honor of the name. (*The Postmodern Condition,* 80–81)

The repudiation of the nineteenth and twentieth centuries, equated with the hegemony of Hegelian thought, echoes Baudrillard's rejection of European "transcendental metaphysics," and signals a total reversal of the traditional view of American culture in European intellectual circles. The critique of humanism and ontotheology leads to the present celebration of the very antimetaphysical consequences of American pragmatism that humanists and Marxists alike rejected yesterday. It is almost as if the "Americanization of the world," which European and Third World left-wing intellectuals so strongly opposed twenty years ago, was taking today, in the realm of high culture, the form of the sweeping colonization of philosophical minds by this most "Anglo-Saxon" mode of thinking, pragmatism. Such an ironic twist of intellectual fate is exemplified by Lyotard's present interest in pragmatics and language games.

Other prominent French poststructuralists exhibit forms of thinking closely related to American pragmatism, often because of their own debt to Nietzsche. Deleuze and Guattari exhort their readers to see philosophical and literary writing as experimentation rather than as interpretation,[7] while Michel Foucault was fond of describing his books not as conceptual systems, but as tool boxes, a metaphor dear to a long line of American pragmatists. It is as though the pragmatization of Western culture were the latest stage in the secularization process which, for Nietzsche, led to the advent of "European nihilism." The effects of this development, which started in Europe, would be coming back to the Old World via America, the historical laboratory of the collapse of transcendence. While in the New World, the movement gathered momentum in the form of the pragmatists' critique of Platonic and Kantian truths.

Richard Rorty offers one version of this story when he contends that the international division of philosophical labor between the Anglo-American and Continental traditions is presently being undermined by what he calls "the pragmatization of analytic philosophy" and by a marked convergence between theoretical movements on both sides of the Atlantic. In Rorty's words, "this convergence shows that the traditional association of analytic philosophy with tough-minded positivism and of 'continental' philosophy with tender-minded Platonism is *completely* misleading" (*Consequences of Pragmatism*, xxi). On the contrary, "the positivistic kind of analytic philosophy" resembles "the Nietzsche-Heidegger-Derrida tradition," since it too begins with "criticism of Platonism" and ends "in criticism of Philosophy as such" (xxi).

The insistence on pragmatism as the distinctive contribution of American culture to Western philosophy and social thought and as the central ideology of contemporary advanced societies is indeed one of the threads linking Rorty's post-philosophical culture, Kojève's posthistorical regime, Lyotard's postmodern condition, and Baudrillard's utopia achieved. In an essay entitled "Nineteenth-Century Idealism and Twentieth-Century Textualism," Rorty draws a parallel between what he called the "textualist" movement (the "Yale School" of criticism, French poststructuralism) on the one hand, and the philosophy of William James on the other. Starting with "the pragmatist refusal to think of truth as correspondence to reality," the textualism of the poststructuralist critics, Rorty says, "adds nothing save an extra metaphor to the romanticism of Hegel and the pragmatism of James and Nietzsche." The best way to understand the role of textualism within our culture is to see it "as an attempt to think through a thorough-going pragmatism, a thorough-going abandonment of the notion of discovering the truth which is common to theology and science" (*Consequences of Pragmatism*, 150–51).

The result of this ironic development is that the pragmatic element in American culture, which, as Sartre put it, "never looks for metaphysical problems," is wedded with the most sophisticated and arcane elaborations of Europe's critical tradition. Rorty sees pragmatism as "the philosophical counterpart of literary modernism"; it is, "to speak oxymoronically, post-philosophical philosophy" (*Consequences of Pragmatism*, 143). Nietzsche and James, Heidegger and Dewey (and their contemporary epigones), through diverging and somewhat incompatible philosophical journeys, end up at the same resting place: the postmodern distrust for the metaphysics of presence, the proclamation of the death of philosophy. Rorty can therefore assert in another essay that "James and Dewey were not only waiting at the end of the dialectical road which analytic philosophy traveled, but are waiting at the end of the road which, for example, Foucault and Deleuze are currently traveling" (*Consequences of Pragmatism*, xviii).[8]

Rorty's postphilosophical culture, then, resembles both Kojève's posthistory and Baudrillard's utopia, with the difference that, for the latter, such a culture could flourish only on American soil. This is the sense of Baudrillard's remark that "we [Europeans] philosophize about the death of a lot of things, but here [in America], they really come to an end" (*America*, 98). Surveying the foreground of what he sees as the radical difference of American culture, Baudrillard refuses to equate "European nihilism" with the practical, utopian hyperreality of contemporary America. Europe can be at best the simulacrum of the United States: "America is the original version of modernity, we are its dubbed or subtitled version" (*America*, 76). Baudrillard's apology for pragmatism leads him to a complete reversal of the traditional humanistic contempt for American "problem solving":

> We criticize the Americans for not being able either to analyze or conceptualize. But this is a wrong-headed critique. It is we who imagine that everything culminates in transcendence, and that nothing exists which has not been conceptualized. . . . They build the real out of ideas. We transform the real into ideas, or into ideology. Here in America only what is produced or manifested has meaning; for us in Europe only what can be thought or concealed has meaning. Even materialism is only an idea in Europe. It is in America that it becomes concretely realized in the technical operation of things, in the transformation of a way of thinking into a way of life, in the "action" of life ("action" in the film-making sense, as what happens when the camera begins to roll). For the materiality of things is, of course, their cinematography. (*America*, 85)

For Baudrillard, and this may be what sets him apart from other postmodern cultural critics, Europe never achieved genuine modernity, let alone postmodernity. It is incurably premodern. Baudrillard's use of "modernity" is therefore quite different from Lyotard's or Jameson's. Modernism does not mean here the aesthetic and cultural critique of bourgeois society to be found in the works of Baudelaire, Van Gogh, or Adorno: this type of thought, enmeshed in "nineteenth-century" metaphysics and historicism, is in Baudrillard's eyes, essentially premodern, and constitutes the ultimate obstacle to the emergence of authentic "modernity." This genuine modernity is not therefore the latest development of the "modernist" movement, but, on the contrary, the result of the historical uniqueness (the "exceptionalism") of the American utopia. In the same way as American liberal culture prevented the rise of a powerful socialist movement, it was never congenial to the critical, "transcendental" aesthetics of modernism. Baudelaire is as foreign to American culture as Robespierre or Lenin. Hence, the exile of successive generations of American artists to Europe, and particularly to Paris. For Baudrillard, America was "born modern," just like Tocqueville's Americans were born equal, instead of becoming so:

> America has never been short of violence, nor of events, people, or ideas but these things do not of themselves constitute a history. Octavio Paz is right when he argues that America was created in the hope of escaping from history, of building a utopia sheltered from history, and that it has in part succeeded in that project, a project it is still pursuing today. The concept of history as the transcending of a social and political rationality, as a dialectical, conflictual vision of societies, is not theirs [the Americans'], just as modernity, conceived precisely as an original break with a certain history, will never be ours. . . . From the day when this powerful modernity was born in all its glory on the other side of the Atlantic, Europe began to disappear. The myths migrated. Today, all the myths of modernity are American. It will do us no good to worry our poor heads over this. In Los Angeles, Europe has disappeared. (*America*, 81)

Modernism has no place in the land of genuine modernity, for this "modernity" of America, as its birthright, is linked to an early exit from history, a capacity to escape the gravitational pull of historicism and dialectical thought, its successful break from Hegelianism.

CONCLUSION

▼

Upon reading French accounts of American culture and society, one is struck at first not only by the size of the textual corpus involved, but also by the diversity of viewpoints, narrative strategies, and descriptive vocabularies used by novelists, poets, or essayists to convey their impressions of the United States. At a second glance, however, some kind of a pattern emerges: these competing versions of America are not unrelated or incommensurable, they often refer to each other, they are connected by relations of complicity and opposition. The main point of this study has been that their connectedness stems from the fact that they were produced in specific historical conditions, in a particular intellectual field, within the borders of a distinct national tradition. These conditions of production imposed their own sets of limits, rules, and constraints upon the narratives of America, defining what was said and not said, seen and unseen, celebrated or anathematized.

The various readings of American civilization I have been dealing with stem from the conflicts and divisions of modern French history as they are reflected within, and reconstructed by, the intelligentsia. They also owe a lot, as I hope to have shown, to the specific position of the intellectuals within French society, and particularly their attachment to traditional models of aesthetic tastes and cultural excellence that have endured for centuries across ideological or political lines. Moreover, the debate over America is an instance of the general struggle over the meanings of modernity that Raymond Williams documented in *Culture and Society*, and although his book focuses on the British intellectual tradition, most of its conclusions hold for other Western European cultures.

In his pioneering study, Williams attempted to show that the history of seminal words such as industry, democracy, class, art, and, above all, culture, reflected the learned public's responses to the changes and challenges brought about by industrial modernity. The author identified three different "phases of opinion" regarding the basic components of the new social order: "In industry, there was the first rejection, alike of machine-production and of the social relations embodied in the factory system. This was succeeded by a phase of growing sentiment against the machine as such, in isolation. Thirdly, in our own period, machine production came

251

to be accepted, and major emphasis transferred to the problem of social relations within an industrial system of production" (296). As for democracy, the main concern was originally directed at the threat to minority values posed by the coming of popular democracy; today the fears of the first phase are renewned in the particular context of "what came to be called mass democracy in the new world of mass communications" (296). At the same time, cultural producers emphasized the independent value of art as well as the "defiant exile" of the artistic community, separated from the values of the "common life." For Williams, the class aspect of the debate shows in the endless wonderings about "mass culture" and "mass consumption."

Clearly the French debates over the American way of life went through similar phases, and the various themes identified by Williams also appear in most of the texts I have examined. A useful periodization of the various reactions to modernity among European intellectual circles should not obscure the fact that these views are extremely durable, that they recurred time and again in slightly modified forms during the past two hundred years. While some of these considerations were more prevalent at certain times, they did indeed coexist throughout the whole period. Williams himself conceded that he had "listed the phases of opinion in the order in which they appeared, but of course opinion is persistent, and whether in relation to industry, to democracy or to art, each of the three phases could easily be represented from the opinions of our day" (296).

The consistency and persistence of these views on modernity, despite momentous changes in the technological and political environments of the Western democracies, derives from the enduring power of the humanistic ethos and the similarity of economic and social situations in which writers and artists found themselves throughout the period of high modernism. The relative autonomy of the intellectual field explains that the (overwhelmingly negative) responses of the literati to changing technical and political conditions have been so similar and so constant, from Rousseau and Carlyle to D. H. Lawrence, Ortega y Gasset, Luigi Pirandello, and Louis-Ferdinand Céline. French cultural life continued well into the twentieth century to be dominated by what Tocqueville had called the literary politics of the intellectuals. The prestige and authority of the humanist tradition, reinforced throughout the school curriculum, the permanence of aristocratic models of cultural taste and judgment, and the centralization of intellectual activities in Paris, helped the literati to insulate themselves from the scientific and economic trends at work in the society at large.

More so than in Germany, Britain, or the United States, French writers and philosophers continued to adhere to precapitalist, antiscientific values and categories of understanding and felt empowered to resist the growing materialism, positivism, and hedonism of the modern world.

At least three different lines of force have informed the French idea of America. The history of the debate over the modernity of the New World is punctuated by such canonical texts as Montaigne's essay on the cannibals, Rousseau's *Discourse on the Origin of Inequality*, or Chateaubriand's *Atala*. It revolves around such issues as the meaning of civilization or the value of the learned tradition, central questions for an increasingly autonomous community of cultural producers. This *cultural* dispute also took the form of *political* conflicts between Right and Left (or rather Rights and Lefts, monarchist, bonapartist, liberal, socialist, anarchist, communist, etc.). These positions were ways for writers and artists of situating themselves on different sides of the question of modernity, in reference to symbolically charged events such as the American, French, and Soviet revolutions.

There is yet another logic at work within the debate over the United States, namely the *aesthetic* struggle between innovation and traditionalism, "classicism" and "romanticism," academicism and avant-garde practices, and the incarnation, or absence, of these artistic principles and creative modes in the space, or body, of America.

Each of these logics in turn implies specific issues and differences, particular lexical registers and metaphoric worlds. The cultural battle over the American way of life, so prevalent in the 1920s and 1930s, has been fought over such notions as egalitarianism, hierarchies of tastes, conformism, and the superiority and fragility of high European culture. It called up cultural chauvinism, reasserted a long tradition of literary excellence, pitted patrician models of aesthetic distinction against the leveling effects of a petty bourgeois, democratic, Protestant, acquisitive populism. French high culture is dominated by the word, the signifier, by style, formalism, and formality, it is filled with anguish over the question of language as an adequate representation of reality, it is saturated with rationalist, Cartesian views of discourse as the mirror of nature. Nothing could be more distateful to its more prominent representatives than American popular culture, with its pragmatic use of language and its fascination for the image and the visual.

The political critique of America revolves around the issue of freedom and is closely connected to the specific history of liberalism in French history. Only during the short period of the July Monarchy was the liberal bourgeoisie able to manage French affairs alone and this was not long enough to have a lasting impact on the national psyche. Never again would liberalism in the classical sense get a chance to dominate French politics and wrench power away from its Legitimist, Bonapartist, or radical Republican contestants. From 1848 on, the Gallic version of the dominant ideology of Britain and the United States would always be an embattled, and largely unlegitimate, view, hemmed in between the forces of reaction and the various components of the Left. The voices of the *juste milieu,* whether in politics or literary culture, have always risked being silenced by their more powerful absolutist opponents, by the numerous idealisms and dogmatisms of right and left, from romanticism and reactionary Catholicism to Jacobinism and its descendants. The "liberal" tradition of Montaigne, Montesquieu, Tocqueville, or Alain, with its emphasis on tolerance and reasonableness was no match for the more exciting, heady ideologies of the contending extremes; it never secured a lasting grip on the minds of the French intelligentsia, it never attained the hegemonic status of its Anglo-American counterpart.[1] Here lies one of the fundamental differences between the United States and France, the former obsessed with consensus and the need to make the various components of its population live together, and the latter racked by centuries of civil wars and revolutions. Some of the postmodern descriptions of America, as we saw, signal a return of the repressed, a reassessment of liberalism, now that the revolutionary alternative has lost its momentum. It is not surprising that this wave of neoliberalism coincides with a positive reevaluation of the American experience, or experiment.

The imaginative versions of America involve desire and mobility, the freedom of the romantics rather than that of the liberals. Chapter 5 explored these poetic readings, whether in their more traditional forms (Claudel, Perse) or in their more innovative ways (Butor, Deleuze, and Lyotard). Here, the imaginary element dominates, following what Edward Said has called, apropos Orientalism, "a detailed logic governed not simply by empirical reality, but by a battery of desires, repressions, investments and projections" (8). The theme of the body of America allows these phantasmatic elements to be fused with mythical reconstructions of the American space, as wilderness or void, tabula rasa, on which to inscribe the words of a poem or to project fantasies of renewal and rebirth. Bodies, fancies, metaphors, energies, and intensities freely flow across the unencumbered vastness of the continent: the American experience is one of mobility and speed, and here the down-to-earth, bourgeois, no-nonsense Anglo-Saxon liberal values of social openness and political tolerance are given a more utopian, metaphysical twist.

A mixture of idealization and demonizing, the French narrative construction of America is in many ways similar to other comparable sets of European interpretations of foreign cultures, such as the French and British Orientalist traditions described by Edward Said. This occurs in large part because they both deal with a long-dominated Other perceived both as inferior and threatening. They are also important differences, however. Although one can find colonialist elements in French (and British) views of the United States, especially in the early nineteenth century, the United States later rose to a political and military prominence never (or not yet) achieved by any other non-European nation. In addition to this, American civilization is part of the "Western tradition": the American Other is often depicted as an interior enemy, a threatening double, a family member who has gone astray, the wayward, prodigal child of the Old World. Representations of the United States illustrate the tensions and contradictions within European learned circles as to the nature of (their own) modernity; in a sense, they are various answers to Kant's famous question: "What is Enlightenment?" In the mirror of America, the cultivated elites looked at themselves, at the culture their forebears had helped fashion, or had resisted, for centuries: the ever-present theme of the sorcerer's apprentice testifies to the fact that most of them did not particularly like what they saw.

To all those who stood outside the liberal camp, whether on its right or left, the fate of America, that most bourgeois of all nations, was a painful remainder not only that Europe was losing its political and military supremacy, but that its traditional clerisies were being swept away in its downfall. America's rise to prominence was not only an effect of capitalist competition. American imperialism carried with it powerful cultural weapons that would eventually bring about the demise of high modernism: an anti-intellectualism rooted in the Protestant egalitarian allergy to the elitist posturing and social privileges of a priestly caste, a deep scorn for the universalist rationalism of the academic mandarins (borne out of British empiricism), a nouveau riche conceit that claimed that anything—even the subtle refinements of cultural distinction—could be bought and sold. The wonders of technology have eventually turned works of art into so many mass-produced commodities whose ultimate value is determined by market forces and advertising strategies: "Art is all over" is postmodernism as the ultimate phase of capitalism. The humanists came to the realization that the humanities, as Zygmunt Bauman puts it, failed to humanize. The culture born of unfettered Lockean liberalism turned out to be the nightmare of the intellectuals: no sooner had they emancipated themselves from the fetters of feudal patronage and monarchic control, than the "masses" themselves started to discount their own authority as tastemakers and purveyors of meaning, turning instead to the market and the expertise of the new professionals. The German mandarins made the ironical outcome of this historical process into a grandiose, metaphysical twist of fate: they called it the forgetting of being and the negative dialectics of reason.

I have shown that things have changed in the past twenty-five years. That a growing number of French intellectuals have been singing the praises of American society as a historical experiment in philosophical or poetic liberation, echoing themes of cultural renaissance found in Emerson or Whitman, attests to the profound changes that have occurred in French society since the end of the 1960s. The "normalization" of political life, with the accepted rotation of conservatives and socialists at the head of the state, the disappearance (or temporary abeyance) of literary politics à la Voltaire or Sartre, and the concurrent growth of civil society and consumerism have brought French culture and society closer to the American model, a condition that fulfills the prophecies of earlier critics of the United States. Is it the end of anti-Americanism? I will briefly examine this question in the form of an epilogue.

EPILOGUE

TRANSATLANTIC THEORIES AND THE CONTINENTAL DRIFT

The U.S. has stopped being an extension of Europe, and has, for better or worse, struck out on its own, an increasingly nonwhite country adrift, however majestically and powerfully, in an increasingly nonwhite world. *David Rieff*

Were I not so frequently associated with this adventure of deconstruction, I would risk, with a smile, the following hypothesis: America *is* deconstruction. *Jacques Derrida*

France is condemned to produce the best ideologues of the liberal West, just as it produced the best theologians of medieval Christianity. *Régis Debray*

Oscar Wilde once quipped that when good Americans die, they go to Paris. I think in Paris, when good theories die, they go to America. *Henry Louis Gates, Jr.*

What could be more American than humbling the highbrow? *Todd Gitlin*

Some recent developments in French culture and society seem to bear out Richard Rorty's claim that there now exists a marked convergence between intellectual movements on both sides of the Atlantic. Post-Enlightenment philosophy is indeed a transatlantic phenomenon. One need only think of Michel Foucault's "tool boxes," a metaphor he borrows from the pragmatists. Gilles Deleuze, as we saw, is very fond of Anglo-American literature, whose superiority over the French literary tradition lies for him in its use of writing as experimentation rather than interpretation. Jean-François Lyotard's frequent use of the notion of language games and reference to social pragmatics in *The Postmodern Condition*, or Jean Baudrillard's celebration of American society as a "utopia achieved," of Americans as people who "build the real out of ideas," and Europeans as those who "transform the real into ideas, or ideologies" seem to support the notion that some-

257

thing like the pragmatization of European thought, which has traditionally been dominated since the Enlightenment by rationalist and universalist models, is indeed taking place. If one takes universalist rationalism and pragmatic empiricism as the most distant poles in French and American cultures (which cannot, of course, be reduced to these two polarities),[1] many recent changes in France would seem to indicate a lessening of the distance between the two intellectual worlds, largely because the rationalist-universalist view is under severe strain.

One way of looking at these cultural and political shifts is to say that French thought, culture, and society have been "Americanized," or, to put it in a less polemical manner, that Western democracies are becoming more alike now that the specific legacies of their respective national histories are being erased by the internalization of capital or the diffusion of the global culture of the media. French society has of late become more "liberal," in the Anglo-American sense of the term: consumer society and the new ethics of instant gratification have eroded old sexual taboos and moral codes, market mechanisms bear directly on the culture industry, the state has lost control of most of the media, and politics have ceased to be a struggle over radically different systems of economic production and social relations. These changes have been accompanied by a collapse of the centralizing, statist, antagonistic political culture that had prevailed in French life since the days of the absolute monarchy. In fact, Jacobinism derived in part from the same universalist rationalism that had informed the models of intellectual practice dear to *les philosophes* and their nineteenth and twentieth century standard-bearers. A few years ago, François Furet sparked off a heated controversy when he claimed that the French Revolution was over and that the political categories and ideological divisions that had governed politics for almost two centuries were fast becoming obsolete, and even meaningless.

Like their Democratic and Republican counterparts in the United States, today's French moderate socialists and middle-of-the road conservatives differ less on ideological or philosophical issues than they do on practical questions of economic or social management, on concrete ways of dealing with worldwide trade competition, inflation, and unemployment. In their reaction to the "recentering" of their national politics, French voters exhibit patterns of electoral behavior well known on the other side of the Atlantic: fewer and fewer people make it to the voting booths, even in national elections. Issues of sexual politics, such as reproductive rights, gender discrimination, or sexual harassment, and divisions along ethnic, racial, and cultural-religious lines have come to the forefront of public awareness, making the good old struggles over collective owner-ship of the means of production or the dictatorship of the proletariat look like ancient history. The clash between Muslim fundamentalists and de-fenders of Third Republic secularized educational ideals over the rights of Arab children to wear a *chador*, or ritual veil, in public schools, and the xenophobic rhetoric of the radical Right, clearly indicate that French soci-ety, like Britain, the new Germany, or the United States, is confronting the thorny problem of how to get communities of diverse backgrounds to live together within the political space of the liberal-democratic nation-state.

The end of French exceptionality, however, means not only that the French have accepted the "alternance" (power changeover) between the Right and the Left, that private radio and TV stations have brought the state monopoly of information to an end, or that most people no longer care about the old battles over the public funding of Catholic schools. The postmodernization of the country is also congruent with im-portant transformations in the intellectual field itself: there is hardly room, in the individualistic, consensual post-Jacobin world, for the Sartrean model of intellectual *engagé*. The critique of Enlightenment reason by the poststructualist thinkers was also a refusal of the old prophetic role of the clerics, thematized by Foucault and Deleuze's distinction between univer-sal and specific intellectuals. The professionalization and academicization of French cultural life in the past twenty years have made French intellec-tuals resemble more closely their counterparts in the United States. Ironi-cally enough, they have turned into the very experts the preceding genera-tion had criticized American intellectuals for having become. Gone are the days when literary prophets such as Zola or Sartre would have nothing to do with the Sorbonne and its scholarly, routine-minded professoriate. The gradual integration of French academics into Alvin Gouldner's trans-national "New Class" (exemplified by the appointments of French critical stars to major American universities) may have played as crucial a role in the recent changes of attitude toward American culture and society as the waning of Old Left anti-Americanism. In any case, the heyday of United States–bashing seems to be over on the Parisian Left Bank.

Do all these developments signal a lessening of the distance between the two intellectual traditions I have been examining in this book? Is the love-hate relationship between French and American cultures finally over? Not very likely. Powerful forces on both sides of the Atlantic resist the adoption of viewpoints foreign to their national traditions. The French have not been converted en masse to pragmatist or empiricist ways at look-ing at the world, and some sectors of the American intelligentsia are now debating the vices of "French poststructuralism" as relevant to the current "crisis in the humanities."

Let us look first at the French side. In *Le Scribe*, Régis Debray proposed a historical account of the relationship between intellectuals and power. One of the central assumption of the book is that might does not make right, that power cannot be exercised in a purely natural, or physical way, as sheer imposition of brute force, but that it always needs a metaphysical justification in order to win the consent of those to which it is applied. The vertical, referential function so essential to the administration of things and people is performed by the intellectual caste: "The cleric is the administrator of the sacred" (71). No human society, Debray contends, can function without the transcendental reference to an outside, sacred, absolute entity ("Law or People, Race or Nation, Class, God, Allah, Progress, Civilization, Humanity, etc."), which legitimizes power and sacralizes those human or institutional agencies that incarnate it. "Just as an arithmetical construction cannot ground the 'inner' demonstration of its truth on its axioms alone, a social body cannot found itself as a body on the basis of its sole social materiality, through a mere addition or totalization of its internal elements. An ensemble which could only rely on its own elements to define itself will never make up a totality" (70).

Although this particular passage in Debray's book does not refer to the American experience, I would argue that statements of this kind point to the major differences on both sides of the Atlantic. What Debray sees as a mathematical, that is, rational or natural, impossibility, is precisely what defines, it seems to me, a good part of the pragmatic project in ethics or politics. What Debray says cannot be absent from any intellectual or political construct, mainly a transcendental principle bringing into being from above the horizontal closure of a mathematical ensemble or social body, is precisely what the pragmatists want to get rid of in their appeal to practical reason and self-validating, "ethnocentric" communitarian values. Most French intellectuals have trouble with the liberal pragmatists' claim to do away with first principles, since "Archimedean points" provide an absolute foundation for ethical conduct or political behavior.

I have suggested in this book that the intellectualist culture of critical discourse in which the French intelligentsia has lived and thought for centuries may be largely responsible for their resistance to what Raymond Aron, in *The Opium of the Intellectuals*, has called the "empirical success" of the United States as a society "which does not embody an historical idea" (227). For its liberal apologists, American culture, in so far as it is pragmatic, succeeded in what Debray deems impossible: to base an entire social body on the "horizontal" interaction of its beliefs and practices, in the absence of any ahistorical transcendental principle. For most French observers of the American scene, the project of a society not legitimized by religious or secularized "metanarratives" is at best an illusion, and at worst a fatal mistake that has turned the best of idealistic intentions into a nightmare.

In a recently published paper, Charles Larmore argues, and regrets, that French neoliberals are unwilling to follow the pragmatic project to its ultimate theoretical and political implications. Larmore commends neo-Kantians such as Ferry and Renaut for defending, against the "class of 68" poststructuralists, the possibility of a nonmetaphysical humanism based on the point of view that "intelligibility is not an intrinsic character of reality, but rather a discipline which we impose on ourselves to look for as many reasons as possible" (187). The main flaw of their argument, however, according to Larmore, is that it is based on a belief in an ahistorical, universal reason, capable of providing by itself a foundation for their humanism. Larmore is skeptical as to the possibility of justifying any ethical or political practice on such a transcendental conception of reason, especially in view of the crisis of normativity that characterizes our fin-de-siècle. "The idea that reason must transcend all historical rootedness to warrant morality is . . . a metaphysical remnant, which hinders Renaut's project to elaborate a 'non-metaphysical humanism'"(191).

In the same way, Richard Rorty has argued in *Objectivity, Relativism and Truth* that the pragmatists' "lonely provincialism, the admission that we are just the historical moment that we are, not the representatives of something ahistorical, is what makes traditional Kantian liberals like Rawls draw back from pragmatism" (30). In Larmore's view, most French critiques of postmodernism are undermined by the opposition they maintain between reason and history. The neo-Jacobin attack on German romanticism in Alain Finkielkraut's *Défaite de la pensée* is paradigmatic of the deep-seated antihistoricism of most reactions to postmodernism. Larmore, for his part, refuses to throw out the historicist baby with the bath water of nihilism, for "morals cannot rest on rationality alone." He commends Herder for having understood that reason is historical through and through and for having searched for "a middle-way between the ideal of transcendence and the capitulation in front of relativism" (199). The best way to surmount the dichotomy between reason and history is, Larmore says, to turn to the "pragmatist model of rationality" based on the notion of a moral tradition. That ethics (and politics) are contingent does not imply that we have to surrender to radical skepticism. The French seem caught within an absolutist view of things, whichever side they are on: if one does not believe in absolute reason, then one is, in a sense, an absolute relativist. If God is dead, then everything is permitted, for nothing can justify any beliefs or ethical actions short of a transcendental principle, which is nonexistent. Montaigne was more consequent, for he said that the true skeptic must doubt even his own skepticism.

Over and beyond the validity of the philosophical arguments deployed by Larmore in his discussion of recent trends in French political theory, I find both his appeal to pragmatism and his characterization of French authors (as still deeply influenced by the metaphysical tradition) indicative of the limits of the "pragmatization of French thought" that I referred to in chapter 6. Although the waning of Marxism and the critique of metaphysics of the 1960s and 1970s, have removed some of the obstacles to the importation of (American) pragmatist views into contemporary French debates, Larmore's foregrounding of the deeply entrenched intellectual habits that are resistant to such transatlantic movements seems to indicate that the conversation between the two intellectual cultures is far from being free of misunderstandings and incompatibilities.

For all the recent redistribution of positions and dispositions within the transatlantic intellectual communities, the exchange of theories has by no means been balanced; France is still the main exporter of interpretive models to the New World.[2] This theoretical export-import business, however, poses serious difficulties in the United States. French poststructuralist theory, so successful in some sectors of the American academy in the past fifteen years, has recently met strong resistance both in intellectual circles and in the educated public at large. What came to be called the de Man affair is a case in point, given the passion it unleashed within the intellectual community. In many ways, the "don of deconstruction" and his defendants fell prey to the antitheoretical drive so central to American culture, whether high or low, from which they had hitherto benefited. At first, a theory like deconstruction, which undermined the notion of origin, questioned established intellectual traditions, and problematized history, was sure to meet with some success in a country whose political mythology still rests on the renewed assertion of self-begetting and the resolute break with any oppressive or decadent past.

As many commentators have remarked, Paul de Man's personal odyssey was prime material for Hollywood mythologizing. It was a perfect example of the American dream turned American tragedy, the story of an immigrant who had succeeded in erasing his past and starting afresh, with no questions asked, in the land of opportunity, until history, posthumously, caught up with him. The very personal qualities that had contributed to his charismatic appeal, his distinction, his accent, his intellectual rigor, and the ascetic ethos he brought to the subtle exegesis of difficult and sacred texts, were classic examples of what arouses the American ambivalent fascination for European sophistication whether dealing with perfume or *écriture*. Richard Rorty, among others, has deplored that American intellectuals have a tendency to let themselves be "buffaloed" by their European counterparts.

The fascination, however, is ambivalent, and conceals a deep resentment that can surface at any moment. Once de Man became associated with the most discredited of all European political traditions, both the liberal and radical academic communities turned against the fallen idol with acrimony. The very same aristocratic dispositions that had contributed to the rise of the Belgian professor were now precipitating his downfall. They were no longer seen as the mark of a superior intellect, monastically devoted to the pursuit of knowledge and the display of critical acumen, but as the product of the decadence of the interwar European intellectual caste, guilty of the most revolting instance of the treason of the clerics. Critics were quick to point out that what likened de Man's later writings to his articles in the collaborationist Belgian newspaper *Le Soir*, was not the contents of his prose, of course, but the high-handed, mandarinal, authoritative—in short, elitist—tone of his pronouncements.

Once again, characterizations of Parisian high culture as the decadent and cynical negation of everything American liberalism stands for filled the cultural sections and literary supplements of mainstream weeklies. For quite some time, deconstruction had regularly been denounced as embodying, as did existentialism a generation earlier, the demonic threat of trendy, high-faluting French gibberish and "apocalyptic hype." But the revelations surrounding de Man's wartime activities lent new fuel to the fire. In *The New York Review of Books* (1 June 1989), Robert Hughes wrote that you cannot make your mark in American academia unless "you add something to the lake of jargon whose waters (bottled for export to the States) well up between Nanterre and the Sorbonne and to whose marshy verge the bleating flocks of poststructuralists go each night to drink."

The resistance to French theory is frequently couched in a broader cultural opposition that pits Gallic illiberal skepticism against Anglo-American common sense. In *Signs of the Times*, a recent account of the de Man affair, David Lehman describes the growing influence of French intellectual imports on American campuses in the following terms: "The American lit-crit profession slowly but steadily shed its tweedy English image in favor of foppish French fashion" (48). Further along in the book, Lehman refers to accounts in the British press that presented debates about deconstruction as a struggle between English common sense and Left Bank abstruseness (90). As the battle over de Man's wartime articles escalated, the defenders accused their opponents of nativistic bigotry. For them, the attacks against de Man were another instance of the narrow provincialism and deep-seated xenophobia of American society, even in the halls of academia.

Even the staunchest supporters of one form or another of French theory in the United States have often been uncomfortable with the cultural and political values that nurtured poststructuralism and are implicit in the theory, as well as the practice, of many of its French proponents. Richard Rorty, for example, likes the antirationalist philosophies of Derrida, Foucault, and their epigones, but does not care much for their illiberal, revolutionary politics. In "Cosmopolitanism without Emancipation: A Response to Jean-François Lyotard," Rorty chastises his French colleagues for their "antiutopianism, their apparent lack of faith in liberal democracy. . . . Even those who, like myself, think of France as the source of the most original philosophical thought currently being produced," he goes on, "cannot figure out why French thinkers are so willing to say things like 'May 68 refutes the doctrine of parliamentary liberalism'" (220).

More recently, Edward Said and Henry Louis Gates, Jr., among others, have denounced the "dogmatic and systematic orthodoxies" and "the New Moralism" that have resulted from the theory craze. Gates argues, with other black intellectuals such as Cornel West, that the (Europeanized) academic Left is out of touch with broader political issues in American society, as a result of "its undialectical, purely antagonistic relationship to liberalism" ("Goodbye, Columbus?" 721). If you do not build on liberalism, Gates, quoting West, contends, you build on air. "One of the most interesting developments in the past decade took place when theoretically sophisticated minority scholarship parted company with its left-theoretical mentors" (721). For Gates, the problem with "massively totalizing" theories is that their all-or-nothing logic breeds paranoia, and that their "Messianic pessimism" discourages "anything so vulgar as overt political action," ruling out "humble amelioration." What Gates's antitheoretical self-criticism ("we [literary critics] have been betrayed by our two-decade-long love affair with theory") shows, is that theories of any kind are eventually soluble in American liberal-pragmatist thought. No matter how bad things get in academia, sooner or later, "common sense" will prevail, and some middle-of-the-road position will emerge: checks and balances are operating in the world of ideas.

The de Man affair crystallized all the misgivings about the illiberal, antidemocratic character of French theory, by focusing on the political consequences of its theoretical assumptions, a move the deconstructionists desperately tried to counter. Even before the 1988–89 debates, a growing concert of voices from the Left had difficulties with the intellectualism of the new critical academicism, which looked to them as yet another form of demagogic, intolerant mandarinate. In *Marxism and Deconstruction*, Michael Ryan, while stressing the usefulness of Derrida's views for a renewal of Marxist thought, contends that for many literary scholars in the United States, deconstruction was a way of saving, by way of rejuvenation, academic studies of canonical texts. While the liberal-humanist camp insisted on the threat deconstruction posed to literary studies, or worse, Western civilization, many academics on the Left countered that to focus on canonical texts, even if it was to denounce their logocentric flaws and self-contradictions, was still to privilege the European tradition; after all, de Man's studies bore on the most consecrated authors, like Rousseau, Rilke, Proust, or Nietzsche, and seldom, if ever, dealt with nonwhite or female writers, let alone popular culture. Sooner or later, the uneasy alliance between deconstructive literary theorists and a younger generation of more overtly (or more traditionally) politicized cultural radicals (with the support of older New Left intellectuals) was bound to break down under the strain.

In an essay written immediately before the outbreak of the de Man affair, J. Hillis Miller, one of the major practitioners of deconstruction, warned his readers of the challenge from neo-Marxist, Foucaultian, and new historicist quarters, which he ironically described as a reassuring, humanistic move away from the anxiety generated by those who were not afraid of staring into the linguistic abyss. "It is as if a great sigh of relief were rising up from all across the land. The era of 'deconstruction' is over. It has had its day, and we can return with a clear conscience to the warmer, more human work of writing about power, history, ideology, the 'institution' of the study of literature, the class struggle, the oppression of women, and the real lives of men and women in society as they exist in themselves and as they are 'reflected' in literature" (quoted in Lehman, 260). One of the most aristocratic aspects of the deconstructive ethos was undoubtedly this Nietzschean theme of the fearless gaze into the bottomless depths of nihilism, of the heroic encounter with the consequences of the death of

God, which, indeed, is reminiscent of the right-wing literary culture of the 1930s. For his admirers, Paul de Man belonged to those happy few who can withstand the disappearance of the gods and squarely face madness and the collapse of meaning. He was apparently referred to as "the only man who ever looked into the abyss and came away smiling." (quoted in Lehman, 156).

Even critics of deconstruction often wonder how it can be attacked as both an elistic circle and a culturally "nihilistic" movement. "Why," Howard Felperin asks in *Beyond Deconstruction*, "would the high priests of a religion of literature want to abolish the source of their status and power?" The answer may be that their status and power derives precisely from their ability to foster, and manage, anxieties about reality and meaning among those who must turn to them for answers and reassurance. In *Legislators and Interpreters*, Zygmunt Bauman, drawing on Paul Radin's anthropological work, argues that the intellectual function, from ancient shamans and prophets to contemporary scientists and New Age gurus, is based, to paraphrase Weber, on the clerical class' monopoly on the manipulation of the mysteries of nature and the uncertainties of human existence. For Radin, "the religious formulator . . . capitalised on the sense of insecurity of the ordinary man" (quoted in Bauman, 10). The priestly caste derived its authority from its capacity to answer the popular demand for ways of coping with the unknown. The history of Western secularized intellectuals is a self-reproducing process: modern science and technology create as many fears and threats as they purport to assuage, thus ensuring the perpetuation of the power and legitimacy of those who have the monopoly of knowledge and decision making. Popular wisdom sees intellectuals, from the epileptic shaman to the neurotic romantic genius, as "different," that is, slightly weird and somewhat frightening. As Bauman writes, while "ordinary people" are usually satisfied with their lot, "the thinkers cannot help but ponder, doubt, invent. Theirs is, by necessity, a very different life—one which non-thinkers would rather not emulate. The thinkers are cultural heroes to be admired and respected, but not imitated" (16). Far from being a consequence of their choice of the intellectual vocation, the very difference, the ascetic trials and social isolation of the cultural producers is the very condition of their power as well as their professional *point d'honneur.*

If Radin and Bauman are correct in their assessment of the genealogy of the intellectual function, one might argue that, by pushing to its limits the disenchanting drive that is the cultural hallmark of modern times, many postmodernist intellectuals heighten the anxieties of their learned contemporaries and thus contribute to produce the social demand for their own products as ways of dealing with those anxieties. The ubiquitous publications, debates, and colloquia about relativism, value-free knowledge, and the deleterious effects of expressive individualism in our fin de siècle, are symptoms of the central role intellectuals, whether in the sciences or the humanities, play in the social management of insecurity and of the profits they derive from it. Pragmatists offer a reassuring product on the anxiety market, telling us that we should not worry about the collapse of values, since radical relativism is an illusion: nobody can operate outside a given set of beliefs to guide one's actions. "Hard-core" deconstructionists, on the other hand, may have pushed the debunking game a little too far, especially in a country like the United States, where the reverence for the priestly caste, and the tolerance for the legitimacy of its separation from common sentient beings, has been eroded by centuries of egalitarianism.

Nietzsche's question, and his test of a free spirit, was: How much truth (i.e., insecurity) about the human condition can an individual tolerate? He also thought, however, that the refusal to shed one's illusions about reality had been one of the conditions of the survival of humankind. Most people, and that includes many intellectuals as well, can only take so much ontological, or epistemological, skepticism: soon they blame the messenger for the message and shop for less disturbing types of intellectual product. Hence the return of the repressed that J. Hillis Miller saw at work in the recent challenges to pure, unadulterated deconstruction: the return of historical agency in new historicism and feminism in the United States, the return of the subject in the neohumanism of many French intellectuals today. If, as Miller himself claimed in *Criticism and Society* (222), "the accommodation and appropriation of deconstruction in the United States was producing something specifically American," if deconstruction was really to become "an American thing" rather than a species of French theory, then the new vulgate would have had to shed the most unacceptable remnants of its highbrow Parisian past and be born anew in the American academic crucible as an Emersonian, or Whitmanesque, blend of democratic pragmatism and nativistic romanticism. After all, as Rorty has contended, French theory merely added a "footnote" to James, Hegel, and Nietzsche.

My second example of resistance to French theory as indicative of the remaining differences between the two national traditions comes from those intellectual quarters who reject the elite views of the fashionable French critical set as incompatible with American popular culture. Camille Paglia, a self-described "child of the sixties," has launched a spirited attack against the "Ninnies, Pedants, Tyrants and Other Academics"—those, she says, who have taken over the humanities in America. First, she takes up

the old fight of the (Europeanized) humanist against the sterile specialization of the new critical experts who are aping their colleagues in the natural
sciences. Those "ignorant professors" have "substituted 'narrow expertise'
and 'theoretical sophistication' for breadth and depth in the world history
of art and thought" (1). The discarded model of comprehensive vision is,
of course, the German philological erudition, based on "universal scholarship," which dominated "belles-lettristic" endeavors in nineteenth-century
American universities and was the antithesis of French literary ama-
teurism.

Paglia then adopts a more romantic line of interpretation, contrasting
the Dionysian, rebellious, psychedelic 1960s, a "short-lived Rousseauistic
dream" complete with regression, violence, primitivism, and anarchic individualism with the "French 1970s," described as a "panic reaction by head-
locked pedants unable to cope with the emotional and sensory flux of the
iconoclastic 60's" (33). Paglia's contrast, by the way, mirrors the traditional
opposition, to be found in many French interpretations, albeit with inverted valuation, between nature (the dynamic, energetic, and primitive
fluidity of American life), and culture (the hierarchical, rational, refined
resiliency of the French tradition). While the 1960s were concerned with
openness, liberation, expressivity, and the exploration of sexual limits, the
French 1970s were about "rigid mental control, power plays by the critic
over the text and the artist . . . a reactionary escape into false abstraction
and rationalism, masquerading as distrust of reason." Sounding at times
very French indeed, like Baudelaire or André Breton castigating the narrow philistinism and utilitarianism of the (petty) bourgeoisie, or Zola and
Péguy jeering at the bookish academicism of the Sorbonne professoriate,
Paglia contends that "academics with the soul of accountants now approached art like a business deal, haggling over negotiable, movable
clauses."

In Paglia's view, the main shortcoming of the French theorists is not
that they are "eros-killers," tyrants (like Lacan), or "totalitarian misogy-
nists" (like Foucault), or that they display a gross ignorance of America,
"which leaped far beyond European thought the moment we invented
Hollywood" (29), but that they have no place in the United States, for
they engage in a pernicious form of un-American activities. "In the United
States, deconstruction is absurd, since we never had a high culture of any
kind. Far from being illiterate, we are still preliterate, accentuated by an
image-dominated popular culture that was the all-embracing educational
medium of my generation" (33). The naturalist and infantile American
personality, with its "booming . . . beaming, bouncing egotism" so repul-

sive to the French high humanists of the 1930s, has of course its dark side, since for Paglia "the titanism of rock" and the short-lived Rousseauistic dream of the 1960s ended in chaos, "a descent into barbarism" (33). Even these excesses, however, are better than the cold, timorous, pedantic intellectualism that have taken their place in Academia.

Popular music, and especially black music, is taken to represent American spiritual energy at its highest. "Black artists are the American paradigm of vivid, vibrant personality, dramatic self-assertion and spiritual magnitude of the individual voice." Indeed, a musical culture rooted in the rural South, "with its evangelical fervor and fire-breathing preachers" (33), is the furthest thing from highbrow French thinkers. Elvis Presley is credited for having brought to the white youth of Paglia's generation "the power, passion, truth of African-American experience" (29). The author's own brand of romantic primitivism, which roots authentic American culture in the black experience, also serves to boost national pride, since the choreographic prowess and physical virtuosity of black teenagers' break dancing are "recorded on music videos and beamed around the world, to the helpless amazement of European and Japanese admirers, who cannot imitate them" (33). The major competitors of the United States in the new global economy may have high culture and achieve higher levels of productivity, but, according to Paglia, they are left to long for the "sacred poetry of the [American] body."[3]

Slavoj Žižek has argued that the Other of cultural chauvinism is always perceived as the outsider who "steals the enjoyment" generated within the gemeinschaft. This enjoyment, although hard for us to define, is what makes us feel that we belong to a particular community, it is what is at stake "when we speak of the menace to our 'way of life' presented by the Other." It is made up of all the rituals, beliefs, and ceremonies through which we reenact our belonging to the group. "We always impute to the 'other' an excessive enjoyment; s/he wants to steal our enjoyment (by ruining our way of life) and/or has access to some secret, perverse enjoyment" (54). Remarking on the obsessive concern of the American media for the workaholism of the Japanese, Žižek (who uses Lacanian categories and hence is another of Paglia's victims of French theory) writes that "the reason for Japan's increasing economic superiority over the USA is located in the somewhat mysterious fact that the Japanese don't consume enough, that they accumulate too much wealth. . . . It is as if they find enjoyment in their excessive renunciation of pleasure, in their zeal, in their inability to 'take it easy,' to relax and enjoy; and it is this attitude that is perceived as a threat to American supremacy. Which is why the American media report with such evident relief how the Japanese are finally learning to consume, and why American television depicts with such self-satisfaction Japanese tourists staring at the wonders of the American pleasure industry: they are finally 'becoming like us,' learning our way to enjoy" (56).

I find strikingly similar elements in Paglia's opposition between the perverse vices of French theory and the redeeming virtues of American popular culture. *Her* Japanese tourists are also staring "with helpless amazement" at black teenagers' physical prowess, while the French theorists (and by extension all French "sophisticated" high culture) are accused of robbing the children of the 1960s of their capacity to enjoy music, dance, and their bodies. With characteristic psychoanalytic irony, Žižek gives a further twist to his analysis: "The Lacanian thesis that enjoyment is ultimately always enjoyment of the Other—enjoyment supposed, imputed to the Other—and that, conversely, the hatred of the Other's enjoyment is always the hatred of one's own enjoyment, is perfectly exemplified by this logic of the 'theft of enjoyment.' What are fantasies about the Other's special, excessive enjoyment—about the Black's superior potency and sexual appetite, about the relationship of Jews and Japanese towards money and work—if not precisely *so many ways, for us, to organize our own enjoyment.* Do we not find enjoyment precisely in fantasizing about the Other's enjoyment, in this ambivalent attitude towards it?" (57).

It is the particular way (cold, detached, cerebral) that European aristocrats of the mind have of organizing *their* enjoyment (the good old *libido sciendi*) that triggers the ire of the American populist. As Žižek points out, the hatred of the Jews in capitalist nations may be directed at the most essential feature of capitalism itself, namely its obsession for money. What the Nazis, who wanted capitalism without its excess, that is, without its capacity to destabilize all social orders and deconstruct all identities, blamed the Jews for was this excess precisely, which they projected on them as 'cosmopolitanism.' "For this reason," Žižek contends, "it is not sufficient to point out that the racist's Other presents a threat to our identity. We should rather invert this proposition: the fascinating image of the Other personifies our own innermost split—what is already 'in us more than ourselves'—and thus prevents us from achieving full identity with ourselves. The hatred of the Other is the hatred of our own excess of enjoyment" (57). Could it be then that what the child of the 1960s detests so much in the theoretical 1970s (in which she sees an anxious reactive formation to the hedonism of Woodstock) is precisely that the decade points to the very excess of enjoyment of the preceding decade, which led to a "descent in barbarism" and "ended in disaster"?

Modern French philosophy was born of the necessity for its proponents and their public to deal with growing state power and endemic political violence. Montaigne's skepticism was a reaction to the bloodshed of the religious civil wars of his time; Cartesian rationalism, which finds its prolongations in Voltaire's plea for tolerance, was an effort to ground thought (and social relations) on a transcendental entity (reason) that would delegitimize, and neutralize, the ideological struggles that had marred France's national history. It is true that many brands of French thought have a strong anti-utopian component, that they view liberation and revolution with cool skepticism and like to remind the reader that some kind of "Master" always returns in the aftermath of the insurrections of desire. This dominating and repressive instance is not only a philosophical fiction dear to Lacan or Foucault, but was embodied in those historical figures named Louis XIV, Robespierre, Napoléon, or Pétain. Unlike European societies, American society, largely because of its overwhelmingly capitalist nature, is dominated by the production of excess in Žižek's sense and has been immune to the return of the master. Because excesses of enjoyment (like the psychedelic 1960s) are part and parcel of the dynamics of consumerism, they can neither really threaten it, nor bring about a successful puritanical, authoritarian reaction, which the same dynamics of consumerism (and their built-in libertarianism) renders unprobable.

Paglia's views are interesting in that, unlike Rorty, for example, she sees French theory as totally opposed to American culture, whether high or low. By dissociating the rebellious, liberating romantic 1960s from the intellectualist, reactionary 1980s, she makes impossible the strategic alliance, advocated by the "anti-foundationalist" camp, between American pragmatic antirationalism and French critical, or deconstructive, antirationalism. At the end of her article, Camille Paglia has a dream, the dream of reversing the flow of imported theory, of invading the invaders, of flooding Paris, the center of the adversary culture, with the liberating tidal wave of the American popular industry. This appears as a mock-heroic pastiche, and reversal, of the French Revolution: "In my dream, based on the diner episode in "The Blues Brothers," Aretha Franklin, in her fabulous black-lipstick "Jumpin' Jack Flash" outfit, leaps from her seat at Maxim's and, shouting "Think!" blasts Lacan, Derrida and Foucault like dishrags against the wall, then leads thousands of freed academic white slaves in a victory parade down the Champs-Elysées" (33).

Nineteenth-century German romantics and cultural nationalists railed the Jacobins for having had the gall to impose their own (Voltairean) local culture on their European neighbors under the pretense that it was universal and emancipatory.[4] In similar fashion, Paglia accuses the late-twentieth-century reincarnation of the French intellectual imperialists of having colonized American minds in the name of a supposedly liberating theory. To reverse the French Revolution in theory, then, means to stress the parochialism of Gallic poststructuralism, to attack it on its own turf, and to wipe it out with the help of the only true universal and cosmopolitan culture of modern times, that of Hollywood, hip-hop, and the Blues Brothers. The children of the 1960s have returned to teach the world (and especially the French aristocrats of the mind) how to have a good time.

Žižek's insights, needless to say, apply as well to the 1930s French humanists' contempt of Hollywood and American kitsch, which is an inverted version of Paglia's impassioned vindication of popular culture made in the USA. What Georges Duhamel and Céline rejected in the land of "materialism," was a way of organizing one's enjoyment that denied their own, and pointed, perhaps, to a secret longing for what they could not, as individuals devoted to the cultivation of the examined life, indulge in. The haste and delight with which their postmodern descendants have embraced "popular" media culture, now that the forbidding barriers of high humanism and Frankfurt school Marxism have been removed, testifies to the power of the literati's formerly repressed desire for the rewards of the (American) pleasure industry. In any case, Paglia's humorous critique as well as the angry debates surrounding the de Man scandal, lead me to believe that the tensions and contradictions I have tried to document in this book are still playing themselves out in transatlantic academic debates. A similar study of the American intellectuals' images, descriptions, or representations of French society and culture would also reveal, I think, the extent, power, and duration of these differences between competing interpretive worlds and ways of intellectual life. The passionate love-hate affair between the two cultures, the reciprocal, fascinated repulsion for their respective organizations of pleasure and meaning, is by no means over.

NOTES

▼

Introduction

1. Throughout this discussion, all translations of excerpts from French books or articles not published in English are mine.

2. On the topic of the "civilization of bathrooms and refrigerators," consider the following remarks by Roger Vailland, a prominent communist writer, at the height of the Cold War (1956): "I have never properly appreciated what purpose a Frigidaire might serve in France, where, except for two or three months a year— and not even that long some years—it is always so cold that one needs no more than a meat safe on the windowsill to keep the left-overs on the Sunday roast fresh until Monday, Tuesday or Wednesday. Those of my friends who own a Frigidaire use it mostly for making ice cubes to put in their wisky [*sic*] and spoil its taste. Anyway with the price of wisky what it is nowadays, their Frigidaire retains no more than a symbolic function" (quoted in Lacorne, Rupnick, and Toinet, 190).

3. Dominique Jullien offers a very detailed and persuasive account of the recurrent nature of all these "topical networks" throughout two hundred years of French travel literature in her recent book, *Récits du nouveau-monde: Les voyageurs français en Amérique de Chateaubriand à nos jours.*

4. Duhamel's essay was an immediate success. According to Pascal Ory "the book had already run to 150 editions by August 1930, having first appeared the previous April" (quoted in Lacorne et al., 49).

5. For a good overview of French public opinion regarding the United States for the last one hundred years, see *The Rise and Fall of Anti-Americanism: A Century of French Perception* (ed. Lacorne et al.). Although it has a few chapters on the literary intellectuals' views of America, most of the volume is dedicated to questions of foreign and economic policy and their impact on the French media and public opinion. See also Tony Judt, *Past Imperfect,* chap. 10.

6. While departments of literature in the United States were swept by a wave of French criticism in the late seventies, in France the "generation of '68" was being increasingly blamed for having contaminated the national philosophical tradition with theories imported from . . . Germany. In *La Pensée 68* (1985), Luc Ferry and Alain Renault characterized Derrida as a French Heidegger, Foucault as a French Nietzsche, and Lacan as a French Freud. So much for "French" theory. By then, Parisian literary reviews were no longer interested in "différance" or "power-knowledge." Confronted with the unexpected rebirth of liberalism and a call to the defense of human rights, the intelligentsia was now polarized by a debate over the merits of modern individualism as opposed to the "holism" of traditional societies.

Chapter One

1. Pascal Ory credits Baudelaire with having introduced the verb "améri-caniser" in the French language (1855), in reference to technical materialism and moral and spiritual corruption. Baudelaire wrote in *Les Curiosités esthétiques* that "The poor man [modern humanity] is so Americanized by the zoocratic industrial philosophers that he has lost all notion of the difference between the phenomena of the physical and moral worlds, and those of the natural and supernatural" (quoted in Lacorne et al., 46). In the preface to his translation of Poe's *More Tales of the Grotesque and Arabesque*, the French poet complained that "Americanomania has virtually become a socially accepted fad." As expected, the most determined opponents of technological modernity were also the most devoted proponents and practitioners of aesthetic modernity. Baudelaire, like Sartre celebrating Faulkner and Dos Passos, was all the more so admiring of American literature as he was dismissive of the cultural climate in which it had come to flourish, apparently against all odds. The Second Empire, like the Gaullist Fifth Republic, was a period of intense modernization. The Saint-Simonian, productivist outlook of the emper-or's technocratic entourage infuriated the literati: the Goncourt brothers wrote in their journal of 16 January 1867, apropos the Second International Exhibition, which was to showcase the industrial and scientific accomplishments of the regime, that it was "the latest blow in what amounts to the Americanisation of France—Industry outdoing Art, steam threshing machines in place of paintings . . .—in a word, the Material Federation" (Ory, in Lacorne et al., 46).

2. The first historical instance of the French elites' claim to cultural promi-nence in Europe (and later in the world) is often attributed to the benedictine monk Alcuin, whom Jacques Le Goff has called "Charlemagne's minister of cul-ture," alluding to the old French tradition of state sponsorship and control of cul-tural production. Alcuin's notion of *translatio studii*, destined to become a topos throughout the Middle Ages, implied that Gaul was called to be the modern con-tinuator of Greece and Rome. The wish came true in the twelfth century, with the University of Paris the beacon of medieval intellectual culture. In the first pages of his *Cligès*, Chrétien de Troyes placed himself squarely within this French culturalist perspective: "This our books have taught us: that Greece had the first renown in chivalry and in learning. Then came chivalry to Rome, and the heyday of learning, which now is come to France. God grant that she be maintained there, and that her home there please her so much that never may depart from France the honour which has there taken up its abode." Later, du Bellay 's *Defense and Illustration of the French Language* (1549) completed the *translatio studii*'s legitimating strategy by claiming to emancipate the national idiom, then no more than a "vulgar" lan-guage, from the domination of Latin and Italian. D. Lacorne and J. Rupnik are right to point out that the struggle to make the French language the privileged vehicle of high culture and intellectual distinction was from the start a defensive and reactional move, aimed at rival, "hegemonic" linguistic entities (24). The equa-tion between language and national identity, particularly strong in French culture,

explains the prominent role played by the threat of linguistic corruption (the recurrent campaigns againt "Frenglish") in twentieth century anti-Americanism.

3. The imposition of the universal model of intellectual excellence elaborated by the courtier society implied the fierce "cultural repression," as Jacques Revel puts it, of peasant and popular ways of life and thought. The classical period of absolutism, the reigns of Louis XIII and Louis XIV were indeed *un siècle de fer* [a century of iron] for the popular classes. In the words of Robert Muchembled: "Popular culture, the rural as much as the urban, suffered an almost collapse under the rule of the Sun King. . . . France of the Reason, and later France of *les lumières*, had room for only one conception of the world and of life: this of the court and the urban elites, the carriers of intellectual culture. The immense effort to reduce the diversity to a unity constituted the very base of the 'civilizing conquest' in France, as witnessed by the drive to subordinate spirits and the bodies, and by the merciless repression of popular revolts, of deviant behavior, heterodox beliefs and witchcraft" (from *Culture populaire et culture des élites dans la France moderne, XVe–XVIIIe siècle*, 341–42; the English translation quoted here is in Bauman, *Legislators and Interpreters*, 60; see also Jacques Revel, "Forms of Expertise: Intellectuals and the 'Popular' Culture in France, 1650–1800").

4. The model of intellectual excellence and the humanistic ideology that makes up its framework are not limited to the French context, of course. One could find instances of them, mutatis mutandis, in other European cultural areas, most particularly in Italy. Historical conditions specific to France, however, have strengthened the cohesion, prestige, independence, and symbolic power of the literati. As I have just said, the early emergence of a monarchic state and the early constitution of a national consciousness and linguistic unity accounts for the importance and duration of the political and ideological role of the intellectuals, as counsels to the prince, administrators, and jurists, as creators of national mythologies and architects of national consensus. On the other hand, *ancien régime* France occupied the middle ground between the feudal regimes of central and eastern Europe (Prussia, Russia, Austria), where the educated elites and the liberal bourgeoisie were subjected to the nobility and the prince, and the constitutional or republican regimes (England, Netherlands), where the relative integration of the aristocratic and bourgeois components of the ruling class left little room for the prophetic role of the intellectuals as torchbearers of free institutions, civil society, and the rational management of human affairs. In France, because of the strength and prestige of the literary tradition, the monarchy was never strong enough, especially after the reign of the Sun King, to stamp out the diffusion of new ideas, as was the case in the "despotic" regimes of central Europe. While the nobility was too attached to its privileges to share its social power with the bourgeoisie, all conditions were conducive to the rise of a relatively autonomous "philosophical party" that would become the vehicle and architect of the discontent of all the excluded groups in the nation and the self-appointed mouthpiece of their demands. The classical study of this remains Tocqueville's *The Old Regime and the French Revolution*, but one finds in

Gramsci's work (especially in his *Prison Notebooks*) valuable elements of comparison between the various historical conditions of the rise of national intellectual fields in Europe and the United States.

5. My colleague Douglas Kibbee brought to my attention the following passage from Durkheim's *Moral Education*, which addresses the French concern with the visible rather than the unseen: "Our language itself is not suited to translate the obscure substructure of things that we may glimpse but do not clearly understand. Precisely because our language is analytical it expresses well only those things that are analyzed, in other words reduced to their elements. . . . But the complex and living unity that these elements form when they are joined together, when they interpenetrate or fuse—all of that escapes because it escapes analysis. Our language seeks the simple. The ideal thing for it would be to have one single word for each indivisible part of reality, and to express the totality formed by everything through a simple, mechanical combination of these elementary notions. As for the aspect that the totality takes on as a totality; as for that which makes its unity, continuity and life—it is in large measure uninterested. This is the origin of the abstract character of our literature" (253). On the cult of style and abstraction in the French tradition, see Tony Judt, *Past Imperfect*, chap. 13.

6. In a recent collection of interviews, several French philosophers complain of this undue emphasis on words, and logos, in their national tradition. Michel Serres questions the disproportionate concern with language in contemporary French philosophy: "In France, Sartre produced *Words*, Foucault writes *Words and Things*, in which language is the chief issue. Recently, a book has come out called *The Grammar of Objects*. In my day little children were given lessons on naming things: it's as if we can only feel or perceive to the extent that we possess language" (quoted in Mortley, 53). Michèle Le Dœuff, who has written extensively on Thomas More and Francis Bacon, ascribes the neglect of the British philosophical tradition in France to the dogmatic, intellectualist bent of the French academic world: "At the beginning of the century, various philosophical dogmas became established. . . . The main one involved a simplistic worship of intellectualism, appraising the philosophical doctrines of the past according to the degree of value or hegemony they give to rationality. Because Kant intellectualizes more than Hume, Kant is thought to be a far greater philosopher than Hume. And amusingly enough, a Kantian professor will look down upon his Humean colleague, but will in turn be looked down upon by any specialist of Hegel" (quoted in Mortley, 84).

7. Andrew Ross's book on American intellectuals, which I find very insightful in many respects, is a recent example of this double-standard in assessing the "popularity" of specific cultural practices. Despite his complex and guarded analyses, and the irony with which he approaches the high-brow "libertinism" of Susan Sontag and the French disciples of Le Marquis de Sade, the postsixties intellectual is not as removed, in his affinities and allergies, from his predecessors (18th century libertines, Baudelairean dandies eager to "shock the bourgeois," transgressive Dadaists, Surrealists, and later disciples of Artaud and Bataille, etc.), as he seems

to imply. In his descriptions of contemporary cultural processes, Ross often displays the familiar phobia of the secularized, modernist intelligentsia for the moral and religious outlook of a large fraction of the "white ethnic" working-class, especially on the divisive issues of abortion and pornography (see Christopher Lasch's cogent analysis of the phenomenon in *The True and Only Heaven*).

8. In a recent review of Ross's book, William Warner remarked, rightly I think, on the author's selective perception of legitimate "popular" culture: "Ross can call for tolerance of popular culture only by restricting his understanding of popular culture so as to exclude the intolerant social movements he would censor" (735). "For Ross, the cultures of certain groups—not the workers, but African-Americans and gays—are extended privileged attention. Others are not. Ross neglects, and therefore implicitly depreciates, cultural icons of popular culture from Frank Sinatra to Sylvester Stallone. Of course, his history does not claim to be anything but selective. But the 'bill of rights' he extends to all popular culture does not conceptualize his own acts of selection" (739). More generally, I would also support Warner's plea for an open-minded, plural, critical assessment of the values of competing interpretations of popular or mass cultures. Critical pluralism, he argues, has more to gain by playing those various theses against each other than by unilaterally siding with one camp. Warner contrasts Ross's version of the popular with Mark Crispin Miller's *Boxed In: The Culture of TV*, which he calls "a strong updating of the Frankfurt School interpretation of contemporary American culture." Warner writes: "Reading Ross and Miller against each other convinces this reader that there is much to be said, and valued, on both sides of the debate. Rather than adjudicating this debate through abstract theses, cultural studies, I suspect, will work through these questions by evaluating what the diverse framing assumptions of different forms of cultural studies allow us to understand" (742, n. 3).

Chapter Two

1. At the beginning of his *Journey*, Céline explicitly plays on the associations between war and butchery: "It was in a cherry orchard dried up by the August sun that the meat for the whole regiment was being doled out. On sacks and on tent canvas spread out on the ground and on the grass itself were pounds and pounds of tripe and whitish-yellow fat and whole disembowelled sheep in a havoc of entrails which oozed curious little streams into the surrounding grass. The carcass of an ox had been cut in two and hung in a tree. The four butchers of the regiment were still clambering around it, swearing and tugging at portions of its flesh. There was any amount of brawling between sections over morsels of rich meat, and kidneys in particular, amid clouds of those flies which are only seen at such moments and are as lusty and clamorous as sparrows. . . . I had to give way to an overwhelming desire to vomit—more than a little, until I fainted. . . . [I could not stomach that war]" (17). (The bracketed phrase is my own translation of the French: "La guerre ne passait pas.")

2. For all his ironical and critical comments on racial segregation in the United States, ("The idea that the unnumbered crimes of the slave-trade and of slavery that were the foundation of American prosperity cannot be expiated, and that those crimes have pierced the side of American happiness with an incurable wound—do you not find that, from the moral point of view, the idea is consolatory, and, all things considered, beautiful?" [151], Duhamel himself was not immune from stereotyping. During a visit to Tuskegee College, the narrator marveled at the diversity of the physical types of the students: "From the anthropoid, all neck and jaws, to the fine aquiline face, pure, open, and tortured by the problems of the mind . . . from the female idol of ebony, fine and beautiful as an Egyptian queen, down to the female servant sculptured in coal—fat-cheeked, broad-hipped, full-breasted and monumental" (146). Later in the book, during a discussion with students in a predominantly white women's college in Connecticut, Duhamel was taken to task by a young African-American student he describes as "a pretty little Negress." "She was charming and well-dressed. In spite of her stigmata she had the self-assurance of the children of the rich. She looked at me proudly. 'Why is it that you, Monsieur,' she said in excellent French, 'who they say have such liberal ideas, spoke in your "Civilization" of your colored stretcher-bearers as "savages"?' . . . 'Well,' I said, 'you see, Mademoiselle, they were Malagasies, if I remember right. And I described them as savages, because this is precisely what at least my stretcher-bearers were.'" Seeing that his answer elicits nothing but "a glance of warm reproach," Duhamel adds, "by way of consolation," that "if it is the word that troubles you, we have savages also among people of our own color." But somehow this does not do the trick. "The young girl went away, shaking her curly head, too full of her just grievance to be reasonable" (149).

3. Céline's description of the fast-food restaurant combines the rationalization of industrial production, the obsessive hygienic concerns of American culture, and the make-believe world of advertisement: "I was looking for a very cheap restaurant and found one of these rationalized places where . . . the business of feeding is simplified down to the barest levels of nature's needs. . . . The waitresses, looking like hospital nurses, stood behind the *nouilles*, the rice and stewed fruits. . . . The strawberries on my *gâteau* shimmered with so many reflections that I couldn't bring myself to eat them" (205–6). For a similarly constructed opposition between the refined sensuality of French cuisine and the Puritan, mindless, collectivistic culture of fast food, consider the remarks of M. F. K. Fischer, the francophile grande dame of American cooking, in her 1937 book, *The Art of Eating*: "France eats more consciously, more intelligently, than any other nation. . . . In Paris and in the village there is a gusto, a frank sensuous realization of food, that is pitifully unsuspected in, say, the college boarding-house or corner café of an American town. In America, we eat, collectively, with a glum urge for food to fill us. We are ignorant of flavor. We are as a nation taste-blind. . . . Ten million men rush every noontime for their ham-on-white and cherry Coke. . . . It might be good if you could go to them, quietly, and say, 'Please, sir, stop a minute and listen to me.'" Some of those

ten million men would listen. Some of them would eat with their minds for the first time."

4. In a similar vein, see the conservative writer and journalist Louis Pauwels's characterization of gender relations in the United States (in a special issue of *Esprit* dedicated to "the American man" [Nov. 1946]): "The American woman is the absolute master of the American man. . . . Of colonial origin, this *de facto* matriarchy daily draws the man without virility—a money-making machine--away from the woman deprived of femininity, transformed into a dominant mother or transposed into this abstract whore: the pin-up girl" (718–19).

5. Compare this view with the reports of Parisian cafés as havens of warmth and nurture in novels by American literary and artistic expatriates of the 1920s and 1930s.

6. True, Morand did not care much for the American cinema either, which he thought had its "eyes fixed on Babbitt, the puritanical onlooker of the 30,000-inhabitant small town." The desire to please the average public seemed to him the main reason why Hollywood was so far behind German or Russian cinema. Morand's description of the "basilicas" of film on Broadway echoes that of Duhamel: "The two most extravagant movie-theaters are the Paramount and the Roxy. The former is a blend of St. Peter's at Rome, the Parthenon, and the Valley of the Kings" (*New York*, 198). As for what goes on on the screen, it is "a complete vision of the end of the world. . . . I find a seat in a deep, soft fauteuil [*sic*], from which for two hours I witness the giant kisses on mouths like the crevasses of the Grand Canyon, embrace of titans, a whole propaganda of the flesh which maddens, without satisfying, these violent American temperaments. It is more than a Black Mass; it is a profanation of everything—of music, of art, of love, of colors" (199).

7. On skyscrapers as on many other aspects of American modernity, Morand was definitely in the minority. In her study of the French reception of American architecture in the interwar years, Isabelle Gournay stresses the resistance to the skyscraper, both in professional circles and in the public at large. Following the first manifestations of enthusiasm of the avant-garde, American modernity fascinated the French much less than it did the Germans and the Soviets. Gournay remarks that the application of literary clichés and familiar metaphors to the description of the American city enabled the French commentators and their readers "to measure the skyscraper following a familiar set of references, which transcended its materialism and undermined its modernity" ("Quand la France découvrait le gratte-ciel," p. 54). As for Le Corbusier, although he ridiculed the new buildings, "his rhetoric on the 'vanity' of the skyscraper was more ambiguous than Georges Duhamel's merciless condemnation in *Scènes de la vie future*. . . . The theme of the 'enchanted catastrophe', which pervades [Le Corbusier's] diary is related to the love-hate feelings most of [his] contemporaries harbored against America" (54). Although new world architectural innovations influenced French urbanism in the 1930s (La Défense, Villeurbanne's Centre Urbain), and after a period of intense 'Americanization' of the urban landscape in the mid-1950s,

Gournay writes that "in the 1980s, the skyscraper represents again the persona non grata it was in 1922, when Le Corbusier presented his diorama of the Contemporary City" (54). See also Gournay's "L'Architecture américaine dans la presse professionnelle française: 1920–1940" and *France Discovers America, 1917–1939*.

8. In its most extreme forms, the Right's antitechnological bent can lead to the assertion that "the computer is the gas-chamber of all culture" (Herte and Nigra, 68).

Chapter Three

1. For the complete bibliography of Sartre's articles on the United States published in *Le Figaro* and *Combat*, from January to June 1945, see Contat and Rybalka's *The Writings of Jean-Paul Sartre* (117–23). The series of articles in *Le Figaro* entitled "Villes d'Amérique" and "En cherchant l'âme de l'Amérique" appeared in *Situations*, vol. 3 (*S III*), with Sartre's introduction ("Presentation") to the special issue (August 1946) of *Les Temps Modernes* (*TM*) on the United States. The English versions of the first two essays appeared in chaps. 8, 9, and 10 in Sartre's *Literary and Philosophical Essays* (*LPE*).

2. In Sartre's philosophical ontology, *being-for-itself* designates the being of (human) consciousness, defined by its self-reflectivity, its intentionality, and its capacity to confer meaning to its activity and to its "world." *Being-in-itself*, on the other hand, refers to the mode of being of all things. While being-in-itself "coincides exactly with itself," human consciousness is capable of transcending (or negating) its physical milieu, its body and itself, in order to constitute itself in freedom, opening up a world of possibilities. This experience of existential freedom, of being projected into a contingent future, creates the feeling of anguish which is commonly associated with the existential hero.

3. The French intellectual Left's uneasy assessment of Chomsky's positions exemplifies the rift between the two cultures. While most French oppositional intellectuals applauded Chomsky's radical critique of American imperialism, they had a hard time reconciling his critical stance in politics with what they perceived as his erroneous positivism in linguistic matters. As Vincent Descombes has remarked in *Modern French Philosophy*, in France, scientific discourse and epistemology (long associated with progressive, republican views) had become, by the 1960s, synonymous with right-wing thinking, while metaphysics and the history of philosophy (formerly denounced by progressive rationalists as the backward-looking purview of reactionary thinkers) were revived and radicalized, via their deconstruction, by left-Nietzschean, neo-Heideggerian, and Freudian-Marxist theories. Hence the puzzlement of how a "positivist, scientistic" thinker such as Chomsky the linguist could be politically correct on issues of world domination. I would argue that it is Chomsky's populist bent in politics, rather than his Cartesian rationalism, that many French theorists found hardest to stomach. Chomsky's populism has led to his renewed attacks on intellectuals as an oppressive social caste, while his pragmatism in politics explains his skepticism as to the validity, and necessity, of critical

social theory. For Chomsky, while the idea of theory is central to the practice of (linguistic) science, all one needs to free oneself from ideological misconceptions of the social and political worlds, and to make sense of history, is a healthy (popular) common sense and the sane exercise of practical reason (see in particular the 1969 debate between Chomsky and Foucault on, among other topics, justice and the power/knowlege nexus in *Reflexive Water*).

4. In her introductory remarks to the English version of "Pourquoi les États-Unis?" (see *The Kristeva Reader*), Toril Moi comments on what appeared as the extreme ethnocentrism of the piece to non-French readers: "Throughout the conversation, the words 'France' (and even 'Paris') and 'Europe' seem to be used more or less as synonyms" (272). Kristeva herself apologizes for the fact that her vision is not entirely French and may consequently appear too idiosyncratic, which contributes toward the "Francocentric" flavor of the debate. Moi goes on to say that American readers "may well feel scandalized at the Parisian trio's somewhat condescending description of the non-verbalized American void, which supposedly is crying out to be filled with the discourse of European (French?) intellectuals." My own point is that this attitude is not peculiar to the Parisian trio, but is constitutive of a great many French discourses on America. Similarly, I think that most of the subsequent criticism of Kristeva from the intellectual Left, who, as Moi puts it, accused her of "abdicating her left-wing politics when confronted with the glamour of monopoly-capitalism," fails to see the deep ambivalence toward American culture that is characteristic of the *Tel Quel* intellectuals, and most of their forerunners since the days of Chateaubriand. As Jacqueline Rose has pointed out, Kristeva's fascination for the nonverbalization of American art cannot be divorced from her anxious wondering whether "that same non-verbalization might not be also the sign of a resistance, the almost psychotic hyperactivity of a violent and overproductive culture incessantly on the go" (quoted in Moi, 8). This is in no way an uncritical endorsement of American "semiotic" culture, and the same goes for Jean Baudrillard's descriptions (e.g., *America*) of the contemporary United States.

Chapter Four

1. The oppositions structuring the ideological field during the Cold War also divided the young intellectuals in training, students at major universities and grandes écoles, and particularly those at the École Normale Supérieure. Pierre Bourdieu reminisced recently on the political conflicts among *normaliens* in the early 1950s: "Those were the days of triumphant Stalinism. Many of my fellow students, who have become today fierce anti-communists, were members of the Party back then. The Stalinist pressure was so exasperating that, we had started at the Ecole Normale, around 1951, a Committee for the Defense of Liberties (with Bianco, Comte, Marin, Derrida, Pariente and others), which Le Roy Ladurie used to attack during meetings of the Ecole's Communist group" (*Choses dites*, 13).

2. A somewhat similar situation is developing today, with the difference that the United States is, ironically, on the defensive and feels threatened in its own

identity. The collapse of the Communist regimes, by making the U.S./Japan alliance less critical, renders it also less bearable, insofar as it is perceived as having mainly benefited the Japanese economy. Although the perception of the Japanese threat is essentially of an economic order, cultural aspects are not altogether absent. Shortly after Sony became the owner of CBS, one could read in *Newsweek* (6 October 1989) that the Japanese had "invaded Hollywood" and had acquired, this time, "a piece of America's soul."

3. The texts from American writers and academicians published in vols. 18 and 19 of *Preuves* were based on a *Partisan Review* survey of the perception of McCarthyism in the U.S. intelligentsia.

4. Denis de Rougemont saw in the subjection of the creative activity to a set of demands proper to journalistic writing one of the roots of the success and originality of American novelists: "The American writes in order to act. . . . If he is a genuine artist, he will write intuitively in order to cast a spell on the reader and on himself through a kind of rhythm or litany of facts—directly connected to the emotionality of his days. Once again, the techniques of American journalism provide one of the secrets of the novelistic art illustrated by the generation of Dos Passos, Steinbeck and Hemingway, who have recently inspired so many younger authors" (*Vivre en Amérique*, 91).

5. In a 1949 lecture on the dangers of Americanization, Sartre had expressed similar views on the alienation and political impotence of American intellectuals and on the threat demobilizing models of intellectual practice represented for the ideal of *engagement:* "In America, the intellectual and the writer are separate. But in our country the intellectual and the writer are one and the same; and since for the moment and in the present state of our society there is no possibility of our seeing writers emerging from different layers of the proletariat and perpetually bringing us a breath of fresh air, if the American influence were to lead us writers to think that out social influence is limited and thereby lead us to estheticism, we would sink into scholasticism" (quoted in Contat and Rybalka, 227)

6. "Indeed, there is a tragic feeling in America. It's been oppressing me ever since I came here but I still do not know what it consists of" (*Journaux de voyage*, 32). Relating a meeting with American students, Camus remarked: "Although, in this country, *everything* attempts to prove that life is not tragic, people feel a void. This grand attempt is pathetic, but one must reject the tragic element *after* having looked at it, not before" (39).

Chapter Five

1. Henry Louis Gates, Jr., sees the same romantic obsession for the authentic at work in the currently widespread belief that individuals cannot cross social or racial barriers and cannot share, let alone portray in art or literature, the experiences of other groups. "The imputation of realness" and the "ideology of the authentic" implies that only people who were born in a given culture can give a true

rendering of it. Building his case on numerous literary challenges to the belief in unequivocal ethnic authenticity (of which the scandal over the best-selling book, *The Education of Little Tree*, a purportedly autobiographical account of a Native American childhood that, in reality, was the product of the imagination of a former Ku-Klux-Klan member, is only the latest instance), Gates concludes that "although our social identities . . . do matter . . . and our histories, individual or collective, do affect what we wish to write and what we are able to write, . . . that relation is never one of fixed determinism. . . . No human culture," he continues, "is inaccessible to someone who makes the effort to understand, to learn, to inhabit another world" (30).

2. At some point, Eco acknowledges that his own ironic comment on American popular tastes must come to a stop, for to prolong the criticism, he says, would constitute "secondhand Frankfurt-school moralism" (52), a refusal to see that this new environment is pleasurable. For all his postmodern irony, however, Eco cannot but find something profoundly disturbing in the latest version of the American dream he has been describing: not on the most immediate level of communication (peace, democracy, contractual relations, etc.), but on that other, allegorical, level superimposed on the literal one, "the implied promise of a 1984 already achieved at the animal level" (52). "What disturbs us," Eco argues, "is not an evil plan; there is none. It is a symbolic threat. We know the Noble Savage, if he still exists in the equatorial forests, kills crocodiles and hippopotamuses, and if they want to survive, animals must submit to the falsification industry. This leaves us upset. And without alternatives" (53). For the Italian critic, we are left with the impossible choice between utopian reconciliation, which will turn us all into ghosts, and the romantic idealization of the past and of nature, which the comsumerism of the fake industry ultimately renders illusory. Such is the dilemma of many postmodern intellectuals, the double bind in which they find themselves in regard to American popular culture: to demonize it is to run the risk of appearing unduly elitist, or even worse, passé and moralistic, an old grouch à la Adorno; to embrace it uncritically is to deny oneself as an intellectual, to renounce the privilege of the critical stance, to assent to the implied promise of 1984, to become oneself a toothless crocodile.

3. In Deleuze and Guattari's *A Thousand Plateaus*, the somewhat difficult notion of the "body without organs" is the result of a dismantling of the organism that allows "intensities" to circulate freely in the body and pass from organ to organ; it is "the unformed, unorganized, nonstratified, or destratified body and all its flows" (43). I find Lyotard's metaphor of the "white skin" of America (in *Le Mur du Pacifique*) quite close to the Deleuzian notion. Both descriptions confirm the perception of the American experience as ceaseless flux and instability (defined as schizoid), in contrast with the static (paranoid) quality of French "landed" culture.

4. I am indebted for much of this analysis to Diana Fuss's application of psychoanalytic theories to fashion photography.

Chapter Six

1. See Marcel Gauchet's "Tocqueville, l'Amérique et nous," Gilles Lipovetsky's *L'Ere du Vide* and *L'Empire de l'éphémère*, and Guy Sorman's *The Conservative Revolution in America*. For a more philosophical celebration of the "horizon of possibilities" opened up by postmodern thought, see Gianni Vattimo, *The End Of Modernity*.

2. The notion of the end of history, long confined to abstruse philosophical works, went mainstream a few years ago when Francis Fukuyama used it to lend intellectual legitimacy to the view that the "Reagan revolution" had brought about the collapse of communism, ended the Cold War, and put the finishing touch on the posthistorical processes hailed by Hegel and Kojève. Fukuyama's essay "The End of History" ignited a heated debate in intellectual and even mainstream magazines (from *The Nation* to *Newsweek*), in the United States and abroad, reminiscent of the fierce "end of ideologies" debate of the 1950s. For a longer version of Fukuyama's views, see his recent *The End of History and the Last Man*.

3. Hegel's own vision of America, born at a time when the future superpower was only a young republic recently emancipated from its colonial status, was, of course, very different from Kojève's. In Hegel's view, the United States, far from having *completed* the historical process, had not yet *entered* it. Since the westward movement acted as an outlet for social and economic discontent and since the new nation had no powerful neighboring enemy (i.e., no negative force to which it was opposed), the American people, unlike Europeans, did not yet "form a compact system of civil society and require an organic state." Hence, America was still "a land of desire for all those who are weary of the historical lumber-room of old Europe. Napoleon is reported to have said: 'Cette vieille Europe m'ennuie.' It is for America to abandon the ground on which hitherto the History of the World has developed itself." But the United States would soon be thrown in the realm of universal history: "America is therefore the land of the future, where, in the ages that lie before us, the burden of the world's History shall reveal itself—perhaps in a contest between North and South America" (*The Philosophy of History*, 86–87).

4. For Bataille's views on Kojève's end of history, see "Hegel, l'homme et l'histoire."

5. For more considerations on the simulacrum in contemporary American popular culture, see Umberto Eco's *Travels in Hyppereality:* "What Disneyland tells us is that technology can reconstruct a fantasy world more real than reality (the 'virtual reality' of computer simulations), or give us more reality than nature can." In the same way "the aim of the reconstructed Oval Office is to supply 'a sign' that will then be forgotten as such: the sign aims to be the thing, to abolish the distinction of the reference, the mechanism of replacement. Not the image of the thing, but its plaster cast. Its double, in other words" (6). Not only is the copy more real, or more authentic than the original, but it is more precious, it has more value, it is endowed with the very aura of which it has deprived the once unique masterpiece, according to Walter Benjamin. This is the ultimate message, the true philosophy of the Palace of Living Arts in Buena Park, Los Angeles, which reproduces in wax,

in three dimensions, life-size, and in full color, the great painting masterpieces of all times: "Not, 'We are giving you the reproduction so that you will want the original,' but rather, "We are giving you the reproduction so you will no longer feel any need for the original" (19). Eco's American metaphysics of substitution, characterized by the erasure of the image and the referent and the assumption of the thing itself as hyperreal simulacrum, which becomes the idolized object of desire, reminds the reader of those (often Catholic) views of Protestantism that contend that the sudden retreat of the Divine from its creation (*deus absconditus*) has left the believer's soul in the throes of anguish: the wrenching metaphysical solitude that ensues has to be peopled with things, artifacts, copies of the elusive Transcendence, all endowed with saving power. Hence the Americans' impatience with words, rituals, and symbolic mediacy, their obsession with efficacy, and their sacralization of artifacts, which foreigners misread as "materialism." The supernatural, Eco concludes, can assume only physical forms, and the same goes for the battle over the salvation of the soul. The ideology of the America of Disneylands, Hearst Castles, and wild safaris aims at giving "a semblance of truth to the myth of immortality through the play of imitations and copies," and at achieving "the presence of the divine in the presence of the natural," even if it is the cultivated, artificial naturalness of the Marinelands. The goal, far from being materialistic, is highly spiritual, urgently cathartic: reassurance through imitation. No longer the imitation of the savior, however, but that of pyramids, centurions, and carriages, of alligators, jungles, and hobgoblins. "Good, Art, Fairytale, and History, unable to become flesh, must at least become plastic" (57). Eco sees this program of salvation as doomed to fail however, for profit, the accomplice of desire, eventually defeats ideology, as in most European stories of America. "The consumers want to be thrilled not only by the guarantee of the Good but also by the shudder of the Bad" (57). Alongside enchanted castles, there are haunted mansions to be found, and bad sharks together with good whales, and Draculas and Frankensteins with the Venuses de Milo. Eco chooses to end his tale of the hyperreal on an equivocal and ominous note, quite appropriate for someone who has been robbed of all alternatives, hopelessly mired in the infinite dream, or nightmare, of the consumption of illusions: "On entering [the] cathedrals of iconic reassurance, the visitor will remain uncertain whether his final destiny is hell or heaven, and so will consume new promises" (58).

6. For a critique of Rorty's "ethnocentrism," see, e.g., Thomas McCarthy, "Private Irony and Public Decency: Richard Rorty's New Pragmatism."

7. Gilles Deleuze, along with Claire Parnet, vaunts the superiority of (British) empiricism, on the grounds that "empiricists are not theoreticians, they are experimenters: they never interpret, they have no principles" (55). And also: "English or American literature is a process of experimentation. They have killed interpretation" (49).

8. Both Nietzsche and Hegel easily lend themselves to pragmatic interpretations, which may or may not diverge from William James's and John Dewey's own

conceptions of pragmatism. Numerous commentators of Nietzsche's philosophy have indeed emphasized the "pragmatic" aspects of his conception of truth. For Walter Kaufman, "Nietzsche's experimentalism may seem suggestive of pragmatism; and as a matter of fact there are in his writings—and particularly in those of his notes which deal with epistemological problems—a great number of passages which read like early statements of pragmatic views" (66). Jean Granier, for his part, although he also draws a parallel between Peirce and Nietzsche, argues that the latter ultimately advocates an "overcoming" of pragmatism: "While the pragmatists see the usefulness of a belief as the criterion of its truthfulness, Nietzsche sees it as the criterion of its nontruthfulness, of its ficticious character" (484). As for Kojève's reading of Hegel, it was also infused with a "pragmatic definition of truth," as Vincent Descombes rightly remarked. Kojève had written in the *Introduction*, "What then is the morality of Hegel? What exists is good inasmuch as it exists. All action, being a negation of the existing given, is therefore bad, or sinful. But sin may be forgiven. How? By its success. Success absolves crime because success is a new reality that *exists*. But how can success be estimated? Before this can be done, History must come to an end" (*Modern French Philosophy*, 15–16). What is best is what comes last. The end of time alone allows for the complete evaluation of truth as success, i.e., for the triumph of a "pragmatic," i.e., instrumentalist and somewhat cynical, view of human history. This particular interpretation of pragmatism as the unconditional acceptance of what *is*, beyond all moral considerations, has been repeatedly rejected by such philosophical heirs to James and Dewey as Sidney Hook, Richard Rorty, or Stanley Fish. While it is true that such a characterization is unfair to pragmatism as a specific philosophical doctrine—namely that of James, Dewey, and their continuators—it certainly can apply to a wider, more ideological, use of pragmatic principles.

Conclusion

1. On the marginalization of liberal political thought in French history, see Tony Judt, *Past Imperfect*, chap. 12.

Epilogue

1. French intellectual history is by no means reducible to its intellectualist and rationalist components. There have always been strong skeptical, empiricist, materialist, or "existential" countertraditions: they have had to contend with powerful idealist adversaries, though, from Cartesianism to Jacobinism.

2. The growing U.S. interest in bridging the gap between the pragmatic tradition and some components of modern continental philosophy is witnessed by the growing number of comparative studies with titles such as Sandra Rosenthal and Patrick Bourgeois's *Mead and Merleau-Ponty: Toward a Common Vision*. It is too early, however, to assess the potential impact of such comparative studies on the reception of pragmatism in French and European philosophical circles.

3. Like that other archenemy of America (the monomaniac Ahab who was bent

on destroying the great whale) the puritanical, overintellectualized French philosophy professors are afflicted with "a low enjoying power."

4. For Žižek, the object of nationalism "functions as a kind of 'particular Absolute' resisting universalization, bestowing its special 'tonality' upon every neutral,
universal notion" (57).

BIBLIOGRAPHY

▼

Adorno, Theodor. "On the Fetish-Character in Music and the Regression of Listening." *The Essential Frankfurt School Reader,* ed. Andrew Arato and Eike Gebhardt. New York: Continuum, 1982.

Arendt, Hannah. *On Revolution.* New York: Viking Press, 1963.

Aron, Raymond. *The Opium of the Intellectuals,* trans. Terence Kilmartin. London: Secker, 1957.

———. *The Imperial Republic,* trans. Frank Jellinek. Englewood Cliffs, N.J.: Prentice-Hall, 1974.

———. *Le Spectateur engagé.* Paris: Julliard, 1981.

Bataille, Georges. "Hegel, l'homme et l'histoire." *Œuvres complètes,* 12:349–69. Paris: Gallimard, 1988.

Baudrillard, Jean. *In the Shadow of the Silent Majorities,* trans. Paul Foss, Paul Patton, and John Johnston. New York: Semiotext, 1983.

———. *Forget Foucault,* trans. S. Lotringer. New York: Semiotext, 1987.

———. *America,* trans. Chris Turner. London: Verso, 1988.

Bauman, Zygmunt. *Legislators and Interpreters: On Modernity, Post-modernity and Intellectuals.* Ithaca, N.Y.: Cornell University Press, 1987.

Beauvoir, Simone de. *America Day by Day,* trans. Patrick Dudley. London: Duckworth, 1952.

———. *Force of Circumstance,* vol.1. Trans. Richard Howard. New York: Harper & Row, 1977.

Bell, Daniel. *The Cultural Contradictions of Capitalism.* New York: Basic Books, 1976.

Bellah, Robert N., et al. *Habits of the Heart: Individualism and Commitment in American Life.* New York: Harper & Row, 1986.

Benjamin, Walter. "The Work of Art in the Age of Mechanical Reproduction." In *Illuminations,* trans. Harry Zohn. New York: Harcourt, 1968.

Benoist, Alain de. *Vu de droite. Anthologie critique des idées contemporaines.* Paris: Copernic, 1977.

Benoist, Jean-Marie. *Les Idées à l'endroit.* Paris: Libre-Hallier, 1979.

———. *Pavane pour une Europe défunte.* Paris: Editions Hallier, 1976.

Berger, Yves. *Le Fou d'Amérique.* Paris: Grasset, 1976.

Blanchot, Maurice. *L'Entretien infini.* Paris: Gallimard, 1969.

Bloom, Allan. *The Closing of the American Mind.* New York: Simon & Schuster, 1987.

Bourdieu, Pierre. *Choses dites*. Paris: Minuit, 1987.

———. *L'Ontologie politique de Martin Heidegger*. Paris: Minuit, 1988.

Boorstin, Daniel J. *The Genius of American Politics*. Chicago: University of Chicago Press, 1953.

Bucher, Bernadette. "Claudel et le monde amérindien." In *Claudel et l'Amérique*. Ottawa: Editions de l'Université d'Ottawa, 1964.

Burguière, André. "Elitisme culturel et révolution des médias." *Contemporary French Civilization* 13, no. 2 (1989): 144–56.

Butor, Michel. *Mobile: Study for a Representation of the United States*, trans. Richard Howard. New York: Simon & Schuster, 1963.

Camus, Albert. "Pluies à New York." In *Essais*. Paris: Gallimard (Pléiade), 1965.

———. *Journaux de voyage*. Paris: Gallimard, 1978.

Cau, Jean. *La Grande prostituée*. Paris: La Table Ronde, 1974.

———. *Pourquoi la France*. Paris: La Table Ronde, 1975.

———. *Discours de la décadence*. Paris: Copernic, 1978.

Céline, Louis-Ferdinand. *Journey to the End of the Night*, trans. John H. P. Marks. Boston: Little, Brown, 1934.

———. *Bagatelles pour un massacre*. Paris: Denoël, 1937.

———. "La Médecine dans les usines Ford." *Œuvres*, vol. 1. Paris: Balland, 1966.

Chartier, Roger. "Intellectual History or Sociocultural History? The French Trajectories." In *Modern European Intellectual History: Reappraisals and New Perspectives*, ed. D. La Capra and S. L. Kaplan. Ithaca, N.Y.: Cornell University Press, 1982.

Chateaubriand, François-René de. *Atala*, trans. Irving Putter. Berkeley: University of California Press, 1960.

———. *Travels in America*, trans. Richard Switzer. Lexington: University of Kentucky Press, 1969.

Chinard, Jean. *L'Exotisme américain dans l'œuvre de Chateaubriand*. Paris: Hachette, 1918.

Chomsky, Noam, and Michel Foucault. "Human Nature: Justice versus Power." In *Reflexive Water: The Basic Concerns of Mankind*. London: Souvenir Press, 1974.

Chrétien de Troyes. *Cligès, a Romance*, trans. L. J. Gardiner. London: Chatto & Windus, 1912.

Claudel, Paul. *Mémoires improvisées*. Paris: Gallimard, 1954.

———. "L'Échange." *Théâtre*. Paris: NRF (La Pléiade), 1956.

———. "American Elasticity" (1936). *Œuvres en prose*. Paris: NRF (La Pléiade), 1965.

———. *Conversations dans le Loir-et-Cher* (1928). *Œuvres en prose*. Paris: NRF, 1965.

————. "Un poème de Saint-John-Perse" (1949). *Œuvres en prose*. Paris: NRF, 1965.

————. *Journal*, 2 vols. Paris: NRF (La Pléiade), 1968 and 1969.

Contat, Michel, and Michel Rybalka. *The Writings of Jean-Paul Sartre*, trans. Richard C. McCleary. Evanston, Ill.: Northwestern University Press, 1974.

Cooper, Barry. *The End of History: An Essay on Modern Hegelianism*. Toronto: University of Toronto Press, 1984.

Crozier, Michel. *The Trouble with America*, trans. Peter Heinegg. Berkeley: University of California Press, 1984.

Cunliffe, Marcus. "European Images of America." In *Paths of American Thought*, ed. Arthur M. Schlesinger, Jr., and Morton White. Boston: Houghton Mifflin, 1963.

Daniel, Jean. "Les Mythes américains de la gauche française." In *Le Reflux américain: Décadence ou renouveau des États-Unis?* ed. Alain Boublil et al. Paris: Seuil, 1980.

Debray, Régis. *Le Scribe*. Paris: Grasset, 1980.

————. *Teachers, Writers, Celebrities: The Intellectuals of Modern France*, trans. David Macey. London: New Left Books, 1981.

————. *Les Empires contre l'Europe*. Paris: Gallimard, 1985.

————. "Un 'antiaméricain' à New York." *Contretemps. Eloge des idéaux perdus.* Paris: Gallimard, 1992.

Deleuze, Gilles, and Félix Guattari. *A Thousand Plateaus: Capitalism and Schizophrenia*, trans. Brian Massumi. Minneapolis: University of Minnesota Press, 1989.

Deleuze, Gilles, and Claire Parnet. *Dialogues*, trans. Hugh Tomlison and Barbara Habberjam. New York: Columbia University Press, 1987.

Descombes, Vincent. *Modern French Philosophy*, trans. Lorna Scott-Fox and Jeremy Harding. Cambridge: Cambridge University Press, 1980.

Dewey, John. *Reconstruction in Philosophy*. Boston: Beacon, 1948.

Dickens, Charles. *American Notes*. Greenwich, Conn.: Fawcett, 1961.

Duhamel, Georges. *America, the Menace: Scenes from the Life of the Future*, trans. Charles M. Thompson. Boston: Houghton Mifflin, 1931.

Durkheim, Émile. *Moral Education: A Study in the Theory and Application of the Sociology of Education*, trans. E. K. Wilason and H. Schnurer. New York: Free Press, 1961.

Duroselle, Jean-Baptiste. *La France et les États-Unis*. Paris: Fayard, 1976.

Eco, Umberto. *Travels in Hyperreality*, trans. William Weaver. New York: Harcourt Brace Jovanovich, 1986.

Elias, Norbert. *The Civilizing Process*. Vol. 1 of *The History of Manners*, trans. E. Jephcott. Oxford: Blackwell, 1982.

————. *The Court Society*, trans. E. Jephcott. Oxford: Blackwell, 1983.

Emerson, Ralph Waldo. "Experience" and "The American Scholar." In *Selected Writings*, ed. William H. Gilman. New York: New American Library, 1965.

Eribon, Didier. *Michel Foucault*, trans. Betsy Wing. Cambridge, Mass.: Harvard University Press, 1991.

Etcheverria, Durand. *Mirage in the West: A History of the French Image of American Society to 1815*. Princeton, N.J.: Princeton University Press, 1957.

Felperin, Howard. *Beyond Deconstruction: The Uses and Abuses of Literary Theory*. Oxford: Clarendon Press, 1985.

Ferry, Luc, and Alain Renaut. *La Pensée 68. Essai sur l'anti-humanisme contemporain*. Paris: Gallimard, 1985. (*French Philosophy of the Sixties: An Essay on Antihumanism*, trans. Mary H. Cattani. Amherst: University of Massachusetts Press, 1990.)

Finkielkraut, Alain. *La Défaite de la pensée*. Paris: Gallimard, 1987.

Fish, Stanley. *Is There a Text in This Class?* Cambridge, Mass.: Harvard University Press, 1980.

————. *Doing What Comes Naturally*. Durham, NC: Duke University Press, 1989.

Foucault, Michel. "Orders of Discourse," trans. Rupert Swyer. *Social Science Information* 10, no. 2 (April 1971): 7–30.

Freneau, Philip. "The Glory of America." *Poems of Philip Freneau*, ed. F. L. Pattee. Princeton, N.J.: University Library, 1902.

Fukuyama, Francis. *The End of History and the Last Man*. New York: Free Press, 1991.

Fuss, Diana. "Homospectatorial Fashion Photography." *Critical Inquiry* 18, no. 4 (1992): 713–737.

Gates, Henry Louis, Jr. "Authenticity, or the Lessons of Little Tree." *New York Times Book Review* (24 Nov. 1991): 1, 30.

————. "Goodbye, Columbus? Notes on the Culture of Criticism." *American Literary History* 3, no. 4 (1991): 711–27.

Gauchet, Marcel. "Tocqueville, l'Amérique et nous." *Libre* 7 (1980): 104–6.

Gellner, Ernest. *Plough, Sword and Book: The Structure of Human History*. Chicago: University of Chicago Press, 1988.

Gouldner, Alvin. "Romanticism and Classicism: Deep Structures in Social Science." In *For Sociology: Renewal and Critique in Sociology Today*. New York: Basic Books, 1973.

————. *The Future of Intellectuals and the Rise of the New Class*. New York: Seabury Press, 1979.

Gournay, Isabelle. "Quand la France découvrait le gratte-ciel." *L'Architecture aujourd'hui* (July 1989): 44–54.

————. "French Writings on American Architecture." Ph.D. dissertation. Yale University, 1989.

————. "L'Architecture américaine dans la presse professionnelle française: 1920–1940." *La Gazette des beaux-arts* (April 1991): 188–200.

Gramsci, Antonio. "Americanism and Fordism." *Prison Notebooks*, trans. Quintin Hoare and Geoffrey Nowell Smith. New York: International Publishers, 1971.

Granier, Jean. *Le Problème de la vérité dans la philosophie de Nietzsche*. Paris: Seuil, 1966.

Habermas, Jürgen. *The Philosophical Discourse of Modernity*, trans. Frederick G. Lawrence. Cambridge, Mass.: MIT Press, 1990.

Hartz, Louis. *The Liberal Tradition in America*. New York: Harcourt, 1955.

Hegel, G. W. F. *The Philosophy of History*, trans. J. Sibree. New York: Colonial Press, 1900.

————. *Selections*, ed. J. Loewenberg. New York: Scribner's Sons, 1929.

Heidegger, Martin. *Introduction to Metaphysics*, trans. Ralph Manheim. New Haven: Yale University Press, 1959.

Herte, Robert de, and Hans-Jürgen Nigra. "Il était une fois l'Amérique." *Nouvelle École* 27–28 (1975): 10–96.

Hondt, Jacques d'. *Hegel, textes et débats*. Paris: Librairie Générale Française, 1984.

Hook, Sidney. *Pragmatism and the Tragic Sense of Life*. New York: Basic Books, 1974.

Horkheimer, Max, and Theodor Adorno. *Dialectic of Enlightenment*, trans. John Cumming. New York: Continuum, 1975.

Irigaray, Luce. *This Sex Which Is not One*, trans. Catherine Porter and Carolyn Burke. Ithaca, N.Y.: Cornell University Press, 1985.

Jameson, Fredric. "Postmodernism, or the Cultural Logic of Capitalism." *New Left Review* 146 (July/August 1984): 53–92.

Jeanson, Francis. *Sartre dans sa vie*. Paris: Seuil, 1974.

Jefferson, Thomas. "First Inaugural Address." *Basic Writings of T. Jefferson*, ed. Philip Sheldon Foner. Garden City, N.Y.: Halcyon, 1950.

Jehlen, Myra. *American Incarnation: The Individual, the Nation, the Continent*. Cambridge, Mass.: Harvard University Press, 1986.

Judt, Tony. *Past Imperfect: French Intellectuals, 1944–1956*. Berkeley: University of California Press, 1992.

Jullien, Dominique. *Récits du nouveau-monde. Les Voyageurs français en Amérique de Chateaubriand à nos jours*. Paris: Nathan, 1992.

Kaufman, Walter. *Nietzsche: Philosopher, Psychologist, Antichrist*. Princeton, N.J.: Princeton University Press, 1950.

Kerouac, Jack. *On the Road*. New York: Viking Press, 1979.

Kojève, Alexandre. *Introduction to the Reading of Hegel*, trans. James H. Nichols, Jr. New York: Basic Books, 1969.

Kristeva, Julia. *Polylogue*. Paris: Seuil, 1977.

———. *Powers of Horror: An Essay on Abjection*, trans. Leon S. Roudiez. New York: Columbia University Press, 1982.

———. "Women's Time," In *The Kristeva Reader*, ed. Toril Moi. New York: Columbia University Press, 1986.

Kristeva, J., M. Pleynet, and P. Sollers. "Why the United States?" In *The Kristeva Reader*, ed. Toril Moi. New York: Columbia University Press, 1986.

Kushner, Eva. "L'Amérique: Une solitude?" In *Claudel et L'Amérique*. Ottawa: Editions de l'Université d'Ottawa, 1964.

La Capra, Dominick. *History and Criticism*. Ithaca: Cornell University Press, 1985.

Lacan, Jacques. *Écrits: A Selection*, trans. Alan Sheridan. New York: Norton, 1977.

Lacorne, Denis, Jacques Rupnik, and Marie-France Toinet, ed. *The Rise and Fall of Anti-Americanism: A Century of French Perception*, trans. Gerry Turner. New York: St. Martin's Press, 1990.

Larmore, Charles. "Histoire et raison en philosphie politique." *Stanford French Review* 15, nos. 1–2 (1991): 183–206.

Lasch, Christopher. Introduction to Charles Dickens's *American Notes*. Greenwich, Conn.: Fawcett, 1961.

———. *The Culture of Narcissism*. New York: Norton, 1978.

———. *The True and Only Heaven: Progress and Its Critics*, New York: Norton, 1991.

Lasky, Melvin J. "American and Europe: Transatlantic Images." In *Paths of American Thought*, ed. Arthur M. Schlesinger, Jr., and Morton White. Boston: Houghton Mifflin, 1963.

Le Goff, Jacques. *Les Intellectuels au Moyen Age*. Paris: Seuil, 1957.

Lehman, David. *Signs of the Times: Deconstruction and the Fall of Paul de Man*. New York: Poseidon Press, 1991.

Lipovetsky, Gilles. *L'Ere du vide: Essais sur l'individualisme contemporain*. Paris: Gallimard, 1983.

———. *L'Empire de l'éphémère: La Mode et son destin dans les sociétés modernes*. Paris: Gallimard, 1987.

Little, Roger. Introduction to Saint-John Perse's *Exil*. London: Athlone Press, 1973.

Lyotard, Jean-François. *Le Mur du Pacifique*. Paris: Seuil, 1979.

———. *The Postmodern Condition*, trans. Geoff Bennington and Brian Massumi. Minneapolis: University of Minnesota Press, 1984.

Malraux, André. *Romans*. Paris: Gallimard (La Pléiade), 1947.

Maritain, Jacques. *Reflections on America*. New York: Scribner's, 1958.

Maurois, André. *L'Amérique inattendue*. Paris: Mornay, 1931.

———. *From My Journal*, trans. Joan Charles. New York: Harper & Brothers, 1948.

McCarthy, Thomas. "Private Irony and Public Decency: Richard Rorty's New Pragmatism." *Critical Inquiry* 16, no. 2 (1990): 355–70.

Mills, C. Wright. "The Cultural Apparatus." In *Power, Politics and People*. New York: Oxford University Press, 1963.

Moi, Toril. Introduction to *The Kristeva Reader*. New York: Columbia University Press, 1986.

Morand, Paul. *U.S.A.—1927*. Paris: Plaisir du Bibliophile, 1928.

———. *New York*, trans. Hamish Miles. London: Heinemann, 1931.

Morin, Edgar. *Journal de Californie*. Paris: Seuil, 1970.

Mortley, Raoul, ed. *French Philosophers in Conversation*. London: Routledge, 1991.

Muchembled, Robert. *Culture populaire et culture des élites dans la France moderne (XVe–XVIIIe siècles)*. Paris: Flammarion, 1978.

Nelson, Robert J. *Willa Cather and France: In Search of the Lost Language*. Urbana: University of Illinois Press, 1988.

Nietzsche, Friedrich. *Beyond Good and Evil*, trans. Marianne Cowan. South Bend, Ind.: Gateway, 1955.

———. *Thus Spake Zarathustra*, trans. Thomas Common. New York: Random House, 1956.

Ory, Pascal, and Jean-François Sirinelli. *Les Intellectuels en France, de l'Affaire Dreyfus à nos jours*. Paris: Armand Colin, 1986.

Paglia, Camille. "Ninnies, Pedants, Tyrants and Other Academics." *New York Times Book Review* (5 May 1991).

Perse, Saint-John. *Exile and Other Poems*, trans. Denis Devlin. New York: Pantheon, 1949.

———. *Winds*, trans. Wallace Fowlie. New York: Pantheon, 1953.

Pierssens, Michel. "Amère Amérique." In *Colloque 1980: Saint-John Perse et les États-Unis*. Aix: Université de Provence, 1981.

Poe, Edgar A. *The Adventures of Arthur Gordon Pym* Vol. 5 of *Complete Works*, ed. E. C. Stedman and G. E. Woodberry. New York: Scribner, 1927.

Popper, Karl. *The Open Society and its Enemies*. Princeton, N.J.: Princeton University Press, 1966.

Rémond, René. *Les États-Unis devant l'opinion française (1815–1852)*. Paris: Armand Colin, 1962.

Revel, Jacques. "Forms of Expertise; Intellectuals and the 'Popular' Culture in France (1650–1800)." In *Understanding Popular Culture, Europe from the Middle Ages to the Nineteenth Century*, ed. Steven L. Kaplan. London: Mouton, 1984.

Revel, Jean-François. *Without Marx or Jesus*, trans. J. F. Bernard. Garden City, N.J.: Doubleday, 1971.

Ringer, Fritz. *The Decline of the German Mandarins: The German Academic Community, 1890–1933*. Cambridge, Mass.; Harvard University Press, 1969.

Romains, Jules. *Salsette découvre l'Amérique*. New York: Editions de la Maison Française, 1942.

Rorty, Richard. *Consequences of Pragmatism*. Minneapolis: University of Minnesota Press, 1982.

———. *Contingency, Irony and Solidarity*. Cambridge: Cambridge University Press, 1989.

———. "On Truth, Freedom, and Politics." *Critical Inquiry* 16, no. 3 (Spring 1990): 633–43.

———. "Cosmopolitanism without Emancipation." In *Objectivity, Relativism and Truth*. Cambridge: Cambridge University Press, 1991.

Ross, Andrew. *No Respect: Intellectuals and Popular Culture*. New York: Routledge, 1989.

Rougemont, Denis de. *Vivre en Amérique*. Paris: Stock, 1947.

———. "Le dialogue Europe-Amérique." *Preuves* 18–19 (August–September 1952): 68–70.

Rousseau, Jean-Jacques. *Discourse on the Origins of Inequality*, trans. Maurice Cranston. London: Penguin, 1985.

Said, Edward. *Orientalism*. New York: Random House, 1978.

Saluzinsky, Imre. *Criticism and Society*. New York: Methuen, 1987.

Santayana, George. *Winds of Doctrine*. New York, 1913.

Sartre, Jean-Paul. "Les Américains tels que je les ai vus." *L'Ordre* (14 July 1945).

———. "American Novelists in French Eyes," *Atlantic Monthly* 178, no. 2 (August 1946): 116–18.

———. *Situations*, vol. 3. Paris: Gallimard, 1949.

———. *Literary and Philosophical Essays*, trans. Annette Michelson. New York: Collier, 1955.

———. *Critique de la raison dialectique*. Paris: Gallimard, 1960. (*Critique of Dialectical Reason* vol. 1, trans. Alan Sheridan; vol. 2, trans. Quintin Hoare, London: Verso, 1984, 1991.)

———. *Saint-Genet, Actor and Martyr*, trans. Bernard Frechtman. New York: Braziller, 1963.

———. "Pourquoi je refuse d'aller aux Etats-Unis." *Nouvel Observateur*, 1 April 1965, 1–3.

———. *Situations*, vol. 8. Paris: Gallimard, 1972.

Servan-Schreiber, Jean-Jacques. *The American Challenge*, trans. Ronald Steel. New York: Atheneum, 1968.

Siegfried, André. *America Comes of Age*, trans. H. H. Hemming and Doris Hemming. New York: Harcourt, 1927.

———. *America at Mid-Century*, trans. Margaret Ledésert. New York: Harcourt, 1955.

Smith, Barbara Herrnstein. *Contingencies of Value*. Cambridge, Mass.: Harvard University Press, 1988.

Sorman, Guy. *The Conservative Revolution in America*, trans. Jane Kaplan. Chicago: Regnery Books, 1985.

Thibau, Jacques. *La France colonisée*. Paris: Fayard, 1980.

Tillett, A. S. "Some Saint-Simonian Criticism of the United States before 1835." *Romanic Review* 10, no. 4 (February 1961): 3–16.

Tocqueville, Alexis de. *Democracy in America*, 2 vols. Trans. Henry Reeve. New York: Colonial Press, 1900.

———. *The Old Régime and the French Revolution*, trans. Stuart Gilbert. Garden City, N.Y.: Doubleday, 1955.

Tucci, Niccolo. "Amérique, éternel refrain." *Preuves* 44 (October 1954): 54–57.

Vattimo, Gianni. *The End of Modernity: Nihilism and Hermenentics in Postmodern Culture*. Trans. Jon R. Snyder. Baltimore: The Johns Hopkins University Press, 1988.

Warner, William. "The Resistance to Popular Culture." *American Literary History* 2, no. 4 (1990): 726–42.

West, Cornel. *The American Evasion of Philosophy: A Genealogy of Pragmatism*. Madison: University of Wisconsin Press, 1989.

Whitman, Walt. *Complete Poetry and Collected Prose*. New York: Library of America, 1982.

Williams, Raymond. *Culture and Society, 1780–1950*. New York: Harper & Row, 1958.

Wolin, Richard. *Walter Benjamin: An Aesthetic of Redemption*. New York: Columbia University Press, 1984.

Žižek, Slavoj. "Eastern Europe's Republics of Gilead." *New Left Review* 123 (1990): 50–62.

INDEX

▼